Hungary's unique 'gradualist' economic transformation has now reached a critical stage. Despite recent upheavals, Hungary has succeeded in attracting foreign capital, and has achieved its first current account surplus in convertible currency since 1984, but it is clear that privatisation will be a lengthy and difficult process, with significant repercussions for the future of the economy and profound social and welfare consequences.

This book presents some of the local arguments and perceptions informing the current debate, and critical examinations of these ideas from an international panel of scholars. The chapters address privatisation; financial, tax and legal systems; integration into the international financial and monetary systems; labour markets, unemployment and the social safety net; and the political economy of the current economic transformation. The analysis and results will be of major interest to economists and policy-makers concerned with transition throughout Eastern Europe.

Hungary: an economy in transition

Centre for Economic Policy Research

The Centre for Economic Policy Research is a network of more than 160 Research Fellows, based primarily in European universities. The Centre coordinates its Fellows' research activities and communicates their results to the public and private sectors. CEPR is an entrepreneur, developing research initiatives with the producers, consumers and sponsors of research. Established in 1983, CEPR is already a European economics research organisation with uniquely wide-ranging scope and activities.

CEPR is a registered educational charity. Grants from the Leverhulme Trust, the Esmée Fairbairn Charitable Trust, the Baring Foundation, the Bank of England and Citibank provide institutional finance. The ESRC supports the Centre's dissemination programme and, with the Nuffield Foundation, its programme of research workshops. None of these organisations gives prior review to the Centre's publications nor necessarily endorses the views expressed therein.

The Centre is pluralist and non-partisan, bringing economic research to bear on the analysis of medium- and long-run policy questions. CEPR research may include views on policy, but the Executive Committee of the Centre does not give prior review to its publications and the Centre takes no institutional policy positions. The opinions expressed in this volume are those of the authors and not those of the Centre for Economic Policy Research.

Hungary: an economy in transition

Edited by
ISTVÁN P. SZÉKELY
and
DAVID M. G. NEWBERY

CAMBRIDGE
UNIVERSITY PRESS

Published by the Press Syndicate of the University of Cambridge
The Pitt Building, Trumpington Street, Cambridge CB2 1RP
40 West 20th Street, New York, NY 10011-4211, USA
10 Stamford Road, Oakleigh, Melbourne 3166, Australia

First published 1993

Printed in Great Britain by Bell and Bain Ltd., Glasgow

A catalogue record for this book is available from the British Library

Library of Congress cataloguing in publication data

Hungary: an economy in transition / edited by István P. Székely
and David M. G. Newbery.
    p.   cm.
   Includes index.
   ISBN 0 521 44018 1
   1. Hungary – Economic conditions – 1989–.
2. Hungary – Economic policy – 1989–.
I. Székely, István P., 1959–. II. Newbery, David M. G.
HC300.282.H86   1992
338.9439 – dc20   92–29669   CIP

ISBN 0 521 44018 1   hardback

Contents

Discussion of Part Seven
David Begg
R. E. Rowthorn
Conclusion
Adam Ridley

Figures

Tables

Preface

This volume contains the proceedings of the conference 'Hungary: An Economy in Transition' organised by the Centre for Economic Policy Research and held in London on 7–8 February 1992.

Financial support for the conference was provided by the ACE programme of the Commission of the European Communities, Citibank and the Foreign and Commonwealth Office, to whom we express our gratitude. We would also like to thank the CEPR's permanent staff for their encouragement and support, especially to Stephen Yeo and Wendy Thompson for organising the conference; Lisa Dowling, Allyson Davies, and Jennifer Jones for making it run smoothly; Kate Millward and David Guthrie for organising the volume's production, and to Richard Portes for his leadership role. We also thank Barbara Docherty for essential editorial assistance. The editors would like to thank the participants of the conference, many of whom are the authors of chapters in this volume, for their contributions. Our thanks go also to the discussants of the chapters, who helped to clarify the nature of the problems and the special characteristics of the Hungarian case. Needless to say, the success or failure of this book depends mostly on their efforts.

Almost all the chapters in this volume have been written by Hungarian scholars and policymakers. The aim was to present some of the local arguments and perceptions informing the current debate to the critical examination of an international panel of discussants. By doing so, we hope to contribute to improved communication and exchange of ideas among economists both inside and outside Hungary, and to the ongoing debate about these matters in the country itself.

István P. Székely   *June 1992*
David M. G. Newbery

Foreword

MARIO SARCINELLI

The CEPR is one of the most active research institutes in the field of economies in transition. In early 1990 it launched a major new research initiative on Eastern Europe and the complex problems of economic reform and system design now faced by its governments. Several research workshops have already generated substantial output.

The transformation of the economies of Eastern Europe and their integration into the international economy is a major challenge for politicians, civil servants, and scholars alike. This is the first reason why we should welcome CEPR's initiative in this field. The second lies in Hungary's role as a pioneer in attempting such an economic transformation, which 'has . . . been instrumental [also] in the acceleration of the transformation in the East–Central European region'.[1] Through the Hungarian experiment, we will be able better to understand what is at stake in other Central and Eastern European economies.

The Hungarian economy

The economic transformation in Hungary has now reached a critical stage. The cost of transition is huge, and higher than expected. It has become clear that economic transformation will take much longer than originally thought. The Hungarian economy is also characterised by both remarkable achievements and some less auspicious tendencies. On the positive side, the current account of the balance of payments in 1991 was in surplus for the second year running; new small enterprises emerged at an impressive pace; further steps were taken to improve resource allocation by freeing prices and liberalising foreign trade: 90 per cent of consumer prices are now free of controls (as compared to 50 per cent in 1988). Imports of goods representing around 70 per cent of industrial production are completely free. The average level of import tariffs has also decreased. The resulting high degree of price and import liberalisation has laid the foundation for competition in the private sector, the significance of which is expected to increase substantially over the next few years. So far, the increase in private economic activities has stemmed mainly from the rapidly rising number of small companies. However, the government aims to complement the process through broad privatisation of large state-owned enterprises. New laws on banking, insolvency and accounting were also passed by Parliament to encourage the move towards an economy based on market principles. The level of direct foreign investment rose sharply, providing the basis for a much-needed accumulation of foreign exchange reserves.

On the less auspicious side, production continued to decline; inflation is under control but has accelerated (at least temporarily); and the pace of privatisation was substantially slower than planned, although the government aims to reduce the state's share of assets in the competitive sector to less than 40 per cent by the end of 1993.

External economic relations and foreign investments

Convertible currency indebtedness remains high (US$19.7 bn by mid-1991, 63 per cent of GDP). The debt service ratio declined to 39 per cent in 1991, from 64 per cent the year before, on account of a smoothing of the maturity structure and a sharp increase in convertible currency exports resulting from the collapse of the CMEA and the switch to convertible currency settlements.

Hungarian debt policy differs drastically from that followed by some of its neighbours. While Bulgaria used to be considered a credit-worthy sovereign borrower, it declared a unilateral moratorium in 1990 and requested the opening of debt restructuring negotiations. Agreement was reached with the Paris Club in May 1991 to reschedule the official debt, but agreement has not yet been reached with the commercial banks which own 85 per cent of Bulgarian external debt. In 1990, Poland put pressure on its public creditors; in April 1991 an unprecedented debt forgiveness agreement was reached with the official Paris Club creditors, which may result in a 50 per cent reduction in the US$33 bn (at the time of the agreement) owed to Western governments.

Hungary's policy has aimed to service her international obligations in full, which the international financial community has greatly appreciated. Such an attitude imposes constraints and requires the definition of appropriate macroeconomic and financial policy objectives. From a theoretical standpoint, two main objectives could be followed: a current account surplus objective or an official reserves target. Many questions immediately arise:

* How should the choice of Hungary with regard to its debt servicing policy be judged from a long-term point of view?
* What has been the prime target for Hungary's macroeconomic and financial policies?
* Which instruments have been relied upon?
* Would another policy have been possible?
* What are the consequences of the choice made in terms of exchange rate policy, and in terms of inflation?
* What will the exchange rate policy impact be on foreign trade and foreign investments?
* How have the interest margins on Hungarian bond issues on the international capital market developed recently? Have they responded to the strong increase in national reserves?

Foreign capital is finding its way into the Hungarian economy in fairly large amounts compared to the other countries in the region, although still not at the pace hoped for. The total number of business entities with foreign participation reached about 5700 by the end of 1990. Foreign participation represented 28 per cent of the equity in these companies and was valued at around US$1.5 bn, of which US$570 mn had been contributed in cash (the remainder in the form of goods, goodwill, and services). The cash contribution alone amounted to US$800 mn during the first eight months of 1991. We may ask here:

* How has the ability to serve its international obligations influenced Western capital inflows?
* Why has Hungary succeeded in attracting more foreign capital than its neighbours?
* What role do the rather high current tax incentives play in this process?

Chapters 8 (Király), 9 (Várhegyi), 11 (Oblath), 12 (Riecke), 13 (Sárközy) and 14 (Koltay) may help us answer the questions of debt servicing and 2 (Csaba), 3 (Mizsei) and 4 (Halpern and Székely) those on issues of foreign trade.

Privatisation

Privatisation has also reached a critical stage. The period of high expectations about a quick and easy privatisation process, based on a massive inflow of foreign capital, is perhaps now over. Here we need to consider:

* How should we assess the contribution of foreign capital to the privatisation process?

* Is there a real threat of a slowdown in the inflow of foreign capital, and if so, why?

Chapters 5 (Járai), 6 (Mihályi), and 7 (Stadler) will help us elucidate the interplay between privatisation and foreign capital. It has already become clear that privatisation will be lengthy and difficult process, and particular attention must be paid to its repercussions on the future nature of the economy.

The role of the SPA

The State Property Agency (SPA)[2] was created in March 1990 with the authority to manage and privatise a large proportion of state assets. It was established in response to a recognised need for firmer central control, as some enterprise managers had been buying enterprise assets without involving independent auditors or open bidding. In spite of many initiatives, the pace of privatisation remains slow: by September 1991, about 15 per cent of the 2200 state-owned enterprises earmarked for privatisation had been fully or partly privatised, although most of these were relatively small. Here we need to ask:

* What judgement should we pass on the change made in SPA procedures and the privatisation methods adopted?
* How does the current process compare with the vouchers' distribution approach developed in Czecho-Slovakia?
* What are likely to be the next steps in the privatisation process, and if it is to be so slow what consequences may be envisaged at the political level?
* To what extent will the continuing public ownership of factories and companies negatively affect the growth of GDP through the persistent inefficiency caused by such things as relatively poor management, lack of incentives, and obsolete technology?

Restructuring and financial discipline

In such an economic transformation, restructuring and imposing financial discipline will have profound social and welfare consequences. Here three final questions must be asked:

* What will be the unemployment consequences of economic restructuring?
* Has a retraining strategy been devised and, if so, with what success?
* Has the government put in place a social security safety net to mitigate the consequences of economic reform?

Chapters 15 (Köllő), 16 (Augusztinovics) and 17 (Ábel and Bonin) may give us some of the answers to these critical questions.

NOTE

1. Béla Kádár, *Rivista di Politica Economica* (June).
2. A Glossary of key acromyons will be found preceding the Index on p. 353.

Acknowledgements

The editors and publisher wish to thank the following for permission to reproduce copyright material.

EUROSTAT, for data in Table DI.1.

OECD, for data in Tables 10.1, from *Country Report on Hungary* (1991); 11A.1, from *Economic Surveys, Hungary* (1991); and 14.4, from *Economies in Transition: Structural Adjustment in OECD Countries* (1989).

IMF, for data in Table 14.4, from 'Fiscal reform in European Economies in transition' (1991)

Közgazdaságy Szemle, for data in Table 14.4.

The European Economy, for data in Table 11A.2, from *Special Edition* (1991).

List of conference participants

István Ábel *Budapest University of Economics*
Philippe Aghion *EBRD and CEPR*
Tibor Antalpéter *Embassy of the Republic of Hungary, London*
Mária Augusztinovics *Institute of Economics, Hungarian Academy of Sciences, Budapest*
Simon Barnes *S.G. Warburg*
David Begg *Birkbeck College, London, and CEPR*
John Bonin *Wesleyan University*
Simon Broadbent *Foreign and Commonwealth Office, London*
László Csaba *Kopint-Datorg Institute for Economic and Market Research and Informatics, Budapest*
Jean Currie *UK Department of Trade and Industry*
Daniel Daianu *Romanian Institute for Free Enterprise, Bucharest*
Renzo Daviddi *Innocenzo Gasparini Institute for Economic Research, Università Bocconi, Milano*
Robert Deane *HM Treasury*
Rumen Dobrinsky *Centre for Strategic Business and Political Studies, Sofia*
Konstantine Gatsios *Fitzwilliam College, Cambridge, and CEPR*
Iota Emil Ghizari *National Bank of Romania*
Stanislaw Gomulka *London School of Economics*
László Halpern *Institute of Economics, Hungarian Academy of Sciences, Budapest*
Paul Hare *Heriot-Watt University*
Hector Hawkins *Foreign and Commonwealth Office, London*
David Hexter *Citibank*
Athar Hussain *London School of Economics*
Lucian C. Ionescu *Romanian Banking Institute, Bucharest*
Zsigmond Járai *James Capel, Budapest*
Júlia Király *International Banking School, Budapest*

János Köllő *Institute of Economics, Hungarian Academy of Sciences, Budapest*
Grzegorz Kolodko *Institute of Finance, Warsaw*
Jenő Koltay *Institute of Economics, Hungarian Academy of Sciences, Budapest*
Michael Landesmann *Department of Applied Economics, Cambridge*
Colin Mayer *City University Business School, London, and CEPR*
Péter Mihályi *UN Economic Commission for Europe, Geneva*
Kálmán Mizsei *Institute for World Economics, Hungarian Academy of Sciences, Budapest, and Institute for East-West Security Studies, New York*
Lyubomir Mitov *Ministry of Foreign Economic Relations, Sofia*
André Newburg *EBRD*
David M. G. Newbery *Department of Applied Economics, Cambridge, and CEPR*
Willem Noë *Commission of the European Communities*
Jonathan Ockenden *Foreign and Commonwealth Office, London*
Gábor Oblath *Kopint-Datorg Institute for Economic and Market Research and Informatics, Budapest*
Joan Pearce *Commission of the European Communities*
Kinga Pétervári *Budapest University of Economics*
Richard Portes *CEPR and Birkbeck College, London*
Stephen Pudney *Department of Applied Economics, Cambridge*
Adam Ridley *Hambros Bank and CEPR*
Werner Riecke *National Bank of Hungary*
Jim Rollo *Royal Institute of International Affairs*
Jacek Rostowski *School of Slavonic and East European Studies, London*
Robert Rowthorn *University of Cambridge*
André Sapir *Commission of the European Communities and CEPR*
Mario Sarcinelli *EBRD and CEPR*
Paul Seabright *Churchill College, Cambridge, and CEPR*
János Stadler *National Office of Economic Competition, Budapest*
György Surányi *Central European International Bank, Budapest*
István P. Székely *Budapest University of Economics and United Nations, Department of Economics and Social Development, New York*
Iván Szegvári *EBRD*
Ede Sziklai *Embassy of the Republic of Hungary, London*
Zdeněk Tuma *Centre for Economic Research and Graduate Education, Prague*
Éva Várhegyi *Financial Research Ltd, Budapest*
David Winter *University of Bristol*
L. Alan Winters *University of Birmingham and CEPR*
Stephen Yeo *CEPR*

Observers

Kasper Bartholdy *EBRD*
Stuart Brown *Georgetown University*
Chris Nicholson *KPMG*
Mark Odescalchi *James Capel & Co*
Paolo Reboani *London School of Economics*
Gareth Thomas *KPMG*

1 Introduction

ISTVÁN P. SZÉKELY and
DAVID M. G. NEWBERY

1 The Hungarian success story

Hungary is now widely regarded as a 'success story'. The most visible evidence for this is the confidence demonstrated by the international business community, which is reflected in the increasing number of conference papers promoting this assessment. First of all, foreign direct investment (FDI) shows signs of a substantial acceleration. In 1991, FDI totalled US$1.25 bn, up from US$0.34 bn in the previous year. Hungary attracted almost half of total FDI into the region (not counting, of course, the former GDR) in 1991. This happened in spite of the fact that Hungarian labour costs are probably the highest in the region (again excluding the ex-GDR), and that the Hungarian forint (HUF) strongly appreciated in real terms (the real effective exchange rate appreciated by about 12–13 per cent in 1991). Although the HUF is officially still not convertible, and there are severe restrictions on exchange for non-business purposes, rates on parallel markets show a rapid strengthening of the HUF. The country has also regained secure access to international commercial capital markets, and this has happened despite the fact that Hungary, while achieving substantial improvements in many of the indicators of indebtedness, still belongs to the group of highly indebted countries.

The strong support on the part of international organisations, most notably the IMF, the World Bank and the EC, also demonstrates a favourable judgement on the country's performance so far. As a result, the share of non-commercial finance in total debt rose rapidly: the level of non-commercial debt rose from US$3.04 bn at the end of 1990 (out of a total debt of US$21.55 bn) to US$5 bn at the end of 1991 (out of a total of US$22.36 bn).

The signs of improved confidence in a successful transformation are visible not only abroad, but to an extent also inside the country. Private unrequited transfers, primarily representing the accumulation of hard currency-denominated deposits of households with domestic banks, remained high, and in fact slightly increased in 1991. Domestic private saving in financial assets increased substantially, although part of this, as just noted, is kept in hard currency-denominated balances. This can, however, be interpreted as portfolio diversification to reduce risk rather than as a distrust of the transformation process itself. Inflationary expectations seem to be gradually calming down, although very slowly.

2   The Hungarian transformation process: prospects and pitfalls

Is this favourable assessment justified by the results Hungary has achieved so far in its economic transformation? Or, put differently, is there any evidence to caution us against being too optimistic about the future prospects of the country? The reform process can best be judged at two levels: that of the macroeconomy, and the more detailed microeconomic structure. The macroeconomy is more visible in the published statistics, and maintaining or restoring macroeconomic stability is an essential step in the transformation process. If we concentrate on the macroeconomic aggregates, there is no doubt that 1991 was a year of major importance in the process of economic transformation in Eastern Europe. It was a painful year, and more so in the countries which started this process later. In the region as a whole (here and hereafter not counting the former GDR) real GDP declined by at least 15 per cent, and probably by even more than that: the figures for individual countries range from a decline of 22.9 per cent for Bulgaria to around 8 per cent for Poland; the latest official figure for Hungary shows a 10.2 per cent decline. It has to be emphasised that the statistical systems in these countries are increasingly unable to cover newly emerging small-scale private activity. However, if this is taken into account (by using business survey-type methods), then the relative position of Hungary further improves. As a consequence of the substantial decline of economic activity, unemployment started to increase rapidly, and this process will certainly accelerate in 1992. In Poland and Bulgaria, unemployment had already exceeded 10 per cent by the end of 1991. In Czecho-Slovakia (6.6 per cent) and Hungary (8.5 per cent) the values at the end of 1991 were lower, but they were also increasing rapidly. Although in Romania unemployment was around 4 per cent, this does not yet fully reflect the decline in economic activity, and there is little doubt that it will rapidly increase after the general elections in 1992. Similar trends can be expected in the republics of the Commonwealth of Independent States (CIS, i.e. the former USSR). One can thus expect a substantial increase in the number of registered unemployed people, amounting to at least 3 mn in the region as a whole at the end of 1991. This, taking account of the fact that unemployment is geographically strongly concentrated, will undoubtedly create enormous social tensions in each of the countries, and in fact has already done so in many regions.

The decline in economic activity in the region is even more pronounced in investment. For the region as a whole, real gross investment was estimated to have declined by 21 per cent in 1991, but this may well again turn out to be an underestimate. In Bulgaria, investment declined by more than 55 per cent, while the same figure for Hungary, most probably representing the other end of the range, was a decline of about 11 per cent. The estimated figures for Poland and Czecho-Slovakia were falls of 16.7 and 30.1 per cent respectively. Although the initial estimated decline for the CIS was about 7 per cent, the final figure will undoubtedly be substantially higher.

Inflation soared in the region during 1991. The expected figures for CPI inflation for 1991 ranged from 480 per cent for Bulgaria to 35 per cent for Hungary. Although Poland managed to bring down inflation substantially towards the end of the year, for the year as a whole it recorded a figure slightly above 70 per cent. Czecho-Slovakia had an initial large step-change in the price level, but this does not seem to have translated into persistent inflation, as the month-to-month inflation was down to 1.6 per cent by October, though for the year as a whole the change was 58 per cent. Although for 1991 as a whole the CPI inflation for the CIS was well below the figure for Bulgaria, the price liberalisation in January 1992 ignited an unprecedented inflation which – in the view of many analysts – could easily reach 700–1000 per cent for the year.

Real wages, incomes and consumption also declined, though to a somewhat smaller extent than the declines in GDP. Estimated figures for real private consumption range from a decline of 27.6 per cent for Czecho-Slovakia to an increase of 6.6 per cent for Poland. The figure for Hungary was a decline of about 6 per cent, again at the lower end of the range.[1]

As this brief overview indicates, the performance of Hungary in 1991 was relatively good compared to the other countries in the region, but the general tendency to a major decline in economic activity characterised Hungary as well. Indeed, there were other factors which were damaging for confidence. The budget deficit reached 4–6 per cent of GDP, depending on what sort of definition was used for the budget. This figure was considerably above the one agreed with the IMF for 1991, and the required reform of public expenditure was further delayed. How, then, given this fall in output, investment and consumption, and the worrying budgetary position, does one explain the markedly improved confidence in the ability of Hungary (or that of the Hungarian administration) to carry out a smooth and successful economic transformation?

First, one should point to some of the successes. Domestic demand management successfully curbed imports to a level that produced a positive current account of some US$0.3 bn. Riecke points out in Chapter 12 that as a result of increasing hard currency export revenues and a further improvement in the structure of foreign debt the debt-service ratio declined substantially, from around 54 per cent in 1990 to around 35 per cent in 1991 (these figures, taken from the somewhat different definitions used by the World Bank, are slightly different from Riecke's, but the trend is exactly the same). International (hard) currency reserves increased substantially from about US$1.02 bn in April 1990 to US$3.4 bn at the end of 1991, now covering more than three months of imports. The increased level of international currency reserves will enable the National Bank to continue the real appreciation of the HUF which, if not excessive and thus sustainable, will undoubtedly further ease inflationary pressure. The prospect of continuing real appreciation should also encourage foreign investors to move in, as investment will be cheaper now than later, and the dollar value of future profits will be higher. However, the policy of real appreciation of the domestic currency is not without risk, as we shall argue below. Although gross foreign debt expressed in US$ increased, totalling US$22.4 bn by the end of 1991, net debt somewhat decreased.

Another, perhaps even more promising result, pointed out in Csaba's Chapter 2, is the substantial increase in the exports to OECD countries, and a remarkable success in weathering the collapse of CMEA trade. Hungarian firms, even the state-owned ones, proved to be fairly successful in finding new markets for their products, and/or changing their production lines to meet demand in foreign markets. This remarkable result was achieved despite a strongly appreciating domestic currency, and with very high domestic interest rates: that is, firms were able to improve their cost efficiency substantially. Some of the reasons for the apparently surprising flexibility and responsiveness are to be found in Chapter 4 by Halpern and Székely, in which they find that enterprises after the reforms of 1968 were quite responsive to market signals (exchange rates, taxes, subsidies), but that this responsiveness was obscured by the opacity of the regulatory and tax system. As exchange rates are unified and adjusted in response to trade deficits, and taxes made more uniform, so these market responses show up at the aggregate level.

At the macroeconomic level, then, Hungary's performance appears creditable when compared with her neighbours, and appears to have satisfied the critical test of international acceptance. We shall return to the credibility of the reform, essential for international confidence, below. Macro-economic stability is a necessary but not sufficient condition for trans-forming a Soviet-type economy into a market economy. For that, institu-tions, laws, and behaviour have to be transformed in profound ways. The next section asks how far these structural reforms have proceeded.

3   Enterprise reform

The objective, shared by all the formerly socialist economies of Eastern Europe, is to transform a Soviet-type economy into a market economy. The distinguishing features of the Soviet-type economy are now fairly familiar. There was little or no private ownership outside small-scale agriculture and services. Enterprises were confined to certain defined lines of production, and the production units were large, creating monopolies either by product or by region or both, under a system of tutelage from the responsible ministry. The guiding ministries had reasonably well-defined targets for the outputs of different sectors, and the negotiated pattern of CMEA trade had first priority as it enjoyed the status of a treaty obligation. In the more decentralised system of planning intro-duced in Hungary in 1968 the enterprises were under indirect but never-theless tight central control implemented through a complex system of taxes and subsidies as well as investment allocations. After-tax wages were determined by political criteria which reflected the objectives for the economy. Wage differentials were relatively narrow, and the degree of after-tax and transfer income inequality was much lower than in market economies. Much of the system of social security was devolved to the large enterprises. Many systemic features of the economy follow from these characteristics.

The highly concentrated structure of industry reduces or eliminates the ability of enterprises to find competing sources of supply, and leads to bargaining rather than market-mediated transactions, as well as to exces-sive vertical integration. The same concentration reduces the quality of information flowing to the centre, and forces the pattern of relationships between the centre and enterprise into one of bilateral bargaining under asymmetric information, likely to lead to inefficient outcomes. Worse, the government finds it hard credibly to commit itself to any agreement reached today, as all future transactions are subject to renegotiation. This in turn undermines incentives for efficient investment, management, and innovation, and creates the whole syndrome of the 'soft budget con-straint'.

If we ask what characterises market economies it is harder to find uniformities, especially in the system of ownership and control over large

B

corporations. Stock exchanges and dispersed equity ownership are characteristic of the USA and UK, while bank finance and more concentrated control are characteristic of Germany and Japan. The extent of state ownership in the productive sector varies widely, as does the choice between regulation and public ownership for natural monopolies. Some countries have very liberal trade regimes and no restrictions on capital mobility, others are at almost the other extreme. Nevertheless, one can make some broad generalisations. The most striking difference between the formerly socialist and market economies of Europe lies not so much in the industrial structure, but in the size of firms and the degree of industrial concentration within each industry. Market economies have many small and medium-sized firms, and few large firms, while the formerly socialist economies have very few small and medium-sized firms, and a predominance of large enterprises. The striking similarity in the size distribution of firms in market economies suggests that there are powerful market forces at work to generate and reproduce this pattern. Where not actively prevented by the state, firms everywhere will seek to establish cartels or monopolies to secure profits. In a market economy the resulting profits will attract entry, and the observed size distribution is the outcome of the more successful firms growing faster and increasing concentration, while new firms enter at smaller scales. In Soviet-type economies, producer interests have captured the state and prevented the competitive erosion of their market power. Entry is impossible if there are no independent sources of finance, such as commercial banks, and if it is illegal to employ wage labour. Firms are prevented from entering different lines of business in competition with incumbents. Unsuccessful firms are subsidised, rather than going bankrupt and being restructured. Stassis rather than success is rewarded, dulling incentives and removing the spur to efficiency.

The economic advantages of the market economy are its flexibility, adaptability to change, ability to innovate, and its efficiency in resource use, both static and dynamic. These result from the coincidence of private gain and public good under competitive conditions, but this coincidence appears to require strong competitive pressure, which rewards success, penalises failure, and reallocates resources from the unsuccessful to the successful. Private property is a key element in providing the incentive for efficiency, but for other than small-scale enterprise there is normally a separation of ownership and control which creates principal–agent problems.

If the state enterprise is profitable, has little debt, and is sold to achieve dispersed equity ownership, as was typically the case for British privatisations (and would be for the various mass privatisations proposed for

Eastern Europe), then the problem of corporate governance is acute, and a change of ownership from the state to private individuals may have little effect on efficiency if the enterprise remains a monopoly protected from serious competition. Evidence from market economies suggests that liberalisation which increases competitive pressure is more effective than a change of ownership. If the firm is encumbered with debt, and not very profitable, then equity owners are likely to be less important than the debt holders who, by refusing to roll over debt (or defer interest repayments) are well placed to insist on restructuring to improve efficiency. In such cases the product market does not play such a central role in enforcing efficiency, and privatisation, even of monopolies, may have a dramatic efficiency effect. It may be that the situation in Soviet-type economies is closer to the second case than to the first, which somewhat reduces the urgency of demonopolising the product market compared to privatisation. However, for this to work, debt holders (banks) need the competence and motivation to play this role, and this may require that they be privatised and subject to competition from foreign banks. It also remains true that privatising monopolies forecloses the option of reducing market concentration, so the impact on efficiency may be ephemeral even if the banks were able to play this role.

One of the main questions under debate in Eastern Europe is the urgency of privatisation, and the method to be adopted. The closely related questions of competition policy, trade liberalisation, industrial policy and reform of the financial sector, all of which affect the environment for privatised firms, are perhaps less salient in the popular debate, but no less important. Three authors in this volume address the key questions of privatisation and competition policy. Járai and Mihályi (Chapters 5 and 6) both examine the progress of Hungarian privatisation, while Stadler (Chapter 7) looks at competition policy. Already one can point to differences in the approach of Hungary and her neighbours. Hungary has a tradition of gradual evolutionary reform, starting with the New Economic Mechanism (NEM) of 1968. Similar reforms in Czecho-Slovakia (the 'Prague Spring') were suppressed and the system remained ossified until the Velvet Revolution.

Hungary's sequence of reforms aimed to reform the management of enterprises, to raise their efficiency and accelerate their productivity growth. On the one hand the government attempted to decentralise decision-making, and use price-guided signals (taxes and subsidies rather than directives and quantity requirements), while on the other hand it attempted to redress the extra market power given to the enterprises by maintaining tight control over the use of profits and the allocation of investment resources. As firms acquired more control over decision-making, the temptation was to raise wages rather than lower prices, and to counter this the government imposed steeply progressive excess wage taxes. This system of individually adjusted taxes and subsidies at penal rates effectively eliminated the incentives provided by the move to more decentralisation, and lead to widespread disillusion with the reforms.

The tax reforms of 1988, described in Koltay's Chapter 14, were an attempt to escape from the bilateral bargaining relationship which so reduced the efficiency of decentralised incentives. As Koltay points out, it is not enough to introduce a tax system modelled on that of a market economy when the underlying industrial structure still resembles that of a Soviet-type economy. Lowering the marginal tax rates on enterprises improves incentives, but the incentive may be to increase profit without efficiency, and to reduce state revenue while increasing consumption. We return to the essential reform – that of imposing competitive pressures on enterprises. Here the Hungarian approach has been one of cautiously increasing competitive pressures by liberalising international trade, while attempting to maintain price control through the Price Office. This institution has now been replaced by a Competition Office, as explained in Chapter 7, and a large fraction of imports are now allowed in without restriction. Restrictions on setting up private firms have been removed, and the necessary legal framework of commercial law and contracts is gradually being put into place, as set out in Sárközy's Chapter 13. Hungary's approach and sequencing differs quite markedly from those of Poland and Czecho-Slovakia, who have deferred tax reform but have moved to rapid liberalisation of foreign trade, partly to stabilise prices, but mainly to increase competitive pressure on enterprises.

Just as Hungary has adopted a gradual approach to reforming institutions, the tax system, and the foreign trade regime, in contrast to the more abrupt liberalisations in Poland and Czecho-Slovakia, so her privatisation programme has been state-guided and gradual, aimed at selling enterprises rather than giving them away to the populace, again in contrast to the aspirations of Poland and Czecho-Slovakia. How well has this gradual approach worked, and how far is it addressing the major sources of inefficiency?

The first point to make about enterprise reform is that it has both macro and micro consequences. As already noted, there is a tension between decentralising decision-making and improving incentives, and losing control over the macroeconomy. Improving incentives means lowering taxes and hence state revenue, and requires corresponding cuts in expenditure if a budget balance is to be maintained. The evidence in Eastern Europe, China, and the heavily indebted developing countries is that cutting public expenditure is difficult and typically slow, while revenue can fall quite fast unless supplemented by transitional taxes (or increased seigniorage from the inflation tax). Worse, where the enterprises have market power and are profitable, they are free to raise prices, and with the extra revenue to increase investment, and/or to raise wages and hence consumption, rather than hold down consumption and increase savings. If enterprises are unprofitable (perhaps because they cannot raise prices in foreign markets, or because they have lost their market), then the state typically has to subsidise the losses (either directly, or through the banking system). Profits are no longer fully returned to the state, but are either consumed or invested, while losses that formerly were counterbalanced by profits are fully transferred to the state, unbalancing the budget. If the budget does not explicitly subsidise loss-making enterprises, but allows state-owned banks to roll over debts and advance additional finance, the capital base of the banking system will be eroded and financial stability threatened. Indeed, one of the problems facing the authorities, international agencies, and foreign investors is that the whole national accounting system becomes less informative as the old system of central accounting is replaced by a variety of often unrecorded transactions, through banks, special funds, and local government accounts.

These macroeconomic consequences of enterprise and tax reform are visible to a greater or less extent in all the reforming countries, and Hungary, like other countries, is finding it difficult to reduce public expenditures in a systematic way. In her Chapter 16 on social security, Augusztinovics draws attention to the lack of any systematic plan to reform and secure the financing of pensions, whose finance at the moment is being used to subsidise other parts of the budget. The conference did not address the important question of local government finance, but Bird and Wallich (1992) give a clear account of the potential problems arising from the devolution of responsibility for important and expensive items, such as education (38 per cent of 1990 local government expenditures), health (21 per cent), and local transport (10 per cent). Local authorities are heavily dependent on the central government for income, and have a limited local tax base, which they are in any case reluctant to use. Property taxes are potentially important and attractive revenue sources, but exemptions and local political resistance make this an unlikely source of revenue in the near future. Local governments own extensive property and housing, but charge so far below commercial rents that they are failing to cover maintenance expenses out of current rents, which are in any case fixed by the central government (and not indexed). While these rent controls may have the desirable effect of encouraging sales to occupants, this will not solve the revenue problem. Faced with heavy expenditure claims and limited revenues, local governments may be tempted to borrow (they have unlimited borrowing authority under the 1990 Local Self-Government Act, para. 88) and are certainly undertaking commercial activities with property transferred to them by the central government. As they have little business skill, and as they will be tempted to subsidise loss-making enterprises, this transfer of state property to local authorities achieves the exact opposite of privatisation: it retains all the undesirable features of state ownership, but with reduced account-ability (because of dispersed responsibility), while unfairly competing with the private sector through these subsidies.

In the short to medium run, the most likely outcome is that many services will be underfunded or will disappear, partly because the revenue allocated to finance them will not be fully adjusted for inflation, and partly because in transferring responsibility for supply either from the central government to local government, or from state enterprises to local government, the necessary infrastructure and expertise to administer the programmes will be lacking. Expenditures may therefore be cut by default, but the pressures to reinstate them will be strong, and will eventually have to be addressed. It is hard to judge whether Hungary has the process more or less under control than her neighbours, though there are certainly worrying political tensions between the central and local government levels.

There is one important sense in which Hungary has taken the fiscal implications of enterprise reform more seriously than her neighbours, and that is in insisting on selling, rather than giving away, state-owned enterprises. Augusztinovics puts one aspect of this case in Chapter 16, by pointing out that previously pensions in Hungary were financed by a *funded* pay-as-you go system, in which contributions were used to finance investment in enterprises, whose returns would pay for future pensions. If these assets are given away, the state loses the income stream that finances those pensions. If it sells them, it can then reduce its public debt (as in the UK), and the interest that would otherwise have gone to the debt holders will be released to finance these pension liabilities. The problem with this solution is that it is slower than mass privatisation or redistributing shares in the enterprises, that it may be prone to manipu-lation and capture, and that it may fail to raise much revenue. It may also tempt the authorities to preserve monopolies in order to raise their market price, though rapid privatisation also means that too little time (or attention) is being devoted to restructuring and demonopolising before sale.[2]

Centralised sales of larger state enterprises have not been a success, and the 'First Privatisation Programme' which was launched in 1990 to sell 20 of the most attractive enterprises completed only two major transactions.

On the other hand, the privatisation of small state enterprises was very successful, and the plan announced in May 1992 is to build on this success by requiring 278 of the larger enterprises to choose consulting companies to manage their privatisation, with the fees to the consultants designed to provide incentives for speedy and profitable sale. This idea of privatising the privatisation process may overcome the previous bureaucratic hurdles, but it is fair to say that the jury is still out on the respective merits of the gradual commercial approach of Hungary, or the swift redistributive approach favoured by Poland and Czecho-Slovakia.

If the macroeconomic consequences of enterprise reform have not been adequately addressed, the microeconomic or incentive issues have at least been identified as central to the success of reform, though there is less agreement among Eastern Europeans about their solution. Enterprises must become consumer-, not producer-driven if they are to be competitive in a market economy. Privatisation is seen as a key step in this process, and to the extent that it removes enterprises from the producer-captured state, it is a necessary step. But consumer orientation requires two elements – enterprises have to produce at least cost, and they have to produce what consumers want. Pressures to lower costs and increase productive efficiency can come from the product market, if the enterprise faces efficient competitors, either at home, or abroad, or waiting in the wings to enter the market. They can come from the capital market if owners or lenders can put pressure on management, and ultimately can replace the management with a satisfactory alternative. The first requires product market competition, and has already been stressed. It can best be achieved by trade liberalisation, deregulation, facilitating entry (which requires that the financial sector is able to finance new firms), and breaking up the existing over-large enterprises into smaller, more focused units, perhaps based on the existing establishment structure of the enterprise. The second requires the even more substantial reform of the system of corporate governance. Neither is automatically ensured by privatisation alone, and premature privatisation with the existing structure (a monopoly with dispersed ownership) may foreclose the possibility of transforming the efficiency of the enterprise.

Arguably the more intractable problem is that of ensuring that enterprises produce what consumers want, and this is where restructuring is most difficult. It may not just mean producing the old product more efficiently (to which the product and capital market reforms were directed), but it may require changing the product, replacing the Trabant by the VW Golf, for example. It typically requires importing the technological know-how and the managerial expertise, and creating a reputation for reliability and high quality, or destroying the previous reputation for unreliability and low quality. There is an irony in observing that the kind of industry-wide restructuring which this requires often seems to need the resources of skilled state intervention, as in Korea (Amsden, 1989), or in the UK as in the case of the state-owned steel industry before privatisation or, arguably, in the former GDR under the Treuhandanstalt. But everywhere in Eastern Europe the incumbent state has lost all credibility as a competent reorganising force, and only in Germany was there an alternative state able to play that role. The obvious solution, which Hungary, and even more Czecho-Slovakia, have been quick to grasp, is to invite foreign firms to provide this restructuring. This is borne out by the observations of Járai and Mihályi that most formal privatisations in Hungary have involved foreign investors.

This then raises a serious question for those state-owned enterprises which are unattractive to foreign buyers. Should they be left intact on the argument that it is more difficult to restructure a dispersed competitive industry than a concentrated oligopoly, and that their market power must be weak if they are so unattractive to buyers? Or should they be broken up to reduce their ability to hold the banks to ransom, and to see which parts are due to survive? The Competition Office is aware of the tension between the need to demonopolise state enterprises and the fear that if broken up, large fractions of the original enterprise will not survive. It is not at all clear that privatising such enterprises will not lead to closure of the unviable divisions in any case, though there is a good argument for forcing the incoming management to take a positive decision to close a division, as opposed to requiring a positive decision to buy a separated division to ensure its survival. The German Treuhandanstalt tries to meet this problem by negotiating with the prospective buyer to undertake restructuring of as much of the enterprise as possible, in return for accepting a lower price. This raises the natural question of whether the Hungarian government (or, preferably, an independent state agency), assisted by international agencies or foreign governments, should buy in foreign expertise (perhaps by forming alliances with comparable firms abroad) and leave them to restructure? To date, too little attention has been devoted to the practicalities of such restructuring, and too much to attempts to privatise the state sector.

At the moment the urgency to privatise effectively means that monopolies are not broken up before sale. This may not matter for enterprises exposed to vigorous international competition, or those that can only (just) survive as monopolies, but the worry is that some privatised firms will acquire unreasonable market dominance. It might be desirable for the Competition Office, supported by the government, to indicate that in such cases, further restructuring will take place in the future. This should not deter buyers, as it will only remove the chance of excessive monopoly profits, which they would probably heavily discount in any case as liable to action by the Competition Office. The advantage of being explicit about future references to the Competition Office is that it removes some of the current tension between competition policy and privatisation, while committing future competition policy.

Finally, there is the politial element in restructuring and privatisation. The problem is that control over enterprises needs to be transferred from the inefficient state to efficiency-oriented owners. If owners are to exercise effective control, they will undoubtedly become rich, since dispersed control is unlikely to be effective without a very competitive market for products, managers and control, and without an efficient financial system, all of which are at best embryonic. The problem is to devise a system of allocating this wealth which is both 'fair' in the sense of not undermining the legitimacy of the process, and which achieves this efficiency. The attraction of the mass privatisation schemes of Poland and Czecho-Slovakia is that they hope to achieve the 'fairness' objective, though there must be serious worries on the efficiency score. The worry in Hungary is that wealth is being captured by insiders, which reduces its legitimacy. The worst of all possible outcomes would be that it also failed to achieve efficiency.

Privatisation is only one of the methods available for improving market efficiency, and it has the limitation that it starts with existing firms who have achieved their current position not by competitive success but by administrative fiat. In the medium and long run, the main source of improvement will come from enterprises that are successful in the market place, and to that extent facilitating entry and ensuring that successful firms have access to capital may be even more important. It is encouraging to observe (though it is hardly captured by official statistics), the sizeable increase in private business activities in 1990 and 1991. A 1991 World Bank survey shows that these mainly small-scale businesses are very export-oriented. The majority of them developed out of (semi-) private business created by previous reforms (most notably from the VGMKs).[3] This meant that many of them have some sort of a track record, and experience with private business activities (or, more important, with activities which were competitive, market-oriented and unprotected by the state). This has enabled them to expand their activities much faster than anybody thought possible even in 1990.

The rapid development of the private sector was accompanied by further important steps in the creation of the institutional and legal structures of a market economy in Hungary. As the detailed account of legal reforms given in Sárközy's Chapter 13 shows, a large number of basic laws were passed and a remarkable deregulation was carried out (with the assistance of the World Bank). Unfortunately, most of these acts were passed in 1990 and the process slowed down considerably during 1991, leaving many key acts to be passed in 1992. Nevertheless, the country now has almost all the necessary basic institutions, regulations and legislation of a market economy in place, in contrast to the other countries in the region. This, of course, does not mean that further improvements are not required. However, these future adjustments can be based on accumulated experience. The gradual approach seems to have paid off in this respect, too. It has made possible the operation of the new system which, in turn, has increased credibility and confidence inside and outside the country.

4   Credibility of the reform process

At this point, we reach the most important issue, the credibility of the administration and reform packages. The Hungarian reform programme, from the very beginning, was rather eclectic and less ambitious than any of the then fashionable packages. But this cautious and pragmatic approach enabled it to build up credibility and confidence. The changes, despite vociferous discussion, and progress sideways and backwards, clearly indicate a direction which is widely accepted by the people inside the country, and which is acceptable to the international financial and business communities. This predictability and consistency seems to have paid off; the best sign of this is that although Hungary has probably the highest labour costs in the region, it still attracts the majority of FDI. Another example is the strong appreciation of the HUF in 1991, expected to continue in 1992, combined with rapidly increasing (hard currency) exports and reserves. This expression of confidence by the domestic and foreign business communities suggests that they at least believe the reform programme to be credible. It should be noted that this confidence was displayed in the face of a substantial decline in real GDP, inflation as high as 35 per cent, and a budget deficit amounting to 4–6 per cent of GDP. The resulting capital inflows were able to cushion the inevitable repercussions of a substantial decline of economic activity associated with the required massive restructuring.

The next question is, why has the Hungarian package and the administration attracted such wide expressions of confidence in the eyes of the international and domestic business communities, or at least more so than any of the others in the region?

The starting position of newly elected Hungarian government in May 1990 had many unfavourable features. These included the dangerously high level of foreign indebtedness, discussed in detail in Chapters 12 by Riecke and 11 by Oblath; the correspondingly high level of domestic public debt; the rather low level of international reserves (about US$0.97 bn at the end of April, 1990, covering slightly more than one month's imports); a substantial budget deficit in 1989 (about 2–2.5 per cent of GDP), an oversized state budget, collecting and redistributing 61–64 per cent of GDP in 1989, the very fragile investment portfolios of the newly created commercial banks, foreshadowing a financial crisis; the overwhelming share of state budget-related loans in total domestic credits; rather high levels of production and export subsidies (amounting to about 13 per cent of GDP at the end of 1989); the distortion in relative prices (although lower than elsewhere), accelerating inflation; the unexpectedly sudden collapse of the CMEA trade arrangement (discussed by Csaba in Chapter 2 and by Mizsei in Chapter 3), and the unsettled position of the social security system described by Augusztinovics in Chapter 16.

In the event, other aspects of the Hungarian legacy were much more important than originally foreseen. Among the more important and useful legacies were the accumulating experience with entrepreneurship and private enterprise going back to 1968, and the gradual changes in the institutional and legal structures discussed by Sárközy. To this one should add the price reform in 1980, which confronted firms with the world price level on both the input and the output sides, instead of letting the highly distorted CMEA prices persist, and the gradual reorientation of foreign trade away from distorted CMEA markets. This process continued with the gradual liberalisation of prices (about 62 per cent of consumer prices and the large majority of producer prices by the end of 1989) and foreign trade (approximately 16 per cent of imports by the end of 1989; by 1992 this had increased to 90 per cent). The major reform of the tax system in 1988, which introduced VAT and PIT at a very early stage, and the Company Act, also passed in 1988, both paved the way for private activities and for the incorporation of state-owned firms, while preserving fiscal discipline. The reform of the financial system in 1987 (dealt with by Várhegyi in Chapter 9), created a two-tier banking system and introduced other elements of a market financial system. These gradual reforms enabled the authorities to learn from experience and to accumulate expertise and confidence in market-oriented reforms.

5   The role of aid and professional expertise

The full and unquestioned commitment of the administration to an uninterrupted and punctual servicing of foreign debts was an important factor in building up credibility abroad. Another important aspect of development was the IMF and World Bank membership granted at an early stage. The inevitable collaboration with these institutions helped to a great extent to design and successfully implement many of the positive reforms mentioned above. Naturally, it was also a key factor in preserving the solvency and credit-worthiness of the country during the liquidity crisis Hungary suffered during the 1980s.

The large and increasing pool of professionals with experience and knowledge of the functioning of market mechanisms and with fairly good command of foreign languages also proved to be vital in the process of transformation. Many of the FDI projects are now attracted to Hungary by this pool which, it seems, is not yet available in the main competitor countries in the region.

6   Potential hazards facing the transformation

It seems that the capacity of Hungary to absorb large changes is relatively high. This is partly due to the advantageous initial conditions and institutions, especially if compared to other countries in the region, and also to the very pragmatically managed transition process. Continuity seems to be a key characteristic of the Hungarian transition, and the rest of the world seems increasingly to appreciate the resulting predictability. There are many examples of new reforms built on previous reforms and of reform measures worked out by the previous administration but introduced by the present administration: Sárközy's Chapter 13 gives ample evidence of this. The capacity of the country to adapt to a market economy is further enhanced by the high level of education and skills of the workforce, documented by Hamilton and Winters (1992, Table 10). They show that Hungary ranked first in achievement in science education of a sample of 12 developed countries at the 14–15 year old level, and third at the final stage of secondary education. To this one should add the relative political stability the country has experienced during the last few years. The smooth manner in which the political regime change was carried out, and the design of the systems of election and parliamentary representation also contributed to the remarkable political stability the country has shown during the transformation.

Industrial relations proved to be rather robust, and the country managed to avoid widespread strikes. Although the famous case of the so-called 'taxi strike' showed how vulnerable a government of a country in transition can be, this episode fortunately led each side involved to compromise rather than to pursue further confrontation. The recent attempt of the (old) trade unions to mount a general-warning work stoppage showed again than both sides have a lot at stake; but these events were of minor importance, and industrial relations seem in general to be an element of stability in Hungary. Naturally, a rapidly rising level of unemployment will test this. Köllő's Chapter 15 gives an excellent insight into the problem, pointing out the likely impacts of economic transformation on individual employees' 'everyday power' at the workplace and the problems of communication between trade union leaders and workers. These changes, he argues, have a profound impact on industrial relations, as shown by the story of the general-warning work stoppage mentioned above. As in many other places, the old system has disappeared, but the new one is not yet in place.

All this is, of course, not to suggest that there are no potential dangers and pitfalls in the Hungarian transformation. Sárközy's Chapter 13 points to a number of essential elements of the legal structure which still have to be introduced, and which are far from being properly worked out. Any serious delay in this respect will substantially slow down the process of transformation, since a properly functioning legal system is a vital element of credibility. Without further substantial improvement in this respect an increasing number of FDI projects will be diverted from the country, and the level of uncertainty in business activities will inevitably increase. Increased uncertainty will naturally lead to a higher risk premium to be paid to (foreign) investors, depressing investment activities.

As Chapters 8 by Király and 9 by Várhegyi point out, there is a need for a further substantial reform of the banking and financial system, dealing with the problem of bad and doubtful loans. The country already had a warning case of a bank's bankruptcy, in practice bailed out by the government, but it must be questionable whether the same can be done in the case of a full-scale financial crisis. A substantial shake-up and restructuring of the large commercial banks is an inevitable step, which eventually will have to lead to privatisation. Delays here again will slow down economic transformation and seriously damage the favourable image the country currently enjoys.

6.1 The budget problem

Another potential source of disruption is the position of the state budget, which, as pointed out in the section on enterprise reform, was bound to come under pressure as revenues fell and expenditures proved hard to cut. Although in 1991 the state budget could be financed without imminent inflationary pressure, the crowding out effect of the high budget deficit is undeniable. If Hungary is to raise its growth rate, she will need public investment in infrastructure as well as private investment. Without a substantial increase in investment activities, there will be no lasting success. Instead of using domestic savings to finance the budget deficit, the major part of domestic saving should be channelled into new, preferably private, but in any case viable investment projects, to generate new jobs and economic growth. Budget deficits of the same magnitude as those of 1991 cannot be sustained in the future without damaging longer-term growth prospects and business confidence.

With an appreciating HUF, the high interest rates likely to be created by a high budget deficit will become increasingly painful for firms, endangering their competitiveness in domestic and foreign markets. Improving export performance is, however, as pointed out by Riecke in Chapter 12, of vital importance for keeping the debt-service ratio relatively low. Without this, the risk premium the country pays on foreign debts, and to foreign direct investors, may become unbearably high. This, in turn, will further increase domestic interest rates, driving many firms out of business and halting the whole investment process.

A drastic public expenditure reform thus seems inevitable and this means cutting public expenditure. As privatisation proceeds, it will be increasingly difficult to collect the necessary finance for the sort of expenditure levels observed in the past. If maintaining the competitiveness of domestic producers is, as it must be, a priority for the administration, then the tax burden and the level of social security contribution should be gradually decreased. This will lead to lower tax revenues, which further underlines the necessity of drastic public expenditure reform. There is no doubt that it will be difficult to reach consensus on expenditure priorities in the new democracy, especially one anticipating both a 'Peace Dividend' and the miracle of the market. The evidence from the former GDR is that restructuring is both painful and expensive. Without a wealthy patron in the form of the former West Germany, these costs will primarily fall on the domestic population in the form of reduced state-provided services. This much is already appreciated – the remaining but large problem is to choose where the cuts should fall.

A further important element of the budget equation is seigniorage (inflationary tax). To date the finance of the budget deficit has relied heavily on this source. If inflation is brought down substantially, as planned, this source will dry up. A major reform of the state budget is thus inevitable, but it is not clear whether the government will be able to carry this out, and do it before a budget crisis emerges. A delay here will force the government to try to resume inflationary finance, seriously damaging credibility, business and consumer confidence and distorting price expectations.

Seigniorage, as argued by Augusztinovics in Chapter 16, is an important element in the financing of the social security system as well. As her simulations show, without further substantial reforms, reducing inflation could create a crisis in the financing of the social security system. If the necessary reforms are not introduced in time, this will create another source of pressure on the government to continue inflationary finance, with the consequences discussed above.

6.2 Exchange rate policy

As touched upon several times already, the further real appreciation of the HUF is not uncontroversial. The present intention of the National Bank of Hungary (NBH) appears to be to achieve an inflation of 22–24 per cent and devalue the HUF by 4–8 per cent. This implies a further substantial real appreciation of the HUF in 1992. This suggests three natural questions: Will this, coupled with very high domestic interest rates, enable domestic producers to preserve their cost competitiveness against foreign producers, both on the domestic and the foreign markets? Will the accommodating monetary policy be strong enough to curb import demand to the level allowed by the export performance? Or, put differently, will this not lead to an undesirable drop in international currency reserves? As pointed out above, it is of vital importance for Hungary to maintain a good export performance; otherwise, international finance will become increasingly difficult to secure and credibility and confidence will be seriously damaged. The real appreciation of the HUF will also increase the costs faced by new FDI projects. Although, as pointed out earlier, some other factors may well offset this impact, one should check carefully whether they will actually do so. Perhaps a slower but smoother appreciation is more desirable at this stage.

Declining international reserves will also, no doubt, delay any plan for convertibility. Convertibility is an issue so far not brought into the picture. In this respect, Hungary seems to be following a more gradual path than some of the other countries in the region. To some extent this reflects an understanding of the importance of sustainability, and the impact of the lack of it on credibility. But it is also due to the very pragmatic approach of the administration. For foreign investors, the HUF is practically fully convertible as far as the principal and the yield of their investments are concerned. For Hungarian investors, 90 per cent of imports are liberalised, but the obligatory exchange of export revenues is still there: essentially they are deprived of a hedging instrument and interest rate arbitrage opportunities. At the moment, with a sharply appreciating domestic currency and with fast-increasing international currency reserves, only the latter seems to be relevant. In fact, if the administration is serious about bringing down interest rates in line with inflation, it should in principle welcome such an arbitrage. Naturally, reserve considerations are much more important at this stage, but if these allow a further move towards a higher degree of convertibility, the arbitrage mentioned above will work for the administration.

The real appreciation of the domestic currency is very useful in bringing down inflation, provided that it is perceived as sustainable. Otherwise, it might even work against this objective. This again points to the conclusion drawn above, namely that a slower but smoother real appreciation may be more desirable at this stage.

6.3   Hungary's position in Eastern Europe

As a general rule, it must not be forgotten that Hungary is in fierce competition with the other countries in the region and, in fact, with many countries in other regions of the world. The modest success of Hungary, so far, has been partly made possible by the relatively poor performance and numerous mistakes of the other Eastern European countries. However one hopes that their economic transformations will also get on the right track soon, this will inevitably worsen the relative position of Hungary, especially if she becomes ensnared in any of the traps mentioned above, slowing down the transformation and/or damaging credibility and confidence. Hungarians in the future will have to keep a very close eye on their competitors, and will have to react as promptly as possible. An important decision in this respect will be on what factor to compete. Competing on the level of real wages would be a serious mistake; after all, labour costs are only one, and not necessarily the largest, component of total costs. It would be wiser to compete in providing a business-friendly, stable and predictable environment, a properly (re-)trained and relatively mobile pool of labour, a reasonable social and economic infrastructure, stable and predictable industrial relations, a serious and predictable administration and a proper legal structure and jurisdiction. The consequences of these elements, or the lack of any of them, for costs will be much more serious than changes in labour costs: more precisely, a proper balance of all of these factors is what is needed to create a 'pro-business' climate.

Needless to say, Hungary's position, in spite of the increasing recognition of the obvious differences among countries in the region, depends to a great extent on the overall local situation. The consequences of Bulgaria's suspension of servicing her foreign debts clearly showed this; any major disruption in the Czecho-Slovak or Polish transformations will have even more immediate repercussions. The civil war in the territory of what was previously Yugoslavia has already shown the nature and extent of potential political and military disruption in the region, and also the possible repercussions of such a development on Hungary (or, in fact, on any other country in the region). FDI, tourism, and even refinance of foreign debts are very strongly and closed influenced by such developments. There is no guarantee that this conflict will be the last of such a nature, nor that future conflicts will not be even more severe. But this is largely beyond the control of the country or government, and one can only hope for the best in this respect.

7   Importance of the EC and the West

To sum up, the Hungarian transformation process is far from being resilient to unfavourable internal and external developments. It is perhaps more robust than many transformations in the region, but may yet be subject to setbacks for the reasons mentioned above, or indeed for other unforeseen reasons. Although Hungary now seems to have a good chance of a relatively smooth and successful transformation, there is no guarantee that this will eventually happen. The international community should therefore do its best to help the country if such foreseen or unforeseen problems arise and perhaps, more importantly, to make the whole process of transformation more robust to such factors.

As pointed out earlier, the relative success of Hungary has depended to a large extent on positive changes in the expectations of domestic and foreign investors. It is thus of vital importance to do everything possible to improve business confidence in Hungary. This is equally true for Hungarian and Western governments, and for international organisations. One such step would be a strong and final commitment on the part of EC governments concerning Hungary's EC membership. What Hungary needs is a precisely defined set of conditions under which she can become eligible for membership. This would give a clear goal, and a strong incentive to carry out the necessary further reforms in the shortest possible time. This would not only make the process more robust, but it would also speed up the whole operation of integrating the Hungarian economy into the European economy and, through this, into the world economy. One thinks of competition policy as a good example where importing best European practice is advantageous, and the same will no doubt be true of banking regulation. The principle has already been accepted for tax reform.

Another less well-defined area in which European firms and institutions may be able to help is the restructuring of those state-owned enterprises which cannot be sold off, but which might be viable at Hungarian wage and skill levels if provided with appropriate products, markets, technology and management. In the former GDR, large firms such as Siemens are playing a crucial role of this sort, and there are similar examples in Hungary, but more needs to be done. Given that the old Hungarian state apparatus has been discredited, there is a vacuum to be filled by a surrogate for state industrial policy which might perhaps be met from outside.

8   Conclusion

As the chapters presented in this volume clearly indicate, the purpose of the volume and that of the conference on which it is based was not to develop a concise and consistent policy package proposal, nor yet fully to explain the relative successes or partial failures of the Hungarian transformation. It was rather intended to highlight some of the more interesting aspects of the Hungarian experience, and to show some of the possible directions of future reforms, as seen from the perspective of early 1992. By doing so, we hope to contribute to improved communication and exchange of ideas among economists inside and outside Hungary, and to the ongoing debate about these matters in the country itself. At many points, the chapters also touch upon the potential dangers and pitfalls of economic transformation in Hungary. The authors express a wide variety of (sometimes even conflicting) views on major economic issues, reflecting the fact that although there is wide consensus on many of the major issues of transformation in Hungary, the country has several choices and possible directions of future development. This rich variety of ideas and proposals has characterised the Hungarian situation since the early days of reforms in the 1960s. Naturally, it became easier openly to express and argue for these views as time passed, especially after 1990. This volume hopes to contribute to this process of a better understanding of different possible options and ideas, and to some extent to help the choice among them. The mere fact that it was easily possible to bring together these views, and to some extent confront them, shows that Hungary, perhaps slightly more than the other countries in the region, has a good chance of success. Last but not least, this volume offers some useful lessons for other countries in the region, with the hope that Eastern Europeans can learn from each others' successes and failures.

NOTES

1 The figures come from United Nations, *World Economic Survey 1992*, and one should be aware of the difficulty of accurately measuring consumption in a period in which the importance of the possibly under-reported private sector is rapidly changing.
2 It should be stressed that it is inefficient *from a government revenue viewpoint* to privatise monopolies, as the same additional revenue as the monopoly profits could have been better achieved by additional taxes on a competitive industry, at lower cost to the consumer, as the competitive industry would have been under greater pressure to lower production costs. The state will certainly have a lower discount rate on these tax receipts than the private sector would have on the less secure monopoly profits, so they have higher present value as taxes rather than as monopoly profits.
3 The VGMKs were set up by enterprises to sub-contract work to their employees, who leased equipment from the enterprise, and were to some extent a way of relaxing the tight wage controls on the enterprises.

REFERENCES

Amsden, A.H. (1989) *Asia's Next Giant: South Korea and Late Industrialisation*, Oxford: Oxford University Press.
Bird, Richard and Christine Wallich (1992) *Financing Local Government in Hungary*, Policy Research *Working Paper*, **WPS 869**, Washington, D.C.: World Bank.
Hamilton, Carl and L. Alan Winters (1992) 'Trade with Eastern Europe', *Economic Policy*, **14** (Spring) pp. 77–104.

Part One

Foreign trade

2   Economic consequences of Soviet disintegration for Hungary

LÁSZLÓ CSABA

1   Overall recession and trade with Eastern Europe: causes and consequences

It used to be a commonplace in Hungarian economics to state that radical marketising reforms foundered owing to the vertical power structure of the party-state as well as to the Hungarian economy's unilateral dependence on the Soviet market. It was therefore widely held that overcoming these fundamental barriers would lead directly to rapid and sizeable improvements.[1] Most political quarters considered this to be an axiom, and the hope of fast political and economic transformation shaped public opinion and expectations across all the Central and Eastern European region.

Econometrically inclined analysts attempted to quantify the potential for 'catching up'. In a study published by the Washington-based Institute for International Economics Collins and Rodrik (1991) estimated that East European countries could triple their market shares in the EC. In another volume, published by the Commission of the European Communities Cohen (1991) put the mid-term growth prospects of post-socialist states in the range of 3–4 per cent per annum in terms of GDP. Applying the conventional postulates of growth theory he put the more advanced countries like Czecho-Slovakia and Hungary into the lower range, and the less advanced Bulgaria, the former USSR and Romania in the upper range.

Against this background it is hardly surprising that policy-makers, business executives and the general public reacted with astonishment to the figures released by the central statistical agencies, which indicated a deepening overall recession in every post-socialist country. According to the KOPINT-DATORG data base – which is the source of all data in this

27

chapter unless explicitly indicated otherwise – net material product in Eastern Europe (save for the former USSR) contracted in 1990 by 11.2 per cent, with a drop of industrial production of 17.5 per cent, a drop of agricultural production of 3.5 per cent, and a fall in investments of 13.8 per cent. In 1991 according to preliminary estimates the drop of GDP in the three Central European countries was 15 per cent, and in the Southeast European countries between 20 and 25 per cent. Industrial output was particularly hard hit by recession: in Hungary an 18, in Poland a 14, and in Czecho-Slovakia a 23 per cent contraction was registered, whereas in the former East German provinces about a third of industrial capacity stayed idle. Meanwhile unemployment climbed to historically unprecedented levels: 6.6 per cent (Czecho-Slovakia), 7.5 per cent (Hungary), 11.4 per cent (Poland), and 25 per cent in the East German provinces, where economic activity also declined sharply. The total number of employed persons dropped from nearly 9 to 8 mn in the former GDR, with some 2 mn unemployed/part-time employed. One of the factors to be blamed for all this is the collapse of COMECON – an issue we shall examine in some detail below.

Recession started in 1990 in the Soviet Union – as far as official statistics are concerned. (Meanwhile, Soviet statisticians and economists dispute whether actual stagnation started at the late 1970s or only in the mid-1980s.) Officially, Soviet national income (NMP) dropped by 4 per cent in 1990, with industrial production registering only a 1.2 per cent drop and investment suffering below average.

The first thing to be observed is that owing to a strong contraction in overall economic activity, which hit industrial production, the backbone of traditional COMECON trade, most heavily a 20–25 per cent – linear – drop in intraregional trade is absolutely normal even if we consider the status quo *ex ante* as ideal and reorientation/opening up to the world economy unnecessary.[2]

Before turning to our subject proper it seems expedient to make a general remark. During the 1970s and 1980s economists learned that the traditional maxim 'more growth means more welfare and more business opportunities', is rather misleading under Eastern European conditions. Artificially accelerated growth in the 1970s, and even the attempt to accelerate growth in the 1980s implied the retention of ossified, internationally non-competitive economic structures. The fact that these structures produce negative returns is reflected in the grave indebtedness of these countries (as measured against their export performance).

The *raison d'être* of all those policy measures and institutional changes, jointly called systemic change, is therefore 'hardening the budget constraint of companies', i.e. putting an end to activities producing negative returns. Entering a new growth path becomes possible only if old patterns of production, specialisation and exchange are being replaced as new, income-generating activities open up. Exposing the production structure inherited from socialism in competitive market pressures, and reorientation of commercial relations from crisis-ridden to dynamic growth implies by definition a recession in overall economic performance which must last two–three years at last. Of course, on paper one may construct a model in which everything is free of friction and governed by economic utility maximisation alone, where a protracted recession is not an inevitable bedfellow of major structural change. However, international experience, especially of less developed countries, indicates that stabilisation is quite costly in terms of growth (Halpern, 1991; Dembinski and Morriset, 1991). The recession startred earlier than a fall of GDP was first observed, and it will last at least two–three years (probably longer than that). As is common knowledge, socialism collapsed among other reasons because it proved unable to maintain the growth on which its distributional systems and social balance rested. From our perspective, in Hungary and Czecho-Slovakia the year 1991, in Poland and East Germany 1990, and in Russia 1992 may be taken as 'initial', when the drop of GDP has to do primarily with a policy choice, not with 'circumstances'.

A drop in economic activity in general and in COMECON trade in particular cannot therefore be interpreted as an unfavourable sign, as a manifestation of crisis. The use of the term 'crisis' either in terms of the business cycle, or in the broader sense (the 'general crisis of capitalism') would be inappropriate and unjustified to describe the subject of our analysis. It is absolutely clear that a totally nationalised economy, whose priorities have been politically–ideologically predetermined for decades, cannot be painlessly transformed, and its transition to a market economy will take several years. Expansion of the private sector, mastering the market rules of the game by tens of thousands of economic actors, is bound to take time. While ossified state economic structures die out 'instantaneously' as the economy opens up and the market begins to bite, the germs of free enterprise are slow to evolve into robust organisms. Even if the latter expand tremendously, overall economic performance on the macro level is bound to be determined by the ailing public sector for quite some time to come. This is not a rationalisation of disillusionment, as it could have been foreseen at the very outset of the process (Csaba, 1990a). The conclusion is thus that in the period of transition other indicators than growth reflect economic performance – such as convertible currency exports, the current account, exchange rate stability and inflation, or the evolution of sales patterns and external market shares.

True, recession remains a fact of life, and the concomitant high rates of interest and depressed demand slow down the spread of private enterprise as well, but it does not change the overall trend.

As a footnote, we should also be clear about the limits of our knowledge of the actual state of the art in Eastern Europe. We do not actually know what the exact size of recession is, as statistical reporting continues to focus on large-scale public activities, while data collection on small-scale and (semi-)private activities is rather inadequate. For Hungary the Central Statistical Office uses tax reports to estimate the share of private activities. On the basis of these reports an average entrepreneur should have earned about 20 per cent less in 1990 than an average state employee, which is contrary to all sociological, economic and everyday evidence. It therefore seems not very biased to maintain that official statistics cover fully the erosion of old activities whereas they heavily underreport private and (semi)private business. This overstates the severity of recession and understates the processes of transformation and recovery.

2   Reorientation and systematic change

Let us now survey the evolution of the geographical pattern of Hungarian foreign trade.[3] As our analysis is macroeconomic in nature it is hardly relevant for us how many litres of wine were being sold, or how many buses were being produced, as these are partial (regional or employment policy) aspects of macroeconomic processes which can be interpreted only in monetary terms.

As is clear from the long-term statistical series, Hungary's trade with the rouble area peaked in 1987. In other words, in terms of domestic currency, trade with the rouble area had already started to *drop* in 1988, when there was no talk of reorientation, when valid five-year and annual interstate protocols should have induced the customary (and actually envisaged) 'uninterrupted growth' of intraregional trade. The export drop of 3 per cent represented a turning point in the long-term historical trend. True, in 1989 exports to the rouble area surpassed the 1987 levels by nearly 2 per cent. However, this was – even then – seen as one of the major mistakes in overall governmental policies, as the unusable rouble surplus was 550 TR mn. In 1990, i.e. in a year when traditional arrangements were still in force (including obligatory interstate quotas and transferable rouble accounting), a drop of 25.3 per cent in Hungarian sales was registered.

This was not because the Hungarian government attempted to balance trade: this applied only to the first two quarters. In the year 1990 as a whole a mixture of unintended processes took place. German monetary union and the resultant artificial DM/rouble rate, converting 1 TR into 2.2 DM, priced out most Hungarian commodities, rendering them non-competitive with better-quality Western produce. Hungarian exports to the GDR thus dropped by a third. Due to the recession, Hungarian exports to Poland and Bulgaria were halved, whereas sales to the USSR fell only by 19 per cent. A balanced annual rouble account thus contained a nearly 600 TR mn Hungarian surplus against the Soviets and a 545 TR mn deficit against Germany. While the latter was mostly an outcome of a *force majeure*, the former took place in the teeth of governmental policies. The erosion of the Soviet market had started and begun to intensify well before convertible currency accounting was introduced on 1 January 1991: the share of the Soviet market was 30.8 per cent of Hungarian sales in 1980, 34 per cent in 1985, 33 per cent in 1987, 24.3 per cent in 1989 and 18.7 per cent in 1990. According to preliminary data, the Soviet share of total Hungarian sales in 1991 was 12 per cent. In other words, the trend of the previous years continued, and – contrary to frequent predictions in some quarters – nothing truly dramatic happened. Exports to the USSR dropped by 19 per cent, just as much as in 1990. Sales to all East Europe (excluding East Germany) were down by 13.5 per cent – even less dramatic.

Looking at the import side, here too the year 1988 was the turning point. True, imports from the USSR had already started to diminish in 1987, by 3.5 per cent. The decline continued in 1988, by 8 per cent; in 1989 it stagnated – despite that year's export 'boom' of 5.4 per cent – and in 1990 it dropped further, by 15.7 per cent. If in 1980 the Soviet share in Hungarian purchases was 29 per cent, and in 1985 31.3 per cent, in 1987 it was 28.6, in 1989 22, and in 1990 17.8 per cent. Reorientation on the import side also took place before dollar trade came in. In 1991 according to preliminary data 13.2 per cent of Hungarian purchases originated from the USSR. In value terms, due to the switchover to dollars and exchange rate effects, an increase of 23.4 per cent was registered, which in nominal HUF terms was somewhere around the 1988 level; imports from Eastern Europe grew by 23.1 per cent for similar reasons. In other words, a year of dramatic events, of dissolution of the Soviet internal empire, was rather undramatic in bilateral trade terms. This is not to say that nobody lost markets, but the share of machinery in Hungarian exports to East Europe in 1991, for example, was 22.3 per cent, nearly twice as high as Hungarian exports to the OECD. Meanwhile, on the import side, machinery imports from East Europe accounted only for 6.1 per cent of purchases compared to 26.7 per cent in imports from the OECD and 39.7 per cent in imports from the non-European OECD. These data indicate that machinery markets for various ex-CMEA countries were not equally soft, and further that not only reorientation, but a modernising change of partners, took place. The reorientation of fuel purchases to developing countries and their concomitant advances also deserves attention.

It is interesting to note that, contrary to oft-voiced fears, the transition to convertible currency accounting proved to be relatively smooth, and the expected enormous deficit in Hungary's trade with the USSR did not emerge. Actually, it was below $400 mn, while expectations ran between $1.5–2 bn. True, in the trade balance a deficit of $1.6 bn occurred, but only a quarter of it fell on the USSR. The lion's share fell on the OECD and developing countries, where purchases grew by 60.3 and 67.6 per cent respectively. This supports the view (Oblath, 1992; Kádár, 1991) that liberalisation of the import regime in 1991 took a larger step than was actually justified. Still, even if we assume that part of the 'Western' and 'Southern' deficit derives from reorientation, this must be seen as a healthy process of redirecting scarce or even failing resources, such as oil, or substituting obsolete 'socialist' imports by more competitive items. The latter fosters competition on the still fairly monopolised domestic market, and improves not only consumer welfare, but also international competitiveness of other producers via better input supply.[4] This explains why convertible currency sales of machinery grew by 13 per cent in HUF and 73.5 per cent in dollar terms, implying much improved prices and currency revenues for those who survived. Moreover, as both total and OECD exports grew – by 17.8 and 42.6 per cent respectively – the overall balance was favourable.

Summing up what has been said so far, it is surprising to see that the fundamental reorientation of commercial relations has been proceeding quite successfully and even without extreme sacrifices. The entire external environment of the Hungarian economy has changed fundamentally from a command and quota-determined to a market-driven one. Hungary's major partner is Germany, the strongest European economy, with 25.5 per cent exports and 26.1 per cent imports, followed by the CIS and Austria, both with 12–14 per cent for exports and imports and Italy with 8.6 and 6.6 per cent. If we add the 5–6 per cent together represented by Czecho-Slovakia's and Poland's exports and imports, we come to the conclusion that in 1991 the share of ex-COMECON countries had reached an economically justifiable level. As was demonstrated by detailed econometric analysis by Nagy (1989), at the present level of development 20 per cent is what the standard measure of trade flows among market economies would imply for Eastern Europe. References to historical trade proportions, known to have been created by artificial political trade diversion, will hardly invalidate this point.

How was it possible at all, one may well ask again in the context of the

Baltic states and the Ukraine, that contrary to the absolute majority of expert opionion reorientation of commercial relations could take place, and so quickly? The answer is partly technical in nature. Traditionally, the TR was artificially overvalued[5] to inflate the importance of trade with 'fraternal' states, which was a political expectation. In Hungary, this was also a form of hidden or implicit extra-budgetary subsidisation of the large uncompetitive firms involved in COMECON trade, having oriented themselves exclusively on these markets. In other words, it was yet another way of postponing the crisis which had been latent even then for more than a decade.

With switching over to trade in convertible currencies the nominal distortion automatically disappeared – about a third of the radical reorientation reflects the correction of exchange rate distortions. This may, in part, explain why other countries, like Czecho-Slovakia, which used to rely even more on the Soviet markets, survived 1991: the larger was the officially reported share of COMECON in total trade, the larger was this type of statistical overestimation of intraregional trade flows (Drábek, 1988).

In sum, the explanation why Hungary survived the collapse of COMECON in 1991 is threefold. (1) Most of the reorientation took place before the new trade and accounting system was in place. (2) Part of the process was a correction of statistical errors in previous reporting. (3) Hungary – similarly to the other two Central European transition economies – is not any more a classical shortage economy. The threat of bankruptcy therefore became real for many firms *before* they could be privatised. Under this pressure even state-owned firms showed a remarkable ability to adjust to market signals.

It would still be difficult to deny that the fundamental change in the system of COMECON trade was a sizeable shock at the microeconomic level. One may speculate that this change provided the impetus for radical changes in the system, which the new government failed to deliver (on political grounds); it thus played a favourable role in accelerating the process of transformation. The practical implications of this adjustment on employment, output, and regional development leads one to suggest that *more state involvement* could and, indeed, should ameliorate the pains of adjustment. Hungarian firms were told openly only at the end of the first quarter of 1991 that state trading was over; that there would be no clearing arrangement; that larger advances that could bridge the liquidity problems of Soviet buyers could be expected from Western intermediary banks only, and moreover it was not a liquidity but a solvency problem that they faced on Soviet markets, which had nothing to do with the top-heavy nature of the bureaucracy in Moscow; and finally that no reorientation funds were being established by the Hungarian government to promote the search for new markets.

3   A 'lame duck' administration?

All in all, these are not the faults that the Hungarian government is customarily blamed for. The most frequent complaints focus on other concerns. It tolerated the disruption of well-established cooperation deals. It withdrew from a market which was huge, promising and which will be hard to reconquer. It was indifferent to the crisis of long-established industrial strongholds. It had no sectoral concept to protect the domestic market. It did nothing to stop recession. It stayed idle while hundreds of thousands of people lost their jobs. Supporters of these criticisms have one thing in common: on the bottom line, the government would in their view act in an appropriate manner if somehow or other it pumped a fair dose of additional purchasing power into the economy. In other words it should *artificially induce a demand* which is currently non-existent for products and services of a given quality at a given price.

It is common knowledge that in a small and open economy domestic demand is not an independent variable to be manipulated by the government according to its own will: the failure of the first Mauroy government or the severe repercussions of the policies of Andreas Papandreou in Greece illustrate this point. If a country is indebted, servicing its debt is possible only if domestic use of GDP lags behind GDP produced. The state can therefore 'help' those in trouble only at the expense of other citizens and economic agents. This economic truism has a long way to go before it is fully reflected in policy-making, but it does seem to be one of the few lessons that the conservative coalition has learned in Hungary, which is remarkable against the background of its expansionary election platform. Critiques of these governmental policies, however, normally fail to pinpoint who is to pay for the costs of a more activist state policy, or what additional inflation an export guarantee, a bailout and similar propositions would involve.

'Socialisation' of the costs of trouble-ridden large firms is anything but a novelty in Hungarian economic practice. On the contrary, this government and its predecessors have a lot in common, inasmuch as a verbal radicalism against uncompetitive companies has coexisted with a rather lenient attitude in practice towards those who still do not believe that doing business in Russia has become a somewhat risky venture. 'Leniency' means in practice that amidst talk of opening up and adjustment to the world economy subsequent administrations have gone out of their way to maintain an economic environment in which exporting to a soft market is still a most lucrative business. Parts of the bureaucracy still believe that it is their job to find and secure markets for existing white elephants.

True, these activities have resulted in the ambiguous situation that the true dimensions of a shrinking Eastern market have yet to manifest themselves for many firms (Szegvári, 1991; Harsányi, 1991). In my view the economic system's ability to mitigate and lessen, and thereby transform, an external shock into a longer-run and thus more manageable challenge, is itself a sign of its viability, as this is parallel to what happens in a living organism. Meanwhile the currently $2 bn Hungarian claims against member-states of the CIS, that look rather illiquid, are illustrative of the costs of practical governmental leniency.

This state of the art prompts us to the conclusion that reorientation and adjustment to the external shock results not so much from a *governmental policy*, which is hardly formulated in this area. Rather it is a *spontaneous process* of decisions of tens of thousands of entrepreneurs trying to find their way under very tough conditions, often in despite of the misleading and contradictory signals coming 'from above'.

Let me give a few examples of how the Hungarian authorities 'promoted' reorientation of commercial relations. The NBH, though maintaining a tight monetary policy, went out of its way to try and find an opportunity to establish a clearing agreement with the central monetary authorities of a disintegrating empire, who were hardly any longer controlling anything. The Ministry of Industry cherished high hopes of the interstate indicative lists of deliveries of commodities, hoping that one way or other a governmental guarantee would cover its items. The Ministry of International Economic Relations (MIER) was fighting for a reorientation fund and for various methods of export promotion (export credit guarantees, etc.) without much success; thus these intentions were never translated into practice. The Ministry of Agriculture did manage to get an export credit facility for grain sales more than double the total funds of the MIER supporting all other convertible currency exports. Last but not least, the Ministry of Defence followed a rather intransigent line on the financial aspects of Soviet troop withdrawal, which was surely patriotic but not terribly efficacious.

In sum, it seems plausible to assume that everything that resulted in systematic transformation depended on enterprise decisions. It was equally expedience when governmental organs either followed anti-inflationary policies, or were simply constrained by an empty Treasury to heed that 'excellent' advice which would have implied more state involvement in the management of transition. Propositions calling for an activist state policy normally mix up the micro and macroeconomic aspects of the process. As many non-competitive firms could flourish under the CMEA they take this as normal and abstract from the static and dynamic costs of being part of socialist economic integration, the latter reflected in secular stagnation and long-term marginalisation in the international economy (Csaba, 1990b). At the macro level, this is the whole point, and if we abstract away from this in discussing the pains of reorientation we miss the purpose of the whole exercise.

There are several areas, of course, when even the most libertarian stance cannot abstract from the need for governmental action. One of them is the issue of outstanding Soviet debts. Originally, a rather simplistic approach seems to have prevailed. In March 1990 an agreement was reached that Soviet debts would be converted into dollars at the rate of TR 1 = $0.92 and repaid in one year by commodities. (The underlying assumption was the automatic emergence of a huge Soviet surplus due to the switchover to convertible currency trade.) The MIER did not seem to have taken seriously the informal statement of the Soviet party about repaying its debts in five instead of one year, which was made in June 1990. Instead, as retroactively confirmed by the responsible official (Timár, 1991) they believed that a growth in rouble debts was not all that bad: 'Let us never conclude an inferior deal to this, when we make HUF 66 out of HUF 27.5 thanks to the conversion rate of 0.92', he noted. This may explain why over 1 bn of the TR 2.1 bn Soviet debt was accumulated under the anti-communist government.

This naiveté or misjudgement made the Hungarian authorities participate in a game in which Hungarian firms went out of their way to export (without any firm guarantee of being paid), Soviet buyers were keen to buy as shortages exacerbated, and Soviet authorities determined to run a deficit in order to be able to pay at least some Western bills. This situation reemerged in 1991, as Hungarian energy imports had to be paid for in cash, whereas over 70 per cent of Hungarian sales were on a credit base without firm commitment of buyers to pay.

It was only in the second quarter of 1991 that ideas of a *debt–equity swap* began to circulate. The general manager of Financial Research, Inc. (Lengyel, 1991) proposed the conversion of outstanding Soviet debts to equities of firms located in the Western borders of the Ukraine, where the Hungarian minority lives. Further he proposed a clearing agreement to promote the use of national currencies between the Ukraine and Hungary.

At the time, i.e. prior to open Russian insolvency, the secondary market value of Soviet bonds was about 70 per cent of the nominal sum – for major Western banks, whose bargaining power is incommensurable with Hungary's; since then, it has dropped further. Even if a kind of triangular deal could have been orchestrated, it seems improbable that the host country would not want to retain a say in which companies were to be sold and which not. Moreover, the Ukraine owes only 16 per cent of total Soviet debt, and the ways of servicing it require separate agreements. For the time being the Ukraine does not possess convertible currency reserves, while in January 1992 it imposed practically a full-scale export ban on all commodities. The hrivna in all probability will be an inconvertible currency, otherwise it cannot serve its major purpose of defending the national market from the rouble overhang. Most Ukrainian firms are yet to be corporatised, and the same holds good for Russian firms.

Thus, while the use of national currencies – both the hrivna and the rouble – is yet to be secured within their respective countries, I do not see that too many foreign businessmen would be prepared to accept them. In kind payments in the current total ban on export items that could be of interest to foreigners will hardly be allowed soon. Thus the circle closes and the rationale of the proposition is gone: neither debt–equity swap nor the use of local currency is feasible or sensible.

More state intervention and a partial socialisation of costs and risks is implied by another popular proposition to create a Central European Payments Union (Van Brabant, 1990, or 'Illés, Mizsei and Szegvári, 1991). The severity of the crisis in bilateral relations with the CIS, shortage of convertible currency, the need to lessen the impact of recession and the Western policy of treating at least the three Central European countries as one entity is mentioned to support the idea. Proponents of this idea rarely reflect on one of the oldest theses of international trade theory, that any restriction of free global flows of commodities and factors is welfare-inhibiting and thus needs to be separately justified. Why should citizens pay for trading with neighbouring countries rather than with their most efficient partners, just when the period of politically motivated trade diversion has ended? Reference to geographical and historical factors is unconvincing as dynamic economies like the NICs tend to trade with more major international growth centres such as Japan and the USA than among themselves.

As we have seen above, the process of reorientation of commercial relations along the lines of international standards is an accomplished fact, and so reference to the need for a mechanism of smooth transition is equally unconvincing. Further, it is hard to comprehend that markets lost due to the collapse of the USSR could be easier to reconquer in countries encountering deep recession than in dynamically growing nations: I do not see anything wrong if Spain is as important a trading partner for Hungary as is Czecho-Slovakia.

Among many ailing white elephants there still is hope and expectation that the government will one way or another reopen soft markets for them. Proclaiming regional cooperation as a policy priority thus gives yet another misleading signal to tens of thousands of economic actors: they may believe that it is the 5 per cent of Hungarian trade conducted with Poland and Czecho-Slovakia which matters, and not the need to adjust overall economic legislation to EC norms, as if there were a 'third way'. What if the 5 per cent increases by 50 or 60 per cent in three years?

Mention should finally be made of a proposition which never gained any publicity in the specialised literature, yet started its career at the highest possible level. The idea was to use the EBRD to bridge the imbalance of Hungarian–Soviet payments. It is yet to be clarified who has come to the conclusion, and on what grounds, that it is only the EBRD and nothing else which is the appropriate institution to overcome this problem. The EBRD was established for an entirely different purpose, to promote *privatisation* and *infrastructural projects* in post-socialist countries *other than* the USSR/CIS; moreover 60 per cent of all placement must go to the *private* sector. The institution is thus tailored to the needs of small countries' transition, and the bottomless barrel of state budgets is to be deliberately eschewed by its activities. One thus wonders why it should have been in Hungary's interest to undermine these principles of the EBRD at the time of its foundation, as the proposition of the Hungarian Ministry of Finance would have implied.

If Hungary and the Soviet Union had each received the $500 mn support, and this had created a precedent for others, the Bank could have hardly avoided being involved in the problems of Polish–Soviet, Czech–Soviet, Bulgarian–Soviet, Romanian–Soviet and even German–Soviet bilateral trade, where similar difficulties emerged. Such an option could have 'secured' the utilisation of all those EBRD funds, which are mostly yet to be collected. But what then would happen to the original objectives, whose importance has been stressed by the Premiers present at the opening session of the Bank?

One actually wonders how such a primitive trick, reflecting nothing other than the vested interests of narrow groups, could have got to the political level. If bilateral trade were indeed such a lucrative business as described by those involved, they should not find it difficult to find financing on normal commercial terms. When no private money is available, one wonders why the state should be re-included just when it has managed to disengage from this particular trade activity.

Such 'minor' priorities as reorientation, as rolling back the state, as transition to the market and credibility of governmental policies could have been sacrificed if this proposition had been implemented in the spring of 1991. Though an influential section of EBRD staff, who have always seen their fortunes in adopting a high profile in world politics (and thus have always been preocccupied with Russia rather than with the original target countries) were receptive to this proposition, it never finally materialised. The fundamental reason for this was the resistance of the Soviet Ministry of Finance to utilising its small amount of EBRD funds for this particular purpose.

The lesson is hardly new: governmental organs can be involved in overcoming business difficulties by socialising costs of mistaken entrepreneurial decisions, meanwhile sacrificing the original objective of government, that of serving public rather than partisan interest. While there are numerous ways and means of overcoming microeconomic disturbances, there is no substitute for the government in following macroeconomic policies.

4   Prospects for the future

With the Minsk agreements of December 1991 the USSR ceased to exist. The CIS inherits the burdensome legacy of incompetent macroeconomic policies and half-hearted reformatory attempts of the Gorbachev period, while no longer constituting a single economic entity. National states with national, inconvertible currencies and with grossly divergent economic strategies have emerged. While Russia has adopted a Polish-type shock therapy, the Ukraine has adopted a phased five-year plan of small and large privatisation. While monetary expansion and populist promises know no limits in Russia, the Ukraine's introduction of coupons replacing roubles seems to maintain traditional Russian financial conservatism and anti-inflationary priorities.

Three factors seem therefore to determine the outlook for Hungarian–post-Soviet economic relations: (1) the inherited recession and a system of bureaucratic coordination; (2) the success or failure of stabilisation policies and the modifications brought about by them; (3) the shock waves of a disintegrating empire which will hardly stop at the present borders of Russian Federation.

4.1   Recession and bureaucracy

Whichever are our priorities and forecasts, the basic economic fact about the CIS is not that it is a market of 300 mn people. It is an openly insolvent area, where a severe contraction of economic activity is already well under way and where stabilisation policies are bound to exacerbate this, at least in the short and medium run. The output of those sectors which used to be the backbone of Soviet exports, like oil production, will contract with above-average severity. The scale of the crisis is such that the need for large-scale external involvement in terms of humanitarian, organisational, technological and financial assistance is no longer a subject of discussion. Therefore, though individuals may, and will, find lucrative business opportunities, macroeconomically there is no reason for us to expect any dynamising or stabilising effect exerted on the Hungarian economy by Eastern markets. Rather the spillover effects of the crisis – from supply disruption to mass migration, to mention just two elements – are bound to intensify. Macroeconomic policy should thus be oriented towards deflecting these as far as possible rather than positively fostering high-risk business deals, although freedom of the export–import regime must imply the liberty of any individual to experiment at his own risk and harvest the fruits, be they exorbitant profits or bankruptcy.

Could the success of the current radical stabilisation policies of the Gaidar team not change this state of affairs? Several declarations of early rouble convertibility have been made, implying an opening up and much greater freedom to do business. One should, however, be clear about the difference between *Dichtung* und *Wahrheit*: while Gorbachev kept on speaking about radical reforms throughout the six years of his tenure, in reality the bureaucratic coordination of economic processes intensified in the last two years (Lányi, 1991). As the Russian minister for foreign economic relations, Petr Aven, openly acknowledged, the system of foreign trade controls imposed in January 1992 bears a fair degree of resemblance to the practices of the Pavlov and Ryzhkov governments (as reported in *Napi*, 7 January 1992). This is hardly by chance, as a system of bureaucratic coordination cannot be transformed through a single stabilisation shock, even if it is successful. Contraction of output, the unresolved issue of who should take what portion of the rouble overhang, stagnant privatisation – except for spontaneous processes (Grigoriev, 1991) – and widespread indexation of incomes, lax monetary and fiscal practices hardly permit giving up the visible hand's role in intercourse with the outside world.

4.2   Stabilisation policies

It follows from the above that several grounds lead us to be sceptical about both the Russian and the Ukrainian transformation plans, at least as they stand now. The most probable outcome of these and of the secessionist movements is an escalation of customs war and export prohibitions, which was already an accomplished fact in January 1992. This implies a radical contraction of intra-Soviet deals and a disruption of traditional channels of commodity flows without their having been replaced with new ones. This explains why the supply situation, especially in major cities, is much worse than the actual size of recession would imply. In this case it is the absurd reincarnation of COMECON rather than anything else (Szamuely, 1991) that is to emerge on the ruins of the single economic space. Some of the successor states – like Turkmenistan and Belarus – have already started signing interstate protocols on compulsory deliveries of commodities. This implies, for outsiders, that there is no hope of expecting that the foreign economic liberalism that would have characterised the Shatalin Plan will stand a good chance of returning in the foreseeable future. Instead, a restrictive bureaucratic import and export regime seems to be a lasting phenomenon in the CIS, general statements of intention notwithstanding.

4.3   Imperial disintegration

The example of proclaiming the Chechen, the Mordvin and especially the 6 mn strong Tatarstan Republics in the last quarter of 1991 was already indicative of the further disintegration of the Russian empire. As local analysts (Migranian, 1992) correctly noted, the Yeltsin team seems to have repeated the mistakes of Gorbachev in starting a reform project without prior clarification of its political feasibility. The boundaries of the rouble area are anything but clearly defined. The role of the local elites is far from secure and integrated into the overall decision-making process, especially now the bonapartist institution of prefects has been imposed upon them. Therefore – remaining with trade issues – it is absolutely unclear who owns what, whose licences are valid for what territory and under what conditions. Until the ethnic and political rivalries are clarified, there will be no clear-cut division among competences, no methods for settling conflicts, no mechanism of arbitration, not even an established safe mechanism for transferring money abroad. In other words, nothing that really matters for business is secure, and this has nothing to do with the competence or the good intentions of the present coalition of Russian populists, soldiers and liberals.

Could not the emerging Western engagement, the foreseeable large injections of fresh money, change this gloomy picture? Governmental quarters in Hungary have been going out of their way to get the idea of *triangular deals* (Western-financed Central European exports to CIS) off the ground. There seem to be at least two minor problems with this choice: (a) EC countries, but also the USA, have a food and agricultural surplus of their own, thus the incentive to finance someone else's overproduction is not particularly strong; (b) Hungarian agricultural exports are hardly competitive given the subsidies and credit lines granted by Western governments to their producers. Even Poland and Czecho-Slovakia apply more direct and indirect support to farming sales to the CIS than does Hungary. As I think we are macroeconomically right in not joining in this competition of budgets, and moreover the need to restructure and reorient Hungarian agriculture was established many years before the CIS emerged (Lányi, 1984), I think the pressure to adjust will only be beneficial for Hungarian farming. Waiting for bureaucrats and politicians to elaborate a strategy has not worked in this field either.

Thus the challenge is thrown down. An empty Treasury and an insolvent partner, where chaotic conditions will last for many years, are two lasting and severe constraints on Hungarian trade with the CIS. The Hungarian government can do precious little to ease these constraints, and a further sizeable drop in the share of CIS in total Hungarian trade, even to the level of 4–5 per cent of total turnover therefore seems inevitable. The real trouble is not the loss of market; the real trouble will come if the present dynamics of transition cannot be maintained, and thus export performance deteriorates. Losing the opportunities inherent in being a marginal supplier on all OECD markets in all sectors – this would be a real threat. In that case exports could not induce Hungary to outgrow her debt, and the transition to the market would become protracted and even more conflict-ridden than it is already.

NOTES

The author is research director at KOPINT-DATORG, Inc., Vice President of the European Association for Comparative Studies and Professor of International Economics at the College of Foreign Trade, Budapest.

Research for this study has been conducted in the framework of an OTKA project, co-ordinated by Dr T. Földi on 'Transition to the market in Central and Eastern Europe, 1988–92'. Useful comments on T. Földi, A. Köves, G. Oblath and L. Szamuely on a preliminary version are acknowledged.

1 Suffice it to recall the Programme for National Renaissance of the present Hungarian government, which has never been formally withdrawn, or the influential paper of Sachs (1991) representing a widely shared view of the international profession.
2 True, in physical units exchanges shrank much more – some estimate a 50–60 per cent drop. Still, as exchange rate and other monetary developments played a decisive role, physical flows can't be taken to indicate the 'final' outcomes especially at the macroeconomic level.
3 Supplement to Hungarian Foreign Trade Statistics (1980–90) and Külkereskedelmi Statisztikai Gyorstájékoztató various issues (monthly report of KOPINT-DATORG Inc.).
4 Those who survived on CIS markets or redirected their output westwards made enormous price gains, which explains the disparity.
5 In 1990, for example, companies were selling and buying TR claims for HUF 14–17, while the official rate was TR/HUF 27.5.

REFERENCES

Brabant, J. van (1990) 'On reforming the trade and payments regime among the CMEA countries', *Jahrbuch der Wirtschaft Osteuropas*, **14**, 2. Halbband, München-Wien, G. Olzog Verlag.

Cohen, D. (1991) 'The solvency of Eastern Europe', *European Economy*, **2**, *Special Issue* (June).

Collins, S. and D. Rodrik (1991) 'Eastern Europe and the Soviet Union in the world economy', *Policy Analyses in International Economics*, **32**, Washington, D.C.: Institute for International Economics.

Csaba, L. (1991a) 'The bumpy road to the free market in Eastern Europe', *Acta Oeconomica*, **42** (3–4).

(1990b) *Eastern Europe in the World Economy*, Cambridge and New York: Cambridge University Press (Soviet and Eastern European monograph series, **68**).

Dembinski, P. and J. Morriset (1991) 'A tentative assessment of IMF policies in Latin America and Eastern Europe', in L. Csaba (ed.), *Systematic Change and Stabilization in Eastern Europe*, Aldershot: Dartmouth.

Drábek, Z. (1988) 'The East European response to the debt crisis: a trade diversion or a statistical aberration?', *Comparative Economic Studies*, **1**.

Grigoriev, L. (1991) 'Ulterior property rights and privatisation: even God cannot change the past', Stockholm Institute of Soviet and East European Studies, *Working Paper*, **32** (June).

Halpern, L. (1991) 'Hyperinflation, credibility and expectations (Stabilisation theories and East European stabilisation programmes)', *Acta Oeconomica*, **43**(1–2).

Harsányi, L. (1991) 'Még nem a fordulat éve jön' (No upswing ahead), *Figyelő*, **41**.

Illés, I., K. Mizsei and I. Szegvári (1991) 'Válaszúton a közép-európai gazdasági együttmüködés' (Central European economic cooperation at the crossroads), *Európa Fórum*, **2**.

Kádár, B. (1991) 'Kétséges az egység' (A questionable unity), interview with Gy. Varga, *Figyelő*, **42**.

Lányi, K. (1984) 'Hungarian agriculture: superfluous growth or export surplus?', *Acta Oeconomica*, **34**(3–4).

(1991) 'A market economy – without commerce?', *Acta Oeconomica*, **43**(3–4).

Lengyel, L. (1991) 'A jövö a vigéceké' (The future belongs to door-to-door salesmen), *Népszabadság* (24 April).

Migranian, A. (1992) See *Itogi* (19 January).

Nagy, A. (1989) 'Külkereskedelmi orientációváltást!' (Let us change the orientation of Hungarian foreign trade!), *Közgazdasági Szemle*, **9**.

Oblath, G. (1992) 'Successes, failures and experiences of Hungarian import liberalisation', *Soviet and Eastern European Foreign Trade*, **28**(1).

Sachs, J. (1991) 'Poland and Eastern Europe: what is to be done?', in A. Köves and P. Marer (eds), *Foreign Economic Liberalization: Transformations in Socialist and Market Economies*, Boulder, Col.: Westview, pp. 235–46.

Szamuely, L. (1991) 'Merre tart a Szovjetinió?' (What is the Soviet Union heading for?', *Népszabadság* (26 October).

Szegvári, I. (1991) 'Válság – dollárban számolva' (A crisis accounted in dollars), *Figyelő*, **23**.

Timár, L. (1991) 'Az NGKM a rubelaktivumról' (The MIER on the surplus in roubles), *Magyar Hírlap* (10 April).

3 Regional cooperation in East–Central Europe

KÁLMÁN MIZSEI

In the fast-disintegrating East European scene it has proved quite difficult to design any kind of trade regime for the whole region, or its parts, since 1989: too many variables have been uncertain and changing quite dramatically. The latest development is the collapse of the USSR and, more particularly, the emergence of new nation states (especially the Ukraine) on the borders of the East European countries.

My understanding is that the basic geopolitical development pattern of Europe has probably not changed fundamentally with the dismantling of the USSR, i.e. the integration processes are still focused around the EC. The fundamental question here is, of course, whether German unification will alter the choice between deepening integration in the EC and widening access to it. Our assumption, of fundamental significance for East–Central European development as well, is that the emergence of a greater Germany will not stop the integration process, that Germany's weight in the decision-making of the Community will grow. The impact of this on the East European geopolitical situation will be significant, because it means in practice that the pre-war reflexes will in the near future no longer prevail.

Nevertheless Germany has become the major trading partner of each of the East European nations, and its proportion in the foreign trade of these countries will probably approach that of the USSR at the peak of its dominance. Germany is the dominant capital exporter into the region, in spite of the short-term consequences of unification. Quite interestingly, this pattern holds for Czecho-Slovakia and Poland but does not, in this period, for Hungary, where major investors from the USA and Japan are even more strongly present.

In retrospect, the establishment of a Central European Payment Union (CEPU), including the USSR, would not have been a feasible idea. Neither could any smoothly working bilateral clearing agreement with that country have been established. The USSR would not have been a

44

reliable trading partner anyway, as the example of the Soviet clearing settlements with other countries of the region for 1991 clearly show. The clearing agreement of Poland with Russia for 1992 shows the same features: the Russians, because of their payments problems, have been unwilling to deliver gas and oil for Polish commodities. the situation gets more complicated if we add the initial experience in 1992 of other republics: some of them, having neither the necessary 'hard' goods, nor the infrastructure for export expansion, are ready to follow the 'indicative lists' in trade with Hungary.

Unfortunately, immediately after the political turnaround in the region there were too many misconceptions about the future of cooperation, including the possibility of a CEPU. Many Western analysts tried to keep together what wanted to fall apart: CMEA could not, and should not, have been saved. It was especially irritating for the new East–Central European policy-makers that many influential people from the West still wanted them to belong to the same 'club' with the USSR. It was politically and economically irrational: everybody should have seen that the USSR was neither a lucrative market, with its rapidly falling purchasing power, nor even a reliable one. Furthermore, institutional development towards a market economy lagged so much behind not only that of Hungary and Poland, but also of Czecho-Slovakia, that this single factor made a CEPU impossible.

Therefore, the big dilemma was what to do in Soviet trade relations, when an all-CMEA solution was impossible. In Hungary, there were two schools among the reform economists. One wing argued that the particular pattern of trade relations with the USSR had been the primary factor hampering reform of the Hungarian economy, and that therefore any kind of prolongation of incomplete market-type relationship was harmful. The appropriate solution in these circumstances was a radical shift towards a fully hard currency payments system without any kind of state-sponsored clearing settlement.

Some other economists, including this author, opted for establishing some kind of buffer mechanisms in the reform process of Soviet trade. We thought that the trade level between the partners would dramatically shrink, resulting in a significant fall of GDP because of the under-developed institutions of trade in both countries, and more especially in the USSR, because of shortage of foreign currencies on both sides.

In this period of sharp political debates any sophisticated rational solution will have much less chance than the promotion of simple panaceas. That happened in this case as well. With no transitional mechanisms, trade volumes fell sharply. In 1990 the fall was still minor: 4.6 per cent in the case of imports and 1.9 per cent for exports (TR/$

cross-rates counted according to the official Hungarian figures). However, in 1991, data for the first eleven months show a sharp decline in Hungarian exports. Keeping in mind the extreme uncertainties concerning both foreign trade evidence and cross-rates, as well as inflation of the domestic currency in Soviet trade, one can estimate that export volumes fell by half. Given the different commodity structure of Hungarian imports from the USSR, the decline was much more modest here, about 11 per cent in value terms.

On the other hand, one can say that Hungarian enterprises showed a remarkable ability to shift their exports to Western markets in 1991. The question in this respect is whether this trade pattern, even with imbalances in Soviet trade, will work as well in future. There is no reason to assume the opposite: the growing Hungarian export potential should easily balance Soviet energy and raw material imports. For the Soviets it is a lucrative business because the infrastructure (pipelines, for instance) are there and Hungary pays in cash.

The idea of a payments union between some of the small ex-CMEA countries had a different perspective in 1990–1. Before discussing this, let us look at the trends in trade flows during the last year. Due to the lack of official figures from the Ministry for International Trade Relations we cannot deliver complete end-of-year statistical tables. The available figures show that overall exports to ex-CMEA Eastern Europe fell by more than 40 per cent, the USSR still accounting for two-thirds of the total. Imports fell less (perhaps by less than 10 per cent), partly because of raw material imports from the USSR.

Data for 1991 in regional trade outside the USSR do not show very clear trends. Trade generally declined more with the Balkan countries and less with Czecho-Slovakia, while the Polish–Hungarian turnover showed an increase in volume. (Polish and Hungarian data differ to a large extent, however.) An interesting phenomenon is that without the strict barter mechanisms of the CMEA a rapid structural change started to occur. The obvious part of the story is that mutual trade in machinery fell sharply; however, the fall in Hungarian machinery exports (and also in exports of industrial consumer goods) was less dramatic than that of former CMEA partners towards Hungary.

As stated before, there is no full data basis available for trade volumes and structures for the whole year. But preliminary estimates indicate a few interesting trends. About three-quarters of Hungarian imports from *Poland* are raw materials and fuels, while Hungarian export is dominated by industrial consumer goods and agricultural products. There is almost no machinery trade between the two countries. Turnover is almost balanced, the Polish surplus reaching less than 15 per cent of total exports.

This is not the case in trade with *Czecho-Slovakia*, where restrictive measures limited the capability to import to a large extent. Czecho-Slovak exports in hard currency trade were about double the size of imports from Hungary, and Czecho-Slovakia still had a sizeable export for roubles because of earlier deficits. Here also, against the expectations of many, Hungarian export structures seem to be more advanced. About a quarter of export is machinery, in spite of a credit requirement of investment imports on the Czecho-Slovak side. In Hungarian import, machines amount to only 18 per cent. More than half of Czecho-Slovak exports to Hungary is raw materials and fuels. This serious imbalance in trade turnover calls for a significant further liberalisation of the import regime in Czecho-Slovakia as a precondition for a free trade agreement.

Rumania is the only noticeable economic partner in the Balkans. The trade volume even with Rumania is, however, only a fragment of that with Czecho-Slovakia. Its structure is even more favourable for Hungary, with a high share of manufactured industrial goods in exports. The export volume to Rumania fell to about half of that of 1990 (itself exceptional because of emergency deliveries to Rumania at the beginning of the year) while imports fell by about 25 per cent. (Here, as in the case of Poland, a drastic fall had already occurred in 1990.)

At the beginning of the process of economic transformation, a payments union seemed a feasible option. The assumption of those considering the idea, including the author, was that only those countries should belong to it which were on a roughly similar level of reformist commitment and were willing to cooperate with each other. Already in 1990 the obvious candidates were Poland, Hungary and Czecho-Slovakia. The purpose of this kind of settlement was seen as having several different aspects. Politically it was thought to be mutually beneficial for each partner to cooperate; all three countries wanted to join the EC as an ultimate target, but knew that they could realise that immediately. It was clear that this would be a long and troublesome process, and we thought that together our countries could achieve more. On the side of mutual trade we found that the recent low level was an artificial consequence of the CMEA. These are heavily indebted countries where a non-cash payments system (accounted in hard currencies) could be useful in avoiding unnecessary trade destruction. We thought that otherwise part of the trade flow would occur with foreign intermediation, increasing the costs of trade. We also believed that the similarity of such an organisation to the post-war EPU would make it attractive and lucrative for Western partners who want to help but are not willing to invest huge amounts of public money in Eastern Europe.

Political willingness as well as an ability to act to organise a concerted effort in the region was lacking in 1990 and 1991, partly because none of the new elites in these countries wanted to belong to a regionally integrated system; all of them, and especially the Czecho-Slovaks and Hungarians, believed that they had the best chance to integrate into Western Europe, leaving the rest behind. The project has in practice now lost its topicality, since trade destruction has been completed (in the case of Polish–Hungarian trade already in 1990). The additional benefits of a lower level of trade destruction, or in the recent situation, some dynamisation of trade and elimination of some third-party intermediaries would therefore be offset by the negative effects of running an undoubtedly bureaucratic system.

Cooperation among the three countries still has scope in other fields. In the area of *trade policy* these countries are in most cases in the same boat, partly because the West treats them so (witness the negotiations with the EC over the association agreements), and partly because of their geopolitical similarities. Concentrated efforts to help the Soviet economy is another good example of the benefits from a common effort. At this point, however, one should also draw attention to the risks of deviation from the dynamic institutional development of one or other country in the near future.

Quite objectively, one has to say that in the recent period it appears once again, that for different reasons, Poland and Czecho-Slovakia are carrying significantly more risk in this respect than Hungary. In Poland the new political parties are attempting to restructure the country's financial system. This has not yet been achieved, and the risk is that the old unreformed system will impede reform elsewhere. In Czecho-Slovakia the unsolved constitutional dilemma about federal or confederal structures makes the future of macro policies uncertain. If the pessimistic scenarios prevail, it will be increasingly difficult for Hungary to slow down the integration of its economy to that of Western Europe to the pace of Poland or Czecho-Slovakia. This is not to say that Hungary's transformation is risk-proof, but the level of uncertainties seems to be quite different now.

The other important field of possible cooperation is *regional trade*. In 1991 (in the case of Poland already a year earlier) two simultaneous shocks occurred. Not only did dollarisation decrease deliveries, but simultaneously the countries introduced customs' barriers against each other. The recognition has emerged only very slowly, and only with the help of the EC, that at least the 'Visegrad-gang', i.e. Poland, Czecho-Slovakia and Hungary, could and should form a *free trade zone*, because of the similar direction and pace of their market reforms.

It is important to emphasise that regional cooperation is not meant to be a panacea for the countries' economic growing pains, nor any kind of substitute for integration into the West European economy (in fact, on the contrary): it is only a modest, but logical, contribution to the reform effort. Free trade can marginally increase trade flows and in this way similarly improve the efficiency of the participating economies. A reliably set trilateral free trade agreement would increase the interest of foreign capital investing in the region, and close regional economic cooperation has additional geopolitical benefits as well. At the same time, it is clear that the risk factors are much the same as in the case of the above-mentioned trade policy cooperation. In addition, the problem of still relatively high subsidies in the Czecho-Slovak economy highlights the importance of anti-dumping regulations in regional trade.

The three partners finally agreed on a timetable of negotiations at the end of November during the meeting of Ministers of Foreign Economic Relations in Warsaw. The methodology of negotiations makes the process unnecessarily complicated: the starting point will not be a free trade regime but the achieved level of concessions of the three countries in their EC agreements. Therefore both during the negotiations and after the agreement, the liberalisation steps will probably be very slow. The rationale for that is that the partners want to be sure that they do not discriminate against each other, as a minimum condition. Only the broad agreement will be trilateral, the concrete regulation and customs' levels will be established in bilateral negotiations. The necessary minimum of final harmonisation is also going to slow down the negotiations.

It will be difficult to keep the target date of end of June 1992 for finalising the agreement. The countries are also losing a good chance of establishing a less controlled agricultural regulation by dealing with the sector with a similar caution to the EC. The only possible advantage of the slow procedure could be that the above-mentioned country risks might in the meantime be tested. However, the participating economies might lose the additional potential benefit of anchoring economic policies to a certain minimum degree of foreign trade liberalisation in the meantime.

The third potential field of cooperation, until now not in practice exploited, is *infrastructure development*. Especially Poland and Czecho-Slovakia, but also Hungary, could decrease their geographical dependence on Germany and Austria by well-designed infrastructure projects, especially road construction. Each of them became significantly underdeveloped in this respect during four decades of communist economic doctrine. It is quite clear that central budgets of the three countries are not in any shape to finance such enterprise; however, cooperation could help to get EC financing. Similarly, private sector funding would be easier if imbedded in a well-prepared regional concept. The overlapping of this with similar ideas in the framework of the Hexagonale cooperation is obvious.

The collapse of Yugoslavia calls, of course, for a proper reaction on the side of the 'Visegrad countries' as well. In the sense of political development, economic reform, geographical and cultural closeness, Slovenia and Croatia might join the project as well. These two countries are now at the beginning of the learning process of identifying their integration strategies, a similar situation to that of the three 'Visegrad countries' in early 1990. My expectation is that the EC will treat Slovenia and Croatia similarly to its handling of Czecho-Slovakia, Hungary and Poland. They might also therefore find it attractive to join the 'Visegrad-club' besides other potential benefits, although at this point it is quite difficult to predict the interests of the potential partners in this enterprise.

Some analysts in Hungary believe that a better area of loose economic cooperation could be the old Pentagonale group (with the Western republics of disintegrated Yugoslavia). The main problem with that is that Italy is not willing, and not able, to give up any of its obligations in the EC to enter into closer cooperation with the region. For Austria, also, joining the EC is a much more important target than its growing, but still relatively minor, engagement with Hungary, Poland and Czecho-Slovakia. Realistically, therefore, the 'Visegrad countries' (not excluding, of course, various forms of closer cooperation with other countries of the ex-CMEA region) should only attempt to integrate with Western Europe in a concerted way.

4 Export supply and import demand in Hungary: an econometric analysis for 1968–89

LÁSZLÓ HALPERN and ISTVÁN
P. SZÉKELY

1 Introduction

The transformation of Soviet-type economies into market economies above all requires that producers respond to market signals rather than to central direction. The main concern of those managing the Hungarian liberalisation is that microeconomic supply rigidities will prejudice the adjustment process, and the collapse of CMEA trade makes such rigidities even more serious. All East European countries have had to redirect a substantial fraction of exports from CMEA to hard currency markets or face a dramatic fall in demand, and hence in GDP. This chapter asks whether the pessimism about supply responsiveness has been overstated, by failing fully to appreciate the signals facing enterprises. Hungary is an important test case, as the reform process has been underway since 1968 with the explicit intention of increasing flexibility at the enterprise level. How successful has this been? Given the salience of the trade balance and the difficulty of servicing the external debt, one of the most important policy questions is how quickly exports respond to incentives – either devaluation, subsidies, or reduced taxes. In this chapter we argue that when the incentives facing enterprises are correctly measured, the Hungarian economy is shown to have a reasonable supply responsiveness of exports to export prices. This suggests that it might be less difficult than it has been thought to judge the future response of a more market-oriented economy to prices. If the supply elasticities observed in the recent past are reasonably close to those observed in market economies, then one can reasonably confidently predict that supply responses in the post-reform economy will lie fairly close to past Hungarian estimates and current market economy responses. If, on the other hand, supply elasticities are shown to be very low, then there will be much greater uncertainty about their future level of supply responses, and their evolution over the next few years. It will be difficult to design macroeconomic and exchange rate policy, and therefore difficult to manage the transition without over- and under-shooting, and consequent instability.

The chapter shows that supply responses are reasonably well identified by the data, but that it is crucial to identify the incentives facing enterprises. If these are ignored, then estimates of the responsiveness of the economy will be seriously misleading – the situation that prevailed until recently. We begin by describing the role of foreign trade in a classic Soviet-type economy, and its management after the 1968 New Economic Mechanism (NEM). This allows us to identify the incentives facing enterprises, and hence to model their behaviour.

2   The regulation of exports and imports in Hungary during 1968–89

2.1   The changing role of foreign trade

The traditional centrally planned economy (CPE) can be regarded as a closed economy, where foreign trade plays a very limited role. Domestic and foreign prices are separated by a multiple exchange rate system, foreign trade is carried on by specialised foreign trade organisations. Neither domestic producers nor consumers are therefore informed about foreign market supply and demand conditions.

In 1968 the NEM slightly modified this closed economy nature of the Hungarian economy. Moreover, the first and second oil-price shocks and the failure to adjust between the two shocks necessarily and dramatically changed the role of foreign trade. In the early years of the NEM, the general approach to foreign trade still preserved the traditional characteristics: (a) the CMEA was intended to assure long-term comparative advantage and international cooperation for the country; (b) hard currency imports were used only as necessary inputs for CMEA exports, intermediate inputs for production and investment; (c) the level of exports to hard currency markets was then calculated as that necessary to balance hard currency trade. The competition between home and foreign markets was very poor, in fact almost entirely absent.

2.2   Foreign indebtedness

The compounded effect of a voluntarist inward-looking economic policy and changes on the international market (radical terms of trade changes and foreign credits with negative real interest rates) was foreign indebtedness. In 1979, the economic policy changed course, dollar exports became the first priority combined with strict import rationing: Hungary managed to service the debt even during the 1982–3 international debt crisis period. Relieved from the debt trap, macroeconomic policy managed to enter the same trap for a second time in 1985–7: due to the acceleration of economic growth, the already high level of dollar debts almost doubled within two years. This proved that survival of the debt crisis had not in itself created the basis for economic growth, and the crisis became deeper than ever.

2.3   The regulation of foreign trade

During the 21-year period under investigation, macroeconomic policy failed to take account of changes in external trade conditions, creating a danger of losing control over the trade balance. Fears about this loss of control encouraged policy-makers to design a whole range of instruments which would allow direct intervention at the enterprise level, but the problem was that such interventions were contrary to the spirit of the GATT and other international organisations to which Hungary belonged (IBRD, IMF). Some ingenuity was therefore devoted to camouflaging the nature of these interventions, particularly after the unification of exchange rates: widespread taxes and subsidies separated domestic from foreign prices in exactly the same way as before. The only regulatory innovation was how to hide these taxes and subsidies, or how to label them in a way that would make international bodies tolerate them. For decades, for example, the CMEA import tariffs were called 'differentiated production turnover taxes' (KÜTEFA), and the export subsidy 'differentiated production turnover tax refunding'. In certain respects this was justified by the large structural gap between CMEA and world market prices, which could not be bridged by exchange rate alignments.

Overall taxation and subsidisation were accompanied by general import licensing, and by wage and credit preferences for exporting firms. The rationing scheme obviously depended on the balance of payments and on the bargaining position of the firm with central authorities. A very full and well-documented description of the import rationing scheme, the bargaining between the intermediator and enterprises, and their effects can be found in Gács (1980a, 1980b). These measures were intended to supplement the effect of taxes and subsidies, and to maintain the confidence of the central planners that in case of need the necessary devices were at their disposal.

3   Previous empirical results on export and import functions for Hungary

Early empirical modelling of foreign trade concentrated on the real side of economic relationships, neglecting the effect of prices and the direct effect of income. This reflected the needs and objectives of central planning methods: the real side of the macroeconomy was regarded as being of primary importance, and prices were treated as a consequence of that. The most important analytical tool was traditional input–output analysis, and this traditional approach was later gradually supplemented by econometric equations and models.

In Simon (1978), the sectoral rouble and dollar exports and imports volumes were explained mainly by real variables, with the one exception of rouble exports of metallurgy, where the relative export price became significant. The estimation period of the equations was 1960–76.

Tarafás and Szabó (1985), using time series methods, showed that the exchange rate had no effect on export supply: on the supply side, the export volume was a function of time trend and domestic demand. The authors were unable to find any specification in which the export price would have been a better explanatory variable than the time trend; on the demand side, the real exchange rate was significant.

In the disequilibrium model of Hulyák (1988), export supply was a loglinear function of the relative export price (the ratio of export prices to domestic prices) and a measure of productive capacities. Preliminary tests yielded an insignificant parameter for the relative price term, supporting the usual hypothesis that in CPEs domestic and foreign prices are formed independently from each other. Only the response to absolute export price could be measured in the observation period. In addition to price and capacity variables, an attempt was made to measure the effects of export subsidies as another explanatory variable in the supply function. Export demand was a loglinear function of relative prices (Hungarian export prices to the export prices of the rest of the world) and the real income of trading partners. The estimation period was 1970–85. In the estimation gross output was used instead of capacity, and both (absolute) price and subsidy became significant. According to Hulyák the small size of the coefficient for export subsidies did not support its explanatory power; the disequilibrium adjustment factors were insignificant in both price and quantity equations. In the demand function the coefficients of neither the price nor the import (used instead of income) were significantly different from zero. The estimation of the food economy showed better results, with the exception of the subsidies, which became insignificant. The adjustment parameter of the demand function remained insignificant.

In a later study, Hulyák (1990) tried to investigate the causality link between inflation and exchange rate. The annual model's estimation period was 1975–88. The final statement (p. 13) was that 'no evidence is given that the devaluation has been effective on volume processes, especially on . . . exports. The bidirectional causality analysis between devaluation and domestic inflation gives rather a surprising result. It suggests that devaluation does not cause inflation, while inflation does lead to the devaluation of the home currency'.

In spite of data and methodological problems, the quarterly model results showed a different picture (p. 14): 'Quarterly time series of exports and imports and those of terms of trade and the balance of trade are causally influenced by quarterly adjustments of the exchange rate'.

In Szentgyörgyvári (1991), the estimation period was 1983:3–1990:4. The volume of export supply was a function of its one-period lagged value, real money supply, volume of gross industrial output, and nominal effective exchange rate index of the Hungarian currency. The export price index depended on domestic producers' prices, the index of world prices of non-fuel commodities and a one-period lagged trade weighted index of domestic wholesale prices of Hungary's most important trade partners. The import demand depended on the nominal stock of money and on home currency import prices. The production function for industrial output included own-one- and two-period lagged values, real money supply and industrial employment as explanatory variables. According to the author: 'The estimation and simulation results . . . seem to confirm the general experience that devaluations of the Forint in themselves brought insufficient, though not negligible balance of payments results in the period considered. The relative price effects of devaluations were dampened by cuts in export sales prices and increases in domestic sales prices . . . Thus, there is no wonder that successive devaluations throughout the period did not result in any significant change in the structure of the economy' (Szentgyörgyvári, 1991, p. 7).

In the model of Neményi (1991), the first estimation period was 1970–87 (Neményi, 1990), and a re-estimation was carried out for 1970–89. The growth rate of export volume depended on one-year lagged export volume, one-year lagged ratio of domestic price of exports to world market price index (from 1983 = 0), one-year lagged ratio of rouble and dollar export price indices corrected by subsidies (from 1983), and on the value and growth rate of the index of export demand (computed as the weighted average of main partners' import growth index, where weights were the shares of the given partner in Hungarian exports). Import demand was a function of domestic demand, one-year lagged foreign trade balance, the ratio of the non-rouble import price index (modified by net import taxes) to domestic producer prices, and the ratio of enterprises not expecting capacity utilisation problems. In both equations the coefficients of the explanatory variables became significantly different from zero with the expected sign, suggesting that supply responses are indeed important.

4   An export supply function for Hungary

The specification used in this chapter is basically a normal supply function, based on a framework in which firms are maximising profit, taking into account exogenously given prices. There are, however, some points where this framework is extended. First, exports are not treated as a homogeneous category; rouble and non-rouble exports are separated, and the present study is confined solely to the analysis of export supply in non-rouble markets. As is widely known, trade in the rouble area was strongly determined by central interventions; although the central economic administration had no formal power to interfere with enterprises' production and export decisions, in order to fulfil contracts between governments there were several hidden mechanisms for the authorities to do so. It is important to recognise that any sort of such intervention had an influence not only on the rouble exports, but also on the non-rouble exports, due to the fact that most firms entered both markets (Halpern, 1991).

Second, export subsidies are explicitly taken into account. As described in section 2, export subsidies played an increasingly important role in economic policies in Hungary, geared to achieving a positive trade balance in the non-rouble area and designed to provide enough incentive for firms to meet rouble export targets. This was accompanied by sizeable changes in the transferable rouble dollar cross-rate, another important instrument of economic policies. Firms' profits, as well as their decisions on supply in each market (domestic, rouble and non-rouble export market) were strongly influenced by the amount and allocation of export subsidies; that is why the ratio of implicit dollar export exchange rate (official nominal exchange rate plus unit export subsidies minus unit export taxes) is introduced as an additional explanatory variable.

Third, not only current production, but also inventories are taken into account. As previous studies indicate (Ábel and Székely, 1988), inventories played an important role in enterprises' production decisions in Hungary. On the input side, they represented supply-side constraints, while on the output side, production smoothing was detectable throughout the period under investigation. Any behavioural relationship related to production decisions should therefore account for these impacts.

Taking into account the factors mentioned above, the specification used for estimation is

$$\log(ESQ) = \alpha + \beta \log(XQ) + \gamma \log(P_{ESQ}/P_{XQ}) + \delta \log(SUB) \quad (1)$$
$$+ \epsilon \log(KQ)_{-1} + \tilde{u}$$

where ESQ is real non-rouble exports,[1] XQ is real gross domestic output, P_{ESQ} is the implicit price index for non-rouble exports, P_{XQ} is the implicit price index for domestic gross output (the price ratio above is denoted by $PR2$ in Table 4.1), SUB is the ratio of the dollar implicit export exchange rate (official nominal exchange rate plus unit export subsidies minus unit export taxes) to rouble export implicit exchange rate, and KQ_{-1} is the real stock of inventories at the beginning of the current period.

The detailed results[2] are presented in Table 4.1. The estimations are for the period 1969–89. The beginning of the estimation period, which is similar to the import function below, is determined by the introduction of the NEM in 1968. As discussed earlier, this reform package is widely regarded as one which substantially changed enterprise behaviour in the Hungarian economy; it would thus be quite misleading to include any period before 1968.

The tests performed, with the exception of the LM test for $AR(2)$, show no sign of misspecification. The results for $AR(2)$ are conflicting. While the LM χ^2 test is significant at the 5 per cent level, the LM-F test is not. Estimating the equation with $AR(2)$, the log-likelihood ratio tests support neither $AR(1)$ against OLS, nor $AR(2)$ against $AR(1)$ (the test statistics' values are 2.5478 and 3.4815 respectively). Thus, we conclude that the estimated equation

$$\log(ESQ) = -5.280 + 1.185 \log(XQ) + 0.573 \log(P_{ESQ}/P_{XQ})$$
$$\quad\quad (5.28)\quad (6.21)\quad\quad\quad\quad (4.52)$$
$$+ 0.347 \log(SUB) + 0.243 \log(KQ)_{-1} + \tilde{u}$$
$$(5.73)\quad\quad\quad\quad (2.71)$$

presented in detail in Table 4.1 can be regarded as one which is free of misspecification. The parameter estimates are all significant, having correct signs and being in the regions accepted by economic theory. The parameter estimate, the T-ratio and the LM test for variable deletion for variable SUB clearly show the importance of export subsidies. The estimated relative price elasticity of 0.573 (which measures the percentage increase in exports induced by a 1 per cent increase in the relative price of exports to domestic sales) indicates a quite reasonable degree of price sensitivity of Hungarian firms. Relative price sensitivity is also captured by variable SUB, showing that the cross-rate between transferable rouble and rouble, as well as the relative changes in export subsidies for rouble and non-rouble exports, had quite a strong impact on export supply. A 1 per cent increase in the relative attractiveness of hard currency as opposed to rouble rewards from exporting will thus increase hard currency exports by 0.35 of 1 per cent. Both ratios were important policy instruments, although their importance varied remarkably during the period under investigation.

The present work is a continuation of the analysis by Halpern (1989). In that study, the export function

$$\log(ESQ) = \alpha' + \beta' \log(XQ) + \gamma' \log(P_{ESQ}/P_{EW}) + \delta' \log(SUB) \quad (2)$$
$$+ \epsilon' DUM78 + \tilde{u}$$

Table 4.1. *Estimation results for export supply equation (1)*
Dependent variable: log(ESQ)   Estimation method: OLS
21 observations used for estimation from 1969 to 1989

Regressor	Coefficient	Standard error	T-ratio
CONS	− 5.2802	0.9996	− 5.2822
$\log(XQ)$	1.1849	0.1908	6.2095
$\log(PR2)$	0.5734	0.1268	4.5206
$\log(SUB)$	0.3473	0.0605	5.7371
$\log(KQ)_{-1}$	0.2428	0.0896	2.7097
R^2	0.9945	F-statistic F(4, 16)	722.3142
$\bar{R}^2$	0.9931	S.E. of regression	0.0333
Residual sum of squares	0.0178	Mean of dependent variable	4.9503
S.D. of dependent variable	0.4017	Maximum of log-likelihood	− 44.4833
DW-statistic	2.5942		

Notes: For the definitions of the variables see equation (1) in the text.

Diagnostic tests

Test statistics	LM version	F version
A: Serial Correlation		
AR(1)	$\chi^2(1) = 2.8045$	$F(1, 15) = 2.3120$
AR(2)	$\chi^2(2) = 6.2761*$	$F(2, 14) = 2.9838$
B: Functional Form	$\chi^2(1) = 0.9534$	$F(1, 15) = 0.7134$
C: Normality	$\chi^2(2) = 1.2343$	
D: Heteroscedasticity	$\chi^2(1) = 1.8264$	$F(1, 19) = 1.8098$
E: ARCHC	$\chi^2(1) = 0.3147$	
F: Variable deletion	$\chi^2(1) = 14.1308*$	$F(1, 16) = 32.9139*$

Notes: A: Lagrange multiplier test of residual serial correlation.
 B: Ramsey's RESET test using the square of the fitted values.
 C: Based on a test of skewness and kurtosis of residuals.
 D: Based on the regression of squared residuals on squared fitted values.
 E: Autoregressive conditional heteroscedasticity test of residuals.
 F: Variable deletion tests (*LM*- and *F*-statistic) for log(SUB).
 *: Significant at 5 per cent level.

Table 4.1 (*cont.*)
Alternative tests for non-nested regression models
Dependent variable is log(*ESQ*) 21 observations used from 1969 to 1989
Regressors for model *M*1: *CONS*, log(*XQ*) ,log(*PR*2), log(*SUB*), log(*KQ*)$_{-1}$
Regressors for model *M*2: *CONS*, log(*XQ*), log(*PR*), log(*SUB*), *DUM*78

Test statistic	*M*1 against *M*2	*M*2 against *M*1
N-test	− 4.6613	− 4.6314
NT-test	− 3.2107	− 3.1807
W-test	− 2.4891	− 2.4432
J-test	2.7510	2.8122
JA-test	2.6835	2.3340

Encompassing $F(2, 14) = 5.5955$ $F(2, 14) = 3.9517$
Model *M*1:   *DW* 2.5942 $\bar{R}^2$ 0.9931   log-lkhd 44.4833
Model *M*2:   *DW* 1.8569 $\bar{R}^2$ 0.9929   log-lkhd 44.1361
Model *M*1 + *M*2:   *DW* 2.6206 $\bar{R}^2$ 0.9949   log-lkhd 48.8357
Akaike's information criterion of *M*1 versus *M*2 = 0.3472 favours *M*1
Schwarz's Bayesian information criterion of *M*1 versus *M*2 = 0.3472 favours *M*1

Notes: For the definitions of variables in models *M*1 and *M*2 see equations (1) and (2) in the text.

was estimated, where P_{EW} is the implicit price index for world exports (the price ratio above is denoted by *PR* in Table 4.1) and *DUM*78 is a dummy variable (1 for 1978, 0 otherwise). This specification combines supply-side (*XQ* and *SUB*) and demand-side (P_{ESQ}/P_{EW}) factors in explaining exports. Other empirical studies for Hungary (e.g. Tarafás and Szabó, 1985) specified pure demand equations. However, as reported by Halpern (1989, p. 296), pure demand equations (world demand for Hungarian exports) do not perform very well.

The specification in the present chapter is confined purely to supply-side factors. It may thus be of some interest to test whether supply-side factors alone can provide a satisfactory description of export flows. A series of non-nested tests carried out for equations (1) and (2)[3] (see Table 4.1) support none of the specifications, suggesting that demand-side factors played a role in explaining Hungarian exports as well.

5   An import demand function for Hungary

Our starting point is the import demand function developed by Welsch (1987), which was based on a dynamic linear expenditure system.[4] However, the original specification, as well as the way in which it is applied for a former CPE, is somewhat modified in order to suit the focus of the present chapter. First, contrary to previous applications for former CPEs (Gajda, 1990), imports from rouble and non-rouble trade (the former being basically the intra-CMEA trade) are treated separately. While non-rouble imports of goods and services are described by the above import demand equation, imports from the rouble area are treated exogenously. As a consequence, the income variable is also modified, since it no longer contains the income spent on imports from the rouble area.

Second, the price index of non-rouble imports is also redefined. For reasons described in section 2, the implicit price deflator derived from national accounts' statistics is at best misleading. It does not reflect the subsidies and tariffs attached to non-rouble imports, and thus does not measure the actual prices Hungarian enterprises face when deciding upon imports. As we shall see later, this is a fairly important point, and models neglecting this distortion can easily be outperformed by the model presented here.

Finally, the specifications previously used for former CPEs did not account for non-price influences (import restrictions) upon non-rouble imports by the central economic administration. The importance of this point and the actual mechanism through which this control was carried out has already been discussed in section 2. Our idea is that the extent of pressure (import restrictions) the central economic administration imposed upon non-rouble import demand was related to (a function of) the degree of indebtedness (as measured by the ratio between net non-rouble foreign debts and export earnings in the previous period).[5] Moreover, it is also assumed that import restrictions worked in a way that attempted to lower the marginal propensity by a given (and estimated) amount for a varying part of the income available for imports in the economy. The part of the income under pressure is assumed to be proportional to the degree of indebtedness (measured as defined above).

Taking the usual specification of this sort of import demand function, and taking into account the necessary modifications discussed so far, we arrive at the following equation

$$MSQ = a + \beta \, MSQ_{-1} + \gamma \, (GDP.P_{GDP} + MSQ.P^*_{MSQ})/P^*_{MSQ} \quad (3)$$
$$- \, \delta \, GDP_{-1}.P_{GDP}/P^*_{MSQ}$$

where MSQ is real non-rouble imports,[6] GDP is real GDP, P_{GDP} is the implicit price deflator for GDP, and P^*_{MSQ} is the adjusted implicit price index for imports, taking into account subsidies.

Introducing import restrictions in the way described above leads to the following additional term

$$\gamma'(DEX/ESQ.P^*_{ESQ})_{-1}.(GDP.P_{GDP} + MSQ.P^*_{MSQ})/P^*_{MSQ} \quad (4)$$

where DEX is net foreign debts in hard currencies, ESQ is real non-rouble exports of goods and services, and P^*_{ESQ} is the implicit price deflator for non-rouble exports. Parameter γ' is expected to have a negative sign. The justification for interpreting import restrictions as a mechanism which attempted to moderate non-rouble import demand, rather than setting an exogenous upper limit to it, is given in section 2. As described there, it was more a sort of bargaining between the central economic administration and enterprises than a strictly exogenous regulation exercised by the administration (Gács, 1980a).

The final specification for estimation is thus

$$\begin{aligned}MSQ = &\alpha + \beta\, MSQ_{-1} + \gamma(GDP.P_{GDP} + MSQ.P^*_{MSQ})/P^*_{MSQ} \quad (5)\\ &- \gamma'(DEX/ESQ.P^*_{ESQ})_{-1}(GDP.P_{GDP} + MSQ.P^*_{MSQ})/P^*_{MSQ}\\ &- \delta\, GDP_{-1}.(P_{GDP}/P^*_{MSQ})\end{aligned}$$

The estimation was carried out for the period 1969–89. For reasons discussed in section 4, it is not advisable to extend the estimation period before 1968. Figures for 1990 are not yet available.

Estimation results are presented in detail in Table 4.2. The tests performed reveal no sign of misspecification. The parameters are all significantly different from zero, having the expected signs and being in the regions suggested by economic theory. A nested model selection test clearly rejects (3) against (5), that is, the results seem to support the idea that import restrictions had a significant influence on import demand. A series of non-nested tests were carried out to see whether the introduction of the modified import price index (P^*_{MSQ}) was justified. The alternative model was the one in which the unmodified implicit import price index (P_{MSQ}) was used, but otherwise was the same as equation (5). The tests seem to support the original specification given in equation (5). Thus we are inclined to accept the equation

$$\begin{aligned}MSQ = &-46.652 + 0.432\, MSQ_{-1} + 0.283\,(GDP.P_{GDP} + MSQ.P^*_{MSQ})/\\ &\;\;(2.08)\quad\;\;(2.65)\qquad\qquad\quad(4.20)\\ &P^*_{MSQ} - 0.012\,(DEX/ESQ.P^*_{ESQ})_{-1}(GDP.P_{GDP} + \\ &\qquad\quad(1.86)\qquad\qquad\qquad\qquad\qquad\qquad\qquad\quad(6)\\ &MSQ.P^*_{MSQ})/P^*_{MSQ} - 0.192\,(GDP_{-1}.(P_{GDP}/P^*_{MSQ}))\\ &\qquad\qquad\qquad\qquad\quad(2.54)\end{aligned}$$

Table 4.2. *Estimation results for import demand equation (5)*
Dependent variable: MSQ   Estimation method: OLS
21 observations used for estimation from 1969 to 1989

Regressor		Coefficient	Standard error	T-ratio
CONS	a	− 46.6517	22.4429	− 2.0787
MSQ(− 1)	β	0.4320	0.1629	2.6516
GDPC	γ	0.2833	0.0675	4.1996
GDPR	γ'	− 0.0122	0.006570	− 1.8572
GDPA	δ	− 0.1916	0.0756	− 2.5360

R^2	0.9498	F-statistic $F(4, 14)$	75.6723
$\bar{R}^2$	0.9372	S.E. of regression	8.4231
Residual sum of squares	1135.2	Mean of dependent variable	150.4333
S.D. of dependent variable	33.6232	Maximum of log-likelihood	− 71.6929
DW-statistic	2.0877	Durbin's h-statistic	− 0.3021

Notes: For the definitions of the variables see equation (5) in the text.

Diagnostic tests

Test statistics	LM version	F version
A: Serial Correlation		
$AR(1)$	$\chi^2(1) = 0.1595$	$F(1, 15) = 0.1148$
$AR(2)$	$\chi^2(2) = 0.3806$	$F(2, 14) = 0.1292$
B: Functional Form	$\chi^2(1) = 0.0091$	$F(1, 15) = 0.0065$
C: Normality	$\chi^2(2) = 0.6908$	Not applicable
D: Heteroscedasticity	$\chi^2(1) = 0.0050$	$F(1, 19) = 0.0046$
E: ARCHC	$\chi^2(1) = 0.0245$	
F: Variable deletion	$\chi^2(1) = 3.7244^*$	$F(1, 16) = 3.4494^*$

Notes: A: Lagrange multiplier test of residual serial correlation.
       B: Ramsey's RESET test using the square of the fitted values.
       C: Based on a test of skewness and kurtosis of residuals.
       D: Based on the regression of squared residuals on squared fitted values.
       E: Autoregressive conditional heteroscedasticity test of residuals.
       F: Variable deletion tests (LM- and F-statistic) for $GDPR$).
      *: Significant at 5 per cent level.

Table 4.2 (*cont.*)
Alternative tests for non-nested regression models
Dependent variable is MSQ 21 observations used from 1969 to 1989
Regressors for model $M1$: $CONS$, $MSQ(-1)$, $GDPC$, $GDPR$, $GDPA$
Regressors for model $M2$: $CONS$, $MSQ(-1)$, $GDPC1$, $GDPR1$, $GDPA1$

Test statistic	$M1$ against $M2$	$M2$ against $M1$
N-test	− 0.6792	− 3.4957
NT-test	− 0.4395	− 2.6233
W-test	− 0.4204	− 2.0746
J-test	0.5277	2.2418
JA-test	0.5249	2.2394

Encompassing $F(3, 13) = 0.3608$ $F(3, 13) = 1.8169$
Model $M1$: DW 2.0877 $\bar{R}^2$ 0.9372   log-lkhd − 71.6929
model $M2$: DW 2.3455 $\bar{R}^2$ 0.9178   log-lkhd − 74.5297
Model $M1 + M2$ DW 1.9289 $\bar{R}^2$ 0.9287   log-lkhd − 70.8530
Akaike's information criterion of $M1$ versus $M2$ = 2.8368 favours $M1$
Schwarz's Bayesian information criterion of $M1$ versus $M2$ = 2.8368 favours $M1$

Notes: For the definitions of variables in models $M1$ and $M2$ see equations (5) and (3) in the text.

as a satisfactory description of Hungarian import demand during the period under investigation.

In order to separate the investigation of the price index used and that of the import restriction term, equation (3) was also estimated and like equation (5) was compared with the equation in which the *unmodified* price index (P_{MSQ}) was used. The non-nested test performed (not presented here) clearly favoured equation (3), showing that if prices are not corrected for import subsidies, the less satisfactory import equation (3) is mistakenly preferred to (5). These results also allow one to assess the impact of neglecting import restrictions on other parameter estimates. Leaving out import restrictions leads to an under-estimation of the habit formation coefficient, and thus to an under-estimation of the price elasticity.

The average short-run price elasticity based on equation (6) for the period of estimation is − 0.5869. This is slightly lower than the estimate given in Székely and Welsch (1986), which was − 0.634. This is a result of the lower parameter estimate for the habit formation parameter for imports. However, it is difficult to judge how much of this difference is due to the changes in the specification, for the estimation periods are different (1961–82 versus 1969–87). Moreover, the study mentioned above estimated the equations for total imports. However, the long-run price elasticities (− 1.033 and − 1.043) are by construction similar.

The price elasticity estimated here is in line with estimations for market economies (e.g. France, the UK, Italy, see Székely and Welsch, 1986) with similar degrees of openness (as measured, for example, by the ratio between imports and GDP).

6   Conclusions and policy implications

During the last two decades, the Hungarian economy has undergone substantial developments concerning her responsiveness in foreign trade. Economic transformation in Hungary will no doubt further change the behavioural characteristics of economic agents. The results presented in this chapter, however, seem to identify stable and sensible equations for the period up to the beginning of economic transformation in Hungary.[7] This fact suggests that even in a relatively fast-changing environment, as was the Hungarian economy in the period investigated, it may be possible to build simple econometric models.

Managing foreign debt will undoubtedly be at the top of the agenda for Hungarian economic policy-makers for quite some time to come. Monetary and exchange rate policies and export subsidy packages – should they opt for this sort of instrument – will have to be designed to accommodate targets on balance of payments. Notwithstanding the importance of other items, this chapter is concerned with the foreign trade balance. A properly designed policy package relies on the understanding of the ways domestic prices, exchange rates and different forms of subsidies and taxes influence export supply and import demand. Previous empirical studies, for the reasons set out earlier, failed to provide either stable econometric relationships, or reliable estimates of price, income or output elasticities. Lacking such information, economic policies were bound to over- (or under-)shoot, and thus contribute to unnecessary excess volatility.

The framework presented in the chapter takes into account some of the special characteristics of the Hungarian economy during the period under investigation (1968–89) not accounted for so far by other empirical (or theoretical) work. In particular, by explicitly taking into account subsidies given to rouble and non-rouble exports, we could identify their impacts on non-rouble exports. At the same time, this made it possible to give a more realistic (and stable) estimate of price elasticities.

As mentioned above, there were many other factors (e.g. credit preferences and preferential wage regulations for exporting firms and preferential treatment of these firms in import licensing) which had an important and sizeable impact on export supply behaviour (see, e.g. Gács, 1980a, 1980b; Oblath, 1988). However, it is almost impossible to quantify these factors. Moreover, if they had had a significant impact independent from that of subsidies, it should have made our equations misspecified.

In case of import demand, the modified price index, which takes into account import subsidies and taxes, was also necessary to get reliable and stable estimates for income and price elasticities. The other crucial element here was that import restrictions, which played a very decisive role especially during the 1980s, were taken into account. This also helped in establishing a stable import demand function and getting more reliable parameter estimates.

The two equations discussed in the present chapter can also be very useful in designing more coherent policy packages. They identify the differences in the way in which, and the extent to which, different policy tools influence exports and imports. Economic policy-makers have a desperate need to understand how, and to what extent, the policy instruments they plan to use (or are already using) influence the economy.

Significant price elasticities revealed by the present study, however, are by no means arguments against or for devaluation (or appreciation). It should be kept in mind that what matters are always relative prices, that is the ratios between domestic and export (or import) prices. Such ratios can improve or deteriorate due both to exchange rate movements (or the lack of them) and to domestic price movements not (or only marginally) induced by exchange rate movement. Monetary and fiscal policy, as well as other factors thought to influence the domestic price level, therefore have an impact on relative prices.

Econometrics, due to its nature, is backward-looking in the sense that it establishes relationships concerning past data. The general question whether it is possible in any way to understand the future from the past is even more crucial for economies undergoing substantial transformation. In the present context, the question is whether one can obtain meaningful and reliable estimates for price and income elasticities of export supply and import demand. Previous work suggested that this was not possible even for the period until 1989. This chapter claims that if correction is made for specific features of export and import policies, stable relationships, and therefore meaningful and stable estimates, can be achieved for this period. If this claim is justified, these estimates can be invaluable sources of information for economic policy-makers.

The present chapter deals with the period 1968–89, that is, with a period not covering the whole process of transformation into a fully-fledged market economy. Naturally, when data become available for 1990 and 1991 the whole exercise must be repeated for the extended period to see whether the relationships identified and estimated here remained stable during the economic transformation. Although it is difficult to foresee the outcome of this exercise, economic policy-makers do not have at present many alternative sources of information when designing policy packages.

Appendix: Description of data

XQ	gross output at 1981 prices, national accounts: 'A gazdaság fejlödésének föbb mutatói 1988' and 'Föbb nemzetgazdasági folyamatok', KSH (CSO), Budapest 1990, HUF bn
I	investments, national accounts (HUF bn, current prices)
C	consumption, national accounts (HUF bn, current prices)
KQ	stock of inventories at 1981 constant prices, national accounts (HUF bn)
MSQ	dollar imports at 1981 constant prices, national accounts (HUF bn)
ER	rouble exports, national accounts (HUF bn, current prices)
ES	dollar exports, national accounts (HUF bn, current prices)
$GDPN$	GDP national accounts (HUF bn, current prices)
MRQ	rouble imports at 1981 constant prices, national accounts (HUF bn)
P_{XQ}	gross output implicit price index (1981 = 1), national accounts
P_{ESQ}	dollar exports implicit price index (1981 = 1), national accounts
P_{MRQ}	rouble exports implicit price index (1981 = 1), national accounts
DEX	the ratio of dollar exports to net dollar debts; own computations using for 1968–81 various estimations on net dollar debt and CSO data for dollar exports; from 1982 computations based on the *Yearbook of Hungarian National Bank* (1990)

SUB   ratio of dollar implicit (or *de facto*) export exchange rate
               (official nominal exchange rate + export
               subsidies – export taxes) to rouble export implicit
               exchange rate, own computations for 1968–75 using
               various CSO publications; for 1976–87 'Devizaegységre
               jutó forintérték alakulása', KSH (CSO), Budapest
               (various years); for 1988–9 own estimation based on data
               of all exporting firms
$P*_{MSQ}$ overall cost (official nominal exchange rate + import
               duties + import taxes – subsidies) of 1 1981 HUF dollar
               import (1981 = 1), own computations for 1968–75 using
               various CSO publications; for 1976–87 'Devizaegységre
               jutó forintérték alakulása', KSH (CSO), Budapest
               (various years)

	XQ	GDPN	I	C	ER	ES	MRQ	MSQ	KQ
1967	995.8	256.8	61.4	184.0	38.4	29.6	62.0	79.0	46.6
1968	1063.6	281.1	72.1	196.4	43.6	30.1	67.4	68.9	53.7
1969	1119.6	210.1	82.0	210.1	49.1	39.4	64.0	74.7	57.6
1970	1200.3	332.4	100.3	228.5	52.1	49.3	81.4	98.8	61.5
1971	1269.8	360.7	113.1	247.4	58.5	51.4	96.2	117.6	82.8
1972	1362.5	391.0	116.8	262.1	73.4	61.9	93.1	109.5	83.4
1973	1437.1	429.0	123.1	282.2	81.5	84.3	95.8	114.0	79.2
1974	1517.9	448.6	139.2	308.3	85.5	103.0	111.0	134.0	93.7
1975	1609.8	481.1	161.0	335.2	103.1	97.0	128.3	129.0	107.4
1976	1687.6	528.7	168.2	359.2	104.8	100.4	124.2	139.6	125.5
1977	1812.5	580.1	197.7	390.4	124.0	116.6	132.2	157.6	139.7
1978	1936.0	628.0	214.4	426.1	125.1	118.8	144.6	182.1	185.7
1979	1979.3	682.0	220.8	470.9	135.6	147.7	152.5	162.3	190.1
1980	1991.9	721.0	207.7	515.3	124.3	157.6	153.3	158.2	200.5
1981	2054.7	779.9	206.6	556.8	136.0	172.3	147.6	168.9	215.3
1982	2110.2	847.9	213.9	599.3	144.3	177.6	148.6	155.9	225.6
1983	2138.9	896.4	220.0	642.1	165.6	195.1	152.6	154.5	227.3
1984	2204.8	978.5	225.4	695.8	182.5	219.5	151.7	158.7	231.3
1985	2217.8	1033.7	232.1	753.8	208.0	228.2	152.3	182.4	234.3
1986	2274.1	1088.8	261.2	811.5	221.3	210.3	157.7	186.0	241.5
1987	2370.0	1226.4	303.5	904.8	221.6	242.8	164.4	189.3	235.9
1988	2373.4	1409.5	295.6	1011.9	214.1	316.3	169.8	185.5	243.1
1989	2348.0	1706.0	345.0	1203.7	222.4	399.2	157.7	200.8	243.8

	P_{XQ}	P_{ESQ}	P_{EW}	SUB	DEX	P_{MRQ}	P^*_{MSQ}
1967	0.5637	0.6004	–	–	–	0.6368	0.4581
1968	0.5977	0.5923	1.3465	1.5350	0.5684	0.6600	0.5481
1969	0.6130	0.6210	1.3574	1.5722	0.2501	0.6995	0.5098
1970	0.6210	0.6378	1.3426	1.5847	0.7411	0.6751	0.5524
1971	0.6400	0.6615	1.3428	1.5693	1.0667	0.6863	0.5673
1972	0.6545	0.6892	1.3333	1.4506	0.8857	0.6966	0.5963
1973	0.6776	0.7913	1.4340	1.2377	0.5083	0.6998	0.6390
1974	0.6991	0.9414	1.2346	1.2500	0.7090	0.7075	0.7390
1975	0.7389	0.8556	1.1443	1.1525	1.0136	0.8926	0.8161
1976	0.7781	0.8060	1.1194	1.3518	1.2141	0.8809	0.8086
1977	0.7998	0.8378	1.0726	1.3220	1.3948	0.9408	0.8391
1978	0.8291	0.8346	1.0941	1.2990	2.1138	0.9511	0.8682
1979	0.8510	0.9123	1.0652	1.2520	1.7841	0.9614	0.9308
1980	0.9442	0.9710	1.0196	1.1835	1.6229	0.9170	0.9908
1981	0.9987	1.0000	1.0000	1.3041	1.6704	1.0000	1.0000
1982	1.0408	0.9847	0.9722	1.4013	1.5436	1.0740	1.0081
1983	1.0948	1.0333	0.9207	1.6175	1.5580	1.1600	1.0087
1984	1.1499	1.0899	0.8850	1.7852	1.4156	1.2240	1.1623
1985	1.2077	1.1026	0.8690	1.8247	1.7601	1.2980	1.1529
1986	1.2506	1.0612	0.8763	1.6839	2.3066	1.3830	1.2382
1987	1.3160	1.1498	0.8259	1.7158	2.6132	1.3120	1.3412
1988	1.4425	1.3390	0.8547	1.8243	2.2267	1.2211	1.5168
1989	1.6588	1.6177	0.8807	2.1264	2.2055	1.2967	1.7835

NOTES

Research conducted under the auspices of CEPR's research project on 'Economic Transformation in Eastern Europe'. The research reported here was carried out while László Halpern was a visitor at the Department of Applied Economics of the University of Cambridge within the framework of the CEPR's Summer Consultancy Programme. László Halpern acknowledges the financial support of the Ford Foundation (grant No. 910-0383) and the SPES programme of the Commission of the European Communities (grant No. E/90100033/PRO).
1 For a detailed description of the variables used in the estimations, see the Appendix pp. 66–8.
2 Calculations presented throughout this chapter were carried out by using DFIT 2.0 licensed at the University of Cambridge, Department of Applied Economics. For the definitions of estimation and hypothesis testing procedures available in DFIT and used here, see the Reference Manual of DFIT 2.0. Data series used are described and listed in the Appendix.
3 Unfortunately, we cannot reproduce the result of the other studies mentioned. No formal test can therefore be applied to compare these equations with the one presented in this study.

4 This specification was used for a wide range of economies (Welsch, 1987; Gajda, 1990; Székely and Welsch, 1986), and proved to be a robust specification performing rather well in a highly non-linear and complex simultaneous model environment (Dobrinsky and Székely, 1990).

5 Naturally, some other indicators could have been used as well. An obvious candidate is the debt–service ratio which is widely used, and which was in fact closely monitored by international capital markets throughout the 1980s. Our original intention was to use this ratio, but due to well-known reasons, reliable figures for this ratio are available only for the period 1982 onward.

6 For a detailed description of the variables included see the Appendix.

7 Naturally, time series analyses must be complemented with investigations based on cross-sections and pooled cross-sections of observations for micro units (enterprises) (see Halpern, 1991).

REFERENCES

Ábel, I. and I.P. Székely (1988) 'Price regulations and inventory behavior of companies under central planning', in A. Chickán and M. Lovell (eds), *The Economics of Inventory Management*, Amsterdam: Elsevier, pp. 3–14.

Dobrinsky, R. and I.P. Székely (1990) 'Growth in an interdependent world economy', in W. Krelle (ed.), *The Future of the World Economy*, Berlin: Springer-Verlag.

Gács, J. (1980a) 'Constraints on imports, shortages and the adjustment of enterprise' (in Hungarian), Budapest: KOPINT, p. 116.

(1980b) 'Regulation of import and enterprise behaviour' (in Hungarian), Budapest: KOPINT, p. 29.

Gajda, J.B. (1990) 'Structural change in foreign trade of CMEA countries', in W. Krelle (ed.), *The Future of the World Economy*, Berlin: Springer-Verlag, pp. 259–75.

Halpern, L. (1989) 'Effects of devaluation in a macroeconomic model for Hungary', *Acta Oeconomica*, **41(3–4)**, pp. 293–312.

(1991) 'Cost and subsidy effects of trade reorientation for Hungarian exporting firms', paper presented at the Cambridge Workshop of the ACE project, 'Economic Transformation in Eastern Europe', Cambridge (1–3 December).

Hulyák, K. (1988) 'The supply and demand for Hungarian export-goods: a disequilibrium analysis', paper presented at ESEM, Bologna (September) p. 19.

(1990) 'The effects of exchange rate adjustments on foreign trade and on domestic prices in Hungary', paper presented at the 6th World Congress of the Econometric Society, Barcelona (August).

Neményi, J. (1990) 'Annual macromodel of the Economic Research Institute', *ERI Working Papers*, Budapest: ERI.

(1991) 'Macroeconomic forecasting in the transition period: The case of Hungary', paper presented at the conference, 'Econometrics of Short and Unreliable Time Series: Model Building, Estimation and Forecasting of Economic Transition in Eastern Europe', Vienna (June) p. 29.

Oblath, G. (1988) 'Exchange rate policy in the reform package', *Acta Oeconomica*, **39(1–2)**, pp. 81–93.

Simon, A. (1978) 'Econometric analysis of foreign trade and output' (in Hungarian), Budapest: KOPINT, p. 31.

D

Székely, I.P. and H. Welsch (1986) 'Dependency and development in LDCs', University of Bonn, *Discussion Paper*, **SFB303**; also paper presented at the World Conference of the Applied Economic Association Istanbul (9–14 December).

Szentgyörgyvári, A. (1991) 'The balance of payments effects of currency devaluation in Hungary', paper presented at the conference, 'Open Economy Macroeconomics', Vienna (November).

Tarafás, I. and J. Szabó (1985) 'Hungary's exchange rate policy in the 1980s', *Acta Oeconomica*, **35(1–2)**, pp. 53–79.

Welsch, H. (1987) 'An aggregate import demand model for long-term projections', *Jahrbücher für Nationalökonomie und Statistik*, **203/204**, pp. 372–82.

Discussion of Part One

RENZO DAVIDDI

Chapters 2, 3 and 4 are quite different in scope and nature. Mizsei's analysis of regional cooperation in Chapter 3 is very much policy-oriented; it reviews various policy propositions, and makes precise recommendations. Csaba's Chapter 2 is more analytical and aims, among other things, to investigate the relationship between macroeconomic performance and trade reorientation. Halpern and Székely in Chapter 4 carry out a useful econometric exercise, estimating in an innovative way hard currency export supply and import demand for Hungary. In this discussion I would like first to identify a couple of features common to all three chapters, and then discuss briefly some specific ideas contained in them, concluding with some comments on a few specific issues.

All the chapters start from a positive assessment of liberalisation and trade reorientation. Negative costs of the stabilisation are recognised in terms of macroeconomic performance and unemployment, but they are deemed necessary for a profound restructuring of the Hungarian economy. The dismantling of the CMEA is considered by all authors to be an essential element for the success of the reform; moreover, the expedient of retaining existing institutions, and to a certain extent even initiating new forms of cooperation with former partners, are considered only to prolong the agony of the past regime, and delay necessary adjustment. Each author takes a clear stance in favour of eliminating subsidies, tariffs and restrictions.

The chapters by Csaba and Mizsei discuss trade reorientation at length.

Csaba shows evidence that such reorientation predates 1989, and maintains that the collapse in intraregional trade is mostly a consequence of the deteriorating domestic macroeconomic performance of the countries in the region. However, he also suggests that the huge fall of trade has had so far only a limited negative impact on the macroeconomic performance of the formerly centrally planned economies (CPEs).

Both Csaba and Mizsei take into consideration the issue of a payments union among former CMEA members, but in the end they discard it. Csaba explains at length why payments' agreements with the USSR did not work, and why agreements with the CIS or individual republics are not likely to work either: the high degree of political instability, as well as the lack of a clear reform strategy in the former Soviet Republics are indicated as the main causes.

Mizsei's attitude towards regional cooperation is less dismissive. In particular he advocates forms of closer cooperation between three countries (Czecho-Slovakia, Poland and Hungary) and identifies three areas of cooperation: trade policy, regional trade and development of infrastructures.

The chapter by Halpern and Székely presents new insights into export supply and import demand functions, two essential relations for a small open economy like Hungary. The novel feature that the authors introduce is the explicit treatment of export and import subsidies and import restrictions in the functions. The authors claim that without the inclusion of subsidies, the implicit deflators derived from national accounts' statistics can be misleading and make econometric equations misspecified. However, not enough evidence is provided on this point, and indeed the comparison with other authors' findings provided in the text points more to similarity rather than differences in results. The implicit assumption on which the chapter seems to rest is that hard currency trade was responding to economic rationality even under the previous trade regime, and results produced in the chapter seem to support this view.

Maybe the authors should have spelled out more clearly what the purpose of the exercise was. Certainly their findings will be of great use for interpreting the past behaviour of Hungarian trade. However, attempts to use the parameters for forecasting purposes can be rather dangerous. I wonder about the predictive capacity of a model whose equations are estimated in the presence of structural breaks and as complete a regime change as those observed in Hungary.

Finally I turn to a number of specific issues. Trade relations with the CMEA have entailed a massive trade diversion with respect to the pre-war situation, when Hungary's main trade partners were Germany and Austria. Furthermore, despite the resource transfer in 1960–80, in the long run the CMEA has damaged the economic interests of Hungary (and more generally those of all the Central–Eastern European countries) through:

* forced patterns of specialisation and normative allocation of industrial output
* trade dependence on the former USSR, both for the import of raw materials and for the export of low-quality goods produced for the Soviet market, and not exportable for convertible currencies.

Indeed, at the beginning of 1990 Hungary seemed locked into the traditional trade dependence with the USSR and stood to lose greatly from an immediate move to trade at international prices settled in convertible currencies. In fact, quite to the contrary, Hungary seems to have responded better than other CPEs to external supply shocks and to the changes in CMEA agreements. The country has been able to respond quickly to a dramatic decline in intra-CMEA trade, reorienting a large part of its exports to the hard currency area; the foreign trade reorientation reflected the government's policy to encourage enterprises to limit their trade relations with former CMEA partners. The progressive opening of EC markets to Hungarian products, the HUF devaluation policy adopted in 1989, 1990, and 1991, the continuing application of subsidies to some export-bound products and a sharp decline of domestic demand facilitated the process.

However, it is difficult to agree with Csaba's view that the CMEA collapse has not had a negative impact on output, inflation and the state budget. Hungary, like the other East European countries, faced two external shocks:

* oil price increases
* further decline in CMEA trade and worsening of the terms of trade.

The increase in the price of oil came primarily from the change in rules for price determination within the CMEA. The price of crude oil increased from an estimated TR13.7 per barrel ($5.89) to $20 per barrel in 1991.

The income effect of the regime change was partially reduced by the sharp decline in volume. But a large part of the deterioration was undoubtedly reflected in the state budget. Future outcomes will depend on how rapidly, and to what extent, Hungarian enterprises are able to reorient their production towards Western markets. It is true that in this respect, performance in 1990 and 1991 was extremely positive: even sectors heavily engaged in CMEA trade, like machinery and light industry, were able to expand the volume of their exports towards Western partners.

Table DI.1. *Hungarian export share of non-sensitive products[a] in the EC,*
per cent

1988	48.3
1989	48.7
1990	51.4
1991: q2	54.7

Note: [a] Non-sensitive products exclude agriculture, steel, and textile products.
Source: EUROSTAT.

The integration process focused around the EC. Trade reorientation
took place in the direction of this area, the final aim being EC membership. All other transitional arrangements, including the creation of a
free trade area, or agreements between some or all former CMEA partners are rejected on the ground that they will delay this ultimate goal.

However, the collapse of intraregional trade can be harmful in the long
run, in particular since no account is taken of the consequences of EC
trade policy. Nobody would deny that a substantial increase of trade with
the EC has taken place. The value of Hungarian exports increased by 13.4
per cent in 1990 and by 23.4 per cent in the first half of 1991. But the
question remains: how much of the increase is due to preferential
treatment by the EC (linked to PHARE and other forms of assistance),
and how much represents a real gain of competitiveness by the Hungarian
industry in the Western European market? As Table DI.1 shows, the
Hungarian export share of non-sensitive products in the EC has remained
almost constant since 1988. The increase in exports can be ascribed to a
large extent to an increase in agriculture, steel, and textile products. These
are sensitive sectors which are strongly affected by trade restrictions; the
increase in Hungarian exports is therefore very likely to have occurred
thanks to specific EC concessions. If this is true the 1991 European
Agreement might actually make things worse for Hungary on the EC
market.

Moreover, the trade surplus recorded in 1991 was achieved under conditions of domestic recession, with a substantial fall in domestic demand.
The great emphasis placed on macroeconomic stabilisation produced a
steeper than expected output decline, but had the positive effect of
alleviating pressures on the balance of payments. This is unlikely to
happen in periods of sustained growth which are, incidentally, an essential prerequisite for a successful policy of running down the external debt.

Finally, the necessity to stimulate exports and to gain competitiveness in
international markets is not consistent with the relatively high level of

domestic inflation. The high inflation currently experienced by the Hungarian economy can be attributed to several factors, but above all to price liberalisation and to the reduction of subsidies. Nonetheless, signs of emerging inflation expectations have recently begun to emerge. Such expectations may be attributed to differences between price targets announced by the government and actual outcomes, as well as to wage pressures (which clearly run counter to the necessity to moderate wage increases for balance of payments purposes). The substantial inflation differential which exists at present between Hungary and its main trade partners results in a constant appreciation of the real effective exchange rate, which in turn induces periodic devaluations. Periodic devaluations of this kind can be easily anticipated, however, with destabilising effects on the economy.

Part Two

Privatisation and competition policy

5   10 per cent already sold: privatisation in Hungary

ZSIGMOND JÁRAI

Nobody knows exactly its rate, but the private sector is undoubtedly growing fast in Hungary. According to official figures 14 per cent of the declining GDP was generated in this sector in 1991. Unofficial estimates, however, suggest that the real rate could easily be double the official figure. The difference is derived from the black or 'shadow' economy, which may be the only branch showing good results in Eastern Europe. While the official privatisation is proceeding more slowly than expected, a layer of Hungarian entrepreneurs, rapidly growing in strength, has not waited for the bureaucrats, but has privatised run-down and state-managed enterprises by one means of another.

The Hungarian government entrusted a daunting task to the State Property Agency (SPA). It is supposed to transfer at least 80 per cent of the Hungarian industry and services into private hands in four to five years, in an environment in which it is exposed to constant criticism from all sides. If the Agency manages to sell off a state-owned company then it is often the workers, who fear for the security of their comfortable 'state' jobs from the new and real owners, that try to prevent such sales. Sometimes public opinion, or perhaps the press, finds the sales price achieved too low, albeit that run-down and loss-making companies are very often difficult to sell. Some of the bigger deals stir up political storms even today although the really big scandals of two or three years were replaced by smaller local scandals in 1991.

Everybody in Hungary appears to be an expert on privatisation. Instead of pursuing their own jobs, some government institutions are very keen on dealing with privatisation issues (even defining asset values). This increased interest is, of course, natural because the stakes of privatisation are high. Privatisation is the stage on which will be decided which social groups will have access to the means of production, and under what conditions and who will eventually get to the sunny or the shady side of this evolving capitalist paradise.

1   Promising results

In spite of the many problems, privatisation is running promisingly in Hungary. Basically, the process takes place on three different 'levels': (1) the centrally directed privatisation, (2) the so-called 'spontaneous' privatisation and (3) the formation and strengthening of new private companies.

1.1   New private companies

Growth is quickest, almost miraculous, at level (3). In 1991 more than 30,000 new private companies were registered in Hungary. It is true that the majority of these companies were established purely for purposes of tax evasion, or at least for purposes of circumventing flexibly interpretable (and interpreted) taxation rules, yet many thousand new and real enterprises set out on their way. Hungarians are full of ideas – almost everyone has two or three conceptions as to what kinds of new enterprises should be launched. Of course, there are only a few who realise their conception, and there are even fewer who get through the first several years. A vast majority would still like to remain employees, even though this is becoming less and less easy.

In this rapidly growing sector high incomes are generated – the tax office often does not know how high they are. This is evident from the number of Mercedes, BMWs and Porsches – the newly rich are living well. But the smarter ones are those who do not consume their easily attained wealth but rather invest and expand their companies. Today there are at least 50 medium-size companies operating in Hungary which were formed only a few years ago, and some of them have already entered the mature category. An example is one of the most successful companies on the Budapest Stock Exchange, the American–Hungarian FOTEX, shares of which are also traded in Vienna, London, and New York, or MÜSZERTECHNIKA, which has become one of the largest computer firms in Eastern Europe. The first private steel mill is fighting with problems, but there are numerous servicing companies in the tourist, catering and in the financial industry, which are showing substantial growth.

1.2   'Spontaneous' privatisation

The so-called 'spontaneous' privatisation became eventually accepted after two years of wrangling, frequent abuse and many political disputes. State-owned companies or cooperatives can be transformed into a joint stock company and look for their own investors: the SPA only supervises the process, and may stop it in the case of any possible violations of the law, but does not otherwise direct it.

Although only 216 out of a total of about 2000 state-owned companies have made use of this opportunity so far, this process is already under way in the case of a further 307 firms and a large portion of the remaining 1500 is also considering the possibilities of transformation, where this transformation is permitted. Some are prevented as the different ministries set up new lists every 3 to 4 months, which mark companies 'remaining in state property for the national interest'. Practical necessity, however, regularly overrules these lists and an observer can thus state that the limits of privatisation are not clearly defined and that the number of institutions dealing with the handling of companies remaining in state hands is growing.

From the point of view of state revenues, 1991 was a year of 'spontaneous' privatisation. The SPA had revenue of about half a billion dollars from selling a part of the shares of the transformed companies, while foreign buyers invested a quarter of a billion in the companies purchased. Several considerable deals can be found among those concluded in 1991; several companies of world-wide reputation have acquired a stake (generally a majority) in medium-size or relatively big Hungarian companies. Some more important transactions were the following:

	Multinational	Company interested in
*	Philip Morris	Egri Dohánygyár (Eger Tobacco Factory)
*	Julius Meinl	Csemege
*	Nestlé	Szerencsi Csokoládégyár (Szerencs Chocolate Factory)
*	Sanofi	Chinoin
*	Elektrolux	Lehel
*	Siemens	Villanyszerelóipari Vállalat (Company for Electrical Installation)
*	Interbrau	Borsodi Sörgyár (Borsod Brewery)
*	Underberg–Zwack	Buliv
*	United Biscuits	Győri Keksz – és Ostyagyár (Győr Biscuits Factory)

1.3   Centrally directed privatisation

The 1991 results of the central privatisation programmes directed by the SPA seem to confirm statements of investment bankers in Budapest, who say that the Hungarian government wants to sell everything that cannot be sold, while it wants to hold on to those companies that buyers would like to buy. Not one of the 50 firms in the two official programmes found a buyer, and some of them have already gone bankrupt in the meantime. The central programmes carry all the bureaucratism inherent in every state administration; ownership rights are often unclear, the different government agencies are referring potential buyers from one to the other and responsibilities are not clarified. It requires a skilled adviser indeed who, finding his way in a jungle of constantly changing legal regulations, eventually carries out a privatisation project.

Looking at this internal disorder and disorganisation it appears that these programmes have been initiated too early and that the necessary rules are not yet in place. And from an economic aspect, the privatisation of mostly medium-size and large companies came too late; the output of these companies had dropped sharply due to the collapse of the Eastern European market and their former profits changed to losses. Large companies could not improve the quality of their products quickly enough, and it is the buyer who must pay the cost of an over-employment of 50–100 per cent.

The recession of the world economy affected these companies in two ways, for on the one hand they got into a worse situation through shrinking Western markets and on the other their potential buyers were also struggling with financial and marketing difficulties.

Under such internal and external circumstances one cannot wonder at the slowness of central privatisation programmes; what is more noteworthy is the relative speed of 'spontaneous' privatisation and the sudden growth of private enterprises.

2   Buyers, sellers and intermediaries

As could have been expected it is the foreign investors in the first instance that participate in the purchase of former state property. In 1991 almost 90 per cent of the privatisation revenues of the SPA came from foreigners, who invested considerable amounts even outside the privatisation programmes, mainly in the establishment of new companies. The involvement of foreign capital in Hungary amounted to about $1.5 bn in 1991, which is more than the sums invested in total in the previous two–three decades. It was this substantial inflow of capital that brought about equilibrium in the balance of payments of the country, as opposed to the planned deficit. In spite of the difficulties, capital is still flowing into Hungary, and many would prefer to see an even higher rate of capital involvement: at the end of 1991 3–4 per cent of the means of production were in foreign ownership, whereas the target figure to be attained by the turn of the century is 25–30 per cent.

In contrast to this foreign investment, local capital is flowing almost entirely to areas outside the official privatisation channels. There are some examples of Hungarian investors also buying a privatised company. Recently, for example, the 'flagship of socialist electronics', VIDEOTON was bought by a domestic group of investors in bankruptcy proceedings. Although foreigners are buying business premises, or possibly several smaller parts of a business, their investments are mainly directed towards establishing new companies. One of the main reasons lies in the fact that this activity generally requires less money and that large local companies still count as 'small' in the international investment environment.

In spite of the repeated promises and experiments of the last four–five years domestic investors still lack support, unless we take the habit of concealment from the tax office as a kind of assistance. Loans are quite difficult to obtain and interest rates often exceed 40 per cent p.a. (The inflation rate in 1991 amounted to 35 per cent.) Because of the under-development of the internal capital market, small investors are basically left out of privatisation and shares of only a small number of companies have been floated on the Stock Exchange. Although one or two years ago one could hear about the privatisation plans of at least 30–40 companies through the Stock Exchange, practically nothing came of these. The development of the Budapest Stock Exchange, resurrected from its 40 years of apparent torpor in 1989, had a spectacular start but 1991 turned out to be worse than expected. The 45 Stock Exchange members are still trading in 20 shares altogether. The total value of the shares is very substantial ($2 billion); turnover, however, hardly exceeded $30,000 a day. Due to the lack of internal purchasing power and the general economic problems rates dropped by an average of 20 per cent during the year and several listed companies came to the verge of bankruptcy. During the whole of 1991 there was only one successful flotation, which related to official privatisation: the 'Styl' Clothing Company; the legal, institutional and organisational frameworks of the Stock Exchange would enable it to deal with a much higher turnover. In spite of this some hope may be offered by the fact that from 1992 domestic share buyers will obtain certain tax benefits. It will, however, be difficult to stimulate the restored machinery of the Stock Exchange to a higher turnover after the sudden downturn in 1991: interest rates are too high, the market is small and sometimes manipulated, information is not always reliable, and it is no accident that investors are cautious.

Given the small importance of the capital market the major role has been played by direct investments and acquisitions. In the case of privatised Hungarian companies the SPA sold a controlling share of stocks to foreign companies operating in the same line of business. The transactions were realised under the mediation of local or foreign investment banks and advisers, these latter rendering help in the valuation of the company to be sold, the collection and systematisation of the necessary information, the selection of the possible buyers and eventually the preparation of sales agreements containing also long-term development plans, with the buyer making the best bid. In the case of some of these agreements the emphasis is not only on the purchase price but also on the assessment of future development opportunities.

Some say that even if Hungary is not yet a paradise for investors, it certainly is for advisers, as besides many hundred small and medium-size Hungarian advisory firms and banks, numerous giant banks and advisers of the world are represented along with Hungarian companies. Almost every large auditing firm, large Japanese, American, British, German, French, Austrian, Italian and Dutch banks and advisers have their offices in Budapest.

3   Prospects for 1992

The Hungarian government hopes that a substantial improvement in the economy will be attained in 1992. They expect the decline in GDP to stop (an unchanged GDP is planned as opposed to a decline of 10 per cent in 1991) and the government wishes to reduce the 1991 inflation rate of 35 per cent to 20 per cent. These factors could provide a favourable climate for the further acceleration of privatisation. The rapid growth in the number of private enterprises and 'spontaneous' privatisation in the sector of small- and medium-size companies will continue, and in all probability will again produce the best results in 1992.

However, both unemployment (at present 6–7 per cent) and the number of bankruptcies of large companies are expected to increase. As a result, social tension will continue to grow between lower and upper social layers, who are becoming increasingly poor and rapidly rich, respectively. Some disputed ownership issues should also be clarified and the conversion of the compensation certificates accepted to compensate the owners of several decades ago should not pose any substantial problems and the division of work among government agencies and their relevant responsibilities will perhaps also become more clear-cut. A large part of the central privatisation programmes will come to an end and the SPA does not wish to launch any new ones. Two new areas are also in sight where one can reckon with serious foreign interest if bureaucratic obstacles can be eliminated: telecommunications (possibly other parts of the infrastructure, too) and the banking sector (see Chapter 9 below). If in addition to existing sectors serious investment activities could be initiated in these sectors (provided that issues related to frequency usage are successfully clarified and the problem of doubtful liabilities of large banks is resolved) the proportion of the private sector in Hungary could expand by another 10–15 per cent.

6 Hungary: a unique approach to privatisation – past, present and future

PÉTER MIHÁLYI

1 Introduction

It has to be noted at the outset that the first freely elected post-communist government does not have a single, comprehensive programme of privatisation. Viewed superficially, the lack of a unified conceptual and legal basis shows merely that the privatisation process itself does not provide the focus of the government's attention.[1] But the lack of a comprehensive strategy supports a more fundamental proposition, an idea which runs right through the present chapter: the past 40 years of Hungarian developments cannot be regarded as a closed book. Vested interests, deeply established forms of thinking, legal traditions and informal connections do not disappear overnight, simply because it is impossible to forge a democratic consensus against the totality of this common heritage.

The countries of Eastern Europe are sailing in uncharted waters. The known examples of privatisation in Western Europe or in some developing countries give little, if any, guidance. The distinctly different Polish and Czecho-Slovak approaches to privatisation have not proved themselves, either. Academic circles in Hungary are divided, too. Paradoxically, the relatively free intellectual atmosphere of the past ten years did not give rise to a crystallised view on 'what is to be done, when it is possible'. On the contrary, such proposals were torn to pieces one after the other, leaving a bad taste in everybody's mouth.[2] In this situation, the Hungarian government – perhaps subconsciously – has drifted towards a 'wait-and-see' position and moves in the direction of least opposition. This is a very cautious approach, something the country perhaps simply cannot afford, but it would be a mistake not to appreciate its origins.

2   Scholars looking for owners

2.1   Models considered

Until the middle of the 1980s, the prevailing view was that, after 40 years of socialism, capitalism could not be restored. There was an agreement in academic circles that the emergence of new private ventures was to be encouraged by all means, including a partial selling-off of state property, but this was viewed only as a partial remedy. Various alternatives were considered as possible ways to improve the existing socialist ownership structure, but the restoration of pre-war property structures or the importation of present Western patterns were never contemplated.

The *leasing* model is associated with Tibor Liska's life-work stretching from the mid-1950s to the present. Liska was the first Hungarian economist openly to question the economic rationality of public ownership. He was, however, equally critical of Western types of private ownership. In the mid-1960s he elaborated a model based on leasing state-owned capital to individuals through a periodically recurring auction process.[3]

The roots of the *holding model* go back to the preparatory discussions of the 1968 reform (New Economic Mechanism, NEM). Already several experts were arguing for the need of separating ownership rights from dispositional rights in order to boost capital flows among state-owned enterprises (SOEs). This school saw the main weakness of the Hungarian economy in its tendency to profit redistribution, whereby every SOE was accorded a minimum possibility of expansion but no one was allowed to go bankrupt or to develop very dynamically. A proposal to corporatise SOEs, through compulsory transformation into shareholding companies, was prepared, but it was not accepted and the publication of such ideas was prevented.[4] A few years later, the same suggestion re-emerged in a seminal article by Tardos (1972). Tardos' idea was to create a small number of profit maximising financial institutions (holdings), as personifications of state ownership; the existing state enterprises would have been randomly distributed among them. The holdings' main tasks would have been to nominate and control the management of SOEs, as well as to re-direct capital flows among the enterprises.

The *self-management* model was viewed even by its advocates with a great deal of reservation. As everywhere else, the Yugoslav example prejudiced this idea in Hungary, too. By contrast, the agreeable experiences of Hungarian agricultural cooperatives gave rise to hopes that some efficiency gains could be achieved if this type of ownership were rooted in industrial enterprises.[5] In the final analysis, the advantage of this scheme was seen chiefly in its merits relative to the alternative proposals.[6]

The *cross-ownership* model was the brainchild of György Matolcsy, a young economist making a growing name for himself by his active involvement in the privatisation efforts of the last three governments.[7] According to his suggestion, SOEs have to be corporatised in a way which allows them to acquire equity stakes in one another's firms. Moreover, the participation of other entities (such as local authorities, pension funds, etc.) must be encouraged. The advantage of this model was seen in the instantaneous creation of a functioning capital market, where ownership rights and dispositional rights could be completely separated.

In this peaceful evolution of academic ideas, János Kornai's (1989) book fluttered the dovecotes. In the past Kornai had never participated in reform engineering, and now he suddenly produced a book-length scenario.[8] Until the publication of Kornai's book, it was fashionable to call for the pluralism of ownership forms. The advocates of the various suggestions were all very aware of the weak sides of their own proposals, and they therefore wanted to secure a place in the sun for all ideas.

First, it was argued that each of the existing proposals would fail to create 'strong' owners. The creation of holdings was discarded because it would not exclude the possibility of state intervention into the management of the SOEs.[9] Cross-ownership was attacked in the same way. It was difficult to see any guarantee that the managers of these newly created corporations would become strong proprietors, with a healthy combination of risk-taking and commitment to their companies' long-term profitability, when transparency in an accounting sense was deliberately reduced by a complicated cross-ownership structure. In addition, it was feared that this ownership structure would encourage monopolistic agreements, reducing instead of increasing competition among existing firms. It was also clear from the very outset that the cross-ownership model could not be easily popularised among workers or the electorate at large, and therefore it could not be the driving force of political movements.

Secondly, there was a suspicion of various forms of manipulation. This was an argument that was particularly relevant to the self-management model. It was feared that the management of the collectively-owned large enterprises would be in a very strong position *vis-à-vis* the workers and employees, who were less qualified to participate in decision-making, and less interested in doing so.

The publication of Kornai's book marked the most conspicuous shift in the debate. Kornai proposed a radically different approach. In his perception, everybody who is risking somebody else's money is essentially a bureaucrat, part of the extended arm of the state: 'those who spend state funds cannot claim the same rights as those who have to rely on their own resources'.[10] He forcefully opposed giving more dispositional rights to enterprise managers. The existing rights of managers in determining output prices, wages, investments and imports had to be taken back without any hesitation, he suggested. Since Kornai was also against hasty squandering of state enterprises to private individuals or foreigners, he foresaw a relatively long period when the lion's share of old SOEs remained under administrative state control. As a good example of how they might meanwhile be supervised, Kornai referred to the practices of the US Congress, where law-makers must sensibly reckon with the Pentagon's proclivity to spend.

In spite of Kornai's wide recognition in academic circles, his ideas were met with strong reservations. Paradoxically, he was accused of attempting to return to the classical model of socialism. It would be impossible, as Bauer (1989) argued, to keep SOEs' inputs under strict supervision without a simultaneous control mechanism over outputs. This, in turn, would require the reinstallation of mandatory plan targets – a system with well-known deficiencies. On paper, it is easy to limit the number of mandatory targets to a minimum. But the experience of the 1960s showed that if there is a single administratively set target, then the internal logic of such a system recreates the need for many others. There is an unbridgeable conceptual difference between keeping an eye on the Pentagon (and a few other big spenders) and controlling a state sector representing 80 per cent of a nation's total output. The Pentagon is a final consumer, whose output is not directed back to the nation's economy. By contrast, the Hungarian state sector encompasses a number of branches whose output becomes the input of others. In other words, if prices, wages, investments, etc. are administratively set within the state sector, it is inevitable that the entire economy will be affected by these decisions.

Levelling his criticism against Kornai's book, Bauer went back to his opponent's well-known theory on 'soft budget constraints'. According to Bauer, soft budget constraints were not the main problem of the traditional state-owned enterprises. In the system of mandatory physical indicators, their role was at best secondary. The real problem was that the mandatory physical indicators themselves were soft and became the subject of bargaining between the SOEs and the centre. This is an intrinsic problem of a nation-wide economic system based on centralised decision-making, and the Pentagon-type solution Kornai envisaged would not fundamentally alter the situation.

2.2   The reform legacy

Hungary has been in the vanguard of the East European reform process since 1968. Today, it is evident and comprehensible that the subsequent reform steps were insufficient to raise the country's overall economic performance and put it on a par with Western market economies. Paradoxically, however, the magnitude and persistence of these steps were large enough to narrow the spectrum of choice in the present.

At the end of 1989, the Hungarian economy had a number of unique features, most of which were perceived as 'advantages' over the other countries of the East European region. Some of these advantages are mixed blessings – at least from a theoretical point of view, but in an overall political context, purely logical arguments do not carry a decisive weight. These 'advantages' were highly publicised both internally and externally, and therefore the 'clean sheet' approach would have required a large amount of political pressure to roll back the consequences of twenty years of Hungarian reform engineering. Moreover, these advantages have formed an interconnected logical network, in which one effect became the cause of others.[11]

2.2.1 Entrepreneurship
When the communist leadership departed from the scene, it left behind a barely serviceable foreign debt burden with an international commitment nevertheless to continue debt service. But even before that, this debt had placed an enormous economic, political and moral pressure on the leadership. One of the valves through which an attempt had been made to reduce this pressure was the increasing tolerance towards *entrepreneurship*. Managers of state-owned enterprises, true private entrepreneurs as well as the population at large were told: 'We give you a challenge: *Enrichissez-vous!*'.

Apart from industry, where the share of private activities was minuscule in 1989, a small but fast-growing private sector soon came into being in the main branches of the economy.[12] Earlier limitations on land ownership, real estate, foreign travel and convertible currency holdings were abolished or eased. In addition to the accumulation of mobilisable private wealth (bank deposits, real estate, motor cars), a large segment of the population gained some entrepreneurial experience – an asset that soon became highly valuable.

As a corollary to this policy, the majority of enterprises became self-governing entities in 1984–5. This development obviated a centrally orchestrated privatisation process, because it would inevitably have met resistance from the management of these firms.[13] Of course, this opposition could have been overcome, but only at a high cost. Output and therefore exports would have declined for this reason alone – something the government could have ill afforded.

2.2.2 Western capital

The inflow of *western capital* was another important part of the reform heritage. Until 1990, the sums involved were not significant – less than 100 joint ventures (JVs) with an estimated value of $500 mn – but they came from influential Western companies.[14] Pondering the possibilities of a *de facto* debt–equity swap, the last communist government had already tried to go beyond the JV type of capital import schemes, suggesting the direct sale of existing SOEs.[15] So foreign investors came into Hungary with an understanding that the recently created legal instruments – the company law, the law on securities, taxation laws, etc. – would not be radically altered from one day to the next.

2.2.3 Monetary constraints

Since 1987 a unique combination of fiscal and monetary regulations has been in effect. On the one hand, the government had left the commercial banks and the SOEs alone to solve their financial disputes in the best way they could. The banks bailed out the troubled SOEs, but not without appropriate collateral. The large SOEs were also eager to institutionalise their links to the banks through portfolio investment. Thus, in the period 1987–90, when the four large banks repeatedly went for extending capital through a secondary issue of equities, these enterprises acquired a considerable share – ranging from 35–49 per cent[16] – in these banks.

On the other hand, little by little *monetary constraints* have become effective both for the banks and for their clients. Subsidies were cut, taxes were increased year after year. These measures were dictated by the elementary logic of prudent state management, though they might easily have been abandoned without the pressure of the country's main creditors. But this pressure was there in many forms (IMF surveillance, frequent negotiations with Western governments and bankers, increased interest of the Western media, etc.) – so the policy of monetary restraint had to be maintained. Now, in 1992–2 the enterprises have started to fall into the hands of commercial banks like ripe fruit.

Through this mechanism, the ownership structure has been shifting towards the cross-ownership model. For many firms the only way to survive was gradual self-liquidation. Under daily financial pressures subsidiaries, real estates and securities had to be sold or given as collateral. This was the beginning of a process which later became known as 'self-privatisation'. Real estate, equities and other types of securities have been – or are soon likely to be – transferred from many medium-size and large SOEs to the banking sector. Cross-ownership has also become relatively widespread among enterprises with firm, technology based commercial links. Given the high level of monopolisation of the domestic market, liquidity problems among these closely cooperating companies were solved through equity transactions.

3   Objectives of privatisation

In a *quantitative* sense, the final objectives of the privatisation process are clearly laid out. They appeared already in the *Programme of National Revival* (1990), the Antall government's work programme for the period 1991–3. This book-size document, published in September 1990, stipulated that the share of state-owned property must fall below 50 per cent of the value of the total assets, ideally with 30–35 per cent owned by private enterprises, 20–30 per cent owned by corporatised owners and non-profit organisations, and the remaining 35–50 per cent in state ownership. A few principals were also laid down in this document:

* Privatisation means transferring property rights to private owners. Without private property there is no free society, and there is no market economy. Cross-ownership schemes are not supported, since the government's objective is to create real owners.
* The government is committed to gradualism, saying that the forms and proportions characteristic of Western market economies would be achieved in three–five years, and not by a cavalry-attack type of action.
* The government is against the widespread use of give-away schemes, and makes a commitment to use the proceeds of privatisation to offset the country's internal debt.

The last two principles were derived from the government's overall set of preferences. Given the country's precarious external financial situation, radical suggestions were discarded from the very outset, as they might shock the country's potential creditors. Give-away schemes were also discarded, largely because of a fear of their anticipated inflationary impact, through the wealth effect. The first back-of-the-envelope calculations suggested that the net worth of SOEs was very close to the value of domestic debt (HUF 1300 bn) – thus there was a strong pressure from the representatives of the financial sector to use the proceeds of sales for the amortisation of this debt.

In a *legal sense*, the government's actions were guided by two laws and a parliamentary resolution – all three prepared by the previous, communist-led government. Acts VII and VIII, 1990 on the establishment of the State Property Agency (SPA) as well as on the protection of state assets were promulgated as laws, while the so-called *Provisional Property Policy Guidelines for 1990* were decreed by a parliamentary resolution (see also Chapter 13 below). The Guidelines' objective was to set priorities and determine the modalities for the SPA during a transitional six-month period. But this is a short document – less than three printed pages in the Official Gazette.

Although the new government has expressed its desire to update or rewrite the Guidelines, not very much has happened in practice. In July 1990, parliamentary control of the SPA was replaced by direct government supervision. Then, as the Guidelines expired, Parliament was asked on two occasions for their further extension. The third deadline expired on 30 September 1991, without any new legislation having been adopted. Thus the SPA (and the entire process of privatisation) was temporarily left with an *ex lex* status.

It was frequently argued,[17] that the privatisation process had to be built upon the widest possible *political* consensus, and that therefore the SPA should be guaranteed a certain autonomy from the government (in a way similar to the privileges of the central bank, the Constitutional Court, etc.). However, the Antall government did not subscribe to this view. The process of systemic transformation – and within this the privatisation measures as well – is being used to buttress the power base of the three parties of the coalition. In other words, this is a battle against the old *nomenklatura*, but in reality the government's attention is focused on filling positions with people loyal to the three coalition parties, rather than with people perhaps equally qualified, but whose hearts are thought to be beating for the parties of the opposition.[18]

In the context of privatisation, this comes to light in a peculiar manner. In theory, one would assume that the principal question of divesting state ownership runs like this: 'Who is the buyer?' Instead, as a Hungarian observer noted, the political struggles were usually fought around: 'Who is the seller?'[19] A great deal of time has been spent on inter-ministerial debates, as well as on a tug-of-war among the coalition parties over the role and the function of the SPA.

The legislation secures a considerable power for the SPA over the state sector and the ruling parties are determined to exploit this possibility to the maximum extent. Parliament has no direct control over the SPA, and citizens or enterprises may not appeal against its decisions. In those cases when the SOEs have been already corporatised and the SPA had a majority holding, the government replaced the old management with its own appointees or pressed for an 'unconditional surrender' from those who remained.[20] There were several incidents when the same happened to non-corporate SOEs. The SPA has simply suspended the mandate of the self-governing bodies and put the firm under its own control. In other cases, premium office buildings in Budapest were taken away from SOEs by an SPA fiat.

3.1   The run-up period: restitution and petty privatisation

The newly-elected government of Hungary felt a moral obligation to restore property rights that had existed before the communist takeover. From the point of view of sequencing, this step seemed to be urgent too. The process of sale of any property could not be started, it was argued, as long as the ownership of the asset was under dispute. Thus the restitution of confiscated property in general, and the future of land in particular, dominated the early part of political debates.[21] The crux of the 'land problem' was that one of the minority partners in the coalition, the Smallholders' Party, insisted – as at least a minimum programme – on a *de jure* restoration of land ownership rights existing in 1947. Accepting this view, the Antall government's programme explicitly referred to the need for a *land reform*. This demand was a very attractive proposition to many people, but numerous legal, economic and technical objections called its feasibility into question.

* In Hungary land was never completely nationalised. Out of 10 mn hectares of agricultural land, state farms owned and occupied no more than 10 per cent, cooperatives had a share of about 35 per cent and the remaining part was owned and cultivated by individual farmers. In reality cooperatives cultivated almost twice as much land as they owned, with the difference being registered in the name of their members. At the same time, a non-negligible part of the cooperatives' land was allotted to their own members and employees, who paid only a nominal or even a zero rent for the use of it.

* Since jurisprudence in Hungary makes virtually no difference between landed property (agricultural land and urban land) and other types of real estate (housing, shops, restaurants, small workshops) it was clear from the outset that the issue of land restitution was inseparably linked to the future of these other types of real estate. While in the case of agricultural land the connection between the existing asset and the asset which was originally expropriated can be easily established, this is much less true for urban land, buildings and apartments, which might have changed hands several times. It was also fairly obvious that while confiscating agricultural land from the existing tenants (i.e. the agricultural cooperatives in most cases) was something worth considering, legislation entailing the confiscation of urban land, houses and apartments from the present tenants was simply not enforceable.

* During discussions on restitution, it had to be acknowledged that political injustice did not start only with the communist takeover; there is a sizeable group within the country's present population whose

suffering had started well before that. Responding to this argument, the government has undertaken the obligation to push this deadline back to 1939; compensation will thus have to be accorded to the victims of the Holocaust, to war verterans, POWs, etc.

Finally, the coalition partners agreed that there would be no in-kind restitution to citizens. Though this was against their own taste, they accepted the Constitutional Court's ruling, issued on 2 October 1990, that the restitution of land would be unconstitutional as it would amount to unlawful discrimination between citizens. The process of re-privatisation, the Court said, cannot be selective according to the type of property in question: 'land is not different from any other type of fixed assets'. The Court specifically stated the private property character of the land owned by the cooperatives effectively prohibited the renationalisation of 'their' land for the purposes of restitution.

Instead of restitution, physical persons – the original owners or their direct heirs – receive freely tradeable, interest-bearing *compensation certificates*. These certificates, denominated in HUF, represent vouchers for the purchase of state assets (including land and urban dwellings), but they can be also converted into a life-annuity contract. As a part of the compensation package, the SPA is preparing a list of 40–50 enterprises where voucher holders may have certain privileges over other potential buyers. Against the backdrop of empty Treasury coffers, even financial compensation would be on a sliding scale with an upper limit of HUF 5 mn per person.[22] In the case of land, the law-makers envisaged positive discrimination so that families permanently residing in agricultural areas can stake a claim proportionate to the value of their previously-owned land and use their vouchers to buy land from cooperatives or state farms. In these auctions, only voucher holders can participate.

These matters, being as complicated as they are, required that the relevant legislation be sent to Parliament in several forms, and the Constitutional Court examined the matter on three occasions – so it will take at least two years to build the legal framework and the necessary administrative infrastructure just to begin the process.[23]

Beyond the moral obligation to compensate individuals, the new government had a commitment to restore *local authorities* to the juridical position they traditionally enjoyed in pre-war Hungary. Fortunately, it was a simple issue, at least in a legal sense. Much of the urban housing stock, building land, the retail trade network and many service related enterprises never ceased to be owned by the local authorities. Nevertheless, the ownership rights of almost 30,000 establishments (buildings, building plots, bridges, roads, waters and waterways, etc.) had to be transferred by way of legal action in order to create a certain uniformity in the starting position of the local authorities.

The situation is more delicate with regard to *religious institutions* and other charitable organisations. With few exceptions, their properties had been ruthlessly confiscated between 1945 and 1949. As a general rule, it was decided that productive assets (factories, agricultural land, forests, etc.) will not be restituted, but the new government accepted claims on buildings and real estate required for the resumption or the expansion of religious, educational, health, and social activities. In the absence of clear principles and codified rules, 6000 restitutions' claims have been taken up on a case-by-case basis at the local level.

Paradoxically, there has been an important flow of capital assets in the opposite direction, too. Property, chiefly real estate, previously owned by non-state organisations were taken into state hands as a follow-up of political changes. The Soviet military authorities alone have left behind assets worth HUF 100 bn, and the estimated value of property belonging to the dissolved political organisations (the communist party, the workers' militia, etc.) is of similar magnitude. For the management of these assets, a separate institution, the *Treasury Property Management Office* was created in January 1991.

In contrast to the heated debates on restitution, there was a clear consensus on *'petty' privatisation*, pertaining to the retail trade and catering sectors, if not by restitution then through other methods, and the faster the better. Indeed, this was so commonly agreed that the relevant piece of legislation had been already prepared by the last communist government and only time prevented them implementing it. So, within a few months, by September 1990, the law on 'pre-privatisation' – as the Hungarian jargon calls it – was put into effect.[24]

In spite of this smooth kick-off, the process itself has had a surprisingly slow start. By the end of August 1991 only 515 units had been sold (see Table 6.1). Preliminary figures for 1991 as a whole show some acceleration, but no breakthrough. Altogether some 3200 shops were auctioned, but only half of them were actually sold. Through other methods, an additional 400 shops were reportedly divested in 1991.

The reason for this fiasco, publicly acknowledged by the SPA itself, are manifold, and important general lessons can be drawn from them.

* First, the scope of privatisation was very narrowly defined by the law. Its declared aim was to privatise retail units employing a maximum of 10 persons (15 in the case of restaurants) through public auctions. In late 1990, the government assumed that out of 54,000 units statistically recorded some 37,000 would fall under the jurisdiction of this law.

Table 6.1. *Progress in pre-privatisation*

	Number of units	HUF mn
PREPARATIONS:		
NUMBER OF STATISTICALLY REGISTERED BUSINESS UNITS in retail trade and catering as of end-1989	*53 502*	
Number of reported business units by the 371 SOEs, falling under the jurisdiction of pre-privatisation law	10 193	
(As of 27 August 1991)		
premises owned by the SOEs	2918	
premises rented by the SOEs	7275	
Not saleable	2977	
Property rights under investigation	2237	
READY FOR PRIVATISATION	*4983*	
RESULTS:		
(As of 31 December 1991)		
Auctions held (first)	2648	
Auctions held (second)	563	
Business units sold through auctions	1729	
with ownership	458	
with tenants' rights	1271	
for cash payments	691	
for cash and credits	1038	
Business units disposed through other ways	391	
TOTAL NUMBER OF BUSINESS UNITS PRIVATISED	*2120*	
Sales price (gross, total)		5088
Reserve price (gross, total)		3900

Source: Statisztikai Évkönyv 1989, p. 174; SPA official data, as reported in *Magyar Hírlap* (13 February 1992).

However, by the time the auction mechanism was actually set up (early 1991), this number was reduced to only 10,000. Given the very low limit on the number of employees (and some other loopholes),[25] this was almost inescapable.

* Foreigners were not allowed to participate in auctions, although there is nothing to prevent them buying shops, or entire commercial chains, which do not fall under the effect of the pre-privatisation law.
* More than 70 per cent of the premises are in buildings owned by the local authorities. In these cases, not the ownership of the shop but

rather the leasing rights were auctioned. Although this is a fairly common practice in the West, in a turbulent, inflationary environment, Hungarian would-be shopkeepers felt defenceless against any future rise in the rent.

* The economy has been undergoing a serious recession. The volume of retail sales has been falling by 15–20 per cent and the upswing is still not in sight. This had an obvious impact on the demand for these business units.

* It turned out that the SPA, as a centralised, small-size, Budapest based body, was ill-positioned to implement this campaign with the required speed in some 3000 localities. The remedy most often applied – to appoint the SOE's themselves for the implementation of the auction – was not a fortunate choice, due to the lack of impartiality.

* When it comes to asset evaluation, the SPA is very much concerned at being attacked for selling out the 'family silver' at bargain prices, and thus tends to err too much on the other side.[26]

* There was a great deal of initial confusion concerning the availability of bank credits for the bidders. For this reason, the process which had been launched in December 1990 had to be suspended and the re-start could not take place until April 1991. In practice, however, these credit facilities have often turned out to be inadequate, as the potential borrowers were not credit-worthy if principles of prudence were taken seriously by the banks.

* Finally, there are signs suggesting that the potential circle of new buyers has been already largely exhausted. People with the necessary skills are already in business,[27] while others with less motivation but still in possession of the managerial talent and the necessary financial resources are doing well in well-paid employee status, be it in the government sector or in the emerging private companies and JVs (see Table 6.2).

As explained above, the future of the *housing stock* was not tackled by the laws on pre-privatisation. Fortunately, there is not so much to be done, since in Hungary the lion's share of the dwelling stock was never expropriated. Nevertheless, this is a very important area, not only because housing is a basic need for the population, but also because privatisation of the housing stock serves the interest of new ventures. In the short run, accommodation for the new companies can be provided for them only through the conversion of apartments into industrial premises or offices.

In contrast to the solutions adopted for privatising the retail trade sector, the housing stock, nominally owned by the state, was not transferred to the SPA. After protracted discussions, Parliament decided to

Table 6.2. *Number of dwellings sold by local authorities, 1987–90*

Year	No.
1987	4300
1988	8700
1989	18 700
1990	54 000

Memorandum item:		
Total number of dwellings (end 1986)	3 891 000	
state-owned	782 900	(20.1%)

Source: Statisztikai Évkönyv 1986 (pp. 250, 251); KSH, Press release (18 June 1991).

transfer the ownership rights to the municipalities. Indeed, this was an almost inevitable decision, since the municipalities had been gradually accorded the right to use and administer these apartments since the 1960s and the sale of the apartments had also started well before the current wave of privatisation.

In this context, the word 'selling' has to be taken with a considerable grain of salt. The apartments were sold well below their market value, either because the buyer was the existing tenant, or because the apartment was divested with a tenant in it, and the new owner had very limited possibilities of removing the tenant. The average sales price in 1990 was 23 per cent of the market value, while in Budapest this ratio was below 20 per cent.[28] In addition, buyers were allowed to take out loans on preferential terms to reduce downpayments. Precisely for this reason, this issue has become a hot potato in several municipalities; in the absence of political consensus at the local level and clear regulations for the country as a whole, further sales were suspended in many municipalities just after these newly elected bodies were formally constituted.

3.2   Land reform in sight?

The protracted legislative battles over the Compensation Act resulted, predictably, in a long delay in decision-making pertaining to the future of agricultural cooperatives. Not until the first days of January 1992 was Parliament able to reach a compromise on this matter – a year and a half after the government had announced its commitment to land reform. In the meantime, Parliament decreed a moratorium: cooperatives and state farms were not allowed to change their legal structure

Table 6.3. *Land and other assets of agricultural cooperatives*

	Present situation	Foreseen by the new law
Agricultural land used by the ACs	3.4 mn ha owned by the ACs	Distributed among members
	1.9 mn ha owned by members	No change
	0.2 mn ha owned by the state	Transferred to local authorities
Other tangible assets valued at HUF 300 bn	Indivisible property	Distributed in shares

or to engage in major transactions which could jeopardise government plans.

The starting point of the law is a decision to create new, autonomous grassroots' associations to replace the old *kolkhoz*-type cooperatives, without questioning the legitimacy of existing property rights (see Table 6.3).[29] Collective ownership will be fully replaced by private ownership. In the new order, every inch of land will have a natural owner included in the land register and in the books of the cooperatives. The lion's share of the agricultural land previously owned by the cooperatives will be distributed among the members, while a smaller part of it will be used for the purpose of restitution. Assets other than land will have to be distributed among members in the form of non-tradeable shares. Members wishing to leave the cooperative can use these certificates for acquiring property rights to these physical assets by direct purchase or auction (see Table 6.4).[30] Existing cooperatives were given a year to liquidate and rebuild themselves on the basis of the decision of their present members.

The future of state farms is a less complicated issue. About half of them – some 80 farms – were placed under direct ministerial control. In these cases, the elected directors will be replaced by appointed privatisation commissars. The government would like to see a quick privatisation of profitable farms while the notorious loss makers will simply be liquidated.

The envisaged changes in land ownership are unprecedented in Hungarian history. Through compulsory distribution and direct auctions 3.4 million hectares of land will be disposed of – twice as much as in the post-war land reform. As many as 800,000 new 'landlords' will be created, at least on paper. However, in reality, much of the land will be likely to remain under collective cultivation, since the small average farm size

Table 6.4. *SPA-initiated privatisation programmes for medium-sized and large SOEs*

	Start	Number of SOEs	Total book value of firms (HUF bn)
First privatisation programme	Sep. 1990	20	70
Investor-initiated privatisation*	Feb 1991	—	—
Second privatisation programme	Apr. 1991	12	14
Coordinated privatisation of state agricultural companies in the wine producing sector*	May 1991	15	14
(First) property management programme	Spring 1991	5	1
Construction industry privatisation programme*	Spring 1991	35	19
Downtown office building programme	Spring 1991	12	8–10[a]
Programme for companies affected by the collapse of the CMEA*	Summer 1991	15	—
Self-privatisation programme	June 1991	348	40
Second property management programme	Aug. 1991	8	—

Notes: Programmes marked with * are abandoned or merged with another programme.
[a] Estimated market value.
Source: SPA (1991); *Népszabadság* (11 June 1991, 24 September); *Figyelő* (7 November 1991).

(4.5 ha) and the age structure of the new owners (70 per cent of them are believed to be over retirement age) will not make individual farming viable.

3.3 The cross-ownership model becomes reality

'Big' or 'real' privatisation usually refers to the divestiture of property rights of medium-size and large SOEs. It goes without saying that the

Table 6.5. *SPA revenues from privatisation*

	1990: March–December (HUF bn)
From foreign clients	0.54
From domestic clients	0.14
Total	0.68

	1991: January–December
From foreign clients	34.0
From domestic clients	5.0
Portfolio revenues	1.0
Total	40.0

Source: SPA, as reported in *Magyar Hírlap* (20 March and 7 June 1991); *Heti Világgazdaság* (18 January 1992).

selection of enterprises to be privatised under 'big' privatisation or 'petty' privatisation depends in large part on the circumstances. As we have seen above, in the Hungarian case relatively small companies of the retail industry (department stores, hotels, food chains, etc.) were deliberately removed from the scope of the pre-privatisation law. Indeed, some of these SOEs were privatised beforehand, while others retained their previous legal status and their future remains to be decided.

At the end of 1989, the total amount of state property accounted for was 2201 SOEs, valued at HUF 1842 bn ($\approx$ \$30 bn) according to their accounts. Since the Hungarian government ventured upon the 'big' privatisation process without an itinerary, it required some time for observers to discern where the process was going. Table 6.4 is intended to give a quick overview of all ongoing SPA programmes, launched between September 1990 and June 1991; a detailed description will be given in the Appendix on pp. 110–11.

For any observers, 'big' privatisation in Hungary has been chiefly evolving through selling out the 'family silver' to *foreign investors*. The view that this method is indeed the most often used instrument of 'big' privatisation can be easily demonstrated by the data released by the SPA on its revenues (see Table 6.5).

As Table 6.5 demonstrates, virtually nothing was sold to domestic buyers in the 'big' privatisation programme. The reported HUF 5 bn revenue came very close to the receipts of the pre-privatisation programme (HUF 3.6 bn),[31] from which foreigners were excluded from the very outset. The Hungarian authorities themselves are inclined to put the role of foreigners in the limelight: there is a lot of talk about 'strategic foreign investors', and news about negotiations with Western firms is announced almost daily. The second often heard observation, namely that privatisation is moving at a snail's pace, can also be supported by these revenue figures: HUF 40 bn is not more than 2 per cent of the initial capital stock.

Note, however, that this assessment is based on a narrow understanding of privatisation (= selling to private individuals or foreigners), which is unsuitable to grasp the crux of the unfolding processes. In Hungary, 'big' privatisation is essentially a domestic corporatisation process without payments, whereby the former SOEs are completely restructured and their hierarchical links to the state administration are cut.

In practice, it is not easy to separate the different methods by which Hungarian SOEs have been privatised over the past few years.[32] Conceptually, the situation is simple. The existing legal framework knows three options:

* outright divestment
* the 'transformation' method, under which a new company is created which takes over in its entirety the business of the state enterprise
* the 'vesting' method, under which assets of the state enterprise are transferred to a joint stock company in return for shares in that company of an equivalent value.

In reality, however, the process is not so straightforward. First of all, the changes in ownership usually coincide with organisational break-ups. Moreover, the transforming companies are, in the large majority of cases, forced by law to allot a certain equity share (25–30 per cent) to the local authorities which own the buildings of the enterprise or the urban land beneath it, as well as to sell equities (8–10 per cent) at a preferential price to their own employees. The reorientation of property rights goes along with a physical restructuring of productive capacity. The capital stock is partly replaced and partly upgraded, and redundant workers are laid off. Foreign capital often functions as a catalyst in these cases, but it would be a mistake to overestimate its importance: its share was 9 per cent if compared to the total value of restructured companies.[33] Financial restructuring is also part and parcel of most deals. In many cases, the burden of such operations is directly or indirectly carried by taxpayers. Sometimes it occurs in the form of debt forgiveness on the part of the Treasury or the social security fund (see Chapter 16 below), in other cases the commercial banks are asked to write off the old debt.

From a monitoring point of view, such a coincidence of changes is

Table 6.6. *Approved transformation cases, 1990 and 1991*

Year	Number of cases	Book value of the shareholder's fund (HUF bn)	Company value recognised at transformation (HUF bn)
1990	27	26	41
1991	189	316	418

Note: These figures are of a preliminary character, since in January and February 1992 important transformation cases were approved by the SPA, with an effective date of 31 December 1991.
Source: Newsletter (December 1991).

undesirable. Sometimes, it is surmised that the whole game is played with marked cards and that individuals are getting rich at the expense of the state. But in most cases these allegations cannot be substantiated. Nevertheless, it is important to note that in all transformation cases beyond a certain threshold[34] there is a built-in mechanism of state control. There can be no property divestment without the approval of the SPA, which is far from being a mere formality.[35]

There are various estimates concerning the speed of the corporatisation process. According to the experts of Finance Research Ltd the original 2200 SOEs were transformed into 8–10,000 corporate entities, with smaller or larger state participation.[36] According to a more recent calculation, prepared in the Privatisation Research Institute, by the end of 1991 assets worth HUF 500–550 bn, some 25–30 per cent of the initial state capital stock, will be transformed into companies, where the state administration, state enterprises or state funds are the majority partners.[37] The SPA's first provisional figures on its 1991 performance record are in line with these estimates (Table 6.6). By the end of 1991, 20 per cent of the old SOEs were in corporate form. However, when allowance is made for direct buy-outs, acquired options and capital increases which occurred *after* corporatisation, the corresponding figure was already above 50 per cent.

In some branches the corporatisation process has been completed or is very much advanced (trade, construction), while in others (industry, transport) the pace of change is considerably slower. In the financial sector, the picture is mixed. At the end of 1991, the state's share in the ownership of all financial institutions mounted to 33 per cent, with another 35 per cent being held by enterprises and cooperatives, 15 per cent by other financial institutions and 11 per cent by foreigners. In the three largest commercial banks, however, the state's share was 30–40 per cent.[38]

Now, there is mounting evidence, and thus a growing consensus among Hungarian experts, that this shift from a relatively monolithic structure of state ownership towards the *cross-ownership model* is a *spontaneous evolution* fed by the energy of the Hungarian managerial class and made possible by the benign neglect of the state administration. It has been an unplanned process which, of course, does not in itself prejudge the outcome. The impression given by Table 6.4 is somewhat misleading. The programmes listed there appear to be initiated by the SPA, but in fact the firms participating in these programmes were chosen on a voluntary basis and their management was playing an active role in implementation.[39]

Originally, the Hungarian government had a strong opposition to 'spontaneous' privatisation,[40] as well as to cross-ownership. This stance was flavoured with both anti-communist and anti-capitalist undertones. There has been a concern that the managers of SOEs, as well as top officials, may unjustly benefit from their positions in the 'old regime'. The problem with this approach, which is shared by many Western analysts,[41] is twofold.

First, it has been confirmed by several field studies that the danger of robbing the state had been grossly over-stated. Apart from a few dozen small cases, these corporatisations did not imply a legal transfer of final ownership rights to Hungarian individuals. The changes were driven by far more complex motivations, even if, for the sake of argument, we focus our attention first only on the pecuniary incentives of the management. In those cases where a large or medium-size SOE was split into 10–15 smaller units, the advantage was in the opening up of new executive positions. When foreign partners were involved, this has held out the prospects of 'almost-Western' salaries, increased travel possibilities, and access to state-of-the-art technologies. After the political changes in late 1989, it very quickly turned out that the position of a successful SOE manager was easily convertible into a high office in state administration, or an equivalent (but better paid) job in those Western firms. In addition to these possibilities, the establishment of hundreds of joint stock companies has created a need for several hundred non-executive directors, members of supervisory boards,[42] etc., and these posts were also filled by the same group of people.

However, the self-interest of managers alone is insufficient to explain the momentum of 'spontaneous' privatisation. In fact, what happened in 1990 and 1991 was nothing else but the continuation of the transformation processes already described. Under the pressure of daily liquidity problems, SOEs continued to be forced to look for additional sources of financing: ownership links with banks, foreign and domestic cooperation partners were extended, subsidiaries and production units were sold or leased.

The second problem with the view that opposes 'spontaneous' privatisation is that there are few people available with sufficient technical and commercial competence who can do the job better than the previous management elite. This is not a specifically Hungarian problem, it applies to other countries of the region as well. After a landslide change in a country's political system it is relatively easy to find a few dozen competent politicians to replace the government, the heads of the armed forces, etc. But there is no back-up to provide 20,000 managers to run 2000 SOEs and an even larger number of civil servants.[43] Independent experts can, of course, be invited from abroad, but this is not a cheap solution and very often these 'foreigners' are in fact expatriates themselves, so their independence can also be questioned. Moreover, experience has shown that the increase in objectivity they bring is not sufficient to outweigh their lack of detailed knowledge.[44] Under such circumstances a centrally-supervised process of de-etatisation can easily degenerate into a very expensive bureaucratic exercise.

With time, the government's hostility to 'spontaneous' privatisation has abated. On the one hand, the government is under pressure to accelerate the privatisation process, and thus it is interested in demonstrating that things are moving. On the other hand, the reservations against 'spontaneous' privatisation did not completely disappear. This explains the fact that both the SPA and the government are inclined to give another name to the baby, such as 'enterprise-initiated' privatisation or 'self-privatisation'.[45]

What can be expected from the emerging cross-ownership structure? What kind of market will come out of the corporatisation process? Is there any basis for believing that at the end of the road the medium-size and large companies of the Hungarian economy will be in the hands of 'strong' owners? Before attempting to answer these questions, it is important to note that the privatisation process is unfolding against the backdrop of an overall *decentralisation* process, whereby the impact of the changes in the (old) state sector are intermingled with the impact of new start-ups (Table 6.7) and the proliferation of joint ventures (Table 6.8).

This increase in the number of domestic economic agents has created a new situation. The arguments against the cross-ownership model, marshalled in the academic discussions *before* privatisation actually started, have thus lost much of their strength. Here, of course, causes and consequences are intermingled. The importance of the Soviet market has

dramatically declined and this is a fatal blow to some of the largest
Hungarian firms whose monopolistic position had been historically based
on their overwhelming weight in the trade between the two countries. As
Western imports are liberalised, and the pressure to increase exports

Table 6.7. *Number of economic organisations, end of period, 1988–91*

	1988	1989	1990	1991
(1) Enterprises	2378	2400	2363	2240
(2) Corporate associations	919	5191	19401	34327
Limited companies	450	4484	18317	37871
Joint stock companies	116	307	646	1040
(3) Cooperatives	7414	7546	7641	7749
In agriculture	1333	1333	1348	1419
Total (1) + (2) + (3)	10711	15137	29405	49316
Memorandum item:				
Private entrepreneurs		320000		400000[a]

Note: [a] End of April.
Source: CSO, *Press Release* (12 February 1992).

Table 6.8. *Number and size of joint ventures, end of period, 1975–91*

	Number of firms	Registered capital[a] (HUF bn)	From which foreign-owned[a] (HUF bn)
1975	3	—	—
1980	7	—	—
1987	123	11	5
1988	227	20	9
1989	1357	125	30
1990	5693	274	93
1991 (Sep.)[b]	9791	378	133

Notes: [a] Aggregated values of statutory capital, accounted for at the moment of
registration. The figures do not reflect changes which occurred later on.
[b] Author's estimate, based on new registrations in the first three quarters.
Sources: New Hungarian Exporter (February 1985); *Hungarian Trade Journal*
(March 1988); KSH, *Tájékoztató* (15 October 1991) p. 8; *Figyelő* (28 November
1991); *Statisztikai Havi Közlemények* (1991, **10**) p. 74; NBH, *Annual Report 1990*,
pp. 35–6.

grows, monopolies are attacked from other sides, too. Monetary austerity also bites – the endemic shortages, which plagued the enterprise sector for decades, disappeared. Once all these considerations are taken into account, there is a basis for optimism. A growing part of the Hungarian economy has already liberated itself from state tutelage and become exposed to the discipline of market mechanism. In practice, many of them tried to escape from these pressures but there is a countervailing pressure from Parliament, the external world, from the domestic banks, and from public opinion at large.

4   Speed: just about right

As far as the future of the privatisation process is concerned, it is very important to recognise that the state can neither abandon its enterprises overnight, nor divest them too quickly to *strong* owners. These enterprises, independently of their legal forms, do need a certain amount of protection, simply because they had been protected for so long. If they fell too quickly into the hand of strong owners, the ensuing losses in output and employment would rapidly undermine the position of the government. Strong owners do not care about externalities, and – more importantly – do not like to pay taxes. Three years after its inception, the Hungarian taxation system is still in its infancy (see Chapter 14 below); working hard and ready to take certain risks, companies and ambitious entrepreneurs can easily find loopholes. This applies chiefly, but not exclusively, to the small firms. The problem with the large foreign investors is that they are *long-term investors* in the best sense of the word. In the first few years of operation, they do not expect to make profits – and if by chance they do, then these profits are usually exempt from taxation as a result of tax-holiday agreements.

Another frequently heard objection against the feasibility of the cross-ownership model (and 'spontaneous' privatisation in general) pertains to the smallness of private domestic capital as compared to the value of the 2200 SOEs. At the dawn of privatisation it was widely believed that the market value of the 2000 SOEs was a given magnitude, somehow intrinsically frozen in land, tangible assets, etc. and once the country had acquired the right accounting expertise, this figure could be arrived at with an unquestionable objectivity. When detailed calculations were made, it turned out that the book value of the 2000 SOEs was five times larger than the stock of gross savings, and 300 times larger than the stock of net savings (savings *minus* consumer debt). It then was widely argued that given these proportions, it would take 50 to 100 years for the Hungarian population to buy up the enterprises of the state sector. After

Table 6.9. *Household savings and the book value of SOEs, end of period,*
1989–91

	Savings[a] (HUF bn)	Loans outstanding (HUF bn)	Net savings (HUF bn)	Book value of SOEs (HUF bn)	Ratio of SOE value to net savings	Ratio of SOE value to gross savings
1989	354	348	6	1842	287.8	5.2
1990	670	369	301	1842	6.1	2.7
1991[b]	865	254	611	1842	3.0	2.1

Notes: [a] Including convertible currency deposits.
        [b] Preliminary estimates.
Source: CSO and NBH.

two years, it can be safely said that these static comparisons were almost meaningless from the very outset (Table 6.9).

First, there is a more sober assessment of the market value of the capital stock appearing on the supply side. It turned out that this value was greatly influenced by factors beyond the control of the privatisation agency or the government; at the present time, in most cases this influence is value-diminishing and not value-increasing. In the case of small shops, for example, the general decline in retail sales exerted a strong downward pressure on auction prices. The experience that the collapse of the Soviet markets is undermining the market value of Hungarian manufacturing firms presents a similar difficulty. Moreover, the price foreigners are willing to pay is largely determined by the availability of similar assets in the other ex-socialist countries. And since privatisation is on the agenda everywhere from Rostock to Vladivostok, the rapidly increasing supply tends everywhere to hammer down the equilibrium price quite considerably.[46]

The second lesson learned over the past two years was that under favourable circumstances the purchasing power of the population might rise much faster than was anticipated. Several factors work in this direction. The protracted inflationary process and the gradual liberalisation of the economy tend to support a healthy concentration process, whereby households and small new ventures quickly enrich themselves through perfectly legal and less perfectly legal real estate transactions, foreign exchange deals, export–import activities, tourism related services, etc.

At the same time, for the reasons outlined in the previous paragraph, the value of the SOEs remain unchanged – i.e. it is diminishing in real terms by 20–30 per cent every year. According to the Privatisation Research Institute over the past three years the cumulated 'devaluation' of these assets might be as high as HUF 1000 bn in real terms. Beyond the reasons already mentioned, the Institute draws attention to the fact that the market value of the state enterprises is constantly undermined by the old but still existing amortisation rules and taxation practices. Compared to the private sector, state enterprises are strongly disprivileged, simply because they cannot hide their revenues, even if their managers were ready to take risks, just as the private owners do. Under such circumstances, the market value of a given SOE is relatively lower (and grows more slowly), than that of a similar private enterprise, if this market value is estimated on the basis of discounted future net profits.

In spite of the progress made so far, the lack of a coherent, consensus based privatisation policy document is being felt more and more strongly every day. Progress in new legislation and in the implementation of the existing laws are both hampered, as debates on seemingly technical issues always find the way back to the same undecided fundamentals. This situation is a hotbed of protracted parliamentary debates, cheap compromises and ambiguously drafted laws.

At the beginning of 1992, there is a long list of laws missing from a comprehensively thought-out privatisation scenario (see Chapter 13 below). Due to the protracted legal debates on restitution, the government was unable to agree on a draft law on *land and housing*: there are many thorny issues around these subjects, the right of foreigners being the thorniest one. The deadline for presenting compensation claims expired in the middle of December 1991. Altogether, 830,000 claims were filed, pertaining to 2.5 mn land ownership cases, 181,000 homes and 64,000 enterprises. Although these numbers are much lower than thought a year ago, it will take a long time to sort out so many cases. The future of agricultural cooperatives also remains unclear. Parliament adopted the necessary laws on *cooperatives* only in early 1992, thus it is too early to see the reactions of the parties concerned.

There is no final decision on the future of the country's *commercial banks*. There are plans to privatise at least part of them, but no definite timetable has been set. In principle, the National Bank is ready and waiting for foreign capital. The law adopted in November 1991 requires that the share of state ownership in any of the financial institutions may not surpass 25 per cent. In itself, this is not an over-ambitious target, since the process of cross-ownership had made significant headway. But in the three largest commercial banks, as noted, the state's share is very high, and this is the area where views diverge. Strictly speaking, foreign ownership is a loss of control not a solution to the monitoring problem. Since these commercial banks have a considerable stake in large Hungarian firms, losing control over the banks means a loss of control over a large part of industry as well. But this argument cuts both ways. The mutual dependence between industrial firms and banks is a hotbed of other dangers, and from the vantage point of bank regulation (see, e.g., Várhegyi, 1992 and Chapter 9 in this volume below), this is a sufficient reason to welcome majority foreign ownership in the banks.

Such a strategy, however, would – *inter alia* – require a radical write-off of non-performing assets. At the end of 1991, the government committed HUF 10 bn to assist the three largest commercial banks to do so, but this is only the first step in the right direction. The trade-off is difficult. On the one hand, the cleaning of the banks' portfolios is an obvious 'must', but this can be done only at the expense of current profits. But these banks are good taxpayers and they also pay dividends into the public purse.

On the fiscal front, the promised overhaul of the social safety net (pensions, health care, education, etc.) has been postponed by at least a year, thus no decision can be made on the forms and the size of property transfer required in favour of the planned *self-governing social security fund(s)* – (see Chapter 16 below).

Political and academic discussions have been going on for a year on the need to set up a *state property management agency*, but so far the government has not made up its mind. For the time being, the SPA is responsible both for the management and the privatisation of state assets, although there is a growing consensus on the need to separate these two jobs. A related question is the identification of those enterprises where *majority state (or national) ownership* is sought, even in the longer run. Various lists were circulated among the ministries, and sometimes they were leaked to the press as well,[47] but the final word has still not been pronounced.

The Antall government has committed itself to open the legal way for *ESOP-type* workers' participation programmes.[48] But in this matter it faces tough opposition both from the entrepreneurs and from the SPA.[49] The question of *investment funds*, or legal regulations of *leaseholds*[50] are much less controversial; here the legislative throughput of Parliament was the chief bottleneck.

The first eighteen months taught many bitter lessons to the SPA and the Hungarian authorities in general:

* It turned out that in a democratic society neither sequencing nor speed of privatisation could be pre-planned. Even relatively simple transformation measures – such a 'petty' privatisation – have their own dynamics, and the government's room for manoeuvre is rather small.[51]

* The otherwise sensible proposition to sell SOEs through the Stock Exchange had to be discarded when it became clear that against the backdrop of falling share prices, it would be suicidal to pour even more shares on the market.[52]
* Experience has showed that Western multinationals are not willing to engage themselves in real competitive bidding. Instead, they tend to apportion the East European market among themselves through behind-the-scenes negotiations, and when the SPA tries to generate competition they resist.[53]

While there is a certain danger of making generalisations on the basis of experiences accumulated in a short period of time, it appears that the Hungarian privatisation process advances at the right speed – neither too slow, nor too fast. Compared to the practices or plans of the other ex-socialist countries, the path Hungary has chosen is unique, but at the same time it is firmly rooted in the country's recent economic history. This is not a guarantee of success, but it does reduce the risks.

Appendix: A summary of SPA-initiated privatisation programmes for medium-size and large SOEs

The *First privatisation programme*, announced in September 1990, comprised 20 of the larger and generally better performing companies. The voluntary registered firms had a combined annual turnover of approximately HUF 100 bn and assets worth HUF 70 bn in their own books. For the privatisation of these companies the SPA sought international consultants. This was accomplished by publishing the conditions of an open competition for the 20 companies' advisors. Approximately 300 offers were received, most representing interest on the part of the world's best known investment banks.

The *Downtown office building programme* was targeted at 12 SOEs which had in the past used, but not owned, premium office buildings in downtown Budapest. In the first phase, the ownership rights were transferred from the ministries or the local authorities to a newly created SPA subsidiary.

In the framework of a programme tailored to fit the requirements of the *companies affected by the collapse of the CMEA* the SPA asked 8 well known investment banks to examine the situation of 15 companies, and to gauge whether or not they had a realistic opportunity of attracting foreign investment.

The *Second privatisation programme*, launched in April 1991, was targeted at 12 'shell' companies, disposing of assets worth HUF 14 bn tied up in 115 limited companies. These subsidiaries had been created during the past two–three years from medium-size and large industrial SOEs, whilst the role of the head office of the original company was confined to that of trustee. While on paper it was never stated, in reality both programmes were tailored to excite the curiosity of foreign investors.[54]

In June 1991, the SPA launched a new programme, called *Enterprise-initiated privatisation* or *self-privatisation*. Initially, 348 medium-size SOEs, each having no more than 300 employees and an annual turnover less than HUF 300 mn, were allowed to privatise themselves with the help of 'authorised' advisors. There is an approved list, containing the names of 84 firms, Hungarian and foreign companies alike. Starting from November 1991, the advisors enter into a contractual obligation with the SPA to privatise their clients until March 1993. Depending on the speed of the process, the consulting company may keep 5.0–15.0 per cent of the sales revenue for itself. At a later stage, the SPA wishes to widen the range of firms entitled to choose this simplified procedure and would like to involve 1000 SOEs in the programme.[55]

NOTES

The author is affiliated with the Division for Economic Analysis and Projections of the United Nations Economic Commission for Europe in Geneva. The views presented here are his own and do not necessarily reflect those of the ECE.
 1 On the list of priorities, the issue of privatisation is clearly preceded by a number of other objectives, such as foreign policy matters, seeking the ways and means to punish the culprits of the previous regime, etc. Among the economic priorities, the government's commitment to service foreign debt and to arrest inflation are also more important than changes in the ownership structure.
 2 On the other hand, it has to be acknowledged that these academic discussions were useful in the sense that different ideas about changes in property rights, and the weaknesses of various types of reform programmes, became widely known. In other countries, the serious professional discussion did not even start until 1990 (or later) and for a long time the air was full of all sorts of untested, naive ideas. (I am grateful to Phil Hanson for this comment.)
 3 Although Liska's views were known to the profession, he remained marginalised for more than two decades. His book advocating an entrepreneurial society, which was written in 1964, was not published until 1988. Though incompletely, his ideas were finally made concrete in the late 1970s, when a large number of shops and restaurants were leased to private individuals. In 1988 about 11 per cent of the shops and 44 per cent of the restaurants were operating this way.
 4 For a recollection of the content of the pre-1968 discussions see Hoch (1991).

5 This argument was used by Tamás Bauer in a 1982 paper that became influential in the process of preparing the 1984–5 reform measures. 'If internal democracy is improved within the (agricultural and industrial) cooperatives, they may become examples of self-regulation. In view of the fact that the cooperative scheme has received favourable political reception in Hungary, while autonomy and the system of workers' councils evoke negative associations, the transition may take place in the following form. A state-owned enterprise is transformed into a cooperative, the members act as "socialist custodians" of the capital equipment, as it becomes the property of the cooperative' (Bauer, 1984, p. 78).

6 Soós (1990), for example, stressed that this ownership form had more chance of obtaining legitimacy in the eyes of the population than any newly invented economic institution haphazardly created by the government.

7 Since the mid-1980s, Mr Matolcsy has been involved in the preparation of new legislation under the auspices of the Ministry of Finance. In 1990, he worked first as a personal economic adviser of the Prime Minister, then as Deputy Minister of Finance. He was sacked in December that year. Later, he founded a research institute, named the Privatisation Research Institute. In September 1991, he was sent to the EBRD as the Hungarian government's representative in the bank.

8 It is worth noting that this intellectual accomplishment remains unchallenged in Hungary. There is a continuous flow of new ideas in the academic journals, but people seem to lack the vision and patience to develop their own ideas into a detailed programme.

9 As Soós (1990) convincingly argued, the solution of this problem 'can hardly be expected to come from anything but a strong stimulation of the holdings' leaders to resist all attempts at interference, which amounts to putting them in a situation that is quite similar to that of private owners. They should be guaranteed that if they increase the value of their firm's capital they could expect high . . . monetary rewards, and they should be assured of job security' (p. 57). The question is, whether this is a socially enforceable proposition for any government.

10 Quoted from the English edition (Kornai, 1990, p. 68).

11 The subsequent analysis relies heavily on Matolcsy (1991).

12 For more details see UN (1990) p. 249.

13 In this respect, the Hungarian developments stand in marked contrast with the experience of the GDR and – to a lesser extent – the other reforming countries. The GDR has lost its political and economic battle against the Federal Republic and accepted unconditional surrender. In Hungary, the systemic change was perceived as a victory for reform-minded intellectuals – managers included.

14 A few names from the complete list of JVs, reflecting the situation as of the end of 1987: Girozentrale, Siemens, Adidas, Volvo, Ikea, Citibank, Societé Générale, Creditanstalt, etc. (*Hungarian Trade Journal*, 3, 1988).

15 In July 1988, Prime Minister K. Grósz touring in the USA told US businessmen that his government was ready to sell a few companies. Six months later, a list of 45 industrial enterprises were presented and made available for potential investors through the West German Deutsche Bank. In Hungary, the full list was published only six weeks later (*Figyelő*, 16 February 1989).

16 Petschnig and Voszka (1991) p. 946.

17 See, e.g., Bokros (1990b).
18 A fine example of this policy occurred when, a few months after the election, the government insisted upon the re-election of chief executives in all self-governing SOEs. Quite surprisingly, 90–95 per cent of the old management were easily re-elected.
19 Voszka (1991a) p. 130.
20 One widely criticised example of this behaviour was when the heads of the commercial banks were 'asked' to sponsor a new daily newspaper which was known to be the semi-official mouthpiece of the government.
21 The future of land ownership is a particularly sensitive issue in Hungary, which is still very much an agrarian country and where a reform-minded agricultural policy has succeeded in maintaining food supplies and generating an export surplus over the past two decades.
22 This sum buys a good house in any village or a medium-size apartment in the town.
23 The first compensation law went into effect in August 1991, the second and the third ones were planned for the first half of 1992. Since all three pieces of legislation give generous deadlines for the people concerned to present their claims, the disbursement of vouchers and public auction of land holdings are not likely to start before the autumn of 1992. The list of enterprises from which voucher holders can choose, as well as the legislation on life-annuity contracts, are still be to worked out.
24 For an English-language summary of the law, see National Bank of Hungary, *Market Letter*, **10** (1990) or *The Hungarian Economy*, **18(3–4)** (1991).
25 E.g. shops constituting a part of a 'chain' were exempted. In a similar way, the law did not have any effect on sales' units operating in factories, army barracks, prisons, etc. Some 2000 pharmacies, a few hundred 'dollar shops', travel agencies and a few dozen pawnshops were also taken out, by arguing that their management required special qualifications.
26 This is not done by the SPA, but rather by outside consulting or auditing firms. This may speed up the process, but it adds to the cost of the operation, which is then reflected in the reserve price. Experience showed, however, that this price was generally too high, and therefore the SPA was forced to reduce prices by 25 per cent on average. Then, a few months later, when the SPA was criticised for the slowness of the pre-privatisation process, reserve prices were cut further. (See the interview with Mr E. Rácz, one of the SPA directors, in *Magyar Nemzet*, 25 September 1991.)
27 Out of the 10,000 shops mentioned above, some 2000 were already 'privatised' for all practical purposes, while an estimated 5000 units are covered by various types of leasing agreements, which cannot be unilaterally abrogated by the SPA. Finally, one should not forget about the circle of registered shopkeepers who had had their own shops for years (50,000) and of those who started from scratch since 1989 (40,000). (These figures are based on estimates prepared in the Ministry of Industry and Trade and reported in *Világgazdaság*, 9 November 1991.)
28 KSH: Press Release (18 June 1991).
29 This applies to all cooperatives – not only agricultural ones, but also those specialised in industrial activities, retail trade or housing estate management.
30 This is, of course, the general rule only. The members of a cooperative will

have the right to assign property rights to the heirs of ex-members or cooperative employees not currently enjoying a membership status. In many cases, special rules will apply to non-agricultural cooperatives.

31 SPA, *Newsletter* (December 1991).

32 The first reorganisation, which served as a model for similar subsequent efforts, was undertaken by MEDICOR, a medical instruments manufacturer which used to be a reputed firm but had accumulated enormous debts by 1986. In early 1987, the firm was transformed into 10 separate joint stock companies and several limited companies. The change gave an opportunity to revalue the enterprise's assets under favourable terms and to reduce indebtedness through debt–equity swaps. The MEDICOR example was followed by five major SOEs in 1987 and by more than 100 in 1988 and 1989 (Móra, 1990, p. 8; Matolcsy, 1991, p. 188).

33 SPA, *Newsletter* (December 1991).

34 This threshold varies from HUF 20–50 mn, depending on the circumstances of transformation and the type of assets concerned.

35 During its first 12 months of existence, the SPA blocked nine transformation cases, seven proposals for JVs and three merger plans. In fourteen cases the SPA vetoed other divestment proposals of different kinds. The total book value of these forbidden transactions was HUF 15 bn (SPA, 1991, pp. 20, 24, 26, 29).

36 This guesstimate figure is the author's extrapolation, based on a careful estimate of Petschnig and Voszka (1991), reflecting the situation on 30 June 1990.

37 Matolcsy (1991) p. 257.

38 See an interview with Mr I. Nádori, an official of the NBH quoted in *Central European* (September 1991).

39 There is one notable exception, the downtown office building programme. This was carried out against the will of the firms concerned.

40 According to Voszka (1991a) the term 'spontaneous' privatisation was first used by Matolcsy in a short article, published in a popular economic weekly (*Heti Világgazdaság*, 28 October 1989).

41 A few citations may give a flavour of their arguments. Walters (1990), the former personal advisor of Mrs Thatcher, argued that 'spontaneous' privatisation 'can be broadly characterized as the existing managements stealing the capital and running off with it'. For Nuti (1990), 'spontaneous' privatisation is simply another name for 'arbitrary appropriation'; Grosfeld and Hare (1991) speak of a need to 'prevent an effective takeover of . . . [the] economy by those in a position to accumulate the necessary funds: this includes crooks, ex-members of the *nomenklatura* and foreigners'.

42 This is the equivalent of the German 'Aufsichtsrat', a prestigious body with little responsibility, but with a guaranteed fix-sum remuneration for its members.

43 In 1949 the first major wave of nationalisation went along with a complete removal of the previous management. Qualified engineers and businessmen were sacked (if not arrested) and reliable party workers were put in their place. In terms of lost efficiency, the price of this takeover was enormous. Today, this event is still very much in the memory of Hungarian decision-makers and they try hard to avoid the same mistake.

44 Western accounting firms appear to have a particularly poor record in this

respect. In many cases, their involvement in the privatisation process has been limited to 'rubber stamping' after Hungarian accountants have done the real job.

45 This dilemma is also reflected in the interdepartmental conflict between the Ministry of Finance and the SPA. In a Ministry of Finance draft prepared for the government, the SPA was heavily criticised for conducting the privatisation in a centralistic–bureaucratic manner. This document, at a later stage, was commented on by the SPA as follows: 'So far, 99 per cent of the ongoing privatisation transactions were launched at the initiatives of the enterprises concerned and 90 per cent of the privatisation revenues came from these spontaneous actions' (quoted in *Heti Világgazdaság*, 28 September 1991).

46 In fact, as a recent survey showed, privatisation programmes of various scale are currently being pursued in more than 70 countries (*The Economist*, 21 December 1991–3 January 1992).

47 See e.g., the list published in *Heti Világgazdaság* (13 July 1991). In three categories the names of 95 firms are mentioned. The 8 firms of the first group are proposed to become public corporations with 100 per cent state participation. The second group comprises 49 firms (including 19 state farms), where the Treasury would seek a 51 per cent equity. In the case of 38 companies, the government's objective is to limit foreign participation to 49 per cent.

48 In June 1991, the government faced the danger of a general strike. In order to prevent this, an accord was signed with the largest trade union, which, *inter alia*, compelled the government to give priority to this issue in its legislative plans.

49 The first outright employee buy-out had already been accomplished in the framework of the first privatisation programme. In a strict legal sense, however, this was not an ESOP operation, due to the absence of proper regulations. In the above-mentioned case, 25 employees of a firm with 165 employees was willing to go for the buy-out.

50 There is already a Law on Concessions, but this is a skeleton law, to be given substance by other laws and statutes. The law enables the conclusion of concessionary agreements in the following cases: national and local highways; basic postal services; the telecommunication main grid and frequencies; public electricity works and transmission lines; mining and prospecting; transport by rail, trucks, buses and pipelines; production and distribution of fissionable and radioactive materials; organisation and operation of games of chance. (For an English-language summary of the law, see *The Hungarian Economy*, 1991, **2**.)

51 This point was powerfully made by V. Klaus, the father of the Czecho-Slovak reform. 'Only an omnipotent monarch, a dictator, or a social engineer operating in vacuum could exercise full control over the transformation. We live, however, in a real world, which imposes many legitimate constraints that must be accepted and dealt with . . . Overstressing the sequencing issue in practical policy-making is nothing other than an attempt to make the world conform to the dreams of ambitious intellectuals' (Klaus, 1991, p. 9).

52 So far, only one firm has been privatised through the Stock Exchanges of Vienna and Budapest.

53 According to Hungarian press reports, precisely this happened when the SPA tried to sell a Hungarian cosmetics' manufacturer. Originally, ten major Western companies had been invited to participate at the tender, but only Colgate–Palmolive sent a realistic offer. About the same time, Unilever was

able to buy a similar Polish company and Procter and Gamble purchased a Czecho-Slovak one in non-competitive negotiations. The above-mentioned two Western firms did not even participate in the Hungarian tender (*Heti Világgazdaság*, 2 November 1991).
54 The figures quoted above are taken from SPA (1991) pp. 7–8.
55 For more details, see SPA, *Newsletter* (October 1991); *Figyelő* (7 November 1991).

REFERENCES

A nemzeti megújhodás programja (A Köztársaság elsö három éve (The programme of national revival (The first three years of the republic), Budapest (1990).
Bauer, T. (1984) 'The second economic reform and ownership relations: some considerations for the further development of the New Economic Mechanism' (Hungarian original published in 1982), *Eastern European Economics*, **3–4**.
— (1989) 'Melyik a reális illuzió?' (Which illusion is realistic?), *Figyelő* (14 December).
Bokros, L. (1990a) 'Az állampolgári részvénytulajdon programja' (The programme of people's shareholding', *Népszabadság* (27 October).
— (1990b) 'Privatisation in Hungary', paper presented at the IMF Institute conference on 'Centrally Planned Economies in Transition', Washington (9–19 July).
— (1991) 'Privatization and capital market development in Hungary', paper presented at the International Center for Monetary and Banking Studies, conference on 'Privatization in Eastern Europe', Geneva (20–21 September).
Csikos-Nagy, B. (1991) 'Privatization in a post-communist society – the case of Hungary', *Hungarian Business Herald*, **2**.
Grosfeld, I. and Hare, P. (1991) 'Privatization in Hungary, Poland and Czechoslovakia', *European Economy*, **2**.
Hoch, R. (1991) 'Formációváltozás és privatizálás' (Systemic change and privatisation), *Társadalmi Szemle*, **7**.
Kiss, K. (1991) 'Privatization in Hungary', *Communist Economies and Economic Transformation*, **3**.
Klaus, V. (1991) 'Dismantling socialism – a preliminary report', *CIS Occasional Papers*, **35**.
Kornai, J. (1989) *Indulatos röpirat a gazdasági átmenet ügyében* (Passionate pamphlet on economic transition), Heti Világgazdaság Kiadói Részvénytársaság, Budapest.
— (1990) *The Road to a Free Economy*, New York: W.W. Norton.
— (1991) 'A privatizáció elvei Kelet-Európában' (The principles of privatisation in Eastern Europe), *Közgazdasági Szemle*, **11**.
Kőhegyi, K. (1991) 'A tulajdonosi szerkezet átalakításának hazai koncepciói' (Hungarian proposals to transform the ownership structure), *Külgazdaság*, **4**.
Macrae, N. (1983) 'Into entrepreneurial socialism', *The Economist* (19 March 1983).
Major, I. (1991) 'Lesz magyar átalakulás?' (Will there be any transformation in Hungary?), *Figyelő* (26 September 1991).
Matolcsy, G. (1990) 'Defending the cause of the spontaneous reform of ownership', *Acta Oeconomica* **(1–2)**.

(1991) *Lábadozásunk évei – A magyar privatizáció* (The years of convalescence – Privatisation in Hungary), Budapest: Tulajdonalapítvány – Privatizációs Kutatóintézet.

Móra, M. (1990) 'Changes in the structure and ownership form of state enterprises (1987–1990)', *Economic Research Institute Economic Papers*.

Nuti, M. (1990) 'Privatization of socialist economies: general issues and the Polish case', paper presented at the 1st Conference of the European Association for Comparative Economic Studies, Verona (27–29 September).

Petschnig, M.Z. and É. Voszka (1991) 'Lefékezi-e a tulajdonosi szerkezetváltás az inflációt?' (Will the change in the structure of ownership relations put a break on inflation?), *Közgazdasági Szemle*, **10**.

Soós, K.A. (1990) 'Privatization, dogma-free self-management and ownership reform', *Eastern European Economics*.

Stark, D. (1991) 'Privatizáció Magyarországon (A tervtől a piachoz vagy a tervtől a klánhoz?)' (Privatisation in Hungary (from plan to market or from plan to clan?), *Közgazdasági Szemle*, **38**.

SPA (State Property Agency) (1991) *Annual Report 1900* (Budapest: SPA).

Tardos, M. (1972) 'A gazdasági verseny problémái hazánkban' (The problems of competition in the Hungarian economy), *Közgazdasági Szemle*, **2**.

  (1982) 'A development program for economic control and organization in Hungary', *Acta Oeconomica* (**3–4**).

  (1990) 'Property ownership, *Eastern European Economics*, **3**.

UN (United Nations Economic Commission for Europe) (1990) *Economic Survey of Europe in 1989–1990*, New York: UN.

Várhegyi, É. (1992) 'The Modernisation of the Hungarian banking sector', Chapter 9 in this volume.

Voszka, É. (1991a) 'Tulajdonreform vagy privatizáció?' (Ownership reform or privatisation?), *Közgazdasági Szemle*, **2**.

  (1991b) 'Homályból homályba – A tulajdonosi szerkezet átalakulása a nagyiparban)' (From dusk to dusk – the transformation of ownership structure in large enterprises), *Társadalmi Szemle*, **5**.

  (1991c) 'Tulajdonosi szerkezet – tulajdonosi érdek' (Ownership structure – ownership motivations), *Közgazdasági Szemle*, **9**.

Walters, A. (1990) 'How fast can market economies be introduced?', *European Business Forum, Financial Times* conference (26–27 November).

7 Competition policy in transition

JÁNOS STADLER

1 Introduction

In market economies, competition governs resource and product allocation. In socialist economies, price control was one of the main instruments influencing economic activity. As Hungary moves to a market economy, competition will need to be established and maintained, replacing price controls. If the law of the jungle is not to prevail, we need clear-cut competition rules and an independent state body to ensure the fairness of competition. That was the target Mr Vissi, then President of the Hungarian Price Office, and his collaborators aimed at in the mid-1980s. Today Mr Vissi is the President of the Hungarian Competition Office, and the Law on Prohibition of Unfair Market Practices was passed by Parliament at the end of 1990 and entered into force on 1 January 1991. This was due to the lengthy endeavours of Mr Vissi and his team – a well-prepared, well-managed action, so rare today in Central and Eastern Europe. More than a year's experience shows that the Competition Law is developing into a good instrument for shaping the new Hungarian economy, and that the new Competition Office (GVH) is successfully enforcing the Law. So the means of competition policy have been brought about, and can be used in the transformation process.

2 Characteristics of the Hungarian Competition Law

The basis of Law No. LXXXVI, 1990, the Competition Law, is to be found in para. 2, article 9 of the Constitution stating that 'the Republic of Hungary recognises and supports the right of enterprise and the freedom of competition'. This freedom could of course not be interpreted as an appeal to 'cut-throat' competition since all enterprises should observe the rules of fair business. Since in Eastern European countries in transition the concept of 'business fairness' is somewhat vague for market actors,

118

legislation must attempt to define the concept in a more practical way. By appropriate legal enforcement these rules are more likely to be accepted by all the parties concerned.

A general clause (para. 3 of the Competition Law) declares that (1) 'entrepreneurs are required to respect the freedom and fairness of economic competiton', (2) 'it shall be unlawful to engage in unfair economic activity, including in particular, any conduct that offends or jeopardises the legitimate interest of consumers or is contrary to requirements of fair business practices'. This clause seems to be expedient for cases which otherwise would not fit well into the more restricted provision (1).

The present Hungarian Competition Law is based to a considerable extent on European legal experience, in large part because Hungary's recent association to the EC requires such an approach in this field. Nevertheless, it encompasses a somewhat broader scope than the usual antitrust laws of fully-fledged market economies where, for example, rules protecting business secrecy, trade marks, etc, can be found in civil law.

Law No. LXXXVI, 1990 is divided up in five main Chapters. Chapter I contains provisions concerning unfair competition practices: harm to reputation, abuse of business secrecy, boycotting, usurpation of trade names, speculative withholding of commodities from sale, tying the sale of one commodity to the purchase of another, and a general ban on fraud in bidding, tenders, auctions and Stock Exchange deals. It is worth mentioning that the Competition Office is entitled only to investigate such cases, while ruling is reserved to the competent court.

Chapter II deals with cases of deceiving the consumer, i.e. deceptive information about commodities, deceptive comparison of goods and services concealing a failure to meet standards, misleading labelling and publicity. Interested individuals or legal persons have a choice of submitting a complaint at the Competition Office or suing the producer/distributor at the court (this latter has a wider scope of legal remedies while the Competition Office has a 60-day deadline to meet the decision, which might include an immediate ban on continuing the deceptive practice).

Chapter III includes provisions applicable to cartel agreements. Para. 14 declares a general prohibition of agreements restricting or excluding competition (price fixing, market sharing, choice limitations, etc., discriminative restrictions or exclusions). There is no prosecution for agreements which aim at stopping the abuse of a dominant position (or monopoly) and if the concomitant advantages outweigh the disadvantages. According to the Law, favourable prices, improvements in quality, in distribution and delivery terms, and technical progress might be regarded as advantages. On the other hand the Law defines the outcome as disadvantageous if the participants' joint market share exceeds 30 per cent of the relevant market. If parties deem that their agreement could violate the Competition Law by setting up a cartel agreement, they may submit a request at the Competition Office asking for preliminary exemption. The Hungarian Law does not distinguish vertical and horizontal agreements, which has been criticised by Western experts. In practice so far there has been no case that could be identified as a 'vertical cartel'.

Chapter IV prohibits the abuse of a dominant position. The most important feature is that a dominant position on a relevant market is deemed prohibitive only when it leads to abuses. The Law gives explanations as to how 'a dominant position' and its 'abuse' is to be understood. Sellers and buyers can each be in a dominant position if the customer is forced to buy from or sell to the other party. An assumed 30 per cent market share of one entrepreneur or a 50 per cent share of three entrepreneurs is already regarded as a dominant position, but the abuse must be proved.

Chapter V regulates the supervision of mergers and fusions of enterprises. A preliminary permission from the Competition Office is obligatory if the joint market share of the commodities in question sold by participants in the previous year exceeds 30 per cent, or if their joint overall turnover of the previous year was more than HUF 10 bn ($125 mn). No merger can be authorised by the Competition Office if it could be harmful to competition. But even a certain limitation of competition might be acceptable if economic advantages outweigh disadvantages (e.g. enabling participants to enter international markets). Guidelines to decide 'advantages' and 'disadvantages' are similar to that of cartel provisions.

The rest of the Law provides for legal procedures and the status of the body responsible for jurisdiction. The Office for Economic Competition is the competent authority to investigate cases concerning commodity markets. (As to the banking sector, the insurance and security markets, a separate legal entity will have jurisprudence but for the time being it has not been organised.) The Competition Office enjoys full independence of the government and is answerable exclusively to Parliament. The President and Vice-Presidents are nominated by the President of the Republic, upon recommendation of the Prime Minister. Funds necessary to run the Office are provided by the budget.

The Office has three main sections: The *Board of Experts* is responsible for investigating cases and the expert in charge sums up his findings in a report. On the basis of the report the *Competition Council* acts as a special arbitration court, according to the rules valid for administrative courts.

Hearings are held by a three-member panel and the decision is enforceable. If a violation of the Law is confirmed, the Competition Council may impose sanctions and:

* declare the act an infringement
* prohibit the continuance of illegal practices
* safeguard the interested party from further illegal practices and damages
* impose fines up to double the value of profits realised or damage caused to competitors or consumers.

Mergers are authorised by the decision of the Competition Council.

The third main section is the *Department of Competition Policy* which deals with theoretical and policy issues. This Department may serve as a consultant to the government or Parliament in questions of economic competition.

Proceedings of the Competition Office may take place either in response to complaints of enterprises (entrepreneurs) or individuals, or upon its own *ex officio* initiative. The Law sets deadlines: decisions regarding cartels shall be made within 45 days, on mergers within 90 days and all other (i.e. the majority of) cases within 60 days. The Competition Office has the right to extend the deadline by 45, 180 or 60 days, respectively. For violations of Chapter I (prohibition of unfair competition, paras 4–10) the Competition Council is entitled only to file a suit at the competent Court of Justice. If the decision of the Competition Council is not acceptable to any of the parties, they may sue the Competition Office at the competent Court of Justice. Until the end of 1991 twelve decisions had been contested: in three cases the judgements are already available (in two cases the decision was overturned, in one approved).

3   Experiences in the first year of the Competition Law

In 1991 176 cases were started by the Competition Office of which 71 reached the Competition Council. A breakdown by case type shows:

* cartel: violations 6, acquitted 14
* abuse of dominant position: violations 12, acquitted 15
* merger control: violations 4, refused 1
* deception of the consumer: violations 7, acquitted 0
* unfair marketing practices: violations 6, acquitted 6.

As mentioned before, in three cases the judgements of the Courts of first instance are available. In one case the unfair business practice was confirmed while in another similar one it was overturned. The third case was a cartel where the Court ruled that the horizontal agreement established was not punishable since it was realised in the framework of a joint enterprise. Moreover, one enterprise cannot make any agreement because the other party is missing. So when – according to the judgement – the most important meat suppliers of the city of Budapest set up a joint enterprise and used this as a vehicle to coordinate market activities (pricing, quotas, sanctions against bypassing, etc.) the coordination embodied the objective of a joint enterprise. This joint enterprise had been established and run according to the provisions of the Company Law, so it became clear that in similar cases the Competition Law could clash with Company Law; establishing a joint enterprise may serve as a back door to avoid cartel charges. Such conflicts occur in the present 'legislation boom', and must be smoothed out either by judicial practice or by modifications of the law. However, similar problems apparently arise in the USA as well; sometimes firms set up a joint venture to justify price fixing or an anti-competitive merger.

Cartels caused difficulties for the Competition Office. On the basis of an overall survey of monopolistic structures and behaviour carried out early in 1991, 17 *ex officio* investigations were started in the most varied segments of industry and services. In thirteen cases no violation could be determined by the Competition Council and only four cases ended in conviction. In each case the convicted party filed a suit (in the case of the meat suppliers' joint enterprise the first level court's refusal was appealed by the Office to the Supreme Court).

Further experience of the *ex officio* cartel investigations suggests that because Hungarian industry is undergoing a confusing period of restructuring and a switch to the market economy, it is hard in the present recession for oligopolistic positions to be created and abused. This means that a lack of competition is not always due to cartel agreements, but can also be caused by economic slowdown. Monitoring markets where there is evidence of a lack of competition is necessary, but before starting any investigation a thorough review of the relevant market is essential. On the other hand, out of the three cartel cases initiated in response to complaints, two were found to show positive abuse. Foreign experts believe that without some collaboration from among the interested actors of the market few antitrust enforcement measures will be successful. So without a reliable complaint procedure only few Competition Office operations are likely to result in efficient investigation and law enforcement.

In post-socialist economies *abuses of a dominant position* are still to be found in abundance since monopolistic practices offer many occasions to make profit (or lessen deficit) in view of the weakness of business partners, sellers and buyers alike. Out of the twenty-seven cases which reached the Competition Council stage, sixteen were initiated upon complaints (ten were found to be unproved allegations) while out of the eleven *ex officio* cases in only six was the abuse confirmed and sanctioned. The lesson can be drawn that in contrast to cartel cases those involving a dominant position are more likely to succeed on the Office's own initiative, so if complaints are abandoned on different grounds (e.g. non-payment of procedure fees) it is worthwhile to re-examine the case and sometimes restart it *ex officio*.

Merger control was weak: five cases altogether and only one was refused. Despite expectations, this type of preliminary request was not numerous, owing to the recession and the fact that restructuring entails more split-ups than mergers. Since the locomotive of restructuring is privatisation which is controlled by the SPA, separate legislation and procedures are applied for this process.

After one year of competition law enforcement (which is not very long) it seems that cases of *consumer deception and unfair business practices* (mostly under the general clauses, para. 3 but also under Chapter I and II of the Competition Law) are the best grounds for producing enforceable decisions. Out of nineteen cases only six were overturned by the Competition Council (seven started *ex officio*, twelve upon complaint). Cases of consumer deception were 100 per cent successful (out of seven cases two were *ex officio*). Complaints claiming unfair business practices (mostly upon the general clause) were not always well-founded.

It appears that the public is not well informed about the aim and applicability of the Competition Law. Breach of a contract and individual injustices are not sufficient grounds for competition law enforcement: they are in the first place subject to civil law application or consumer protection procedures. Nevertheless, if certain entrepreneurs, certain businesses, and certain economic activities show certain *tendencies* which are jeopardising the fairness of competition, action by the Competition Office might be justified. In the transitional circumstances we are living in, close cooperation with quality control institutes, consumer protection state bodies, municipalities, trade and entrepreneur associations could contribute to placing antitrust activity on broader foundations. The public should also be educated by pamphlets, informative articles in the daily and professional press, television programmes, etc.

I would conclude by saying that the Office is new and the number of cases small. More will be learned from the experiences gained over a longer period of time.

4   The role of competition policy in shaping markets

First of all it should be stressed that even though competition legislation and law enforcement is one of the indispensable facets of a market economy, several other processes such as privatisation, association to the EC, trade liberalisation, and reducing state aid are also important. There is a certain interdependence and interplay between these processes which should be taken into consideration when we review the role competition policy might play in the transition period. It seems that privatisation is a key part of transformation. Nevertheless, it should be kept in mind that this involves a redistribution of properties which means that irreversible changes are taking place which differ essentially from the normal market processes. Unlike Poland, the Hungarian Competition Office has no legally designated task to split up monopolies. The SPA has full responsibility and competence in putting state assets into private hands (through different but always business-like deals). In order to prevent the formation of new private monopolies (replacing previous state monopolies) the SPA and the Competition Office are in permanent contact but decisions are made by the SPA alone.

A special case of privatisation might happen if a resident entrepreneur (not an individual person, but a company) obtained a decisive influence over the privatised asset (e.g. by buying 50 per cent or more of the equity). If the company in which it acquired decisive influence together with the existing company controls 30 per cent or more of the relevant market, an authorisation similar to that needed for mergers must be obtained from the Competition Office at the time of privatisation. But this is very rare since the merger control rules of the Competition Law prescribe that applicants be already active entrepreneurs (i.e. companies, etc.) and registered in Hungary. Because of this double condition, neither non-residents (including companies) nor resident individual persons are obliged to apply for a pre-merger authorisation.

Privatisation may sometimes produce threats to competition. Some retail chains (e.g. ready-made clothes, stationery, etc.) acquired by one foreign company changed their image and limited the choice of former shops to the products they were distributing abroad, thus excluding many Hungarian and foreign goods.

The recent association of Hungary, Czecho-Slovakia and Poland to the EC will surely entail consequences in competition matters, first of all in mergers and cartels. The contract is still 'fresh paint', so it is under study together with protocols, etc. because provisions concerning competition will be effective from 31 March 1992 onwards. Once the comparison of Hungarian laws (together with procedures) and EC rules and usages has been completed and tasks defined, studies on typical cases will be undertaken in order that all aspects of probable situations caused by the association may be simulated and scrutinised.

The breakup of CMEA and its controlled allocation system should be one of the greatest benefits to East European countries. It should therefore be of prime interest to liberalise trade and banking operations between these countries. Unfortunately, each country is making separate efforts to enter the world market as fast as possible. But in view of shortsighted priorities (e.g. to find markets for unprofitable companies' products) tariffs and restrictions, instead of decreasing are being increased in response to what is perceived as apparently unreasonable competition in these goods. This results in the shrinking of East–East trade. The West should stress how important it could be to liberalise commodity markets and lift monetary retrictions in order to create broader markets in the states of the former Eastern Block. It seems that operations similar to the recently decided 'triangle-deal-construction', where food purchases of the republics of the former USSR from East European suppliers will be financed by the industrially developed countries' may help open up new markets.

Of course, the bulk of the work must be done by the East European countries themselves. Reducing state aid to unprofitable backward manufacturing units producing obsolete machinery, lifting monetary restrictions and thereby liberalising local currencies enabling these to serve as a vehicle for foreign trade, etc. and other carefully prepared and managed operations are still necessary for the shaping of properly functioning markets. These cannot be run by actors who ignore fairness and proper conduct. The major tasks of anti-trust bodies – including the Hungarian Office for Economic Competition – is to teach participants this fairness, and monitor them so that competition rules are always observed.

Discussion of Part Two

JOHN P. BONIN

Chapters 5 (Járai) and 7 (Stadler) discuss the regulatory policies of two agencies in Hungary, the State Property Agency (SPA) and the Competition Agency (GVH). Each agency can initiate proceedings; this authority is important as the problems of creditor passivity in bankruptcy proceedings indicates. The information provided by Járai suggests that whether the company takes the initiative or the SPA provides initial assistance (impetus) has little bearing on the eventual outcome (103 out of 124 of the company-initiated proposals were approved). On the other hand, from the perspective of the GVH, Stadler indicates that the outcome may depend on the initiative of the aggrieved party. Cartel damage claims initiated by the aggrieved party were successfully prosecuted in two out of three cases whereas GVH-initiated cases were successful in only four of seventeen tries. Since cartel damage is difficult to document, information from the aggrieved party is crucial. Interestingly, in the twenty-seven cases of abuse of monopoly power pursued, the success rate was not dramatically different when the aggrieved party initiated the case. Although the legislation defines monopoly structure as a dominant position, it requires conduct or 'abuse' to be proved for prosecution. As Western experience indicates, abusive conduct is often difficult and costly to demonstrate.

The two agencies find themselves on common turf concerning privatisation and foreign investment. Although tensions are likely to arise, legislation has anticipated some problems. When privatisation involves a merger (or demerger), the GVH must be 'consulted' but the SPA has final authority. The GVH has no mandate to split up monopoly positions based on structure prior to privatisation. Furthermore, special treatment is accorded foreign investors by both agencies. Járai is surely correct when he remarks that everyone is an expert of privatisation; however, Hungary has a clearer vision on how to privatise than do other transforming Central European countries and the SPA has the authority to carry out this vision.

The 'equity versus efficiency debate' still continuing in many countries involving the issue of vouchers as opposed to sale and compensation to previous owners have been resolved in Hungary. For the majority of the twenty large companies in the first privatisation programme, placing with a strategic foreign partner is the recommended method. As Járai indicates, fragmented ownership rights have slowed down privatisation; local councils claim ownership of about 15 per cent of the estimated value of the assets of state-owned companies. However, in the celebrated case of the sale of Gundel, the SPA and the Budapest City Council agreed to sell the restaurant to a foreign owner and resolve their dispute after the deal was completed even if they had to go to court to do so. The successful prosecution of a case of accepted business conduct by United Technologies against Malev Airlines in a Budapest court sent an important signal to the international business community. Hungary's relative success in attracting foreign investors as compared to other transforming countries is undoubtedly due in some part to its regulatory and legal environment.

However, tensions exist as the Hungarian small capitalist is at a decided disadvantage with respect to the foreign investor. Once the subsidised preferential loans are exhausted, domestic interest rates are high and loans are rationed. No investment vehicle for the small investor to diversify risk (e.g. a mutual fund) exists. Domestic household savings rates have been extremely low and household portfolios are relatively illiquid. Consequently, the dominance of the foreign investor at this stage is inevitable and a clear understanding by the regulatory agencies of the motives for foreign investment is essential. The typical Western investor wishes to pre-empt competition from Hungarian companies in existing markets and to penetrate new markets in the transforming countries. It is therefore likely that foreign partners will be in the same business as the privatising Hungarian company. Monopoly positions are likely to be strengthened rather than reduced in the privatisation process, a fact yet to be recognised by the GVH. Járai identifies telecommunications and banking as two areas ripe for foreign investment. The SPA has placed many telecommunications' companies in a category in which majority state ownership is desirable and put several banks (including the large Hungarian Commercial and Credit Bank) in a category in which majority national (state and domestic private) ownership is desirable. Both agencies have a watchdog function to perform.

Privatisation is fraught with problems in all of the transforming countries. The transition process generates significant non-diversifiable risk for an investor. The existence of substantial interenterprise trade credit means that firm-specific risk that is normally diversifiable may not currently be so. Hence, reasonable risk premia are required. If companies are delinked and uncertainty is reduced by moderately favourable outcomes over time, the actual returns to the early investors will seem excessive. Regulatory agencies must be mindful of the regrets that will then be expressed about selling the national patrimony to foreigners. Whether companies should be restructured first or privatised first is vigorously debated. A particularly attractive approach suggested by Jean Tirole (1991) is to consider competition-oriented restructuring before privatisation and leave efficiency-oriented restructuring to the new owners. Such a policy would lessen the possibility of foreigners capitalising monopoly rents and provide better market signals for the second stage of restructuring. In Hungary, close cooperation between the SPA and the GVH would be required in the competition-oriented restructuring phase, with more authority given to the GVH in privatisation matters.

REFERENCES

Tirole, Jean (1991) 'Privatization in Eastern Europe: incentives and the economics of transition', paper prepared for the NBER conference (March).

RUMEN DOBRINSKY

The transformation from centrally planned to market economy is very often a process of 'groping in the dark', where the questions are much clearer than the answers. Moreover, most of the economic and, hence, political, problems are open-ended ones whose trade-offs can hardly even be envisaged in advance.

Privatisation is undoubtedly one of the hottest issues in the process of transition to a market economy. On the one hand, the ownership structure is the fundamental of any economic system. On the other hand, as Járai puts it in Chapter 5, 'the stakes of privatisation are high'.

One of the central problems in privatisation is to identify the social groups, or agents, participating in the process in accordance with their own interests. Seven typical agents in the transforming Eastern European countries are:

* the political power(s)
* the groups of former owners
* the workers in the privatised enterprises and their unions
* the managers of the privatised enterprises
* the state administration controlling the SOEs and implementing the privatisation
* the large private investors, and especially the foreign ones
* the public, or the potential small investors.

These groups have contradictory and sometimes even opposing interests. The violation of the interests of one group by another will undoubtedly cause conflicts and, as Járai mentions, scandals accompanied the Hungarian privatisation from its very beginning. It seems that privatisation scandals will be inevitable in Eastern Europe (and this has also been the experience of all countries which have undergone privatisation), because in principle it is not possible simultaneously to satisfy the interests of all the parties participating in this process.

However, it might be possible to diminish the social tensions by implementing appropriate policy tools such as:

* clearly and openly stated goals of the privatisation
* full transparency of the process
* careful planning of the privatisation in terms of achieving a certain balance among the interests of the different participating parties.

Other problems which were touched on in Part Two concern the macroeconomic environment of the privatisation process. Privatisation of SOEs constitutes a part, and a substantial one, of the emerging capital markets in the Eastern European countries. In this regard the process can be clearly defined in terms of supply and effective demand. Since the supply side is almost completely manageable and controllable, most of the problems arise from the demand side.

The information and figures concerning the distribution of ownership in the Hungarian privatisation as given by Járai are really striking: 90 per cent of the privatisation revenues of the SPA in 1991 came from foreigners; local capital is flowing almost fully to areas outside official privatisation; small investors are basically left out of the privatisation process.

This is the consequence, on the one hand, of the lack of effective domestic demand (in the form of private savings) and, on the other, of the reluctance of the Hungarian authorities to introduce any form of free distribution of property as practised in most of the other Eastern European countries. If the domestic accumulation of capital continues at the same rate, foreign ownership may soon outpace the target figure of 25–30 per cent indicated by Járai.

Another aspect is the legal framework of the privatisation process. It is sometimes argued that privatisation has been successful only in countries which did not create cumbersome legislation regulating the process. The reasoning behind this argument is that the more complicated the legal environment, the more privatisation is hindered by bureaucratic obstacles. If we follow this rule of thumb Hungary has more chance of implementing successful privatisation that the other Eastern European countries because, at least up till now, the legal environment for privatisation is simpler than elsewhere (see Chapter 13 below).

The analysis of Járai in Chapter 5 seems to confirm this paradox. In comparing the different modes of privatisation he clearly concludes that the 'spontaneous' privatisation which is less subject to bureaucratic control was obviously more successful than the official privatisation programme which in 1991 was almost a failure.

We need also to consider the speed of privatisation. Although the goals of privatisation and the expectations in Hungary might have been higher, what has been achieved up till now should be regarded as a big success. Most probably the goals have been over-optimistic, but we have to bear in mind that, as with any other economic development, privatisation has its own logic and driving forces.

The main driving force for privatisation is privatisation itself, i.e. the income generated in the private sector. Hence, following conventional logic, we can anticipate that the trajectory of privatisation over time will be similar to a logistic curve with a period of close to exponential growth at the beginning. The problem is not only to identify the factors which may influence the speed of the process, but also to match the goals concerning speed with the other privatisation goals. Here there is an obvious link to the problem of foreign ownership. If foreign ownership occupies a substantial share at the beginning, this share is likely to increase much faster later on. So the easing of the access of local investors to the process of privatisation is likely to have a serious impact not only on the speed of privatisation but also on the future ownership structure of capital in Hungary.

Finally, the issues of competition. Western legislation has solved this problem and there is no better approach for Eastern Europe than to follow the conventional rules. The Hungarian Competition Law, as presented in Stadler's Chapter 7, seems to provide a good example of this. In particular, this law should be an efficient tool to prevent the emergence of new monopolies.

However there still remains a very serious and unresolved problem which is largely outside the scope of this Law. This is the problem of how to deal with existing 'unnatural' monopolies created under central planning. Forcing them to follow the rules prohibiting the abuse of dominant position means direct administrative control over their activity (maybe to an extent hardly bearable for a private company). The eventual breaking-up of such monopolies might be unreasonable from the point of view of economic efficiency and international competitive positions. But the alternative of transferring monopolistic SOEs into private monopolies seems unacceptable. As usual in such situations, the solution of each case should be tailored individually.

PAUL SEABRIGHT

Privatisation and competition policy have a close relation to each other that is particularly important for an economy setting out to devise policies from scratch rather than tinkering with the trappings of a market economy that is already in place. Privatisation is important for the former command economies to the extent that it changes the opportunities and incentives for the control of enterprises. Different forms of ownership transfer (sales by auction, management buy-outs, mass bidding for shares against vouchers) will have radically different implications for enterprise control and can hardly be evaluated in the same fashion even if they all happen conventionally to go under the name 'privatisation'. Private ownership would not matter if it did not give a real opportunity for improving upon the perverse incentives of the command economy. Conversely, to the extent that large-scale changes of ownership may take a long time to accomplish, changing incentives in the enterprises that are still state-owned must be tackled directly and not postponed.

Yet it is precisely because ownership changes cannot be expected to resolve all, or even most, of the present failures of corporate control that competition policy is important for reforming economies. Conventional analyses have always had difficulty reconciling the zeal of antitrust policy with the paltry empirical estimates of the deadweight losses due to monopolistic pricing (typically at fractions of a percentage point of GDP). When one takes into account the known failures of credit and securities' markets to finance investment (especially in research and innovation), the possibility that market reforms might create some buccaneering capitalists who would make large profits that they would then reinvest has seemed a consummation devoutly to be wished rather than an inefficiency to be deplored. More recent work in industrial organisation, however, has warned us that the real costs of market power come not from high profits but from high costs, from cosy cartel arrangements that allow their members to enjoy the quiet life, free from pressure to cut costs, to innovate, to adapt to a changing world. The real villains of capitalism are not usually buccaneers but corporate bureaucrats, who regard running companies as a reward rather than a trust and think of competition as something they encounter more often on the golf course than in the market place. Again and again European and American companies with secure domestic markets have gone to sleep for several decades, only to discover that their place in world markets has disappeared and that their own customers have lost patience at being ignored. Hungary faces this risk in an even starker form, since on any realistic view the ability of the owners of its enterprises to motivate and monitor their managers and workers is going to be even more restricted than in the developed financial systems of Britain and the USA, let alone the closely-knit bank-driven systems of Germany and Japan. In the absence of effective means of corporate monitoring and control, competition policy becomes a regrettable necessity.

The more we have understood the rationale for competition policy in recent years the harder, alas, has it been to design and implement. Recent research has suggested increasingly that optimal competition policies are highly sensitive to the conditions in particular industries, and highly dependent on facts that are intrinsically difficult to observe (such as the presence of potential rather than actual competitors, of tacit rather than overt collusion, of threats of predatory behaviour that are sufficiently credible not to need carrying out). Yet at the same time, public choice theories of the state have emphasised the importance of simple and easily verifiable policies, of rules rather than discretion, of the desirability of arm's-length relations between firms and regulators so as to minimise the risk of 'capture'. What does this mean for firms designing competition policy from scratch? Are there no robust prescriptions?

Fortunately, there are some. One is that questions of consumer protection should be kept separate from concerns about monopoly power. Consumer protection is usually motivated (rightly) by a concern that firms may exploit the informational disadvantages faced by their customers and thereby expose them to loss or harm. There are a number of means of dealing with such dangers, but guaranteeing secure markets to 'responsible' firms and presuming that all potential rivals are irresponsible has proved to be one of the most ineffective and counter-productive ways of doing so. A second lesson is that conventional measures of monopoly power in terms of the size of firms in relation to their markets, or in terms of their levels of profit, are often worse than useless. The presence or absence of barriers to entry by rival firms is a much better guide. Breaking up large firms purely because they are large can do great damage to their efficiency, especially in engineering and heavy manufacturing sectors. It is much better to ensure that retail, distribution and financial networks are not monopolised so that rivals (including foreign rivals) can mount a credible challenge. Likewise, if regulators investigate firms whenever they make high profits, it will soon be discovered that profits can be massaged downwards by inflating costs, sometimes in ways that managers find very pleasant. Any profit regulated Hungarian firms lacking the ingenuity to inflate costs by themselves will find no shortage of Western consultants to help them to do so.

A third lesson of recent research is that new entrants into an industry face many natural obstacles, a point that has two main implications. First, and most obviously, these should not be compounded by unnecessary artificial obstacles in the form of trade barriers, licensing arrangements and red tape. It is also worth remarking that adverse macroeconomic conditions tend to bear much more heavily on small firms and new entrants to an industry than on their better established rivals. Secondly, there are high social returns to a number of public sector activities (such as the provision of information and training, efficient employment exchanges, and the availability of start-up finance) that can offset these natural obstacles to some extent.

One of the frequent obstacles faced by new entrants is the threat of takeover by their rivals. Contrary to the image of takeovers as a means of correcting managerial failure, takeovers of small firms are frequently the product of their success, and it is only once firms become significantly large that the threat of takeover diminishes. Competition authorities that are reluctant to break up large firms should be a little less reluctant to scrutinise the behaviour of firms that seek to become large chiefly through swallowing their rivals. There have been some interesting proposals in recent years to make use of two-step procedures to screen out quickly those proposals that do not threaten competition, while applying a much more stringent test to those that appear to do so. Putting the onus of proof on mergers that, after initial screening, appear appreciably to reduce competition, has the additional advantage of ensuring that firms provide better information upon which the authorities may base their decision.

A fourth lesson, though in some circles a more controversial one, is that considerations of what are usually called 'industrial policy' (which in Western Europe is code for the desire to diminish competition in order to reap countervailing benefits such as economies of scale) are often legitimate considerations, but should be evaluated separately from competition policy *per se*. For a single body to assess both the competition and the industrial policy aspects of, say, a merger proposal, is often a recipe for fudging and confusion, and for the outcome to be determined merely by those interested parties with the loudest voice and the deepest pocket. A system for separating these considerations exist in Germany, where the Bundeskartellamt must address only competition questions; this has not prevented it from being overruled on numerous occasions by the minister concerned, but such overrulings at least make visible the tension between the principles at stake.

F

There is a sense in which the term 'industrial policy' will inevitably have different connotations for the reforming economies of Eastern Europe than it does in Western Europe. In Western Europe a completely *laisser-faire* approach to industry is more or less a feasible, if an unattractive, option. In the East it is not even remotely feasible, for the simple reason that the state is currently the owner of most of the industrial assets, and many of them cannot be sold for a positive price without substantial restructuring. It is entirely right and desirable that the state should wish to ensure, after privatisation, a level field of competition in which the state itself, though a referee for the process, should not again become heavily involved as a player. But while it continues to own many of the players it is involved whether or not it wishes to be. Tackling the failures of corporate control inherited from the command economy will have to be done on two fronts: both through mechanisms to ensure competition in product, capital, and labour markets (the conditions external to the firm) and, for the foreseeable future, through ensuring that adequate motivation and monitoring mechanisms are in place within firms themselves.

Part Three

The financial system and private savings

8   A short-run money market model of Hungary

JÚLIA KIRÁLY

1   Introduction

Two issues are usually discussed in monetary economics: the problem of the transmission mechanism, i.e. the way 'money' affects the economy; and the problem of the 'money creation mechanism' itself, i.e. the institutional and economic functioning of the monetary sector. Most early studies were devoted to the first problem, the second issue being covered by the simple multiplier mechanism. Recently, however, interest has shifted toward the second issue, reflecting a situation of strengthening disintermediation, deregulation and financial innovation. Banks are no more considered as 'money creating automata' but as profit maximising enterprises in a special market environment. Both the spread of various game–theoretic models and the more sophisticated theoretical and econometric models of money supply reflect this shift of emphasis.

In former centrally planned economics (CPEs) money usually played a passive role, and neither the transmission mechanism nor the monetary sector attracted much attention from modellers. Hungary, however, could be considered an exception to the rule, since in past decades money has been much more active than in neighbouring countries and research work has in consequence been intense in this field. In recent years empirical research focused on the money demand function, the causality relationship, and the transmission mechanism in general (Portes and Winter, 1978; Portes, 1981; Nadrai et al., 1985; Ábel and Székely, 1988; Charemza and Ghatak, 1989). Nevertheless, until the birth of the two-tier banking system the money supply mechanism was of little interest, and the Central Bank represented only the 'monetary account' of the government.

The reform of the financial sector, the most significant economic reform of the past few years, has highlighted so far neglected questions, and

137

created a new challenge for researchers. Unfortunately, one of the most crucial challenges of the recent past was that time series-based econometric models gradually lost their relevance, since the Hungarian statistical system has collapsed: not only are comparable time series missing, but reliable actual descriptive data (GDP, income, consumption) are missing as well. Under these circumstances an econometric model builder is tempted to abandon hope.

If we do not abandon hope, we have to begin to collect data, to put together a comprehensive data base, to build and analytically analyse draft models. In the present chapter an experimental money market model, or rather a 'skeleton model' will be presented, which may serve as a basic model for further research. The discussion concentrates on narrative and mathematical description of the monetary sector, taking into account the implicit assumptions already made about the transmission mechanism.

In section 2 a short description of the Hungarian money market is given, while section 3 gives an overview of the tools of short-run monetary policy. In section 4 the framework of a short-run monetary model is outlined, section 5 draws some conclusions.

2   The segments of the money market[1]

The tools of monetary policy are not independent of the structure and liquidity of money markets. Beside other measures – refinance credit, the reserve ratio, the prescribed interest rate or credit ceiling, rediscount policy – market intervention usually forms a significant part of monetary policy, if there is a liquid and well-developed market in which to intervene.

The most widely-spread money market models reflect the particular circumstances of the US monetary system (e.g. Papademos and Modigliani, 1990). It assumes that the (government) securities market is the core of the money market, and that it is liquid and wide enough that open market operations can play the decisive role in monetary policy. Nevertheless, it is well known that in other countries both interbank relationships and the links between the Central Bank (NBH) and commercial banks differ significantly from this simplified picture. In some cases the market for foreign currencies is the core of the money market (e.g. Switzerland and, a few years ago, Norway); in other cases the interbank market (i.e. the overnight deposit market) is of central importance (Italy).

In analysing the Hungarian monetary system we should bear in mind that the two-tier banking system was introduced only a few years ago, and that consequently the development of money markets has had a very short history.

Table 8.1. *Segments of the Hungarian money market*

Vertical markets
 – security markets:
  – auctions of discounted Treasury Bills
  – auctions of the HNB's CDs

 – foreign exchange market:
  – swaps and forward

 – market of HUF funds:
  – intermediated interbank market
  – auction for Central Bank loans

Horizontal markets
 – interbank market of HUF funds

The key segments of the money market can be characterised as in Table 8.1. This characterisation may seem a little artificial and, perhaps, a little obscure; however, it accurately reflects the present features of the Hungarian monetary system. A segment is called 'vertical' when (most of the) transactions take place between the Central Bank and the commercial banks, and 'horizontal' if transactions take place among commercial banks with or without the intermediation of the Central Bank. The 'good' on a market segment may be securities, HUF funds or foreign currency.

2.1 Market for Bills of Exchange

Bills of Exchange form a negligible part of commercial banks' portfolios, and are usually immediately rediscounted at the Central Bank; the interbank sale of Bills of Exchange is not significant either. The rediscount rates declared by the Central Bank follow the movements of the discounted Treasury Bills. Consequently, we cannot really speak about a market for Bills of Exchange.

2.2 Auction of Treasury Bills

The auction market for discounted Treasury Bills was first organised by the NBH in December 1988. Discounted Treasury Bills with a maturity of 30 and 90 days are offered for sale; participants in auctions make their bids for the volume and price they wish to purchase, while the Treasury announces the volume and the lowest acceptable price of Treasury Bills to be auctioned. Bids are ranked and are accepted as long as bills to be auctioned remain. In the case of every accepted bid, settlement is made at the specific bid price and not at the average price of the auction. Non-competitive bids can be accepted during the period between two auctions at the previous auction's average price.

Yields emerging at the auction are determined by the level of the money market's liquidity and the objectives of monetary policy. Auction sales provide an opportunity for the Central Bank to collect useful information on market conditions; with the application of marginal yields and value limits determined for each auction, the NBH is able to influence short-term interest rates. In 1991 the average volume of Treasury Bills to be offered was HUF 1 bn, the average outstanding stock was around HUF 10 bn.

The auction market for Treasury Bills is a typical 'vertical' market. A liquid and concentrated secondary market of such Treasury Bills does not exist; commercial banks have the opportunity to resell the Treasury Bills to their partners or to the Central Bank before maturity, but these operations are not concentrated and are limited in volume, so that open market operations in their classical form cannot be pursued.

2.3   Certificates of deposit (CDs) of the NBH

Since 1989, the NBH has regularly issued its own money market instruments. These instruments have been offered for sale to financial investors with repurchase arrangements: CDs provided the possibility for the Central Bank efficiently to reduce market liquidity according to its monetary objectives. The limits of this market are the same as those of the discounted Treasury Bills' market: it is a vertical market with no secondary market for CDs. In 1991 the average outstanding stock was about HUF 10–25 bn, 90 per cent of which was in the portfolio of the National Savings Bank.

2.4   Auctions of NBH HUF funds

Since the beginning of 1991, after significantly reducing the amount of short-run normative refinance credit the Central Bank has offered liquidity to the commercial banks through the auction of short-run (two-week maturity) Central Bank loans. In 1991 auctions were organised every second week with an average volume of HUF 4 bn. The interest rate of the auctions keeps pace with the interest rate of discounted Treasury Bills.

2.5   Foreign exchange market[2]

This 'market' involves the possibility of immediate sale and forward repurchase of foreign exchange receipts to and from the NBH. The risk originating from changes in the HUF exchange rate can be covered by this operation, and HUF funds gained as a result of the conversion can be utilised for domestic credit extension. Forward rates are calculated by the NBH, with the aim that implicit interest rates and discount rates should not differ significantly from each other.

The market is intended to change under the new deregulated foreign exchange regime when a limited interbank foreign exchange market is introduced and the Central Bank ceases to quote forward rates. In the near future the foreign exchange market may thus become an important segment of monetary policy.

2.6   Market for funds (interbank market)

A spontaneously organised interbank money market was for a long time almost non-existent due to shortage of liquidity, poor liquidity management and the significant risks of default. Nevertheless, the major practical obstacle to a spontaneous interbank market was the lack of confidence among participating banks. The initiative for the development of an interbank market was taken by the NBH by organising a so-called 'intermediate market' of short-term HUF funds. Under this arrangement both the lender and the borrower are bound to the Central Bank by contract, and the Central Bank consequently bears the risks of settlement.

Since 1989 the 'non-intermediated' interbank market has developed significantly. In 1991 the average interbank loan stock quintupled, while the volume of intermediated credit almost doubled. The reason is that though the intermediated credit is riskless, the interest rate is limited: interest rates obtainable on the non-intermediated market are usually higher. The NBH had no other option but to limit interest rates in order to cool inflationary expectations, dozens of brokerage firms, however, entered the market and offered new channels for both suppliers and demanders. The higher than equilibrium interest rate on this market is due to the imperfections of the market and the risk resulting from these imperfections.[3] Brokers collect excess funds through repurchase agreements and deposit the funds through repos, which means that securities of these repos can serve as collateral.

This overview of money market segments demonstrates that these segments are separate. Any links between the segments are usually made by the Central Bank. A more thorough analysis should have been supported by quantitative data, but we have little available statistical evidence, and the data that are available are sometimes contradictory. Figure 8.1 exhibits the co-movements of yields on the different markets.

These co-movements demonstrate that the interest rates on the different vertical segments do not differ significantly from each other. There are

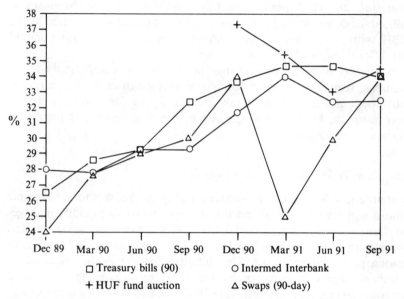

Figure 8.1   **Interest rate movements, money market segments, 1989–91**

some exceptional periods, such as the period of introduction of the
auctions of HUF funds, or the periods before and after the centrally
regulated devaluations. After a significant increase in 1989–90 interest
rates ceased rising in 1991.

3   Tools of monetary policy

Our analysis of money market segments in section 2 suggests that through
auctions of Treasury Bills and CDs the Central Bank can reduce the
liquidity of commercial banks, and through auctions of HUF funds
increase it. Beyond these quasi-market tools traditional control
mechanisms are also applied by the NBH.

3.1   Required reserves

A unified reserve requirement policy was introduced in 1988; the reserve
requirement, for all types of banks and deposits, became a uniform 15 per
cent. In the third quarter of 1989 the Central Bank raised the reserve rate
to 18 per cent; in the third quarter of 1990 the reserve ratio was reduced to
15 per cent, only to be raised to 16 per cent in the fourth quarter of 1991.
  It would be difficult to say that these rapid shifts in the required reserve

ratio reflected a related monetary policy. They rather illustrate the uncertainties the monetary authorities used to face, and still do face.

3.2 Refinancing and rediscount policy

Transforming the banking system into a two-tier framework a strong refinancing channel had to be established between the Central Bank and largest commercial banks, which can be regarded as a structural rigidity.

Refinancing credit has various forms: overdraft credit, rediscount of commercial bills, long-run refinance credit for investment, refinance credit with foreign exchange collateral and preferential refinancing credit. Overdraft credit and the rediscount of commercial bills are usually short-term credit and – usually – limited in an amount prescribed by a set of rules. In 1991 the stock of this type of short-run credit was reduced by 66 per cent. On the other hand, during the same period the importance of a special form of short-run refinance credit significantly increased. Banks can now have access to Forint refinancing credits, pledging foreign exchange account balances as a collateral. This facility makes it possible for the banks to acquire HUF liquidity without definite swap operations, on the basis of their foreign exchange accounts kept with the NBH. In 1991 the stock of this type of credit increased from HUF 7 bn to HUF 94 bn. Note that in this case there is no definite limit, the NBH can use only interest rate conditions to make this form of liquidity 'unfavourable' to banks. Note, also, that in essence this form of refinance credit does not differ from a formal swap transaction.

The restructuring of the refinancing channels means that the NBH faces a serious dilemma. When there is an unexpected surplus on the current account of the balance of payments it is converted automatically into excess HUF funds without any possibility of sterilisation. This will lead to a subsequent increase in the required reserve ratio.

4   A simple money market model

I do not aim to produce here a comprehensive monetary model, rather I wish to concentrate on the commercial banks' behaviour on the money market, and on their response to interest rate and monetary policy signals. The model is simplified, some properties of money market segments are stressed, while others are neglected.

Banks are supposed to be asset managers who face the following basic constraint:

$$RR_j + ER_j + I_j + L_j - D_j - Z_j = RC_j + N_j \tag{1}$$

where

RR_j: required reserves of bank j

ER_j: free reserves of bank j

I_j: investment of bank j (including Treasury Bills, commercial papers, CDs of the Central Bank)

L_j: business loans of bank j

D_j: deposit of bank j

Z_j: miscellaneous items of the balance sheet (e.g. equity and other long-run resources)

RC_j: short-run refinance credit of bank j

N_j: interbank loan (if N_j is positive then received, if negative then advanced).

If variables are replaced by behavioral relationships then the right-hand side of (1) may be interpreted as the supply of, and the left-hand side as the demand for, HUF funds, on a micro level.

Three relevant interest rates will be distinguished: the interest rate of refinance credit (r_F), the interest rate of swap transactions, and of refinance credit with foreign exchange collateral (r_s), and the interest rate on the interbank market (r_i). The first two will be considered as policy variables, the third as an endogenous variable and will be determined by market conditions. It will be assumed that the interbank money market is unified. This assumption is rather crude, and should be replaced in the future. We should bear in mind also, that actual market interest rates should be higher than those predicted by the model due to the existing imperfections. It is assumed, too, that normally $r_F < r_s < r_i$.

The model aims to investigate the money market equilibrium; the micro level equation and its variables will consequently be replaced by their aggregate counterparts. Equations and variables are summarised in Table 8.2.

The functions determining deposits and loans are part of a public portfolio model, where both assets (deposits) and liabilities (loans) are determined as fraction of the total wealth ((2)–(5)). It is supposed, therefore, that the elasticity of demand of deposit and loans with respect to wealth is 1. Demand for deposit and loans depend on the expected rate of inflation, the interest rates offered by banks and the alternative interest rates. HUF deposits are distinguished from deposits in foreign exchange, the latter also depending on the expected foreign exchange rate. Demand for HUF deposits increases if interest rates on deposit and wealth increase, and alternative interest rates and expected inflation rates decrease. The demand for foreign exchange deposits behaves in the same way, except that it decreases if interest rates on HUF deposits increase

Table 8.2. *A simple money market model*

Equations of the model

$$D_{F_t} = D_{F_t}(r_D, r_A, \pi^e)^* W \tag{2}$$

$$D_\$ = D_\$(r_\$, r_A, \pi^e, e^e)^* W \tag{3}$$

$$D = D_{F_t} + D_\$ \tag{4}$$

$$L = L(r_L, r_A, \pi^e)^* W \tag{5}$$

$$r_D = r_D(r_F, r_s, r_i) \tag{6}$$

$$r_L = r_L(r_F, r_s, r_i) \tag{7}$$

$$RR = \beta^* D \tag{8}$$

$$ER = ER(r_F, r_s, r_i) \tag{9}$$

$$I = I(r_s, r_i) \tag{10}$$

$$Q(r_F, r_s, r_i, \mathbf{x}) = RC \tag{11}$$

Variables of the model

D:	deposit	(END)
D_{F_t}:	the HUF deposit of the public	(END)
$D_\$$:	foreign exchange deposit of the public	(END)
L:	business loans	(END)
RR:	required reserves	(END)
ER:	free reserves	(END)
I:	investment (including Treasury Bills, commercial papers, CDs of the Central Bank)	(END)
r_i:	interest rate on the interbank market	(END)
r_D:	interest rate of HUF deposits	(END)
r_L:	interest rate of loans	(END)
Z:	miscellaneous items of the balance sheet (e.g. equity and other long-run resources)	(EX)
RC:	short-run refinance credit	(EX)
r_F:	the interest rate of refinance credit	(EX)
r_s:	the interest rate of refinance credit with foreign exchange collateral	(EX)
W:	total financial wealth of households	(EX)
r_A:	interest rate of alternative form of financial investment	(EX)
π^e:	expected inflation rate	(EX)
e^e:	expected foreign exchange rate	(EX)
$r_\$$:	interest rate on foreign exchange deposits	(EX)
β:	required reserve ratio	(EX)
END:	endogenous variable	
EX:	exogeneous variable	

more than expected foreign exchange rates. In a more refined version of the model the portfolio equations should be replaced by their dynamic versions.

The interest rates on HUF deposits offered by banks and the interest rates asked by them depend on their cost of funds, i.e. the three relevant interest rate of the model ((6)–(7)).

The required reserves are determined by the monetary policy variable (8), while the excess reserves depend on the various interest rates (9). Excess reserves decrease in the first two variables and increase in the third one.

The investment in securities – i.e. Treasury Bills and CDs of the Central Bank – will depend on interest rate differences. If we assume, which is not far from reality, that the interest rate of investment is equal to the interest rate of swap transactions then we arrive at (10), where I is increasing in the first variable and decreasing in the second.

If now we turn back to our initial equation and sum it up over all banks taking into account that:

$$\Sigma N_j = 0 \quad \text{and} \quad \Sigma RC_j = RC$$

we reach our final behavioural equation that determines the interbank market interest rate r_i (11) where $\mathbf{x}$ is a vector of all other exogenous variables.

$$
\begin{aligned}
Q(r_F, r_s, r_i, \mathbf{x}) = &(\beta - 1)* D(r_F, r_s, r_i, \mathbf{x}) \\
&+ ER(r_F, r_s, r_i, \mathbf{x}) \\
&+ I(r_F, r_s, r_i, \mathbf{x}) \\
&+ L(r_F, r_s, r_i, \mathbf{x}) - Z
\end{aligned}
\tag{12}
$$

The model works in a very simple way. If demand for funds increases by an exogenous shift and the Central Bank does not intervene then the market interest rate will increase which, in turn, increases or reduces the demand for funds. This final step depends on the reaction parameters. Let us take an example:

$$dQ/dr_i = (\beta - 1)\partial D/\partial r_i + \partial ER/\partial r_i + \partial I/\partial r_i + \partial L/\partial r_i \tag{13}$$
$$\quad (-) \qquad\qquad (?) \qquad\quad (+) \qquad (-) \qquad (?)$$

The final result, and therefore the comparative statics of the model, depends on the model parameters which should be estimated by econometric methods or by experts. The subsequent step will be to determine realistic parameter values and analyse the actual behaviour of the model.

5   Conclusions

Quantitative prediction is not an easy business under the present circumstances. It is difficult to formulate the basic features, since the financial markets described by the model are changing from day to day. The attempt was made to overcome this difficulty by classifying the money market segments (section 3) and reflecting these characteristics in the model description.

The actual situation in Hungary can be described as an interim period. On the one hand, money market segments are underdeveloped, so that market-oriented monetary policy is not yet effective. On the other hand, direct tools of monetary policy have been weakened by the NBH itself, so that their effectiveness has consequently been reduced. The transformation of the monetary sector has required a shift from direct towards indirect control, and the painful interim period has somehow to be managed.

The other problem Hungary faces is the lack of reliable data. The former statistical system cannot cope with the new requirements, and there is little hope that the data needs even of the above over-simplified model can be satisfied in the near future.

Thus, for quite a while, applied econometric researchers will not be in a position to produce empirical results which could support monetary policy design. Still, a model describing the framework within which monetary policy operates can be a useful start. It can help policy-makers to understand the likely nature of the impact their policy will have on financial institutions. Although monetary policy is bound to resort to some sort of trial-and-error approach in fine-tuning policies, the sort of model offered by the present chapter can make this learning process faster.

NOTES

1 In my overview of the money market segments I have relied on the more detailed description given by István Szalkai (1991); some of his statements are quoted verbatim.
2 In Hungary the major part of foreign exchange banking activities was traditionally performed by the NBH. Following the establishment of the two-tier banking system domestically-owned commercial banks and bank-like financial institutions had no foreign exchange licenses at all. Since then, several stages of decentralisation have occurred; for example, at the end of 1991 a limited interbank spot market for foreign exchange was put into operation. Foreign exchange decentralisation is to be continued dependent on banks' readiness, market developments and the country's foreign exchange liquidity position.
3 I am very grateful to Colin Mayer for this valuable remark.

REFERENCES

Ábel, I. and I.P. Székely (1988) 'Money and causality in CPEs', Budapest University of Economics, *Working Paper*, **88/3**.
Charemza, W.W. and S. Ghatak (1989) 'Demand for money', *Working Paper*.
Nadrai, L. *et al.* (1985) 'Monetary policy and balance of payments', *Szigma*, **18**, pp. 69–88.
Papademos, L. and F. Modigliani (1990) 'The supply of money', Chapter 10 in B.M. Friedman and F.H. Hahn (eds), *Handbook of Monetary Economics*, Amsterdam: North-Holland.
Portes, R. (1981) 'Macroeconomic equilibrium and disequilibrium in CPEs', *Economic Inquiry*, **19**, pp. 559–78.
Portes, R. and D. Winter (1978) 'The demand for money and for consumption goods in centrally planned economics', *Review of Economics and Statistics*, **60**, pp. 8–18.
Szalkai, I. (1990) 'Monetary policy and recent developments in financial markets in Hungary', Budapest, ITCB, mimeo.

9 The modernisation of the Hungarian banking sector

ÉVA VÁRHEGYI

1 Introduction

The modernisation of the banking sector in 1987 was one of the most important elements of reform in Hungary in the 1980s, contributing to the restructuring of the previous institutional framework aimed at centralised capital allocation. However, like the other reform packages of that period, it could not change the basic characteristics of the previous system, namely the concentration of economic control in one centre, and the domination of state ownership. It is necessary to overturn these taboos in order to achieve further modernisation; this will hopefully be undertaken by the 'second' banking reform now taking place.

However, the recent reforms may still fall victim to shortsighted political interests. A delay caused by political struggle could make the further development of the banking sector more difficult. If there were such a delay, the distorted market and corporate structure created by the 'first' banking reform in 1987 could become entrenched to an extent which would seriously jeopardise the success of any later reform.

Section 2 of the chapter pinpoints the drawbacks of the banking reform in 1987. Based on the conclusions of this section, section 3 outlines the desirable elements of a 'second' banking reform.[1]

2 The limitations of the first banking reform

The 'first' reform, which took place in the 1980s, created the institutional framework within which the issuing bank operated as the Central Bank, and the commercial banks and other financial institutions as business enterprises. Since 1987, the National Bank of Hungary (NBH) has had no direct connection with companies, and takes deposits from and advances loans to financial institutions (and the central budget) only. This enables the NBH to focus its monetary policy on achieving macroequilibrium

149

targets (targets on inflation and foreign debt, for example). In the past, these targets were much too frequently sacrificed in order to keep the inefficient large state-owned firms and even whole production sectors alive. This sort of conflict of interest was part of the daily management of credit policy.

In the first period after introducing the reforms, the Central Bank used refinancing as the main monetary policy instrument. Later it relied primarily upon indirect instruments: interest and exchange rate policies, and open market transactions. Commercial banks, under the market conditions created by the Central Bank, collected the deposits and channelled this and other financial resources to the enterprises.

This separation of roles not only enhanced the Central Bank's ability to carry out monetary policies, but to some extent also improved the credit allocation mechanism. The commercial banks and specialised financial institutions, created from the commercial banking arms of the NBH, or established in other ways, have been independent since 1987, and are thus supposed to operate as profit maximising enterprises. In theory, their interest is to place loans and make other investments in ways which maximise profit, also taking into account the risk attached to these investments. This is the only way for them to remain competitive; otherwise, they could not offer competitive rates to their depositors, and proper dividends to their shareholders (owners).

In practice, however, little of this actually happened. The reforms carried out in 1987 were undoubtedly necessary to achieve this target, but definitely not sufficient. The modernisation of the banking sector in 1987 had the same characteristics as other reform packages introduced in the 1980s: it left the domination of state ownership and central control untouched. The former meant that the commercial banks were created as state-owned enterprises, and that the corporate structure in banking remained highly distorted. The latter meant severe restriction on the sovereignty of the Central Bank and the hands-on management of commercial banks. For all these reasons, modernisation of the institutional and regulational frameworks, and adaptation to forms characteristic of market economies, created only a field of play without adequate motivation.

2.1   The Central Bank

The Central Bank remained under the supervision of the government. Its president was appointed by the Prime Minister. Although the formulation and implementation of the monetary and credit policies were the tasks of the bank, the right of approval rested with the government. That is why monetary policy was formally subordinated to the government's economic policy.

2.1.1 Pressure of the state budget

The maintenance of the Central Bank's dependence upon the government hindered the efficient operation of the banking sector. The first constraint was the substantial finance the state budget deficits required. This was the result of the vigorous redistribution of incomes by the state budget, resulting from a largely oversized state budget. The crowding out effect thus created placed an enormous pressure on the whole banking sector. Between 1987 and 1989, three-quarters of the Central Bank's financial assets went to finance the state budget, depriving the commercial banks of their credit sources. (Only in 1990 was this tendency of previous years reversed; this change was due partly to a decline in state investment, and partly to the fact that an increasing proportion of the budget deficit was being financed from the capital market, through the issue of state bonds.)

Until very recently, there was no legislation limiting the Central Bank's share in the financing of the state budget deficit. This depended basically upon the bargaining power of the bank management and the government. Monetary policy was thus subordinate to fiscal policy, potentially increasing inflationary pressure and/or foreign debts. The Central Bank, in trying to maintain the stability of the domestic currency, could restrict enterprises' access to finance, only by increasing the refinance rate, or by introducing ceilings on refinance credits (see Chapter 8 above). Only the new National Bank Act, which was passed in 1991 and which came into force at the end of December, will break this vicious circle. The Act sets a limit to the financing of the state budget by the NBH. However, this limit will be effective only in 1992.[2]

2.1.2 Dominance of the government's economic policy

Another problem related to the lack of Central Bank independence was the influence the government's economic policy exerted over credit allocation. In a fully fledged market economy, the government typically uses fiscal instruments to help out troubled enterprises. The extent to which credit instruments can be used for this purpose is fairly limited. That is why a restriction, such as the one which requires the Central Bank to support the government's general economic policy, does not make much difference. In Hungary, since the bank reform in 1987, significant political changes have occurred, though the danger still remains that the government may exert politically motivated pressure upon the Central Bank's monetary and credit policies.

In 1989 and 1990, the autonomy of the NBH grew in spite of the fact that the legal status of the bank did not change. The refinancing credit lines, created to ensure the survival of certain companies and sectors, were increasingly restricted in the bank's investment portfolio. This, presumably, was mainly thanks to the power vacuum which appeared between the dismantling of the old political system and the construction of the new one, that is, in the short period immediately before and after the change of administration. One of the manifestations of this can be seen in the authorisation given to the new President of the Bank appointed by the new Prime Minister, which gave him a high degree of autonomy.

The sudden collapse of the administration and its slow reconstruction afterwards made it possible for the Central Bank management drastically to reduce the extent of preferential loans. Previously, these loans had played a major role in achieving the government's industrial policy targets. During 1990 and 1991, preferential loans were in practice given 'only' to assist exports, small enterprises and for privatisation.

With the gradual formation of the new state administration, the efforts to subordinate the Central Bank's credit policy to the government's economic and fiscal policies intensified. As a result of these efforts, in the summer of 1991, the draft National Bank Act was approved by the government, with significant modifications limiting the rights of the Central Bank Chairman and the autonomy of monetary policy. This version was in sharp contrast with the earlier versions of the draft Act, giving a much higher degree of independence to the Central Bank.

2.2   The commercial banks[3]

The development of commercial banking, (re)created by the reforms introduced in 1987, was also severely hindered by the heritage of a centralised allocation of capital. Although the newly created commercial banks, at least in principle, did not directly serve economic policy interests, and their placement was supposed to be based entirely on business expediency, in practice, the numerous ties working against this remained unsevered.

2.2.1 Inherited fragile investment portfolios
One of these ties was due to the inherited fragile investment portfolios of the large commercial banks, which dominate the commercial banking sector. A large number of the bad and dubious loans granted by the commercial banking arm of the NBH before 1987 to the present clients of the three large commercial banks – MHB (Hungarian Credit Bank), OKHB (Commercial Bank) and BB (Budapest Bank) – have not so far

Table 9.1. *Doubtful claims of Hungarian commercial banks, 1989 and 1990*

a Total claims

	1989		1990	
	HUF mn	(%)	HUF mn	(%)
Large banks*	21 227	88.7	38 838	84.3
Medium banks	2352	9.8	6377	13.8
Small banks**	349	1.5	854	1.9
Total	23 928	100.0	46 069	100.0

Notes:
 * Without the National Savings Bank.
** Specialised financial institutions.

b Proportion of doubtful claims, 1990

	Doubtful claims in the % of		
	Profit	Own capital	Deposits
Large banks*	126.4	63.8	11.9
Medium banks	54.7	24.4	7.3
Small banks**	39.1	9.9	15.5
Total	100.7	47.9	11.0

Notes:
 * Without the National Savings Bank.
** Specialised financial institutions.

been repaid. Given the present financial position of the firms involved, these loans cannot be expected to be fully serviced. Due to the lack of sufficient provisioning, the commercial banks, even if they had wished to do so, could not have written off the non-performing loans frozen in insolvent companies.

The sum of the doubtful claims in the commercial banking sector amounted to HUF 46 bn in 1990, equal to 4 per cent of total assets and to 48 per cent of own funds. The doubtful claims of the four largest commercial banks amounted to HUF 39 bn, 9 per cent of their total assets, and 65 per cent of their own funds (see Tables 9.1a, 9.1b). In these banks' investment portfolios, some 40 per cent of bad loans and 20 per cent of doubtful claims were inherited from the monobank system. Since 1990, a part of them have been written off by the banks, but at the same time further losses and doubtful claims have accumulated. This was mainly due to the collapse of the CMEA markets, to which these firms were heavily exposed.

On the other hand, until the end of 1991, when the new Financial Institutions Act and the new Accounting Law came into force, it was not in the interest of the banks to write off non-performing loans. With the prolongation of these loans, they were able to earn, at least in their books, the same interest income (or even more) as from loans given to good (solvent) debtors. Previously, the Hungarian regulations – in contrast to international practice – made it possible to keep non-performing loans on the books without having to provision against them. That is why the banks were able to show massive profits in their balance sheets, and from these, to pay substantial taxes to the state budget and high dividends to their owners (including the largest one, the state), while in reality never being able to realise these profits. Put differently, while being highly profitable, the quality of the investment portfolios of the large commercial banks deteriorated substantially.

Another element of the legacy hindering the development of the commercial banking system was the very high degree of foreign indebtedness. High debt service forced the administration to adopt a tight money policy. This, together with the expansive fiscal policy meant that there were practically no financial resources left to be channelled by the commercial banking system.

2.2.2 Segmentation of the loan and deposit markets

The lack of new sources and the legacy of bad loans still impede the efficient operation of the banking system. This is true in spite of the fact that the institutional structure has been modernised. The competition among the increasing number of commercial banks (now more than thirty) was primarily for funds, while the quality of service and the security of operation were forced into the background.

The banking market was heavily segmented, which hindered competition and, thus, efficient capital allocation. The major part of the business sector, including the large state-owned enterprises, were divided exclusively among the four largest commercial banks. Moreover, the market was also divided by industrial sectors. The small- and medium-sized banks (due to their low capital strength) were able to service only the smaller companies. Households and small enterprises formed a separate sector, and were mainly the clients of the savings bank and cooperatives, which had the necessary branch networks (see Table 9.2).

Table 9.2. *The segmentation of loan and deposit markets, 1989, per cent*

	Share in loans to		
	Households	Enterprises	Small ventures
Large banks	1	80	10
Medium banks	1	14	4
Small banks	0	2	1
National Savings Bank	98	4	85
Total	100	100	100
	Share in the deposits of		
	Households	Enterprises	Small ventures
Large banks	1	70	12
Medium banks	2	9	2
Small banks	0	2	0
National Savings Bank	97	19	86
Total	100	100	100

Since 1989, the segmentation of the bank markets has gradually diminished. Due to the liberalisation of the regulations, there is an increasing competition among banks for funds, especially for households' deposits.

2.2.3 Corporate structure in banking

The corporate structure of the banking sector reflects the distorted company size structure of economy as a whole. It consists of a small number of large enterprises with substantial market power, and a relatively large number of small companies, unable to compete with them. The banking sector clearly lacks the medium-sized banks which would be able to put competitive pressure on the larger banks. The market share of the four largest commercial banks, regarding balance sheet size, is still about 70 per cent (disregarding the National Savings Bank which inherited a special monopolistic position in the household sector). The large state-owned enterprises, which were given preferences over decades, still take up the lion's share of total bank loans. The large banks financing these enterprises utilise the Central Bank's refinancing loans (primarily with long-term maturity), regardless of the credit-worthiness of the firms. At the same time, the generally more efficient small and medium-sized

Table 9.3. *Concentration of the banks' assets and liabilities, 1989–90, per cent*

	Assets		Own funds		Refin. credits	
	1989	1990	1989	1990	1989	1990
Large banks*	82	73	65	63	94	88
Medium banks	15	23	26	27	6	12
Small banks**	3	4	9	10	0	0
Total	100	100	100	100	100	100

Notes:
 * Without the National Savings Bank.
** Specialised financial institutions.

companies, due to poor access to bank finance, are forced either to capitalise their own profits, or to rely upon higher interest rate loans from small banks, utilising more expensive credit sources. 88 per cent of the NBH's refinancing credits was given to the four largest banks in 1990, while their total share in the banks' own funds was only 63 per cent (see Table 9.3).

The small banks, which were originally created as SFIs to fulfil certain special financial functions, are able to maintain their market positions only by diversifying their activities. Their strategy to break out of this situation – according to experience so far – is to increase their capital with the participation of foreign capital, and to expand their market share accordingly.

The position of the large banks, on the other hand, due to the growing financial problems of the large enterprise sector, is becoming increasingly difficult. The insolvency of the Eastern markets is causing serious liquidity problems for the large state-owned enterprises incapable of switching markets. This has been accompanied by the decline of payment discipline, and by a consequent increase in creditors' losses.

2.2.4 Ownership structure of the banks
The mutual dependence which developed between the large enterprises and large banks in their credit relations is reinforced by the ownership structures of these banks (see Table 9.4). Alongside the 42 per cent direct state ownership in the four largest commercial banks, a significant proportion of the owners of these banks happen also to be their main debtors. Although prudential regulation was increasingly restricted the range of

Table 9.4. *Ownership structure of the banks' share capital, 1990*

	State enterprises	State-owned sector	Private (domestic)	Foreign
Large banks*	42	58	0	0
Medium banks	7	29	48	16
Small banks**	0	58	28	14
Total	27	49	17	7

Notes:
* Without the National Savings Bank.
** Specialised financial institutions.

possible transactions between banks and their owners, due to the inherited interdependence and bad quality of loans it is not yet possible genuinely to reduce these links. The debt–equity swaps carried out by banks in an attempt to reduce their bad loans (e.g. in Tungsram) creates cross-ownership connections between banks and enterprises; the privatisation of the large state-owned enterprises will probably further increase the extent of cross-ownership (see Chapters 5 and 7 above). Although this process could in principle help companies to solve their restructuring, control and management problems (Corbett and Mayer, 1991), its short-term effect on the banks' portfolios would be unfavourable, and would in many cases lower their quality.

The direct and indirect ownership dominance of the state has an influence on the behaviour of the banks in a number of ways. Concerning bad loans, the state had conflicting interests. On the one hand, as direct owner, it has an interest in preserving the market value of its shares. It was thus interested in the banks' stable profitability, the long-term growth of their assets, and their ability to pay dividends. In this respect, the state could be regarded as a 'good' owner – at least a better one than the rest (Bokros, 1990). So far, the 'hunger for dividends', characterising many of the enterprises holding bank shares, was not observable on the part of the state. On the other hand, it was in the state's best interest to let banks produce massive fictional profits from non-performing assets, because through taxation a significant part of these profits was collected by the state itself. That is, while in its first role the state regularly voted against high dividends enabling the banks to provision against bad and dubious loans, in its second role, by collecting taxes on fictional profits, the state largely contributed to the deterioration of the banks' market value.

The third role of the state is connected to the realisation of economic policy targets. In this capacity, during the period until now, the state has preferred to maintain the status quo, that is a highly distorted corporate structure in the economy. Any settlement on bad loans would have endangered this target; thus, by its attempt to keep large enterprises alive, the state largely contributed to the banks' present problems.

Finally, as a supervisory authority, the state has performed rather poorly. Although it has gradually 'hardened' prudential regulations, it has had no real interest in their implementation. Its interest as a fiscal authority in practice precluded it from enforcing prudential regulations.

Beside the direct ownership of the state, the ownership of state-owned firms has also had an important impact on the behaviour of commercial banks. These firms not only lacked any interest in cleaning up the banks' investment portfolios, but they themselves were largely responsible for a massive part of the bad loans. In reality, their interest in having access to easy loans was much stronger than their interest as shareholders.

2.2.5 Political influence on banks

Beside the inherited fragile investment portfolios, the mutual dependence created by cross-ownership and the distorted ownership structure, the struggle for political control over banks after the regime change is another important factor that must be analysed. The demand for, and promise of, the 'creation of order' – both prior to and following the parliamentary elections – had its impact on the discussion of the (actual and imagined) anomalies of the banking sector. Individual party ideologists, in their attempts to win the support of a society raised on an ideology alien to the market to their political objectives, were frequently tempted to foster anti-trade and anti-bank sentiments. The anti-bank and anti-banker populist campaigns (e.g. the condemnation of banks because of their interest rate policies, or because of the fact that they had turned down certain business loan applications), quite understandably, made members of the banking community (both Hungarian and foreign) cautious.

As well as the ideological overtones, the quest for a power base on the part of the coalition parties also made the situation of the banks, in particular that of the large banks, uncertain. In a pseudo-market, with eight-tenths of the economy state-owned, the government is strongly tempted to resort to such practices. The initiation of new elections of enterprise councils, and the replacement of the management of enterprises under state administrative control, also pointed in this direction. It was (and still is) feared that the process would be completed by the open or less open 'harnessing' of the banks, either by shaking up management, or by appointing board members on political grounds.

This atmosphere primarily threatens the management of the large banks, where the state holds a significant proportion of shares. As pointed out earlier, these are exactly the banks which still carry the heavy burden of inherited loans, and which so far have not been able to work out independent recovery strategies. They will thus have skilfully to manoeuvre among the political parties, the Government, and the various professional bodies.

The banking system, due to the fact that it inherited many of the characteristics of the earlier monobank system, has preserved the segmented nature of financial markets. In spite of a significant increase in the number of financial intermediaries, and a liberalisation of the regulations, the banking sector continues to bear the marks of the structure formed at the beginning of the reform.

3   The beginning of the 'second' banking reform

Any further reform of the banking sector has to address these issues and change the conditions, which it was not possible (e.g. ownership), did not seem possible (e.g. the inherited bad and dubious loans), or was not desirable (e.g. the introduction of European norms) to change in 1987. In the course of the reform, the banking sector must be freed from its dependence upon large and inefficient state-owned companies. Moreover, the segmentation of the system, as well as the framework which enabled political forces to exert influence upon banks, must be removed. Otherwise, the system will not provide efficient capital allocation, and monetary policies will be rendered ineffectual. Such a reform assumes a strong self-restraint by the political forces standing behind the government, and the reinforcing of independent supervisory authorities.

Much of the recent legislation and the actual management of issues pursued by the government reflects the recognition of these facts. The National Bank Act and the Financial Institutions Act create the opportunity for a central bank with a greater legal autonomy than before, and for a system of financial institutions operating according to European norms (see Chapter 13 below). The government proposal for the writing off of the inherited bad loans, with the budget taking on the burden, will help the banks to escape from their former imprisonment. Similarly, the government's privatisation programme does not seem to raise any theoretical barriers to majority private ownership in the financial system. Moreover, it stipulates national majority ownership only in the cases of the largest commercial banks. However, as anywhere else, the devil is hidden in the details. The stated intention to take reform measures may easily be lost in the unsatisfactorily defined, sometimes disproportionately complicated labyrinths of governmental licences, or in the reconstructed fortresses of authoritarian positions.

In the course of formulating the Financial Institutions Act (see, e.g., State Banking Supervision, 1991), stretching back now over some two years, the emphasis has been placed not only – and not even primarily – upon the conceptual argument over the desirable direction of banking system development, but rather on the extent of the supervisory authority's and the government's intervention rights.

The conceptual debate concerning the type of banking system to be created in Hungary eventually led to a compromise. The system created deviates somewhat from the European trend (in as much as it erects some barriers to universal banking). However, in practice, it provides the opportunity for commercial banks to pursue securities trading and investment fund management activities, excluded from their licences, through subsidiaries they may own. No doubt sooner or later, in the process of integrating into the EC, the legislation will be forced to abandon these restrictions and to comply with European banking regulations which allow universal banking.

The second – and perhaps more important – point of dispute during the formulation of the Act was the rights of the bank supervisory body and the government in granting new licences. The final text of the law empowers the government to consider a contribution to 'economically necessary' competition by granting a licence only in cases which involve the acquisition of more than 10 per cent of shares by foreigners. The foundation of all other financial institutions is governed by normative conditions set out to ensure the unbiased and secure operations of banks.

The third point of dispute was the question of the position of the state as an owner of financial institutions. In Hungary, as pointed out above, the capital allocation mechanism was rendered inefficient by the conflicting interests of the state as the direct and the indirect owner of the large commercial banks. Thus, it would be dangerous to exempt the state from the 25 per cent limit on shareholding, generally applicable to any single owner of a bank. However, it is quite clear that the dismantling of the 35–50 per cent share of state ownership cannot be achieved overnight. For numerous reasons, the legislators gave the state a five-year transition period to reduce the extent of its presence in the banking sector. Moreover, a special provision was made, giving the state the right to own a higher than generally stipulated share in particular financial institutions established to serve certain special purposes in the public interest, or in special (stipulated) cases in order to handle certain problems.

The Financial Institutions Act gives the right of appointing the Chairman of the nine-member Banking Supervision Committee to the Prime Minister, who also nominates three further, so-called 'independent experts' to the Committee. As from the outset two of the remaining five members will also fill political positions (Deputy Under-Secretary of State at the Ministry of Finance, or Minister without Portfolio), the supervision of financial institutions remains decisively within the sphere of government authority. This, in itself, would cause no problems if the Act did not allow ample scope for individual decisions (see, e.g. the licensing of new institutions) and banking supervisory provisions.

According to the Act, the Banking Supervision Committee is authorised to issue vital directives concerning prudential regulation (e.g. the methods of assessment of capital adequacy and liquidity, as well as aspects of debt evaluation). This way, the government has the opportunity of controlling the banking sector to an extent which, in the light of international tendencies, is hard to justify. Moreover, in the case of a government effort towards centralisation, it can be actually dangerous.

The National Bank Act and the Financial Institutions Act, as well as the government's intentions and measures taken so far only partially ensure that the second phase of the banking reform will eventually bring about far-reaching changes. The sort of autonomy provided by the National Bank Act ensures the pursuit of a responsible monetary policy only if the Bank Chairman and vice-chairmen are really independent from the government and other political forces. This independence is necessary for the NBH to be able to perform its basic task, namely to preserve the purchasing power of the national currency. However, after the appointment of the new Bank President we cannot be sure that this condition will be fulfilled: it is questionable whether a member of the main coalition party, who was previously a member of the government, will be able to withstand government pressure to loosen the tight monetary policy required in the present situation.

In spite of these worries, the intent to regulate the Hungarian banking system in accordance with standard European legislation is to be welcomed. It is also reassuring that some form of consensus has been reached between those concerned and the government on the handling of the inherited problems of the large banks. Perhaps the most important condition of a 'radical' change is the reform of bank ownership. In this respect, too, judging from various government statements, one may have positive expectations.

According to the Financial Institutions Act, the state has to sell a great part of the its shares in the large banks during the next five years. However, at least three questions still remain. First, who can buy them? Due to the weakness of domestic institutional investors, and the lack of considerable private demand for the banks' shares, foreign (mainly professional) investors must play a significant role in the privatisation of the largest banks. Second, what type of owner will be able to control the management of these banks efficiently? One can suppose that professional investors would solve the serious structural and managerial problems of the large banks in the most efficient way, but restructuring these banks needs not only capital but also special skills. The danger of excessive influence of foreign investors on the domestic economy can be reduced by offering proper terms for acquiring significant proportions of shares (e.g. an obligation to preserve the level of the bank's activity, etc.). Concerning the question of sequencing restructuring and privatisation, simultaneity seems to be a reasonable solution. The present owners of these banks, in particular the largest one, the state, are short of sufficient financial strength to clean up the banks' portfolios before privatisation.

In the present state of the reform process, there are two possibilities. There is a chance that the banking sector may separate off from the state administration, and occupy the position it deserves in a market economy. However, it still cannot be excluded that the authorities will once again attempt to gain a tight control over the large banks, and use this position to achieve their political targets: we can only hope that the 'enlightened' wing of the political forces will get the upper hand.

NOTES

1 The figures featuring in the chapter are taken from the annual reports of the National Bank of Hungary (NBH). A more detailed discussion of the topic is given in Spéder and Várhegyi (1991).
2 The National Bank Act stipulates that the increase in the total stock of loans granted by the NBH to the central budget cannot be greater than 3 per cent of the planned income of the central budget. This clause will, however, come into force only in 1995; for 1992 there is no limit at all, and for 1993–4 the limits are 5 and 4 per cent respectively.
3 This chapter deals only with the commercial banking sector. Savings institutions are mentioned only in connection with the problem of market segmentation.

REFERENCES

Bokros, L. (1990) 'Ideas on the reform of the financial institutions' (in Hungarian), *Bankszemle 1990*, **9–10**.
Corbett, J. and C.P. Mayer (1991) 'Financial reform in Eastern Europe: progress with the wrong model?', CEPR, *Discussion Paper*, **603** (September), London: CEPR.
Spéder, Z. and É. Várhegyi (1991) 'On the threshold of the second banking reform' (in Hungarian), *Jelentesek az Alagutbol, Penzugykutato* (September).
State Banking Supervision (1991) 'New Banking Act in Hungary I. Act No. LXIX, 1991 on Financial Institutions and Financial Institutional Activities'.

10 Changing structure of household portfolios in emerging market economies: the case of Hungary, 1970–89

ISTVÁN ÁBEL and ISTVÁN P. SZÉKELY

1 Introduction

Savings and portfolio allocation decisions of households are critical determinants of the transformation to a market economy in Hungary. While private (personal) savings has attracted a great deal of attention (Portes and Winter, 1978, 1980; Hulyák, 1983; Nadrai *et al.*, 1985; Riecke, 1985; Király, 1988; Mellár, 1990; Rappai, 1990), portfolio allocation has been until quite recently neglected. The only paper related to the portfolio allocation of Hungarian households is Csunderlik (1985), who tried to analyse the interrelationship of private housing investment and personal savings. In this chapter we outline the basic characteristics of portfolio allocation of Hungarian households in the 1980s. Special attention is paid to factors which will play an important role during the transformation, namely inflation, real interest rates, price and income uncertainties, changes in the financial markets, in the social security system and in housing finances. Many of these factors have so far not been candidates for explanatory variables in any analysis of savings and portfolio allocation in Hungary. This was understandable and acceptable in the period of relative economic and social stability; it is, however, no longer acceptable, as the economic transformation will increase both volatility and uncertainty.

Furthermore, one can say that these factors will become even more volatile soon, and thus that they will be even more important in explaining savings and portfolio allocation. This chapter, however, will not speculate about the future; rather we show that most of these structural elements were already present, and had a strong impact on the economy, well before the economic transformation of the late 1980s started. The data compiled here may serve further econometric testing, but the information gained from the raw comparisons of the related time series is also instructive.

In section 2 we describe the effect of changes in interest rates on real and financial assets and debt instruments in the Hungarian households' portfolios since 1970. Sections 3 and 4 deal with the structure of household assets and section 5 gives an overview of the effects of financial reforms on their liquidity, riskiness and yield. Section 6 will summarise the results of raw comparisons and specify hypotheses for future empirical work as well as their relevance and implications for constructing a transformation policy.

2   Interest rates and the accumulation of financial assets

Until 1983 when bonds were reintroduced in Hungary, the structure of household financial assets was indeed extremely simple. It consisted of cash; time and saving deposits; saving notes; concessional and 'commercial'[1] loans (so-called 'bank loans'); housing loans (mortgages); and hire purchase and personal loans. Households were serviced exclusively by the National Savings Bank (OTP) and by the Saving Co-operatives (Takarékszövetkezet). Both institutions were under direct and stringent central control. Financial products were completely standardised and issuing conditions were set directly by the central authorities. The same applies to the debt instruments available to households. The amount of net credit these institutions could issue was centrally planned; this mechanism helped to keep the household sector in a net lending position.[2] Net personal savings were channelled directly to the Hungarian National Bank (HNB) (the 'Central Bank' of the monobank system). Nominal interest rates on assets and liabilities given in Table 10.1 were centrally set by this bank and were kept practically unchanged until 1986. In fact, the central authorities regarded nominal interest rates as absolutely unimportant since, in their opinion, they had no impact whatsoever on personal savings.[3] The reasoning behind this viewpoint is simple. Households, having no other more attractive alternatives for investing their savings, were forced irrespective of the actual interest rate to put their unconsumed income into households' bank accounts. Had consumption been completely planned and controlled, and the (legal and illegal) private sector eliminated, this reasoning would have been correct. However, nothing was farther from reality than this assertion. As previous analyses clearly revealed, consumption plans were not *exogenously* set and were soft targets (Charemza and Király, 1988). Furthermore, the accumulation of financial wealth was quite strongly influenced by changes in the real *interest rates* on financial assets (see Figure 10.1).

To get a more realistic picture one has to correct the stock of financial assets by the inflationary losses on *nominal* financial assets. In the corrected

Table 10.1. *Interest rates on households' deposits and credits, 1981–90, per cent*

	1981	1985	1986	1987	1988	1989	1990
Deposits[1]							
Slight deposits	2	2	2	2	2	8	8
Operating account	5	5	5	5	7	12	17
Time deposits							
1-year	5	5	5	9	13.5	13.5	19
2-year		6	6	10	14	14	19.5
3-year		8	8	12.5	15	15	20
Savings notes							
6-years	7	9	9	13.5	16.5	16.5	24
Young people's deposits							
5-year	6	6	6	8	14	14	18
7-year	6	8	8	11	18	18	25
CDs					18	16.8	20.8
6-month TBs					9	17.5	23
Credits[2]							
Housing loans							
subsidised	0–3	0–3	0–3	0–3	0–3	19.5	25.5
commercial		8	8	8	12	22	31
Hire purchase	6–8	5–9	5–9	12	13	24	35
Personal loans	8–10	8–12	8–12	13–15	15–17	24	35
Memorandum item							
Inflation (CPI)	4.6	7.0	5.3	8.6	15.5	17.0	28.9

Notes:
1. Interest rates on deposits and CDs as of 1988 are net rates (20 per cent withholding tax is deducted).
2. Interest rates on credits as of 1988 include fees.

Source: OECD, *Country Report on Hungary* (1991).

series the fluctuation in net financial accumulation is even more pronounced, as is shown in Figure 10.2. This observed fluctuation in real savings kept in financial assets may also be a result of changes in real incomes. To determine whether the change in real interest rates or the change in real income had the stronger effect on the accumulation of financial assets one would have to make extensive econometric analyses. Our hypothesis is that real interest rates were as important as, or probably even more important than, real income in explaining portfolio behaviour in Hungary as early as the 1970s.

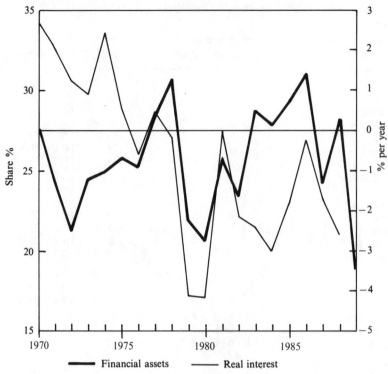

Figure 10.1   **Financial saving share in total saving and real interest rate**

3   Structure of households' assets

The relatively low level of financial service industries in Hungary is reflected in the dominance of *cash* transactions.[4] The ratio between cash and deposits is fairly stable in Figure 10.3, and the share of cash holding is fairly high by international standards.

Bank *deposits* were absolutely free from any risk and were also absolutely liquid. They were guaranteed by the state. This was a mere formality, however, as the failure of the OTP was simply inconceivable; on the other hand, this guarantee was worth nothing against the state itself. In case of serious difficulties, a sudden freezing of deposits was by no means inconceivable: as recent events in the former USSR have shown, even cash is not immune to the confiscatory intentions of central authorities. Liquidity, however, was constrained only by the underdeveloped nature of the financial service industries. For quite a long period there was no checkable account and deposits were accessible only at the branches where they were administered.

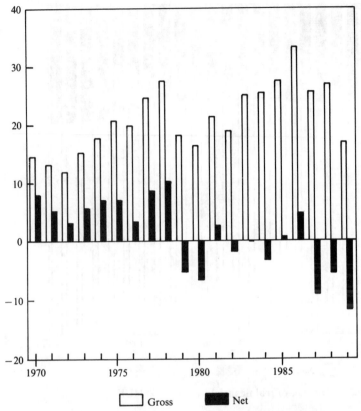

Figure 10.2   **Real annual saving in financial assets, 1980 HUF bn**

Mortgage instruments, like the other financial instruments available to households, were completely standardised and centrally controlled. A strictly limited amount of housing loan with a subsidised and fixed interest rate (the so-called 'concessional housing loan') was available to the purchasers (or prospective owners) of newly built dwellings. For quite a while, the amount available under these conditions varied also according to the type of the dwelling, giving more finance to dwellings in large apartment houses. A larger family with more children also had preferential treatment in the form of larger allowances. Consequently, this sort of mortgage had to be rationed, which led to different restrictions. First, quite a large downpayment was required.[5] Secondly, this type of mortgage was available only for newly built dwellings. The point of this restriction, apart from the apparent interest in increasing the number of

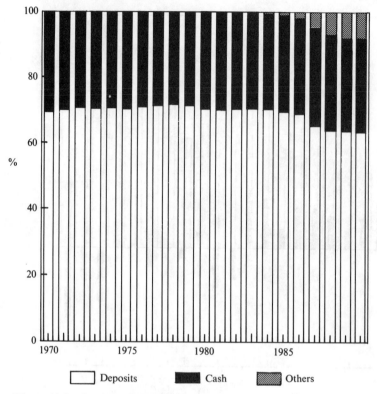

Figure 10.3   Structure of real financial wealth, 1980 HUF

residential units, was that the production and imports of building materials, as well as the capacity in the state-owned part of the residential building services' industry, was centrally planned.[6] For most of the 1970s the number of newly built houses (including owner-occupied ones) were effectively planned by central planners. The amounts of subsidised and the additional 'commercial' mortgage were consequently also kept under control.

Before 1988, a subsidised mortgage typically covered 45–50 per cent of the total price (value). This was then supplemented with the 'commercial' housing loan (also called 'bank loan'), a standardised mortgage product with a higher and variable rate. The amount made available to a household was restricted by the downpayment requirements, and by the ratio between total money earnings and total debt service of the family. In addition, employers were entitled to provide interest-free credit facilities to their employees. The employer decided the amount given, but this type

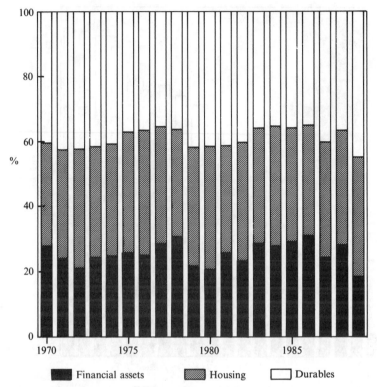

Figure 10.4   Breakdown of annual saving by asset type, in nominal terms

of credit was not eligible to be used as part of the downpayment. Finally, the state budget also provided a one-time capital transfer to first-time buyers (or builders) of new dwellings. The amount of this transfer increased with the number of children, and no money was given to families with no child.[7] Altogether buying (or building) a newly built house or apartment was heavily subsidised, and after the changes in 1991 it is still subsidised, though much less so.

It is widely believed that as a result of the adverse impact of negative real interest rates and inflationary uncertainties, households gradually switched to real assets, abandoning financial ones. Another argument says that part of the financial wealth accumulation was a result of the persistent shortage in housing and reflected forced substitution between real and financial assets. In Figure 10.4 the structure of gross wealth accumulation (without corrections for depreciation in real assets and for inflationary losses in financial assets) does not seem to support this

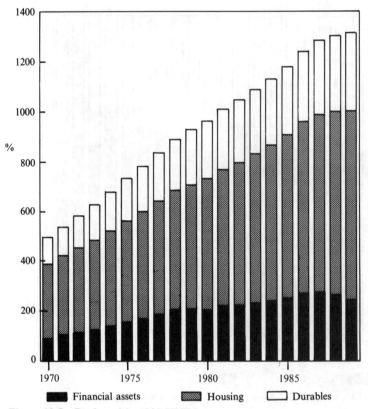

Figure 10.5   Real wealth, 1980 HUF bn

theory. Gross accumulation of financial assets fluctuated around 25 per cent, with no clear trend in either direction. The other important observation demonstrated in Figures 10.4 and 10.8 is that the share of housing investment was more or less stable. This clearly points to a trade-off between consumer durables' investment and investment in financial assets.

Calculating with real rather than with nominal values the structure is somewhat different. Although total real wealth increased throughout the whole period, this is not the case for *real financial* assets. Real financial assets decreased first in 1980 and continuously and increasingly after 1986, as shown in Figure 10.5. The share of financial assets in total (gross) wealth steadily declined after 1978, the only exception being 1986.[8] These tendencies become even more apparent if *net real financial wealth* is considered (see Figure 10.6). This graph shows the cumulative impact of

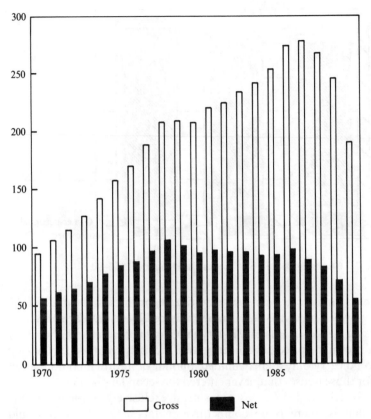

Figure 10.6   **Real financial wealth, 1980 HUF bn**

real net financial wealth accumulation already shown in Figure 10.2. It thus seems fair to say that the restructuring of households' portfolios of real and financial assets in the last twenty years has indeed been remarkable.

4   Factors influencing real asset accumulation

The most important real asset of Hungarian households is their housing stock. The owner-occupation rate was high and increasing in Hungary throughout the whole period (see Figure 10.7). The number and the value of privately-owned dwellings (being almost exclusively owner-occupied) is fairly high. There is no official estimate for the value of this stock. The figures used here are our own estimates based on information on housing investments and costs.[9]

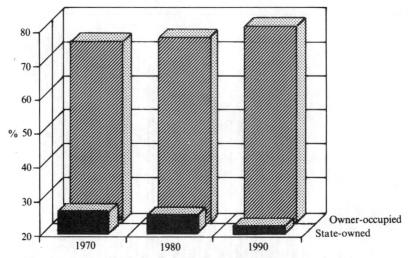

Figure 10.7   Changing structure of housing in Hungary, 1970–90

The lack of any more sophisticated estimate for the market value of the privately-owned housing stock can be explained by several facts. First, as the housing market in Hungary is very thin, very imperfect and, thus, very volatile, prevailing prices, even if they were precisely recorded (as they are not), would carry only a fairly limited amount of information on market values for those houses that never entered the secondary market. Furthermore, privately-owned houses are almost exclusively occupied by the owner, that is, there is no competitive rental market[10] which would determine some sort of market rate. Without market-determined rents, it is difficult to calculate the value of this asset derived from the yield it offers. Clearly, the centrally controlled and artificially low rents in the state-owned sector (the municipal apartments) is of no use for this purpose.

Subsidised rents in the state-owned apartment buildings and subsidisation of purchase (or building) newly built dwellings effectively killed the secondary market for housing. The supply in the state-owned rental sector, however, was rationed. The option to sell a privately-owned house and rent another one was therefore simply not readily available. The only option was to sell and buy a less expensive one, but in this case the transaction costs were extremely high. Furthermore, while this could still have been a way to withdraw equity for individuals, for households as a whole it was hardly possible, because the business sector was not allowed to invest in this market: it was strictly forbidden to convert

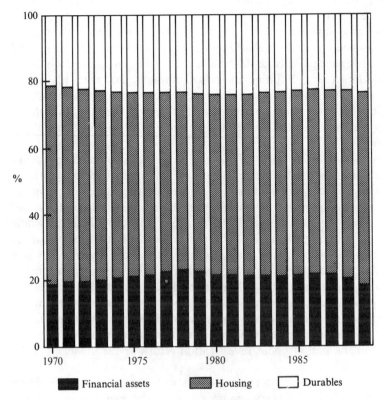

Figure 10.8   **Structure of real wealth, 1980 HUF**

residential houses to business offices. So the only way to reduce equity holdings in housing was to defer maintenance, and use the implicit income from this source for other purposes. Equity holding in housing was therefore a highly illiquid asset.

Investment in this asset was mostly motivated by demand for housing not met by the thin rental market. The pressure on families to go for owner-occupied housing increased in the 1980s. Figure 10.7 shows that the level of state provision in housing steadily declined; the number of state-owned rental apartments, as well as the newly built ones, decreased substantially after 1970. Furthermore, such rental apartments were not available in rural areas. In explaining private (personal) investment in housing one should thus also pay attention to demographic movements and other non-financial factors. Naturally, financial factors were important to moderate or encourage aspirations; nonetheless, to explain housing investment by financial factors only would probably be an ill-fated exercise.

Supply was quite inelastic due to price controls and central planning of capacities and input materials. Excess demand was bound to emerge, and in fact in many periods could be detected using empirical techniques (Csunderlik, 1985). Building materials' imports, however, played an important role in mitigating the impact of excess demand; private supply of building services was also expanding at a rapid pace. Acute shortages were consequently not overwhelming in the market for relatively cheap apartments.

Similar observations apply to *consumer durables*. The data for stocks are again our own estimates.[11] As shown in Figure 10.8, the share of investments in consumer durables, as well as the share of consumer durables in total wealth, has steadily increased. Purchase of consumer durables was the largest component in investment throughout the whole period, as shown in Figure 10.4. There is no evidence that for consumer durables as a whole there was a significant excess demand. In one particular market, the car market, however, excess demand was clearly detectable throughout the whole period (Kapitány, 1989). Certain other goods were sometimes also in very short supply for shorter periods, but no disequilibrium analysis could establish the presence of overall excess demand for the consumer durable markets in any sub-periods in the period under investigation (Hulyák, 1983; Mellár, 1990; Rappai, 1990).

Liquidity of consumer durables is also very limited, and transaction costs are high in Hungary, comparable to the experience of other countries. Selling of used cars was the only exception, making the car market very liquid, with a fairly low level of transaction costs and high profits for dealers. Often as a result of rationed supply in new cars and excess demand secondary (free) market prices of used cars exceeded the prices of new ones. Although for many people this appeared as a capital gain, in fact it is not clear whether it really was. To buy a new car one had to register for it with a heavy advance payment (50 per cent of the prevailing purchase price). This advance payment was kept on a non-interest-bearing account which was not transferable. As the purchase prices at which the actual transaction took place were not fixed, and the waiting time on the average was two–three years, a substantial inflationary loss accrued in most cases for households. Approximately free market prices fluctuated around the present value of the purchaser's investment plus some premium depending on market conditions.

5   The impact of reforms of the financial system

The first important financial innovation in the 1980s was the introduction of bonds in 1983. The first bonds issued to households appeared in 1984, when the secondary trade was also started; the introduction of bonds followed the segmented pattern of the financial sector. The bond market for households and for corporate investors developed in different ways. Until 1985, bonds issued to households could finance only community investment projects and they embodied contributions to these projects rather than financial investments. Accordingly, the amount of this sort of bond was negligible (1.1 per cent of total household deposits). In 1986, these restrictions were lifted and bonds became financial assets heavily demanded by private investors. Until 1987, the market grew very fast and there was an excess demand on the market. Since, due to the excess demand, bonds were perfectly liquid and, due to the state guarantee, very safe, households regarded them as higher interest rate deposits. The only visible difference was that some minimal amount of investment was necessary. Yields, also set by the Ministry of Finance, were as much as 3 to 4 points higher (around 11 per cent) than the then prevailing interest rates on deposits, or the inflation rate. Yields on bonds, similarly to yields on other financial assets, were not subject to income tax. Not surprisingly, the market boomed, bonds issued in 1987 totalling HUF 12.7 bn (more than the increase in total household deposits), and the value of bonds in circulation reaching HUF 19.6 bn.

This situation changed dramatically in 1988, and there are several important conclusions to be drawn from what happened. Bonds issued to households suddenly lost all their advantages, while the risk attached to them became clear. Rates on household deposits were increased by 3 per cent in October 1987 and by a further 2.5 per cent in June 1988 (including premium). The interest rate on one-year deposits reached 13.5 per cent net of tax (see Table 10.1). The state guarantee on bonds issued to households was terminated, and the bond market collapsed. Although underwriting banks (mainly the Budapest Bank) tried to preserve the liquidity of bonds by repurchase, the capital loss on bonds amounted to 10 per cent. With the introduction of personal income tax, bond yields, similarly to yields on other financial assets, became subject to a 20 per cent withholding tax, while the risk attached to the bond was not recognised by tax regulations.

As a consequence, the amount of new issues returned to the level of 1984 and secondary trading was almost exclusively confined to the repurchase by underwriting banks (holding 25 per cent of bonds of this type by the end of 1988). Commercial banks took several steps to keep the secondary market alive but the inflationary expectations were (and still are) too high and volatile and yields on alternative short-term financial assets too high to make bonds competitive.

The next step in the development of the Hungarian financial markets was that commercial banks were allowed to issue certificates of deposits (CDs) to households, and by the end of 1988 the value of CDs in circulation reached HUF 5.6 bn (almost seven times more than the value of bonds issued to households and 28.6 per cent of the increase in household deposits in savings institutions in 1988). In addition new and popular financial assets issued to households emerged (e.g. Treasury Bills, see below) while the households' propensity to save in domestic financial assets declined. In 1989, the value of new issues increased dynamically, while household deposits decreased.

A further important measure taken in January 1989 was to lift the restriction on commercial banks dealing with households. This step, however, did not mean that interest rate ceilings on household deposits were abolished immediately. They remained policy tools until 1992.

The next step in opening towards households was the implementation of Treasury Bills (TBs) in March 1988. Due to liquidity and competitive rates (8, 9, 10 per cent for three-, six- and nine-month TBs, see Table 10.1), TBs became quite popular. By the end of 1988, the value of TBs in circulation had reached HUF 4 bn (15 per cent of accumulation of financial assets in 1988). By that time, interest rates on TBs had been substantially increased (to 16, 17.5 and 19 per cent respectively) keeping the competitiveness of this form of investment.

It is important to notice that the financial instruments which became popular were all perfectly safe, highly liquid and artificially high-yield assets.[12] If any of these characteristics changed they were immediately abandoned: the best example is the history of bonds. Currently, households do not seem to be willing to buy long-term illiquid financial assets, but changes in inflationary expectations will probably bring about changes in this respect.

6   Conclusions

Transformation and restructuring in the Hungarian economy requires resources. Although an important but relatively small part of investment will undoubtedly be (direct) foreign investment, it is not likely that foreign investment will provide sufficient financing for the transformation. Domestic private savings will consequently play a crucial role, and saving and portfolio allocation decisions will be of foremost importance for monetary policies. This is even more the case if we take into consideration that the Hungarian economy inherited a distorted saving pattern and households' portfolio allocation mechanism. Starting in the late 1970s, inflation has accelerated and real interest rates on (time and saving) deposits (being centrally controlled) and also on concessional housing loans (and some other loans given to households) have become negative. This has had a strong impact on savings in general and on portfolio allocation in particular. The saving ratio dropped dramatically in 1979 and only slowly recovered during the first half of the 1980s. Households continuously restructured their portfolios, gradually abandoning financial instruments and favouring consumer durables and real estate.

The general belief that interest rates cannot play any role in the economy has rendered the problem of portfolio allocation irrelevant for Eastern European economies: this view, however, is not justified by empirical analysis and cannot any longer be supported. There is a vital need to investigate the impact of interest rate(s) on savings and portfolio allocation in transforming economies.

Economic transformation, at least in the short and medium run, will inevitably lead to increased uncertainty. There are potentially substantial uncertainties inherent in holding long-lived real assets and financial equity investments during the transformation period. Some of the real assets and financial equities may depreciate, or appreciate less than the overall rate of inflation. So the traditional assumption that inflation, depreciating money's purchasing power, makes it unwise to hold money unnecessarily (beyond what is needed to finance current transactions), or any other asset denominated in nominal terms, may not be operationally correct. Households and firms might react to higher expected inflation by increasing their demand to hold money and short- and long-term debt assets.

During the transformation debt assets may depreciate if the issuer goes bankrupt, or threatens to do so. All marketable debt assets will fall in nominal and real value if nominal interest rates rise (as is likely in the transformation). On the other side of the balance sheet, debt liabilities have their own dangers: the payments owed may become more burdensome than expected if inflation is less than expected. The somewhat unorthodox consequence is that risk-averse households and firms may respond to inflation by increasing their demands for money and debt assets over time.

For existing asset portfolios at any point of time, the conventional assumptions are plausible: higher expected inflation should encourage households and firms to hold more real assets and financial equity claims to real assets, while decreasing their holdings of long- and short-term debt assets and money, and increasing their indebtedness.

If expected inflation increases stock demands for real assets and equities, then the stock demands for debt assets and money must decrease. Within existing portfolios, households and firms cannot hedge the uncertainties of holding more real assets and financial equities by holding more debt assets and money. Saving flows alter this portfolio liquidity constraint over time as additional demand for real assets and equities can be satisfied without a concomitant decrease in the stock demand for additional debt and money. Households and firms may simultaneously decide to increase their demand to hold all components of their asset portfolios, provided that saving flows are positive.

This possibility, however, is not always advantageous. What will households and firms want to do with whatever saving flows there are? The answers to this question are very important in determining the outcome of the transformation process.

Alternative policies for reducing uncertainties and disadvantageous portfolio adjustments are an important – if not the most important – element of the transformation strategy, but most of these questions have remained unexplored until now.

NOTES

1 We use the term 'commercial' loan, to underline the difference between this type of loan and the concessional loan. The difference, however, was only minor. 'Commercial' loans carried a higher and variable interest rate but at the same time they were controlled in exactly the same way as any other loans earmarked to households.
2 Partly because of the backwarded financial intermediation and also because of job and social security guaranteed by the state, the long-term savings' motive was very weak and the net lending position of households was rather low in the 1960s and 1970s.
3 Furthermore, personal savings were also considered unimportant. A surprising position, but explained by the fact that financial resources were mainly channelled to investors through non-market mechanisms.
4 Checkable accounts were introduced only in the 1980s, and the first ATM in Hungary was installed in 1989. It is notoriously difficult and slow to transfer money balances even inside the country.
5 In the case of self-managed projects and/or houses built by the prospective owners – being the dominant case in the villages and smaller towns, but quite frequent in the larger towns as well – own-cash contribution (upfront payment) had to be spent first before any money could be drawn on the credit line provided.
6 The only affordable housing option for the majority of households in towns was to buy a cheaper (but consequently rationed) apartment in an apartment house built exclusively by large state-owned construction companies.
7 Currently, the amounts involved are as follows. For a family with one child it is HUF 50,000, with two children 150,000, and with three children 400,000. Any additional child adds 100,000 to this amount. These amounts should be

compared to cost of approximately HUF 30,000–35,000 per square metre in an average Budapest apartment.

8 This happened as a result of the combined impact of the change in the structure of nominal and real wealth accumulation and the inflationary losses on financial assets.

9 The estimations were made as follows. The estimated cost of a square metre of dwelling in 1980 was taken as basis. A quality improvement of 2 per cent a year was allowed for. This gave the constant value of one newly built square metre. This was multiplied by the amount of newly built square metres. The existing housing stock in 1950, from which year the recursive estimation started, was estimated to be equal to the real value of stock built between 1950 and 1960. The Hungarian CSO publishes figures on depreciation of private housing stock. The constant depreciation rate was set to match this figure for 1980. Parenthetically, this provides a fairly low real depreciation rate (around 1 per cent a year), and even with this rate, the figures by the CSO for the recent years seem grossly under-estimated. This might be a very rough estimate, although nominal values per dwelling derived from this estimation and information on housing price index seemed quite realistic.

10 There was a tiny market niche for foreigners, with soaring rents frequently denominated in hard currency. The segment, however, is highly distorted due to the nature of the housing market as a whole; it provides no reliable information on rents in general. In spite of the soaring rents, it was exceptional to build houses for rental purposes in this market; most of the apartments were rented out by people temporarily abroad.

11 The initial stock of 1960 is assumed to be equal to four times the constant price purchases in that year. This assumption is based on information available for certain types of consumer durables per household and on the numbers of purchases of these goods in the same year. The depreciation rate is taken to be 10 per cent in line with other estimates known in the literature. A consumer price index was used for deflating current price data.

12 'Artificially high' in the sense that it was the state itself who offered (or entitled others to offer) rates, which were higher than the controlled rates on deposits.

REFERENCES

Ábel, I. and I.P. Székely (1990) 'Credit, imports, and inventories', *Engineering Costs and Production Economics*, pp. 11–17.

Charemza, W.W. and J. Király (1988) 'Plans and exogeneity: the genetic-teleological dispute revisited', University of Leicester Department of Economics, *Working Paper*, **71**.

Csunderlik, Cs. (1985) 'The interrelationship of private housing and personal savings: an econometric disequilibrium analysis of the Hungarian housing market 1960–1983', paper presented at the Fifth World Congress of the Econometric Society, Boston (August).

Hulyák, K. (1983) 'Disequilibrium in consumption' (Egyensúlyhiányok a lakosság fogyasztásában I. II.), *Statisztikai Szemle*, **61(3)**, pp. 229–43; **61(4)**, pp. 369–80.

Kalocsay, T., G. Papp, and W. Riecke (1988) 'Household saving and accumulation of financial assets in Hungary' (A magánháztartások megtakarításai és pénzvagyonképzése Magyarországon) (in Hungarian), mimeo.

Kapitány, Zs. (1989) 'Kereslet és kínálat a 80-as évek autopicán, *Közgazdasági Szemle*, **36(6)**, pp. 592–611.

Király, J. (1988) 'Aggregate household saving: empirical evidence for Hungary', Institute of Methodology and Information, National Planning Office, *Working Paper*, **2181/1/XX/1988**.

Király, J. and G. Kőrösi (1990) 'Consumption, housing, and money demand in Hungary', paper presented at the World Congress of the Econometric Society, Barcelona (August).

Mellár, T. (1990) 'Disequilibrium and spill over' (Egyensúlytalanság és a piacok közötti kapcsolatok) (in Hungarian), *Közgazdasági Szemle*, **37(12)**, pp. 1333–50.

Nadrai, L., I. Szalkai and J. Száz (1985) 'Credit policy and the balance of payment position' (A hitelpolitika és a fizetési mérleg egyensúlya) (in Hungarian, *Szigma*, **18**, pp. 69–88.

Portes, R. and A. Santorum (1987) 'Money and consumption goods market in China', *Journal of Comparative Economics*, **11(3)**, pp. 354–71.

Portes, R. and D. Winter (1978) 'The demand for money and for consumption goods in centrally planned economies', *Review of Economics and Statistics*, **60**, pp. 8–18.

(1980) 'Disequilibrium estimates for consumption goods markets in centrally planned economies', *Review of Economic Studies*, **47**, pp. 137–59.

Rappai, G. (1990) 'A disequilibrium model of the consumption goods market' (A fogyasztási javak piacának nem egyensúlyi modellje) (in Hungarian), *Statisztikai Szemle*, **68**, pp. 663–77.

Riecke, W. (1985) 'About the money saving of households' (A lakóssági pénzmegtakarításról), *Szigma*, **18**, pp. 9–26.

Santorum, A. (1987) 'Expenditure and portfolio behaviour in China, London: Birbeck College, mimeo.

Discussion of Part Three

JOHN P. BONIN

To characterise household portfolios in Hungary from 1970 to 1989, Ábel and Székely in Chapter 10 construct estimates of the values of the housing stock and the stock of consumer durables (real assets). The authors concentrate on demand-side explanations for changes in the stocks and resulting flows. They describe the restructuring of real and financial assets over a twenty-year period as 'remarkable' and claim to debunk the myth that households switched to real assets because of negative real interest rates. However, the institutional changes in financial markets during this period which are thoroughly described in the chapter seem to support an alternative explanation.

Ábel and Székely identify a strong positive relationship between fluctuations in the real interest rate and the share of financial assets in savings by plotting these series in Figure 10.1 where the percentage of savings allocated to financial assets is related to changes in the real interest rate. Taking the period from 1978–87 where the correlation seems strongest, an alternative explanation focusing on institutional changes and policy is equally plausible. In a previous work, Ábel and Székely (1988) have shown a close relationship between fiscal deficits and household liquidity. In 1979, restrictive fiscal policy led to a drop in living standards for the first time in the decade (as the adjustment to changes in the external environment could no longer be avoided). Austerity measures and the second oil shock affected household liquidity significantly so that the sharp drop in the share of financial assets in 1979 and 1980 could be attributable to policy changes rather than to changes in the real interest rate. Furthermore, the increase in the share of financial assets from 1984 to a peak in 1986 occurred during a time period in which households were provided with a new financial instrument, secure high-yielding bonds. Subsequently, the government guarantee on these bonds was removed and relative yields fell due to inflation and an increase in deposit interest rates. By 1987, the bond market had collapsed and the share of financial assets dropped precipitously. In 1988, even though the real interest rate declined, this share rose again due to the introduction of two new instruments, bank CDs and Treasury Bills, to household portfolios. Consequently, supply-side phenomena may explain the changes in the percentage of savings allocated to financial assets at least as well as the demand-side changes in the real interest rate.

From 1975–8, the real interest rate was essentially zero and from 1979 it has been negative. Does the data in Chapter 10 support the claim that households moved toward real assets in response to a negative real interest rate? Using the nominal flow data in Figure 10.4, the share of financial assets in savings peaks in 1985 and 1986. In 1989, this measure drops precipitously by almost ten percentage points to its lowest value over the period. By that time, the real interest rate had been negative for ten years. Regarding the distribution between real assets, the share of housing peaks in 1976 with a second milder peak in 1980 and fluctuates about 6 per cent over the entire period while the share of durables peaks in 1989 and is more volatile than the share of financial assets. In essence, durables seem to bear the brunt of volatility of both financial assets and housing in the flow data and the only appreciable downturn in the share of financial assets occurs at the very end of the period. The authors' data does debunk successfully the myth that households fled from financial assets during the long period of negative real interest rates.

To analyse the restructuring of household portfolios over the twenty-year period, we consider the (real) stock data in Figure 10.8. Financial assets begin and end the period at about 19 per cent of the portfolio with a peak at 23.3 per cent in 1978 (and an immediate drop in 1979 to 21.5 per cent which equals both the 1975 and the 1985 value). The trough in housing corresponds to the peak in financial assets in 1978 at a value of 53.2 per cent compared with beginning and ending values of 59.7 per cent and 57.5 per cent respectively. By 1975, durables equal 23.5 per cent of the stock and vary less than 1 percentage point from that year until the end of the period. What seemed to be fairly volatile behaviour in the flows is not reflected in volatile movements in the stocks due to the low volume of savings and the adjustment for inflation. From 1970–5, durables and financial assets each gained about 2.5 per cent as housing dropped almost 5 per cent. In 1988 and 1989, housing regained about 2.5 per cent almost entirely at the expense of financial assets. Consequently, from 1975 to the present the only major restructuring of household portfolios occurs in the last two years when the percentage of financial assets falls and housing increases. It is perhaps remarkable that such a restructuring took place when new financial instruments were made available to households.

Although Chapter 10 is quite ambitious, it does not address a tantalising policy question regarding the most recent period. In 1991, the government announced the end of long-term housing mortgages at 3–3.5 per cent and required from January 1992 that holders of these mortgages either pay market interest rates on half of the outstanding debt (the other half is forgiven) or pay 15 per cent on the entire debt. If the trend observed in Chapter 10 until 1989 continued through 1991, the housing component of household portfolios would be approaching its 1970 level of almost 60 per cent. The impact of the government's new mortgage policy on the structure and liquidity of household portfolios would be an interesting issue for the authors to analyse.

REFERENCE

Ábel, I. and I. Székely (1988) 'Money and Causality in CPEs', Budapest University of Economics, *Working Paper*, **88/3**.

LUCIAN IONESCU

History has always been a mixture of continuity and discontinuity: the evolution of the Hungarian economy is typical in this respect. I think that Éva Várhegyi's Chapter 9 has especially succeeded in depicting the intricate nature of a transition period.

As regards the continuity aspect of contemporary history, I would prefer to quote János Kornai's opinion, according to which, after the dramatic events of the 1950s,

> Hungary became a peculiar blend of more consumer-oriented economic policies (called 'Goulash communism' in the West) and belt-tightening, of more autonomy for the state-owned firms (in the spirit of 'market socialism') and thousands of interventions in their affairs, of rigid central controls and free markets, and also of more permissive attitudes towards the bureaucratic restrictions on private property and private activities. The same ambiguity existed in the political sphere (Kornai, 1990, p. 14).

I also agree that this 'peculiar blend' mostly explains the pioneering role of Hungary both in trying to reform the former socialist system ('the limitations' of the first banking reform being included here) and in starting, after 1989, a radical transformation of the whole political and economic system. But even in the latter case, I think 'that long prehistory' has somehow immunised Hungarian society against the 'Big Bang' fashion of the early 1990s. This makes a striking contrast with the Polish case, which was a *wunderkind* in 1990 and almost a failure at the beginning of 1992.

As Ábel and Bonin (1992) have put it, 'the gradualist policies in Hungary . . . were successful in producing less volatility than the Polish "Big Bang". Significant institutional and legal changes accompanied the gradualist policies in Hungary, while the "Shock Therapy" in Poland may be suffering from a lack of institutional development and legislative lag'.

Another strong feature of Éva Várhegyi's chapter consists in the well-balanced way in which it has dealt with both the fallible and the promising aspects not only of the first banking reform, but also of the ongoing second one. So, stimulated by the rich content of the chapter – in both ideas and information – I will particularly comment on the role of the banking system (including the Central Bank) in the transition period to a market-oriented economy. First of all, I will refer to the problem of autonomy and efficiency of the Central Bank's monetary and credit policies. I will try to synthesise some remarks based on more general traits of the transformation process in East European economies.

It goes without saying that a high degree of autonomy of the National Bank is a 'necessary precondition for the pursuit of a responsible monetary policy'. This is a necessary but by no means a self-sufficient warrant for the way in which a Central Bank should play its role and fulfill its tasks. On the one hand, I have in my mind the rather surprisingly high variance in the autonomy of the Western developed countries' Central Banks (from the Banque de France to the Bundesbank, passing through the Bank of England or the US Federal Reserve System). On the other hand, beyond this variety of particular cases, mainly due to national traditions, there are institutions and mechanisms specific to all mature and developed market economies.

A (more or less) autonomous monetary policy could therefore really be efficient only as an organic component of a 'policy mix' specific to the 'fine-tuning' process within developed market economies. As for East European countries, they are facing quite another sort of a challenge: how to create – or, in some cases, to recreate – the structure, infrastructure and operational mechanisms of a market economy.

Under these circumstances, the necessary autonomy and the role of the East European central banks have specific needs. I will mention only what I consider as major characteristics and responsibilities:

(a)   to correlate the stabilisation policy with the structural adjustment process
(b)   to contribute to the coherence between monetary policy, fiscal policy and the industrial restructuring process
(c)   to favour the privatisation and demonopolisation strategy at a macroeconomic level

This approach may seem contradictory but, in fact, it is only complementary to fulfilling the 'normal' functions[1] of a Central Bank with the environment characteristic to the transition from a centrally planned economy to a market-oriented one. I would also emphasise that my approach should not be taken as pleading in favour of an alleged subordination of the National Bank to the government.

My main concern is to work out a scenario able to avoid jumping from one extreme to another. It is a well-known fact that the former socialist economy obsessively relied on the material aspects of production, while the monetary dimensions were neglected, minimised or even distorted. The other extreme would now be to feed the illusion of an efficient

Western-like monetary policy pursued by a 'neutral' Central Bank, indifferent to what is happening in the 'real' economy.

Obviously, one of the hardest legacies of the command economy is the rift between the so-called real and monetary aspects of economic life. This is why a Central Bank in an East European country should accomplish a function different from the 'classical' ones: to contribute to recreating the normal link between the monetary and the real economy. Otherwise, the increasing tensions between a restrictive monetary policy, based on criteria specific to mature market economies, and a still rigid transition economy, will ultimately provoke and amplify 'the anti-bank and anti-banker populist manifestations'.

In my opinion, the key to the above-mentioned tensions and pitfalls consists in a three-pronged approach:

(1) passing from a *de jure* to a *de facto* stage in the operation of the two-tier banking system, by setting up and developing monetary and financial markets
(2) founding a new type of relationship between the banking community and 'real' economic activity, based on an ever-denser and more experienced network of banking and financial consultancy
(3) creating and developing an interconnected banking infrastructure at the level of Eastern Europe, as a precondition favouring the integration into the EC single financial market.

There are therefore two 'internal' dimensions and an international one. Finally, I consider the paradox of a European evolution characterised by two opposing processes: the deepening of West European integration (under the auspices of the Maastricht agreement) and the dangerous fragmentation of Eastern Europe (with Yugoslavia as the most dramatic example). Neither politics and ideology nor arms and violent conflicts can solve this European paradox. I believe that one of the few hopes for a peaceful and prosperous future lies in evolving a real banking and financial community[2] comprising the whole continent, even though I am aware, as Dr Várhegyi writes, that 'the devil is hidden in the details'.

NOTES

1 By 'normal functions' I mean anti-inflationary monetary and credit policies; supervision of the commercial banks and other banking institutions; equilibrium of the balance of payments; stable exchange rate policy.
2 I had the opportunity to deal more with this subject in a paper included in John Williamson (ed.), *Currency Convertibility in Eastern Europe*, Washington, D.C.: Institute for International Economics (September 1991), pp. 270–1.

REFERENCES

Ábel, I. and J.P. Bonin (1992) 'The "Big Bang" versus "Slow but Steady": a comparison of the Hungarian and the Polish transformations', CEPR, *Discussion Paper*, **626** (January), London: CEPR.
Kornai, J. (1990) *The Road to a Free Economy*, New York: W.W. Norton.

COLIN MAYER

Éva Várhegyi's Chapter 9 surveys the progress that has been made in reforming the Hungarian banking system, and what still remains to be done. She describes how reform was introduced in the form of two-tier banking to replace the old monolithic banking system. However, serious problems remained in at least five areas.

First, there was too much domination by the state of the appointment of the Chairman, in the use of the Central Bank as an instrument of government deficit financing, and in the direction of finance and credit policy.

Second, the existence of bad debts undermined the operation of the commercial banks and resulted in too little competition in the provision of services. Accounting measures provided little guidance on the scale of the problem because they allowed banks to record large profits while a high proportion of their loans were non-performing.

Third, there was too much concentration in banking. The four largest banks, excluding the National Savings Bank, accounted for 70 per cent of the value of assets on bank balance sheets. 80 per cent of the National Bank's refinancing served the four largest banks.

Fourth, there was too much segmentation of the banking market, resulting in inadequate competition. Most loans went to large companies; small companies had to rely on own funds or high interest rate borrowings.

Finally, there was poor regulation, and risks were exacerbated by the fact that a high proportion of bank ownership was associated with companies to which banks lent.

Recent reform is introducing:

* Greater independence of the Central Bank from government
* The writing off of bad loans
* Privatisation of banks
* The ability of banks to undertake some universal banking functions
* An attempt to introduce European-style bank regulation.

The chapter argues that what is still required is:

* Full universal banking
* Less state ownership
* Limitation of the power of government over banks, in particular, that
  the Chairman and vice-chairman should be made independent
* Less dependence of banks on lending to large enterprises.

I am fully in agreement with Dr Várhegyi's assessment. The factors that
she has identified – excessive state ownership and control over banking,
too much concentration of banking, and too much segmentation of
banking – are precisely the ones that differentiate Western from East
European banking. For example, while most banks have the legal form of
joint stock companies, they are owned by the state, by other banks or by
enterprises. They may have several shareholders but all are themselves
state-owned. Furthermore the dominant shareholder is the State Property
Agency (SPA). The banking sector is therefore for the present state-
owned and controlled.

There are a number of other problems that I would mention: shortage of
skilled personnel and inadequate training of bank staff; absence of proper
credit evaluation of prospective borrowers; absence of properly functioning bankruptcy laws that permit banks to liquidate poorly performing
loans; inadequate regulation of banks and investor protection; and poor
accounting by enterprises.

There are a few areas where Dr Várhegyi could have given some more
attention to the linkages that should exist between the state and the
Central Bank, between the Central Bank and private banks, and between
private banks and the enterprise sector.

First, on the relation between the state and the Central Bank, questions
about the appropriate degree of independence of the Central Banks from
government, and in particular fiscal policy, have been much debated in
the West in the context of European Monetary Union. I agree with the
proposition that the primary objective of the Central Bank should be the
control of inflation and that this requires a high degree of independence of
the Central Bank from government. However, there are a variety of forms
of independence, and attention needs to be given to other areas: these
include the composition of the board of the Central Bank; the appoint-

ment of the Chairman; periods of appointment of members of the board and senior executives; rights of government to be consulted about policy; and limitations on the extent to which governments can intervene in decision-taking. Care needs to be taken to determine precisely what form 'independence' should take.

Second, there are some areas in which state involvement in Central Bank activities cannot be avoided. This is primarily associated with regulation. There is much debate about what type of institution is best suited to regulation. There are questions about whether regulation should be undertaken by Central Banks or by independent institutions. It is clear that two types of regulatory function can be distinguished: interventions that are restricted to the provision of liquidity to otherwise solvent banks, and the treatment of insolvency.

Problems of liquidity are appropriately dealt with by Central Banks but insolvency problems, in particular those that can give rise to widespread bank failures, may have fiscal implications arising from the finance that is needed to bail out the banking system; that is precisely what occurred in the USA. Those ministries that are responsible for bailing out banks will wish to be able to take control from the Central Bank when financial systems appear to be vulnerable. Governments will also wish to express concern about activities that may threaten banking systems as a whole, such as concentration of lending in particular sectors of the economy. Separation of government and Central Bank should be increased but cannot be expected to be complete. While there are threats to banking systems from poorly performing enterprises then separation will be particularly difficult to achieve, which is a further justification for writing off loans.

Third, regulation creates an interlinkage between Central Banks and commercial banks. The Central Bank needs to be involved in the evaluation (screening) of banks and their subsequent monitoring. Central Banks should be able to intervene where there is evidence of potential bank failure to correct poor management and, if necessary, arrange mergers. One lesson that we have learnt from US savings and loans failures is that intervention should not wait until banks are insolvent: problems of bank failures can be diminished by prompt intervention while banks have positive present values.

Finally, there is no discussion in the chapter about one of the most controversial areas of interlinkages, that is between banks and enterprises. The question that arises here is the extent to which bank control of firms dominates that of financial markets. There is a longer history of close relations between banks and industry in Hungary than in many other East European countries, and there are some signs that it is re-emerging. Evidence from the West suggests that ownership of enterprises by banks is of limited significance. Control by banks is restricted to periods of corporate failure and restructuring. However, banks may be particularly important in stimulating the interlinkages that exist between enterprises themselves in most of Western Europe. In other words, banks have been important in forming networks of firms and financing the development of those networks.

Turning to Júlia Király's Chapter 8, this identifies three main sources of finance for the Hungarian banking sector: the rediscounting of overdraft credit and commercial bills and credit with foreign exchange collateral, deposits of HUF and foreign exchange, and interbank borrowing. It identifies four main uses of finance: required reserves which are a fixed proportion of deposits, investments in Treasury Bills and CDs of the Central Bank, loans, and accumulations of free reserves.

It then discusses the interest rates that are relevant to these flows. The rediscount rate of domestic and foreign currency deposits is taken as set by the Central Bank. The deposit rate on domestic and foreign exchange and the loan rate are endogenously determined. The interest rate on Treasury Bills and CDs are assumed to be the same as the interest rate on foreign currency transactions; however, this does not accord very well with the diagram of interest rates that is presented in Figure 8.1. The model solves for the interbank rate from the sources and uses identity with the restriction that the aggregate of interbank lending has to be zero. Endogenous interest rates are deposit rates on domestic and foreign exchange, the loan rate and the interbank rate which clears the market.

This is a brave attempt to set out how a money market model should be constructed for Hungary though no attempt is made to provide any estimates. My one concern is that the problems associated with doing this are rather greater than the chapter suggests; these concerns in part stem from considering Chapters 9 and 8 in tandem. The first concern comes from the particularly risky nature of a high proportion of loans in Hungary. The relation between the endogenous (deposit and loan) and exogenous interest rates is a function of risk: risks of corporate failures determine lending/interbank rate margins; risks of bank failure affect the deposit/interbank rate margin. It may be possible to identify some measure of riskiness of bank loans which varies across banks and time, but clearly that will not be easy to accomplish.

Second, differentials depend on levels of government guarantees to the banking sector and to the corporate sector, in particular to large corporates. The greater the implicit guarantee by government of corporate borrowers and banks, the lower the risk premia. But that means that a large part of the determination of interest rates involves evaluating the behaviour of government and the central bank.

Third, the involvement of the state is felt still more acutely in its direct ownership and control of firms. Intervention by the state will limit the degree to which financial flows can be linked to interest rate differentials. Optimising behaviour along the lines suggested in Chapter 8 will become a reality only when some of the proposals for independence that Chapter 9 considers are implemented.

I learned a lot from both these chapters, which make an important contribution to our understanding of the problems of Hungary's transformation in this area.

Part Four

Foreign debt and monetary policy

11 Hungary's foreign debt: controversies and macroeconomic problems

GÁBOR OBLATH

1 Introduction

External debt is perhaps the most onerous economic legacy of the 'pre-democratic' regime that ruled in Hungary for more than forty years. By 1989, Hungary had become the country with the highest *per capita* foreign debt (US\$ 1950). There are grounds for questioning the relevance of this particular indicator, but other economically more meaningful debt indicators also point to the country's extremely heavy indebtedness in international comparison (see Tables 11A.1 and 11A.2 in the Appendix, p. 220).

The special feature of Hungary in this respect is that, in contrast with other similarly (or even less) indebted developing and Eastern European countries, it has at all times fully serviced its foreign debts; no attempt has been made to renegotiate (reschedule) external payment obligations. Whether this is an asset or a liability is one of the issues to be treated in this chapter.

But for the present, continuing to service fully external debts accumulated by the pre-democratic political system is one of the top priorities of the democratically elected Hungarian government. This policy is firmly supported not only the National Bank of Hungary (NBH) (the formal debtor) but also by the parliamentary opposition. However, this does not imply full agreement everywhere on the government's debt strategy. Some political organisations in the country and independent experts both in Hungary and abroad have repeatedly questioned both the feasibility and the rationality of adhering to the present debt strategy. To be sure, the proponents of an alternative approach to debt management are far from unanimous in their proposals and in their perceptions of the situation and prospects of the Hungarian economy. This chapter, besides presenting evidence on the process of debt accumulation, discusses some of the macroeconomic implications of foreign debt management, and addresses the pros and cons of both maintaining, and breaking with, the present debt strategy.

Since the chapter treats not only present issues but also past trends, the reader should be reminded that Hungary, until March 1991, had two types of external trade and payments regimes: one with the East (the COMECON), accounted in (transferable) roubles, and another with the rest of the world, mostly in convertible currencies. The subject of this chapter is the country's debt in convertible currencies. While Hungary is heavily indebted in convertible currencies it is a new creditor towards ex-COMECON countries (primarily the republics of the former USSR).[1] Although one section deals with interrelations between Eastern (non-convertible) and Western (convertible) trade, the focus is on trade and payments in convertible currencies. Therefore, unless indicated otherwise, all data, statements and explanations concerning the country's external trade and payments refer to the non-Eastern (non-rouble) part of Hungary's external sector. The share of the latter was roughly 50 per cent in the early and mid-1980s, but it steadily decreased during the late 1980s. In 1991, Hungary, like other former COMECON countries, switched over to convertible currency payments in intraregional transactions. Partly due to the switchover, and partly because of the economic collapse of East European trading partners, mutual trade declined sharply: in late 1991 the share of Eastern trade (now in dollars) was close to 15 per cent of Hungary's total trade.

The chapter is organised as follows: first the process of Hungary's foreign debt accumulation is discussed (section 2). Next various approaches to the treatment of the debt problem are presented (section 3). Third, the macroeconomic consequences of debt management are treated under different assumptions (section 4). Finally, the issue of revising the present debt strategy is addressed in the context of the Western approach to providing assistance for the East European transformation (section 5).

2   The accumulation of foreign debt

The accumulation of foreign debt has not been a gradual process in Hungary: there were two waves leading to sharp increases in indebtedness. The first started in 1973, when gross and net debt stood at US$ 2.1 and 0.8 bn respectively, and lasted till the early 1980s, reaching US$ 11.4 and 7.5 bn respectively.[2] Between 1980 and 1984, there was a lull: external debts even declined somewhat. The second wave started in 1985:

by 1990 the country's indebtedness had increased more than twofold. Gross debt reached US$ 21.2 bn, net debt grew to US$ 15.9 bn.

In 1991, a decline of foreign debts could be observed: in the third quarter gross and net debt stood at US$ 20.4, and 14.2 bn respectively. The decrease was partly due to changes in cross-exchange rate and partly resulted from the significant improvement of the current account and an increase of international reserves.

In general terms it is fair to state that the reasons for debt accumulation have to do with both mistaken policy responses and unfavourable changes in the external economic environment. After the sharp increases in energy prices in the first half of the 1970s, the recession and stagflation in the OECD region and the sharp deterioration in the terms of trade, economic policy in Hungary tried to 'protect' the domestic economy from the consequences of external shocks. This protection in practice meant the insulation of the Hungarian economy from effects originating in the external sector. Moreover, several economic reform measures introduced in 1968 had been withdrawn. Both factors hampered the adjustment of companies and households to changes in the international environment. Worse, attempts were made to offset price and income changes by inducing the growth of domestic demand and of non-convertible exports to the East. These policies led to large and growing deficits in the trade balance and to the rapid increase in foreign indebtedness in the 1970s.

The beginning of the second wave of indebtedness was the result of other circumstances. Though it may seem strange, Hungary managed to improve its trade balance and halt indebtedness in the early 1980s, during and immediately after the second oil price explosion, at a time of international recession and soaring interest rates. The factors explaining the temporary pause in debt accumulation are partly exogenous, i.e. the radical contraction of the availability of new credits.

The policy reasons behind the second wave of debt accumulation that started in 1985 have to do with domestic pressures for stimulating economic activity by means of increasing both the growth of exports to the East (non-convertible trade) and domestic demand. This attempt again lead to the deterioration of the convertible trade balance which, combined with the higher interest rates and unfavourable changes in cross-exchange rates resulted in a sharp increase of Hungarian external debts.

When studying the reasons for foreign debt accumulation, it is, however, useful to go beyond such general statements. Policy-makers evidently made grave mistakes, but this is only a part of the story, and the other part should be reconstructed from available statistics. In what

Table 11.1. *Components of Hungary's foreign debt accumulation, 1970–90, US$ bn*

Years	ΔGFD (1)	ΔFA (2)	ΔNFD ((3) = (1) − (2))	$-NICA$ (4)	$-I_N$ (5)	$-CA$ ((6) = (4) − (5))	$-ER$ ((7) = (3) − (6))
I 1970–9	9.51	2.81	6.70	3.06	1.44	4.50	2.20
II 1980–90	10.76	1.94	8.82	−4.27*	10.86	6.59	2.23
III 1970–90	20.27	4.75	15.52	−1.21*	12.30	11.09	4.43

* The − sign indicates a surplus.
The calculations are based on the following formulae:

$$\Delta GFD = \Delta FA + \Delta NFD$$
$$\Delta NFD = -CA + ER$$
$$CA = NICA + I_N$$

where:

GFD = gross foreign debt.
  FA = foreign assets.
NFD = net foreign debt.
  CA = current account.
  ER = valuation effect due to changes in cross-exchange rates.
$NICA$ = non-interest current account.
  I_N = net interest (factor) payments.

Source: calculations based on NBH statistics.

follows, we shall try to identify the statistically observable factors contributing to debt accumulation.

2.1 Components of debt accumulation

A simple analytical framework is applied for analysing debt accumulation. On the one hand, the change in gross foreign debts (GFD) can be divided into changes of foreign assets (FA)[3] and net foreign debts (NFD)

$$\Delta GFD = \Delta FA + \Delta NFD \qquad (1)$$

On the other hand, the growth of net foreign debts can be decomposed into the cumulative balance of the current account (CA) and effects of changes in exchange rates (ER).[4] The current account, in turn, has two significant components from the point of view of debt accumulation: net interest payments (I_N) and the non-interest current account (NICA).[5] Therefore,

$$\Delta NFD = -CA + ER = -(NICA + I_N) + ER \qquad (2)$$

Several important features of Hungarian debt accumulation are displayed in Table 11.1. First, the difference between the two decades should be noted. Though the increment of gross debt was quite similar in both the 1970s and 1980s, in the early period the growth of net foreign claims was more significant; this partly explains the larger growth of net debts during the 1980s.

But the more interesting issues have to do with the composition of the growth of net foreign debt. In the 1970s, roughly two-thirds of the increment of net debts are explained by the cumulative current account deficit and one-third by exchange rate changes (see Table 11.2 below). In the 1980s, in turn, about three-quarters of the growth resulted from the negative current account and one-quarter from exchange rate effects. The composition of the cumulative current balance deserves special attention. While in the 1970s the non-interest current account (the deficit on the visible and invisible trade balance) represented roughly 70 per cent of current account deficits, in the 1980s a radical change took place. The cumulative non-interest current account displayed a substantial *surplus* (roughly US$ 4.3 bn), but since interest payments totalled US$ 10.9 bn, the current account was in a deficit of US$ 6.7 bn.

Thus, in the period as a whole, the major component of net debt accumulation was net interest payment on foreign debts: this factor alone explains almost 80 per cent of the increment of net debts between 1970 and 1990. The contributions of various factors to net debt accumulation are presented in Table 11.2.

H

Table 11.2. *Contributions to the growth of net foreign debt (NFD),*
1970–90, per cent

	ΔNFD	$- NICA/\Delta NFD$	$- I_N/\Delta NFD$	$- CA/\Delta NFD$	$- ER/\Delta NFD$
1970–9	100	45.5	21.5	67.0	33.0
1980–90	100	− 48.5	123.0	74.5	25.5
1970–90	100	− 8.0	79.0	71.0	29.0

Source: calculations made from the data of Table 11.1.

Table 11.2 reveals that the period 1970–90 is not homogeneous from the point of view of debt accumulation. In the 1980s debts grew in spite of significant non-interest current account surpluses. As a result, in the period as a whole, the non-interest current account did not contribute to the growth of net foreign debts.

Although this conclusion may be correct in accounting terms, it is not sound in an economic sense. Adding up annual net flows at an (implied) zero interest rate is certainly questionable. To remedy this problem, in Table 11.3, the components of the current account are measured relative to GDP as well.

Relative to GDP the non-interest current account surplus increased continuously between 1980 and 1984. It grew from 0.5 per cent of GDP to 4.5 per cent; it declined in 1985 and turned negative in 1986. Later it returned to surplus, but again there was a slight deficit in 1989. In 1990 an unprecedented surplus was registered. The point is that throughout the 1980s, with the exception of 1985 and 1989, the country reached significant surpluses on its non-interest current account in relative terms as well.

Whether or not Hungary performed similar *net resource transfers* during this period requires further analysis.

2.2   Net resource transfers

Net resource transfer (NRT) can be interpreted and measured in several ways.[6] One of the accepted and theoretically supported interpretations[7] identifies NRT with NICA (non-interest current account) surpluses. There are four problems with this interpretation. Since most of these are directly relevant for the analysis not only of past but also of future Hungarian debt management, they need to be discussed at this point. These problems are: (a) the interpretation of unrequited transfers; (b) the use of payments or customs (commodity trade) statistics and the

Table 11.3. *Hungary's current account in convertible currencies, 1970–90, US$ mn*

	1970–5	1976	1977	1978	1979	1980	1981	1982	1983	1984	1985	1986	1987	1988	1989	1990	Sum 1970s	Sum 1980s	Sum	1991:1–11
Trade balance	-963	-176	-359	-782	-169	276	445	668	772	891	127	-482	36	498	537	348	-2449	4116	1667	206
Shipment (net)	-369	-114	-148	-180	-187	-237	-216	-222	-164	-154	-156	-237	-308	-300	-309	164	-998	-2139	-3137	-72
Tourism (net)	250	47	39	34	72	84	133	180	167	165	147	199	368	41	-349	345	442	1480	1922	528
Net factor income	-548	-109	-164	-252	-366	-409	-1100	-1118	-758	-815	-833	-963	-987	-1077	-1387	-1414	-1439	-10861	-12300	-1242
Other current items	318	-11	-121	-62	-175	-82	11	193	54	-20	-132	-12	15	31	77	1012	-51	1147	1096	1061
Current account	-1312	-363	-753	-1242	-825	-368	-727	-299	71	67	-847	-1495	-876	-807	-1437	127	-4495	-6591	-11086	481
Net res. transfer[a]	-1082	-243	-468	-928	-284	123	362	626	775	902	118	-520	96	239	-121	529	-3005	3129	124	748
NICA[b]	-764	-254	-589	-990	-459	41	373	819	829	882	-14	-532	111	270	-50	1541	-3056	4270	1214	1723
GDP HUF bn	2507.9	528.9	582	629.7	682.3	721	779.9	847.9	896.4	978.5	1033.7	1088.8	1226.4	1409.5	1706	2080.9	4931	12769	17700	
HUF/USD exch. rate	52.5	41.6	41	37.9	35.6	32.53	34.3	36.6	42.7	48	50.1	45.8	47	50.4	59.1	63.2				
GDP USD mn	47770	12714	14195	16615	19166	22164	22738	23167	20993	20385	20633	23773	26094	27966	28866	32926	110459	269704	380163	
Current account items/GDP %																				
Trade balance	-2.02	-1.38	-2.53	-4.71	-0.88	1.25	1.96	2.88	3.68	4.37	0.62	-2.03	0.14	1.78	1.86	1.06	-2.22	1.53	0.44	
Shipment (net)	-0.77	-0.90	-1.04	-1.08	-0.98	-1.07	-0.95	-0.96	-0.78	-0.76	-0.76	-1.00	-1.18	-1.07	-1.07	0.50	-0.90	-0.79	-0.83	
Tourism (net)	0.52	0.37	0.27	0.20	0.38	0.38	0.58	0.78	0.80	0.81	0.71	0.84	1.41	0.15	-1.21	1.05	0.40	0.55	0.51	
Net factor income	-1.15	-0.86	-1.16	-1.52	-1.91	-1.85	-4.84	-4.83	-3.61	-4.00	-4.04	-4.05	-3.78	-3.85	-4.80	-4.29	-1.30	-4.03	-3.24	
Other current items	0.67	-0.09	-0.85	-0.37	-0.91	-0.37	0.05	0.83	0.26	-0.10	-0.64	-0.05	0.06	0.11	0.27	3.07	-0.05	0.43	0.29	
Current account	-2.75	-2.86	-5.30	-7.48	-4.30	-1.66	-3.20	-1.29	0.34	0.33	-4.11	-6.29	-3.36	-2.89	-4.98	0.39	-4.07	-2.44	-2.92	
Net res. transfer[a]	-2.27	-1.91	-3.30	-5.59	-1.48	0.55	1.59	2.70	3.69	4.42	0.57	-2.19	0.37	0.85	-0.42	1.61	-2.72	1.16	0.03	
NICA[b]	-1.60	-2.00	-4.15	-5.96	-2.39	0.18	1.64	3.54	3.95	4.33	-0.07	-2.24	0.43	0.97	-0.17	4.68	-2.77	1.58	0.32	

[a] Balance on trade, shipment and tourism.
[b] Non-interest current account.
Source: Calculations based on NBH statistics.

treatment of foreign direct investment (FDI) in kind; (c) changes in value or volume terms; (d) the effect of COMECON trade on resource flows.

It should be emphasised that no attempt is made to mystify or politicise the concept of NRT (examples for the latter are given in section 3 below). Countries receiving foreign resources may have to transfer a part of the returns of these resources at one time or another; this is why credits are extended. However, if foreign resources have not been utilised efficiently, the source of net transfers is not the income deriving from these resources, but rather the country's consumption and capital investment foregone. The fact that Hungary's economy was stagnating during the 1980s is an indirect indication of zero or even negative returns on previously transferred resources from abroad. If the country has to perform net resource transfers by means of decreasing absorption in real terms, this should be a cause for serious concern.

First the concept of resource transfer should be clarified. From the balance of payments identity,

$$X - M + T_N - (I_L - I_A) + (C_L - C_A) - (P_L - P_A) = \Delta R \qquad (3)$$

the relationship between NICA and financial transfers can be derived. In the above formula X indicates exports of goods and services, M imports of goods and services; T_N net (private and official) unrequited transfers and other current payments; I_L factor payments for foreign liabilities; I_A factor incomes from foreign assets; C_L and P_L inflow of new credits and principal payments on outstanding debt, respectively, C_A and P_A credits extended and principal payments received, respectively; ΔR represents the change in international reserves. Denoting net interest payments $(I_L - I_A)$, net inflow of credits $(C_L - C_A)$ and net principal payments $(P_L - P_A)$ by I_N, C_N and P_N respectively, the two sides of net transfers can be represented as follows:

$$M - X - T_N = C_N - (P_N - I_N) - \Delta R \qquad (4)$$

The left-hand side of the above equation represents the inverse of the non-interest current account; the right-hand side indicates the components of the financial transfer in a given period. The financial transfer is defined as the difference between net inflow of foreign credits and debt service (the sum of net principal and net interest) payments, corrected for changes in official reserves.

From (4) it is clear that a country has to perform a net financial transfer abroad, if $C_N < P_N + I_N$, and receives net financial transfers from abroad, if $C_N > P_N + I_N$. Net financial transfers abroad have to be covered by the surplus of the non-interest current account and/or by using up the country's international reserves.

Departing from the above relationship, the problems of identifying net resource transfers with the non-interest current account can be separated into four different, yet related, issues. The first two problems are methodological; these are relevant mainly for future debt management. The other two issues that follow are important from the point of view of interpreting past trends.

(a) The first problem has to do with the interpretation of *unrequited transfers*. Equation (4) above gives the impression that unrequited transfers to the country are, like exports of goods and services, sources of resource outflows. Although, as will be discussed, this is not a completely implausible assumption in the case of Hungary, it is certainly not self-evident as a general proposition. Equation (4) may therefore be rewritten as:

$$M - X = (C_N + T_N) - (P_N + I_N) - \Delta R \tag{4a}$$

indicating that larger inflows of unrequited transfers permit larger deficits on trade on goods and services.

It is difficult to establish whether the left-hand side of (4) or that of (4a) gives a better representation of net resource transfer from Hungary. The item T_N turned into a significant surplus in 1990, mainly due to the large increase in foreign exchange deposits of households (see Table 11.3). It is not clear, however, to what extent the growth of foreign exchange deposits is due to unregistered current account transactions on the one hand, and to informal capital flows into the country on the other. To complicate the issues somewhat, actual unrequited transfers may be looked upon as potential sources of imports, rather than sources of interest payments. These are the reasons why Table 11.3 gives two measures of net resource transfers: one that includes, and one that leaves out, unrequited transfers.

(b) When measuring and interpreting the net transfers of resources, the second difficulty is related to the use of *customs'* (i.e. commodity trade) *or payments'* (i.e. cash flow) *statistics* of foreign trade. This issue has become significant in Hungary mainly because of the recent increase in the inflow of foreign direct investment.

A comparison of the first column of Table 11.4 and the first row of Table 11.3 indicates that there were gaps between commodity and payments statistics for foreign trade, but until recently these had to do mainly with leads and lags in payments for exports and imports.[8]

Although it seems logical to use customs' statistics for foreign trade when trying to estimate net resource flows, this would be inconsistent with using (the only available) balance of payments statistics for measuring the balance on services. Consistency requires that the payments' (cash flow)

Table 11.4. *The cumulative trade and current account and foreign debts in convertible currencies, 1973–90*, US$ mn*

	Trade balance**	Tourism	Interest	Other	NICA	Current account***	Net debt	Gross claims	Gross debts
1973	65	46	− 85	27	138	53	805	1313	2118
1974	− 577	75	− 201	139	− 363	− 564	1338	1524	2861
1975	− 1177	134	− 383	289	− 749	− 1131	2000	2199	4199
1976	− 1586	187	− 489	257	− 1142	− 1630	2614	2599	5214
1977	− 2229	226	− 653	173	− 1830	− 2483	3530	2672	6253
1978	− 3441	262	− 905	121	− 3058	− 3963	6141	3327	9468
1979	− 3835	334	− 1365	79	− 3422	− 4787	7123	3384	10 507
1980	− 4002	419	− 2228	291	− 3292	− 5520	7571	3884	11 453
1981	− 4130	553	− 3195	554	− 3023	− 6218	7477	3264	10 740
1982	− 3721	733	− 4313	784	− 2204	− 6517	7267	2949	10 216
1983	− 3167	900	− 5071	892	− 1375	− 6446	6994	3751	10 745
1984	− 2564	1065	− 5886	1006	− 493	− 6379	6549	4434	10 984
1985	− 2410	1212	− 6719	691	− 507	− 7226	8046	5909	13 955
1986	− 2880	1412	− 7682	429	− 1039	− 8271	10 668	6239	16 907
1987	− 3204	1780	− 8669	496	− 928	− 9597	13 683	5901	19 584
1988	− 2709	1821	− 5746	230	− 658	− 10 404	13 967	5636	19 603
1989	− 2169	1472	− 11 133	− 11	− 708	− 11 841	14 900	5490	20 390
1990	− 1224	1817	− 12 571	264	857	− 11 714	15 938	5332	21 270

* Till 1981 non-rouble, since 1982 convertible currencies.
** Customs statistics.
*** Between 1973 and 1981 does not include the following items: differences due to valuation, conversion and corrections.
Source: NBH.

statistics be applied. However, as foreign direct investment (FDI) becomes increasingly important for the country, the interpretation of the difference between the balance of payments and the commodity trade (customs based) statistics is becoming a highly topical issue.

FDI may take the form of financial investment (e.g. buying the shares of Hungarian companies, involving an inflow of money through the banking system) and/or investment 'in kind' (imports of goods and/or services). While the first type of FDI (to be denoted as FDI_F) influences only the capital account of the balance of payments (BOP), the second form (FDI_M) should, in principle, show up in both the current and the capital account. Since Hungarian BOP statistics cover only actual payments related to trade flows, the value of FDI_M is included in commodity trade (customs') statistics, but not in the current account. However, for a clear view of net resource transfers, FDI_M has also to be accounted for. Including both FDI_{MN} (net FDI in kind) and FDI_{FN} (net financial FDI) in (4a) we get

$$FDI_{MN} + M - X = (C_N + T_N + FDI_{MN} + FDI_{FN}) \qquad (5)$$
$$- (P_N + I_N + FI_N) - \Delta R$$

where FI_N denotes net factor payments (profit repatriation) related to FDI. By rearranging (5), the effect of FDI on resource and financial transfers can be clarified:

$$M - (X - FDI_{MN}) = (C_N + T_N) + (FDI_{MN} + FDI_{FN} - FI_N) \quad (5a)$$
$$- (P_N + I_N)$$

That is, the larger the volume of FDI_{MN}, the smaller the pressure to achieve an excess of exports over imports to cover net financial transfers by a net resource transfer. If FDI_{MN} is sufficiently large $(FDI_{MN} > X - M)$, the performance of a net financial transfer abroad may be compatible with a net resource inflow. On the other hand, the larger $(FDI_{MN} - FI_N)$, the larger the net financial transfer that can be performed without a net resource transfer. This relationship will be important when analysing the prospects for Hungarian debt management.

(c) Finally, two remarks on the interpretation of *past resource transfers* are in order. First, beyond analysing net resource transfers at current prices, it is useful to take a look at *changes in volume* as well. During the 1970s the volume of exports in convertible currencies more than doubled, while the volume of imports grew by 60 per cent. Meanwhile the terms of trade deteriorated by 20 per cent; thus the 'net resource transfer to the country' represented only a partial compensation of the terms of trade loss. In the 1980s, the volume of convertible currency exports and imports increased by 65 and 25 per cent, while the terms of trade deteriorated by approximately 10 per cent. Thus, in the period 1970–90 as a whole export and import volumes in *convertible currencies* increased by about 250 and 100 per cent respectively, while the terms of trade deteriorated by almost 30 per cent. Although these statistics do not include invisibles and other services, they give a more or less accurate picture of the volume and price changes underlying the cumulative change in the non-interest current balance in the last twenty years.

To be sure, these figures are not intended to give the impression that exogenous factors are responsible for all negative trends in the Hungarian external sector in the last two decades. They simply point to the fact that the accumulation of foreign debts was not matched by real resource inflows into the economy.

(d) A closely related problem of interpreting convertible currency debt accumulation has to do with clarifying the respective role of *trends in rouble and convertible currency trade*.[9] During the 1970s the volume of exports in roubles increased by 119 per cent, while imports grew by 85 per cent; in this period the terms of trade deteriorated by 20 per cent. In the 1980s the volume of rouble exports and imports *declined* by 5 and by 15 per cent respectively; in these years the terms of trade did not change significantly. But in the period as a whole the volume of exports grew by more than 100 per cent, while that of imports increased by about 55 per cent. In the meantime the terms of trade deteriorated by 20 per cent.

It is clear from this that the country performed resource transfers in volume terms with respect to both the rouble trade area (COMECON) and the rest of the world during the 1970s and 1980s. On the basis of the evidence, there are no grounds for claiming that net financial transfers from the West would have been used to finance resource transfers towards the rouble area, though this issue needs further research. The simple fact is that while Hungary accumulated foreign debts amounting to US$ 20 bn in convertible currencies, the country had net claims in roubles. This happened in spite of the fact that the volume of convertible exports grew much more rapidly than that of rouble exports. The source of the problem seems to have been in the stagnation of rouble imports during the 1980s. Given that both economic structure and economic policies were aimed at supplying Eastern markets, the country had no problems whatsoever in increasing rouble exports. However, due to the difficulties inherent in purchasing from the East, Hungary was forced to reorient imports to the West in the 1980s, in a period when it had to increase net exports in convertible currencies to meet debt-service obligations. As a result, the country transferred a significant part of its GDP to both the rouble and the convertible currency area during the 1980s. Net exports

Table 11.5. *Total (convertible and rouble) net exports per GDP at constant prices and GDP growth, 1980–90, per cent*

	1980	1981	1982	1983	1984	1985	1986	1987	1988	1989	1990
GDP growth (previous year = 100)	2.7	2.9	2.8	0.7	2.7	− 0.3	1.5	4.1	− 0.1	− 0.2	− 4.0
Net exports/GDP	− 2.5	− 1.1	1.9	4.1	6.4	5.7	3.5	4.3	7.1	7.2	—

Source: NBH (1990).

(production − absorption) relative to GDP at constant prices and indices of GDP growth are presented in Table 11.5.

2.3   Implications of past trends and questions for the future

The country received a significant net financial transfer in the 1970s, but this was used for covering terms of trade losses and for trying to maintain existing activities. Thus these credits were not used for enhancing long-term export potential, and in this sense they were wasted. During the 1980s significant adjustments were made. However, Hungary's debt soared due to the radical decline of the growth of imports from Eastern Europe, to the lack of a firm export-orientation to the West and to policy errors, such as the stimulation of exports' growth to East European neighbours during the mid-1980s, which happened in spite of significant net resource outflows from the country. Adverse developments in external conditions – the increase of international interest rates, and changes in cross-exchange rates – also contributed to the sharp increase in external debts in the 1980s.

The implication of this analysis is not to blame anyone or any circumstance for the unhappy state of Hungary in terms of its extremely high indebtedness, but rather to point out that the financial resources once transferred to the country are simply not there or, having been 'wasted' (e.g. used for large investments designed for the Eastern markets), are irrelevant from the point of view of servicing the debt.[10] The 1970s are now in the distant past, and during the 1980s Hungary did not receive net resource transfers from abroad. Therefore it is no wonder that the question whether Hungary can – or, for that matter, should – keep on fully servicing its debts after a decade of almost continuous resource outflows is often raised by some academic economists and political organisations.

3   The official debt strategy and its critics

As already mentioned, the special feature of Hungary as a debtor is that it has serviced all payments' obligations fully and maintained creditworthiness, in spite of the extremely high debt indicators by international comparison. Most countries with similar (or often much lower) debt/GDP and debt/export ratios were forced to give up: they stopped paying and rescheduled their debts. Some of these countries managed to reach an outright reduction of outstanding debts or debt service obligations.[11] Are these examples relevant for Hungary?

Before trying to answer this question, the present official position of the Hungarian government on the debt strategy should be clarified. That is followed by some Hungarian and foreign criticism of this strategy.

The official view leaves no question about the intention of the government to keep servicing foreign debts fully and thus maintaining the credit-worthiness of the country. This was the policy of the pre-democratic regime, and has simply been followed by the democratically elected government. The strategy of remaining credit-worthy in order to be able to raise finance from the private markets has worked until now: in 1991 Hungary managed to treble its foreign exchange reserves (to US$ 3 bn) and decrease net foreign debts, while the inflow of foreign investment reached US$ 1.3–1.4 bn.

However, doubts still remain. There are several different criticisms of the official debt strategy. In what follows, these will be classified into 'political' criticisms and 'economic' ones. 'Political' critiques of the debt strategy refer to the fact that foreign debts have been taken by a communist dictatorship, therefore the democratic government should not accept the obligations deriving from them. A similar line of criticism proposes an appeal to the West to cancel these debts, since the credits were extended in order to stabilise the power of a non-democratic regime. Therefore, the reasoning goes, the West has no right to redeem these debts or accept debt-service payments in respect of them.

There is also another kind of politically based criticism. According to this, 'global political–economic' critique, Hungary's debt is just a small drop in the ocean of the global international debt crisis hitting most developing and East European countries. The proponents of this view would like to see some sort of cooperation between Hungary and other severely indebted countries in order to put pressure on creditors to make concessions.[12] I consider these views and suggestions to be naive and irrelevant from the practical point of view, but beside the above, outright political type of criticism, doubts concerning the debt strategy of the Hungarian government were also formulated on economic grounds, both in Hungary and abroad.[13]

These point to the fact that an unchanged debt strategy requires that the country keep on performing significant debt-service payments and thus suffer the consequences of the continuing the resource outflows that characterised the 1980s. Given the inevitable economic and social costs of economic transition and the negative effects of the collapse of COMECON trade, fully servicing outstanding foreign debts involves both an extremely high burden for the country and risks for its creditors. According to this reasoning, the country should try to reach some kind of an agreement with Western governments, international financial organisations and private creditors on a new arrangement. There are different views as to what this new arrangement would involve, but the common point is the need to achieve a *temporary* reduction in payments' obligations, and as a result, a drop in the burden of debt service. Almost all experts subscribing to this recommendation propose that it be done without any kind of open rescheduling of, or default on, outstanding debts.[14]

To formulate this proposal in terms of policy options means in practice looking for a third way between fully servicing the debts and default. (It should be remembered that all international experiences related to 'alternative debt management strategies', i.e. debt reliefs, buy-backs, debt–equity swaps, etc. were preceded by open defaults on foreign debts.)

According to proponents of this 'third way', there is a scope for reducing the burden of debt service by negotiation, but that this possibility will not last long. The government should, therefore, approach potential partners while the improvement of the external performance and debt indicators of the country can still impress the world. According to this reasoning, the favourable image and relative position of the country in comparison with Eastern European should be used as an asset in negotiations on debt (service) reduction.[15]

The position of the government is exactly the opposite: the improvement of external performance should be used to impress private creditors and investors. From this perspective, any attempt at negotiation on debts is disastrous from the point of view of credit-worthiness and, therefore, the terms and amount of new credits that can be raised for running the Hungarian economy. At this point no attempt is made to judge whether the opponents or proponents of the present Hungarian debt strategy have stronger arguments on their side: at present only questions are being posed.

On the one hand, considering the idea of negotiation on foreign debts, it is very important to clarify: Who are the partners? Who should negotiate with whom and on what? Given the structure of Hungarian debts, presented in Table 11.6 below, it is clear that governments are the least represented among foreign creditors, and a very significant portion of the latter are holders of Hungarian bonds. According to the official view in Hungary, in contrast with banks, having extended syndicated loans, it is extremely difficult (or practically impossible) to approach all bondholders for negotiation. Since the technical and institutional details of recommendations on debt renegotiation have not been clarified, the government and the NBH both claim that even if negotiations were feasible, a leak of information would be inevitable, leading to serious difficulties in day-to-day debt management.

Table 11.6. *Composition of gross foreign debts of Hungary in convertible currencies, US$ mn*

	1987	1988	1989	1990	1991:Oct.
Total	19 584	19 602	20 390	21 270	20 902
Short-term	3103	3363	3306	2941	1819
Long-term	16 481	16 239	17 084	18 329	19 083
Financial loans	17 509	17 469	18 060	17 587	17 060
Commercial credits	1652	1626	17 084	1980	2057
Governmental	0	0	0	472	899
Other	423	507	567	1231	886

Source: Based on NBH statistics.

On the other hand, the time horizon of proponents of the official debt strategy is not really clear. As discussed above, they are certainly right in claiming that any major disruption of credit flows and/or withdrawal of deposits, induced, for example, by news of the Hungarian government's 'new approach' to debt management, might have very serious effects on the short-run cash flow position of the Hungarian economy. The existing credit lines of trade financing could be temporarily cut, leading to a decline of imports and a further drop in economic activity. Moreover, domestic holders of foreign exchange accounts, amounting to US$ 1.7 bn, might decide to *legally* carry their savings to Vienna. The statement that a break with the existing debt strategy would imply serious short-run costs is not questioned; what seems more problematic is the enthusiasm of several Hungarian policy-makers about performing the payments' obligations on foreign debts. As if it were not a burden, but rather the 'stick' necessary to stimulate adjustments in the Hungarian economy. Actually, two questions have to be addressed. This first is: Is the government's present debt strategy feasible (sustainable) and if so, under what conditions? The other question tries to clarify this: Even if feasible, is this the best strategy? Are there better options?

4   The official debt strategy: expectations, assumptions and implications

4.1   Outlook, concepts and issues

In the next few years Hungary's foreign debt-service payments will remain very significant. In the period 1992–4, annual principal payments are expected to be around US$ 2.5 bn, while net interest payments, assuming more or less constant interest rates, are forecast to fluctuate between US$ 1.4 and 1.5 bn per year. This implies that relative to 1990 GDP, annual total debt service will reach 12.5 per cent, of which interest payments will be over 4 per cent.

It should be recalled that in 1990 and 1991 Hungary's output declined by 4 and 6–7 per cent, respectively. This decline followed a decade of negligible growth, close to stagnation. The fall of production in these years was the result of several factors. First, structural changes, shifts in government policies related to economic transition (i.e. drastic cuts in direct and indirect subsidies) lead to a decline of real domestic demand and output. Second, the collapse of the trade with Eastern countries (partly as a result of the collapse of their economies, partly due to the switchover to dollar payments in this trade in early 1991).[16] The third reason may have to do with macroeconomic policies geared to achieving an improvement (and, moreover, a surplus) in the current account in a *relatively* non-inflationary manner.

Although no estimates are available on the relative importance of these factors (calculations of this sort are very problematic), it is likely that the third factor also played a role in the decline of production. The importance of this issue derives from the fact that, in order to reduce the domestic burden of debt service, the economy has to grow. Only then is it possible to diminish the relative costs of foreign payments' obligations, while avoiding a new wave of indebtedness.

Inflation is the other aspect of macroeconomic performance worth mentioning in this context. As Table 11.7 indicates, inflation has been accelerating more or less continuously since 1985. The other question that will therefore have to be addressed is the relation between debt service and inflation.

Before turning to the interrelation between debt service, real growth and inflation, it would be useful to clarify three interrelated concepts: (1) debt-service obligations, (2) the *actual* (current) burden, i.e. net transfers necessary to cover debt service and (3) the *relative* total and current burden of debt service.

(1) The interpretation of *debt service* is straightforward: the sum of interest payments and principal. This can be measured against GDP (as above) or against the country's receipts from exports of goods (or goods and services). Time series on the latter are presented in Table 11.8.

These figures show a significant improvement in 1991, but what about the other indicators?

(2) *Net transfers*, indicating the actual current burden of debt service obligations, may be much lower than total debt service. First, if the

Table 11.7. *Price indices in Hungary, 1985–91, previous year = 100*

	1985	1986	1987	1988	1989	1990	1991*
CPI**	107.0	105.3	108.6	115.5	117.0	128.9	136.4
IPI***	104.4	102.0	103.7	104.5	114.6	120.9	133.6

*   10 months.
** Consumer price index.
*** Industrial sales' price index.
Source: Hungarian Statistical Office.

Table 11.8. *Debt service indicators, 1986–91, per cent*

Total debt service	1986	1987	1988	1989	1990	1991*
Relative to exports of goods and services in convertible currencies	75.1	55.3	46.7	38.5	45.5	31.5
Relative to exports of goods in convertible currencies	97.3	71.8	61.4	52.9	62.7	39.5

* Preliminary.
Source: NBH.

country is credit-worthy, principal payments can normally be rolled over. If no new credits or other sources are raised to cover interest, the net transfer corresponds only to interest payments; it is paid from the surplus of the non-interest current account (NICA).

But even if interest payments have to be met by a NICA surplus, net transfers may be lower than the surplus on goods and services. This is so because a NICA surplus may include an item that does not necessarily represent a resource outflow from the country (unrequited transfers) and (in Hungary's case) may leave out an item representing a resource inflow (FDI in kind). Thus, net transfers = NICA − (unrequited transfers + FDI_{MN}); or net transfers = NICA = FDI_{MN}.

The current actual burden of debt service also depends on the inflow of FDI (in cash). If FDI_F (say, from privatisation revenues) is sufficiently large, it may cover a significant part (or all) of interest payments. If the current account deficit equals net interest payments (the balance on goods and services is zero and unrequited transfers are disregarded), and there is an inflow of FDI_F corresponding to the deficit of the current account, then $I_N = FDI_F$. But paying interest from asset sales and/or capital inflows might be considered a shortsighted and hazardous policy. It is certainly true that using these revenues for making current interest payments is similar to the policy of raising new foreign credits for covering interest obligations due – precisely the policy line that was followed in the years 1980–9 in Hungary. However, there are two important points to be considered.

On the one hand, the equation

$$(X - M) - I_N = - FDI_F \tag{6}$$

can be read in two ways. If $X - M = 0$, i.e. there is no net resource outflow from the country, one of the possible ways at looking at the above formula is stating that $I_N = FDI_F$. But there is another possibility as well:

$$(X - I_N) - M = - FDI_F \tag{7}$$

implying that the part of imports not covered by exports (due to using a part of export revenues to finance interest payments) is met by the inflow of foreign direct investment. This is by no means just a game of rearranging the terms. According to the second reading, FDI may be used for financing essential capital imports or for simply avoiding further resource outflows.

On the other hand, the inflow of FDI_F, with unchanged external debt, means that while net foreign liabilities, NFL (the inverse of net foreign assets, NFA) of the country remain at the same level, a healthy type of rearrangement may take place within the portfolio of net foreign liabilities: an increase of foreign direct investment corresponding to a decline of net foreign debts.

The factors that may reduce the actual burden of the interest payments on foreign debt (i.e. lead to a decline or to an outright reversal of net transfers) without new net credits and thus avoid any additional increase of foreign debts are summarised below:

$$(X - I_N) - (M + FDI_M) = - (FDI_F + FDI_M + T_N) \tag{8}$$

Equation (8) implies that if FDI and T_N are sufficiently large, the making of interest payments does not require a corresponding excess of exports over imports. With a given interest obligation, exports may be lower or imports higher than they would otherwise have been.

(3) The third concept, the *relative* current burden of debt service leads us back to our point of departure: the *growth of the economy*. The burden of

debt service declines if the economy grows. But can it really start to grow under the constraint of non-increasing foreign debts while interest payments amount to more than 4 per cent of GDP? Proponents of the present debt strategy claim that it can; opponents state that it cannot. Alternative answers to the question are likely to be supported by different assumptions and expectations concerning the actual current burden of debt service. In what follows, we shall take a closer look at the prospects for and problems of macroeconomic management under two assumptions. First interest payments abroad have to be financed by net exports of goods and services (no FDI, no T_N); and second FDI and T_N are at least as significant as interest payments.

It is important to note that although FDI and T_N flows in 1991 corresponded to the second assumption, the net resource transfer abroad was close to the magnitude implied by the first. The reason for this discrepancy is to be found in the more than US$ 2 bn increase of international reserves.

The analysis below is therefore based on a mixture of counterfactual assumptions, observed facts, intuitive and theoretical reasoning. No attempt has been made to construct a complete macroeconomic model for capturing all possible factors, effects and interrelationships; this needs to be the result of further research.

4.2 Debt management without FDI

In 1991, Hungary's current account was much better than exected (about US$ 0.4 bn surplus, instead of US$ 1.2 bn deficit forecast by the government's economic programme). This could push the government to draw on further credits, but it does not intend to increase foreign indebtedness.

In this case the inflow of FDI becomes extremely important. If it becomes insignificant[17] in 1992 and in the years to come (relative to the US$ 1.3–1.4 bn registered in 1991) then the burden of servicing foreign debts fully will become a major problem for the domestic economy. Interest payments will continuously have to be made from the surplus of exports over imports, that is, from total domestic savings (S) exceeding total investments (IN) by the measure of net interest payments abroad:

$$X - (M + I_N) = S - IN \tag{9}$$

Decomposing the right-hand side into net government and private savings:

$$X - (M + I_N) = (T - G) + (S_P - IN_P) \tag{10}$$

implies that under the conditions stated above, exports have to exceed imports by I_N: foreign interest payments have to be covered by a non-interest budgetary surplus $(T - G)$ and/or an excess of private savings over investments. Both of these factors might involve further declines in domestic demand and investment. The implied contraction of domestic absorption might take place at different levels of inflation. However, the monetary aspect of interest payments indicates the resulting inflationary pressure.

From the identity $NFA^B = \Delta M - \Delta DC$ (where NFA^B, M and DC, denote net foreign assets of the banking sector, money and domestic credit, respectively), it can be seen that the larger the surplus of the current account, the narrower is the scope for the increase of domestic credit, if a given target for money supply growth is to be kept. Simplifying the issues somewhat, let us identify ΔNFA^B with ΔNFA for the whole economy, i.e. the current account (CA). Under this assumption,

$$NICA = \Delta M + (I_N - DC) \tag{11}$$

The non-interest current account directly increases the money supply. If interest payments abroad (I_N) were made by the private sector, this component would decrease the growth of money, and domestic credit could expand to meet the target for M. However, if I_N is paid by the public sector, a similar decrease in domestic credit is needed to assure that money growth corresponds only to the NICA surplus.

In Hungary's case, the foreign debtor is the NBH. Interest payments on foreign debts do not therefore represent a direct withdrawal of money. This is the reason why, other things being equal, either domestic credit has to decline or a primary (non-interest) fiscal surplus[18] has to be achieved for financing the domestic counterpart of the foreign transfer abroad, *without inflation*. But it is difficult to avoid the inflationary consequences, especially at a time of economic contraction.

There are several options for raising (financing) the domestic counterpart of the NICA surplus (US$ 1.7 bn in the first 11 months of 1991, see Table 11.3 above). Some of these are openly inflationary, some are contractionary; their combination is likely to be stagflationary. The first, non-inflationary, but contractionary, way is increasing taxes and/or reducing public expenditures to the point where the non-interest budget surplus covers interest payments (or, alternatively stated, the budget, inclusive of interest expenditure, is balanced). However, increasing taxation and reducing public expenditures might actually decrease the tax base by inducing a further decline in activity. The original problem is thus not solved, but aggravated as the relative burden of the transfer (interest/GDP) increases.

A second option is monetisation, leading to higher inflation. In this case the inflation tax is used to cover the domestic counterpart of the foreign transfer.[19] This solution is extremely dangerous, since it might result not only in higher, but in accelerating, inflation. A reason why this would be very likely is that in order to maintain the competitiveness of exporters and companies competing with imports, periodic devaluations would be inevitable, 'blowing up' the domestic counterpart of the foreign transfer. This, in turn, would imply additional monetisation, inflation, devaluation, and finally very high inflation, or even hyperinflation.

The third option is the one already mentioned above and close to recent Hungarian practice: financing the public deficit by money creation and by strictly restraining the growth of total domestic credit. This implies cheap money for the government and high interest rates for the private sector. The implication is lower inflation than would otherwise be the case, but also lower private investments and real economic activity.

The effects of the fourth option, financing the budget deficit by the issue of domestic government debt to the public, has some similarities with the previous one. While it solves some problems, it creates new ones. The direct consequence of this solution is well-known: increasing interest rates and crowding out private investments from private savings (this is the similarity with the former solution). It also depresses the prices of other domestic financial assets, which is extremely dangerous at a time when a domestic capital market is being established. On the positive side, it has to be noted that this method is the safest from the point of view of controlling inflation. However, what this option actually amounts to is substituting higher domestic debt for lower than otherwise foreign debt.[20] It is useful to recall that in the 1980s the growth of foreign debt was used to finance higher foreign interest payments. Now financing the domestic counterpart of interest payments (net transfers) abroad by increasing domestic public debt involves the creation of a new problem without getting rid of the existing one (foreign debt). Moreover, the real interest rate on domestic debt may easily exceed the interest rate on the foreign one, foreshadowing even more serious fiscal problems for the future.

4.2.1 Implications

From the preceding discussion it should be clear that the serious problems and difficulties with raising the domestic counterpart of the net resource transfer abroad derive from the lack of economic growth, or rather from outright economic contraction. It is easy to see that if the economy started to grow, both the monetary and fiscal aspects of the problem would become much easier to manage. In a growing economy the revenues of the budget could increase significantly and/or there would be much less need for counteracting the monetary effects of the export surplus (the net transfer) by strongly restricting domestic credit growth.

But is it correct to consider economic growth as an exogenous factor from the point of view of net resource transfers and the accompanying monetary and fiscal policies? Certainly not. As presented above, policies that are intended to avoid (or at least control) the inflationary consequences of the net transfer abroad have contractionary effects, either directly (increase of taxes, decrease of expenditures) or indirectly (higher interest rate, lower credit growth). This is not to say that domestic macroeconomic policy measures related to foreign debt management are solely responsible for the economic decline in Hungary. But, other factors being equal, they do exert contractionary effects. In the absence of exogenous factors inducing the growth of activity, the economy might be caught in a vicious circle. Restrictive monetary and/or fiscal policies designed to control the inflationary effects of net transfers abroad might induce a further decline of the economy which, in turn, would lead to higher public deficits, more restrictive policies, further decline and so on. Choosing a higher rate of inflation instead of more contraction is an option only in the very short run. Thus, in the situation described above (which, it should be emphasised, is only a very stylised and simplified representation of the actual state of affairs and policy options in Hungary), sound options are simply unavailable: without economic growth only bad and worse decisions can be taken.

4.2.2 The foreign side of the transfer

But this is not the end of the story. While the recession increases the difficulties related to extracting and managing the *domestic* counterpart of net foreign transfers, at the same time it eases the performance of the actual transfer in *foreign currency*, i.e. achieving a surplus on the balance of goods and services. This is so because the decline of domestic demand restrains the growth of imports, while it forces producers to turn to external markets. A turnaround, involving the growth of the economy, could easily halt the improvement in the foreign trade and service balance, and lead to the deterioration of external performance. In this case, the difficulties with net foreign transfers would shift to the external side, i.e. to raising the necessary foreign currency income from net exports. Either foreign debts would increase, indicating the start of a new wave of foreign debt accumulation to the limit of the country's creditworthiness (this option was assumed away at the start, but even if chosen, it would be very short-lived), or economic growth would have to be blocked by macroeconomic policies, in order to reestablish the NICA surplus corresponding to interest payments abroad.

A *real devaluation* might seem a a plausible option under these circumstances, but if the inflation rate is already high, imports represent a major component in domestic absorption and if, moreover, inflationary expectations are closely linked to nominal exchange rate changes, exchange rate policy may turn out to be an extremely costly and inefficient instrument (in terms of inducing additional inflation) for improving the external balance. On the other hand, the implications of real devaluations for managing the domestic monetary counterpart of net foreign transfers have to be recalled: the larger the devaluation, the larger the inflationary effect of net exports. Counteracting these effects would need increasingly restrictive monetary and/or fiscal policies – leading back to the original problems and to the vicious circle described above.

From the above it would seem logical to draw this conclusion: the Hungarian economy is trapped and there is no way out without a significant debt-(service) reduction. Although not totally implausible, this would be a premature judgement; the preceding analysis was based on several explicit and implicit assumptions. Of the implicit ones, the potential efficiency gains from fundamental institutional changes (e.g. privatisation of the economy, establishing a healthy financial and banking system; structural reforms, domestic and foreign economic liberalisation and deregulation) have not been accounted for. These may offset the negative trends discussed in this section.

On the other hand, we should recall the explicit assumptions: no inflow of FDI and no unrequited transfers. But these two items together are likely to reach more than US$ 2 bn in 1991 (roughly US$ 0.5 bn more than interest payments on foreign debts). It is therefore necessary to take a closer look at the potential effect of these items.

4.3   Effects and implications of the inflow of FDI and unrequited transfers

In the light of the significant inflow of FDI and unrequited transfers (used for increasing international reserves by more than US$ 2 bn in 1991), the pessimistic conclusions reached above may have to be revised. The seemingly irreconcilable conflict between domestic growth (with the resulting inability to achieve the necessary amount of net exports for servicing foreign debts without an increase of these debts) on the one hand, and domestic recession leading to the necessary external surplus, but resulting in public finances getting out of hand, on the other, might be resolved if the country has access to FDI and other revenues (unrequited transfers) that do not imply the outflow of domestic resources.

If the financial inflow continues, and more important, is channelled into productive uses, there is an effective possibility of reconciling domestic and foreign economic equilibrium, i.e. getting out of the bind described above. Although, as already hinted, a part of unrequited transfers might actually constitute exports of goods and services, it is important to see that if there is no need to maintain the outflow of resources, a major constraint on economic growth can be removed. If a balance or, moreover, a deficit on the non-interest current account (involving a deficit on the current account) can be financed by foreign investment, there is no need to apply such harsh macroeconomic policies as might feed the vicious circle of contraction. Investments, imports and the whole economy could thus start to grow. As a result, public deficits and the external debt burden would decline.

The policy involving a higher growth of investments and imports has to be backed by incomes policies as well (based on agreements with labour unions on nominal wage growth), otherwise inflation may easily get out of government control. But the major shift in economic policy requires that no further real transfers be made in terms of net exports of goods and services. If a deficit on the balance of goods and services emerges, and it is covered by the inflow of FDI and unrequited transfers, there is no reason for concern.

The inflow of FDI, combined with a decline of net foreign debts, should be considered as healthy and positive change in net foreign liabilities of the country. Profits on foreign investments may be repatriated (which, by the way, is much less certain than the need to transfer interest payments). However in order to repatriate incomes on foreign investment, profits have first to be earned, which is not the case with the interest on financial loans.

To conclude: with a sufficiently large inflow of FDI and T_N, the Hungarian economy has a chance of climbing out of the pit that it is at present in. There are two basic questions regarding this strategy. The first is the feasibility of attracting further significant inflows of FDI. For the time being, this does not seem to be a problem. In 1991, according to reports in the press,[21] the total inflow of FDI in Eastern Europe was around US$ 2 bn; more than half of this came to Hungary. If the present trend continues, the Hungarian economy will not face an external constraint.

But there are serious risks. In the proximity of Hungary, a civil war is going on in Yugoslavia and the outlook of the post-Soviet republics is also extremely dark – these political factors might frighten potential investors, especially in case of a serious crisis.

As to the other question, it has to be asked whether an inflow of FDI (plus T_N) covering interest payments is sufficient to solve the economic and resulting social problems of the country. The country's economy might need more: a significant net foreign resource inflow to support both the necessary structural changes and manage their social consequences. Is there a hope for such an inflow over expected FDI flows?

5   Hungarian debt strategy and assistance from the West: what is to be expected?

This chapter demonstrated that if nothing goes wrong, Hungary can manage its foreign debts with a sufficient amount of private capital inflow. This would imply that there is nothing whatsoever for the Western community to do. However, this is not the conclusion that I would draw.

Due to the debt overhang of the past, there is a very large drain of resources from Hungary. Beside some academics, no serious authority in the West has considered any kind of debt relief for Hungary, in spite of the fact that this country is unique in adhering to its debt-service obligations at a time of the extremely large burden of economic transition.

Two years ago, it seemed to be self-evident that the West would rush to assist Eastern European countries in overcoming the difficulties of economic, social and political transition. I thought that it went without saying that the earlier assistance was offered, the better the results to be expected. Today, I am extremely sceptical. My impression is that the Western community does not really understand what is at stake in Eastern Europe. Although Hungary is stable at the moment, and can perform its heavy debt-service obligations, it is by no means certain that difficulties of debt service can be avoided forever. The Western community has the clear possibility of assisting Hungary in avoiding domestic crises. But instead it waits. If a crisis emerges, help will be offered – but strategies aimed at avoiding crises are not on offer. This is why I am sceptical of any kind of a 'third way' in debt management. Hungary might need it, but the partners are simply not there.

The country has to base its plans on realistic expectations. If private capital continues to flow in, the debt problem will remain manageable. If it stops, a crisis will develop, necessitating the revision of the present debt strategy. But at this point a new approach to debt management is likely to do more harm than good. It would be different, of course, if the West offered new and promising options. But since it appears unwilling to do so, Hungary should do its best to remain credit-worthy.

Appendix: Hungary's debt in international comparison

Table 11A.1. *Debt-related indicators of Hungary and other indebted countries, 1989*

Countries	Gross debt (US$ mn)	Debts service (US$ mn)	Debt/ GDP (%)	Debt/ exports (%)	Debt service/ exports[a] (%)
Argentina	59 890	10 882	92.5	510.6	92.8
Brazil	114 731	15 691	23.8	296.2	40.5
Chile	18 863	2811	74.7	195.7	29.2
Mexico	97 417	12 601	48.5	271.4	35.1
Nigeria	31 951	2 909	109.0	305.4	27.8
Philippines	29 642	3383	66.9	238.9	27.3
Venezuela	32 931	4487	75.1	207.3	28.3
Average			70.1	289.4	40.1
Hungary	20 391	3455	71.3	239.8	40.6

[a] = Trade and service exports.
Source: OECD Economic Surveys, Hungary (1991) p. 38.

Table 11A.2. *Per capita debt of Hungary, Eastern Europe and some indebted countries, 1989*

Countries	*Per capita* debt (US$)
Bulgaria	1052
Czecho-Slovakia	444
Poland	1 102
Rumania	44
USSR	172
Yugoslavia	930
Hungary	1939
Argentina	1443
Brasilia	644
Chile	1117
Mexico	996
Nigeria	221
Philippines	437
Venezuela	1298

Source: D. Cohen (1991), p. 301.

NOTES

1 Net foreign claims in non-convertible currencies were over US$ 0.3 bn in October 1991 according to the statistics of the National Bank of Hungary (NBH). In addition, rouble claims were converted to dollars (US$ 2 bn), but whether these claims can be redeemed is still an open question.

2 In 1989 an official announcement was made on the inaccuracy of the published data on foreign debts. Following this announcement, new figures were published for the period from 1982. For the previous decade, we shall have to rely on a combination of original and revised statistics, and this may result in some inconsistencies.

3 Foreign assets include foreign exchange reserves and non-rouble credits extended (mainly to developing countries). For a caveat see n. 5 below.

4 Since ER is a residual, it actually contains all potential factors not included in the official current account statistics.

5 This framework does not include foreign direct investment (FDI). The latter became significant only after 1989–90. If FDI were taken into account, the complete formula would be

$$\Delta NFD = -CA + \Delta FDI_N,$$

or alternatively

$$\Delta NFD - \Delta FDI = -\Delta NFA = CA,$$

where NFA indicates net foreign assets. The latter formula becomes important at a later point.

6 See OECD (1990), World Bank (1991).

7 See Dornbusch (1988, 1989).

8 Table 11.4, besides using commodity trade statistics, displays cumulative figures for trade and payments, while Table 11.3. relies on payments' statistics of the NBH and involves annual figures. The differences between Tables 11.3 and 11.4 are mainly due to differences of sources on the period 1970–80.

9 On an early exposition of the interrelations between the two types of trade see Köves and Oblath (1983).

10 When claiming that these credits have been wasted, it should not be forgotten that, even if unintentionally, they represented an important factor drawing Hungary closer to the Western community. They also meant that living standards in Hungary could be higher than they would otherwise have been.

11 See, e.g., IMF (1991), Van Wijnbergen (1991a and 1991b).

12 Examples of the 'political' criticism are presented in the volume edited by Vígvári (1990).

13 Examples are: Inotai and Patai (1991), Portes (1991), Dornbusch (1990), Szakolczay (1991), Köves and Oblath (1991), and Hare and Révész (1992).

14 Dornbusch (1990) is an exception; he suggests that non-payment of obligations is the cheapest way of financing a country with debts as high as Hungary's.

15 This is the main idea underlying the proposals of Inotai and Patai (1991).

16 On this issue see Oblath (1991) and Oblath and Tarr (1992).

17 In the following T_N is also assumed to be insignificant.

18 The Hungarian budget does include the item of 'debt service', but this refers to the debt of government versus that of the Central Bank. The budget deficit in

1991 reached 4 per cent of GDP, closely corresponding to foreign interest payments relative to GDP.
19 The issue of seigniorage and inflation tax is treated in Oblath and Valentiny (1992).
20 On this and related problems, see Reisen and van Trotsenburg (1988).
21 *Newsweek* (13 January, 1992) p. 14.

REFERENCES

Cohen, D. (1991) 'The solvency of Eastern Europe', in 'The Path of Reform in Central and Eastern Europe', *The European Economy*, **2**, *Special Edition*.
Dornbusch, R. (1988) 'Balance of payment issues', in R. Dornbusch and L. Helmers (eds), *The Open Economy*, Oxford: Oxford University Press for the World Bank.
    (1989) 'Debt problems and the world macroeconomy', in J.D. Sachs (ed.), *Developing Country Debt and Economic Performance*, Chicago and London: University of Chicago Press.
    (1990) 'Economic reform in Eastern Europe and the Soviet Union priorities and strategy', paper presented to the OECD Conference, 'The Transition to a Market Economy in Eastern Europe', Paris (28–30 November).
Hare, P. and T. Révész (1992) 'Hungary's transition to a market economy: the case against a "Big Bang"', *Economic Policy* (April).
IMF (1991) *World Economic Outlook* (October), Washington, D.C.: World Bank.
Inotai, András and Mihály Patai (1991) 'Adósságkezelési stratégia a kilencvenes évekre' (Debt strategy for the 90s), Washington, D.C. 16 (May) mimeo.
Köves, A. and G. Oblath (1983) 'Hungarian foreign trade in the 1970's', *Acta Oeconomica* (**3–4**).
    (1991) 'Stabilization and foreign economic strategy', *Acta Oeconomica* (**1–2**).
Oblath, G. (1991) 'Unresolved issues of COMECON trade in convertible currencies', in L. Csaba (ed.), *Systemic Change and Stabilization in Eastern Europe*, Aldershot and Brookfield: Dartmouth.
Oblath, G. and D. Tarr (1992) 'The terms of trade effects from the elimination of state trading in Soviet–Hungarian trade', *Journal of Comparative Economics*.
Oblath, G. and Á. Valentiny (1992) 'Seigniorage and inflation tax in Hungary', KOPINT/DATORG *Discussion Papers*, forthcoming.
OECD (1990) 'Financing and external debt of developing countries, 1989', Survey, Paris: OECD.
Portes, R. (1991) 'Magnarországnak enyhítenie kell az adósság terheit' (Hungary should get debt relief on foreign debt), interview with R. Portes, *Beszélő* (25 May).
Reisen, H. and A. van Trotsenburg (1988) 'Developing country debt: the budgetary and the transfer problem', *OECD Development Center Studies*, Paris: OECD.
Szakolczay, György (1991) 'A magyar adósságprobléma' (The Hungarian debt problem), *Világgazdaság* (27 March).
Vígvári, Tamás (ed.) (1990) 'Adósság' (Debt), SZGII (Institute of the Trade Unions of Research on the Economy and Society), Budapest.

Wijnbergen, S. Van (1991a) 'The Mexican debt deal', *Economic Policy* (April).
(1991b) 'Debt relief and economic growth in Mexico', *The World Bank Economic Review* (September).
The World Bank (1991) *World Debt Tables, 1991–92*, Washington, D.C.: World Bank.

12 Managing foreign debts and monetary policy during transformation

WERNER RIECKE

This chapter is by no means a scientific one; it simply outlines the pragmatic approach of the National Bank of Hungary (NBH) to the issue of debt management. It goes behind the single question of debt management insofar as it tries to explain the role of domestic monetary and fiscal policy that caused the serious increase in Hungary's convertible foreign debt to the level of approximately US$ 20 bn.

Long-term analysis always raises the problem of availability of reliable data for the period to be examined. In the case of Hungary there are data on GDP and related items, on prices and some aggregate data on the balance of payments and debt for a period of almost twenty years, but useful monetary statistics exist only since 1982. Unfortunately, while monetary statistics are improving there is an increasing doubt among Hungarian economists regarding the reliability of the GDP and income statistics; this is due to the fact that the observation methods of the Central Statistical Office are not yet fully attuned to a situation in which the small and medium-size private and privatised sector has become the driving force of the economy. The under-estimation of economic performance is crucial for our analysis, because we may therefore over-estimate the debt burden of the Hungarian economy.

1 Hungary's convertible foreign debt, 1973–91

Hungary's gross foreign debt in convertible currency was US$ 2.1 bn at the end of 1973. The rise of raw material world market prices at that time and the lack of any adjustment effort in Hungary's economic policy led to a steady increase of this debt to US$ 10.5 bn at the end of 1979. From 1979 to 1984 the nominal level of the amount of gross debt was relatively stable, ranging between 10.2 and US$ 11.5 bn. The period from 1985 to 1987 showed almost a doubling of this debt to US$ 19.6 bn at the end of 1987. Since that time the debt level has been around 20; it was 21.3 at the end of 1990, but this was mainly an accounting issue, related to the weakness of the dollar at that time. Hungary's gross debt was less than US$ 22 bn at the end of 1991, accompanied by a comfortably high level of foreign exchange reserves.

Per capita debt can be easily calculated, because of Hungary's 10 mn population: US$ 20 bn debt means a US$ 2000 *per capita* debt. This number is often used in international comparisons, but in my view it is a little misleading. This approach would expose the USA and Hungary as highly indebted countries, but China and the former USSR would get always a good rating. South Korea is risky, but Rumania is a reliable candidate for loans, etc.

Export performance and future growth prospects seem to me a better starting point for the evaluation of the debt situation, but before analysing debt-service ratios let us look more closely at developments in the past, raising and at least partly answering the usual questions regarding resource outflow, the debt trap, etc.

'Resource outflow' is defined as a trade surplus and other items of the current account which have to be maintained at a certain level simply to cover interest expenditure for the existing amount of debt. This trade surplus of course can be inflationary in the absence of sufficient voluntary saving, but it is first of all more an ideological than an economic term. If one thinks about the resource outflow created by the interest burden of outstanding debt, one observes two important facts:

* resource outflows are preceded by serious resource inflows, which created the foreign debt, and
* interest rates are simply minimum requirements on the expected return of investment.

Regarding the first aspect we may calculate cumulative time series from 1973 to 1990. Such series show that in 1991, after only fifteen years, the cumulative outflow exceeded the inflow of resources. The question of causality may also be raised here. Economies such as the Hungarian one are considered to need forced saving (or inflation, shortage, high domestic interest rates, etc.) in order to be able to cover interest payments on foreign debt by trade surpluses. On the other side nobody says that Germany or Japan 'suffers' from its trade surplus, which is probably created by the fact that in these countries there are more incentives to save than to invest. However, economic policy-makers in Hungary – in contrast to its neighbours – often made a choice during the 1970s and 1980s between austerity (an option very rarely chosen), higher inflation or an increase in foreign indebtedness. There was no serious increase in shortage on the goods and services market.

Regarding the return on investment aspect, the analysis also has a political dimension. From the purely economic point of view it is true that there is no direct relation between the increase of foreign debt, domestic investment and export performance: the latter was much more dependent on the restrictiveness of monetary and fiscal policies than on the former two variables. In other words, investments based on government decisions during the 1970s and 1980s frequently proved to be inefficient and not justified by the demand of international markets. A large part of the trade deficit in several years served only to avert serious downturns in the standard of living of the Hungarian population. In fact, in Hungarian economic statistics nothing is smoother than the time series of real private household consumption. This fact leads us to the political return on investment: US$ 20 bn is the price for the most peaceful transition in Eastern Europe, for the fact that Hungary is still an island of stability in this region and, because of this, for the fact that more than half of foreign direct investment in Eastern Europe is attracted by Hungary. Taking this all together, this is a price worth paying.

The question remains of course – returning to the purely economic approach – whether Hungary will be able to pay such a price in coming years.

The debt trap approach says that after a certain debt level is reached – as compared with the possible economic performance of a country – the interest payments will themselves be the driving force behind a further and unavoidable increase of the country's debt. This may be true for some countries, but time series for Hungary show that the largest increases in foreign debt were never connected with the interest payments of those years. The periods with the largest increase in Hungary's foreign debt are closely connected with government budget-initiated big investment decisions, large budget deficits and loose monetary policy.

The years beginning in 1989 show in many regards a new, and for many experts unexpected, picture of the Hungarian economy. Two of these aspects are worth mentioning. First, import liberalisation (1989 40 per cent, 1990 70 per cent, 1991 90 per cent of the volume of convertible imports) did not lead to an uncontrollable increase of imports, but did help to double exports in the last 3–4 years. Second, the inflow of foreign direct investment, which exceeded US$ 1.2 bn in 1991, has become a new counterpart for the financing of current account deficits and has reduced the pressure on economic policy to improve the external balance at any price.

2   Monetary policy behind the increase of debt

Before examining the future prospects of Hungary's monetary policy one has to look at the past. The increase of foreign debt in the past has its counterpart in domestic monetary and fiscal policies. The monetary approach to the balance of payments seems to be an appropriate framework for this analysis.

In terms of pure economic theory the amount of money in the economy is the sum of domestic credit and net foreign assets:

$$M = DC + NFA$$

In a small open economy with a fixed exchange rate the amount of money is determined purely by the demand for money. This is a function of real GDP and the price level. The latter equals the world price level times the exchange rate:

$$M = f(\text{real GDP}, P)$$

$$P = PW^* ER$$

This means also that the instrument of monetary policy is domestic credit creation, and in terms of change (D) the increase or decrease of foreign debt depends on whether or not domestic credit creation exceeds the increase of demand for money:

$$DNFA = DM - DDC$$

Hungary, of course, was different from the usual case of a small open economy because of its trade regime. If there is an administrative control on imports, there could not be a direct link between the world market and the domestic price level.

What happened in all those years prior to import liberalisation? The increase of domestic credit exceeded the increase of the demand for money and so the excess demand on the domestic market could be channelled into two possibilities: the further increase of foreign debt or the increase of the domestic price level.

I call this the 'inflation–current account trade-off' of Hungary's economic policy. This trade-off can be very clearly shown in time series or graphs of the 1970s and 1980s.

The exchange rate policy had its own justification in this trade-off. Since the exchange rate was fixed, but the domestic price level could increase independently from the rise of world market prices (because of the limited access to imports) exchange rate adjustment was from time to time unavoidable. But in our approach these devaluations did not add to the inflation rate, but were caused rather by the difference between world market and domestic inflation. Of course, with 90 per cent of imports liberalised, the price level stabilisation function of the exchange rate has been increased.

It is worth mentioning that in this trade-off relation the third way to respond to excess demand could have been the increase of shortage in the domestic market. This never happened in the 1970s and 1980s in the Hungarian economy because excess demand was in fact covered by excess imports, and because, even under administrative price controls, prices did follow the signals of the markets, although with some delay. The fact that there is no 'monetary overhang' in Hungary is a big advantage in the transformation process.

Before analysing the prospects of Hungary's monetary policy let us have a look at two questions:

* Is the debt manageable now and in the near future?
* How dangerous would any rescheduling attempt be for Hungary?

Looking at different debt-service ratios, time series show an improvement in the last two years and an even more dramatic improvement is expected in the future. This will be caused mainly by three factors:

* increase of foreign debt stopped in 1990–1 (in terms of net debt),
* NBH succeeded in improving the maturity profile of its long-term debt, and the share of short-term debt may be reduced, and
* there has been a large increase in convertible export revenues in the last two years. Exports now exceed the US$ 10 bn level.

With the debt-service ratio reaching the 30 per cent benchmark, there should be no serious problem in financing Hungary's outstanding foreign debt in the next few years. 'Financing outstanding debt' is the key phrase: if there is no doubt of the country's willingness and ability to service its debt, then no problem will arise in replacing maturing loans by new ones. In the case of a non-increasing debt, the debt burden reduces to the interest payments, which will represent in the case of Hungary less than 15 per cent of exports in the next years.

Credibility is crucial to this approach: in the case of an attempt to change this attitude – no matter whether it is called rescheduling, debt relief, maturity extension or whatever – there would be an enormous increase in adjustment costs. Let me list the main factors:

* Amortisation and new credits ranged between US$ 2.5 and 4 bn yearly. A change in Hungary's debt policy would bring only a small reduction in principal payments, but would cause a loss of access to

private capital markets, which are the main sources of debt refinancing. Attempts to ease the situation would thus result in a much larger outflow of resources.

* Moreover, the inflow of foreign direct investment would slow down.
* There would be a capital flight from the US$ 1.5 bn foreign exchange deposits of Hungarian private households.

Taking all this into account, to pay on time seems to be the cheapest solution in the medium and in the longer term. It does not seem reasonable to build up a civil society and a pluralistic democracy based on a free market with massive foreign aid.

3 Prospects for Hungary's economy

If we look only at the debt issue, the question regarding Hungary's future prospects has a simple answer: with increasing exports and with a real growth of GDP we will 'grow out' of this debt. Increasing the denominator is the simplest solution. We had a debt of US$ 20 bn with 5 bn exports – which looked very dangerous. Now we have a US$ 20 bn debt with 10 bn exports, which seems to be manageable. If we are to succeed we need to have exports of 20 bn yearly; Hungary's foreign debt will then be no longer the main issue of economic policy.

But – since the debt was created by, or at least with the assistance of, monetary and fiscal policy – the problem will not disappear without appropriate monetary and budgetary policy. And this is the real challenge for the future.

From the monetary point of view we can recall the monetary approach to the balance of payments. Let us look at the structure of the monetary survey:

	Assets	*Liabilities* (HUF bn)	
NFA	− 1000	M	1500
DC	2500		

(This balance sheet is highly stylised but it indicates the appropriate magnitudes.)

The problem of indebted countries is that the amount of domestic credit is much greater than the amount of money. And, of course, a large share of domestic credit is the liability of the budget. In such a situation monetary policy aiming at external equilibrium has to ensure that the nominal increase of domestic credit equals the nominal increase of demand for money. A simple calculation: 5 per cent real growth plus 5 per cent inflation with stable velocity would mean a 10 per cent increase in the demand for money, according to our monetary survey a HUF 150 bn increase. Targeting a HUF 150 bn increase of domestic credit, which is a 6 per cent increase in outstanding domestic credit, in fact means a very restrictive credit policy, because of the 10 per cent growth of nominal GDP.

As an example: monetary policy was considered successful in 1991, but external and internal equilibrium was achieved with a 27 per cent increase in broad money and a 10 per cent increase in domestic credit. In the longer run such a policy can be maintained only if the share of the budget in the increase of domestic credit is reduced year by year, in other words if the budget deficit is decreasing, or even switching over to a surplus. This was not the case in 1991: the approved budget for that year had a deficit under HUF 80 bn, but the outcome will be a deficit around HUF 100 bn. In 1991 this could be financed by relatively high – and unexpected – saving by private households. The price is paid in the form of a relatively high level of interest rates.

The 1992 budget also includes a HUF 70 bn deficit, but even raw calculations show that at least another 50 bn should be added. This may have differing outcomes:

* inflation may not decrease from 35 per cent in 1991 to 20–25 per cent in 1992, or
* the level of domestic interest rates may remain high even while the inflation rate is decreasing, or
* a new period of increase of foreign debt may begin (together with a decrease in the presently comfortable level of foreign exchange reserves).

Taking all this into account the future of Hungary's foreign debt problem depends on the public sector (budget) reform, which has been postponed by the Hungarian government and the likelihood of it is decreasing as we come closer to the date of the next election (1994).

Monetary policy on its own – even with an independent Central Bank – will be hardly able to ensure the internal equilibrium needed to achieve external equilibrium.

Discussion of Part Four

L. ALAN WINTERS

Part Four of this volume contains two excellent and interesting chapters. They start from very similar perceptions – Hungary has built up a stock of foreign debt without building up a corresponding stock of productive assets – and end with similar conclusions – Hungary should keep up her debt-service payments. In between they diverge somewhat, but even so share – perhaps contrary to the stereotypical Hungarian character – a marked degree of optimism: Werner Riecke in Chapter 12 says there is no problem, while Gábor Oblath in Chapter 11 says there is a problem but also a solution. My comments, on the other hand, are typically British: they reflect a fatalistic acceptance of the prospect of austerity in arguing that there is at least a high probability that the two authors are being over-optimistic. I shall not directly challenge their policy conclusion – to keep paying up – but I shall argue that the dangers and discomfort that it entails are great. I also note at the outset that if there is any case for renegotiating Hungarian debt, my scenarios make it relatively stronger.

Riecke stresses the need to continue debt service in order to retain access to capital markets, and he shows that, in the past, Hungary's exemplary record policy has allowed old debt to be readily renewed when it falls due. This is true, but in isolation it is insufficient to justify the policy. If the debt is a problem, keeping up the payments just in order to be able to enter next year with the same level of debt as last is not good economics. Riecke also argues that rescheduling may cut off the flows of foreign direct investment – which I do not find inevitable, nor even particularly plausible – and of trade credit – which may indeed be a temporary difficulty. Of course, if there is to be a rescheduling it should be quick and complete: protracted negotiations would at least temporarily have the effects Riecke fears, as well as possibly causing capital flight.

Riecke is sanguine about Hungary's debt-service ratios. I do not want (ever) to involve myself in the arguments about the usefulness of the various ratios but, at 30 per cent, Hungary's debt-service: exports ratio is among the world's higher values. Moreover, I would not draw much comfort from the fact that Hungary's *per capita* debt approximates the USA's: the USA has got problems and she is both richer than Hungary and favoured by running the world's principal currency. I also feel the fragility of Riecke's argument that the future looks better on the debt front. His figures show that debt has stopped expanding and that exports are buoyant, and he states that the maturity structure of debt is much improved. That is all well and good, but the debt problem – if such it is – is a medium- to long-run one, and two years is an awfully short period over which to identify new trends.

I have one major worry about Gábor Oblath's analysis – his identification of unrequited transfers (UT) and foreign direct investment (FDI) as saviours. When private individuals receive UT they may be forced to convert them into local currency, but they are still likely to increase their demand for imports and hence reduce the authorities' net 'gain' of foreign currency. If conversion is not forced, this leakage is likely to be greater.

Similarly, FDI seems likely to entail leakages into imports. If FDI amounts merely to selling off existing Hungarian assets with no associated purchases of foreign equipment, intermediate goods or services, the leakage will remain small. This process is essentially a debt–equity swap; it will allow a more convenient scheduling of payments abroad – to when firms are making profits – but, of course, at the expense of raising the average rate of return. If, as seems more likely, FDI entails substantial imports of equipment and inputs, the leakage abroad will be large, leaving little over for debt finance.

The previous paragraph appears to suggest that FDI would be better if it eschewed extra imports, but that interpretation is wrong. In the longer run FDI is the medium for industrial restructuring, technical change, acquiring management skills, etc. all of which are essential to long-run recovery. Anything which discourages these inflows will ultimately be counter-productive. Moreover, foreign investors will be far more likely to come to Hungary if they feel that disinvestment and/or the repatriation of profits will be permitted, and both sorts of outflow look less likely if the FDI flow has been previously 'wasted' on debt service.

Hence I am less optimistic than Oblath that UT and FDI will, let alone should, provide for future debt service. If they do not, the outlook is not comfortable. Rescheduling will be difficult to negotiate for three reasons: Hungary is too small to threaten bank portfolios; one cannot really see Hungary as the magic ingredient missing over the 1980s in the formation of debtors' cartels; and Hungary appears more determined than, say, Latin American debtors to reform and improve its economic performance regardless of its debt position, reducing the force of Krugman's (1989) elegant argument for debt relief. The most plausible argument is moral and political – regime sustainability: if renegotiation is to be avoided I agree with Oblath and Riecke that substantial discipline will be required in the public sector, and that hurts: maybe so much that even the Hungarian commitment to reform will be undermined.

REFERENCE

Krugman, P.R. (1989) 'Private capital flows to problem debtors', Chapter 15 in J.D. Sachs (ed.), *Developing Country Debt and The World Economy*, Chicago: Chicago University Press, pp. 285–98.

RICHARD PORTES

The chapters by Oblath (Chapter 11) and Riecke (Chapter 12) are two excellent and in many ways complementary studies. Werner Riecke defends the official position with skill and force, while Gábor Oblath gives arguments and counter-arguments concerning the need for debt reduction, with illuminating analysis. I disagree with the conclusions of both authors: I have for some time been on record as favouring substantial debt reduction for Hungary, along the lines of the Mexican debt reduction agreement – though more generous. But that is not the only issue to discuss in these wide-ranging chapters.

The authors give us a large amount of useful data, so it is perhaps unappreciative to ask for more. Nevertheless, some of the series stop in 1989 and could be updated with the new *World Debt Tables*; we ought to have a series for secondary market prices of Hungarian debt; and I should also like to see an estimate for the shares of Hungarian debt in bonds as well as in bank debt.

The chapters might have given some attention to the history of the build-up of debt. The commodity price shock in the early 1970s hit the resource-poor Hungarian economy particularly hard, and the authorities chose not to adjust, but to finance the resulting excess absorption from the international capital markets. The build-up of debt was already worrying by 1977–8, and the supply of funds dried up after the Polish debt crisis. Even before Mexico stopped debt service in August 1982, Hungary came very close to being forced to declare a moratorium. Both the authors disregard the supply of loanable funds from the international market: it was not just due to Hungarian policies that debt stopped growing in 1979 and was effectively constant for five years, then was permitted to double in 1985–7. Hungary was credit-constrained for a period, and when the constraint came off, it over-borrowed again.

What did the borrowing accomplish? Not much in the way of building up a modern capital stock, but rather support for consumption, which doubtless helped to maintain political stability. That could not last, and the key question now is how long the current squeeze on consumption – and the crowding out of investment – can be maintained in the cause of faithful debt service. Riecke contends that Hungary can grow out of its debt overhang by continuing to expand exports at the rate of the past couple of years. But the share of exports in GDP cannot grow indefinitely, and the country cannot grow out of its debt unless output grows. The record of the past few years and the prospects for investment and growth are not encouraging; and I would maintain that this is primarily due to the immense pressure that debt service exerts on the economy.

Debt service must be financed internally as well as externally: it is a considerable burden on the budget. The authors do not tell us how heavy the burden is, but simply to pay interest must amount to 4–5 per cent of GDP – as an expenditure item in the budget. That entails some combination of heavy pressures on tax rates, real interest rates, and the money supply (to obtain seigniorage). It is hardly surprising that investment and output are down.

The external counterpart is the transfer of resources abroad in the form of net exports. There is an interesting contrast between the two chapters in their interpretation or denial of the political significance of this net resource outflow. Surely one cannot say that there is no economic or political negative consequence of net resource outflow, so long as it is covered by 'voluntary' saving. This view is not far from mercantilism. And the saving is not all voluntary, except in an accounting sense, since debt service does require budgetary expenditure; moreover, the required combination of saving and taxation may imply distortions of intertemporal allocation.

I would prefer a variant of the absorption approach to Riecke's monetary approach to the balance of payments. He argues that excessive expansion of domestic credit causes excess domestic demand, which requires an increase in foreign borrowing or domestic inflation. But what causes the excessive expansion of domestic credit? And if it is held down, what happens to output?

Foreign direct investment is the current hope – not to say panacea. But it, too, has to be serviced. Oblath is right to say that some substitution of equity for debt is healthy for the Hungarian economy, but that should tend to raise the average yield to foreigners on their holdings of Hungarian assets; and if FDI does not in due course earn a sufficient yield, it will certainly dry up. FDI is important for know-how and technology, but it is not a macroeconomic solution to the debt-service problem.

Hungarian policy-makers should study the example of Mexico – they might even discuss it discreetly with friends at the IMF. Like Hungary, Mexico went through a lengthy and difficult process of reform, established its commitment and credentials, and achieved much. *Then* it went for a Brady-style debt reduction. Once that was agreed, everything fell into place. Interest rates dropped dramatically, capital flowed into the country at an amazing rate, and Mexico quickly returned to unhindered access to the international capital markets. That is a tremendously encouraging and instructive success story. If it were explicable simply by Mexico's geographical position, it would have happened much earlier.

Werner Riecke hopes that Hungary is not viewed in the context of the rest of Central and Eastern Europe, or of Latin America, or in the historical perspective of countries that obtained debt reduction and went on to rapid growth. I share his view that Hungary is special, but not that special. There are lessons to be learned from both historical and contemporary experience.

Part Five

Legislative and tax reform

13   A legal framework for the Hungarian transition, 1989–91

TAMÁS SÁRKÖZY

1   Introduction: now that the wall has been pulled down

Hungary always had a special way of adopting the Soviet legal system in the last two decades. This was partly due to a more sophisticated commercial regulatory system (based on the Commercial Code of Act No. XXXVII, 1875 and its supplements) which had existed since before the Second World War. The Commercial Code (hereafter Com.C.) had been continuously developed, and in 1930 the limited liability company had been introduced. The Com.C. was never formally repealed, even after 1948, but it was rarely applied under Stalinist circumstances. The economic legislation of 1988–9, particularly the Act on Companies, revoked a major part of the Com.C., although several of its more efficient provisions were incorporated into the new legislation, and some are still in force (e.g. relating to warehousing).

The development of the present Hungarian commercial law is constrained by the so far vestigial civil liberalisation: despite some remarkable changes a comprehensive commercial and legal culture has failed to grow. This fact, with other controversial anti-trade and anti-cultural consequences of a Soviet-type socialist system, is rendering the transition of Hungary into a modern civil society very difficult. Hungary's distinctive adoption of the Soviet system was also due to the fact that developments officially viewed with disfavour in practice throve after 1956. Both civil rights and autonomy of enterprises were much broader than in the former USSR in 1953–6, and during the Kádár era a relatively wide 'liberalism' (rising living standards, the so-called 'goulash communism') and higher artistic and cultural level spread. Legislation played a significant role in this – the Civil Code (Act No. IV, 1959), Penal Code (Act No. V, 1961), Labour Code (7/1951 Law Decree); Act No. IV, 1957 on

Administrative Procedure and Act No. III, 1952 on Civil Procedure were also codified. Several areas of the economy were also governed by statutes.

2   Attempts to create a 'socialist market' model, 1967–88

2.1   The 1 January 1968 reform

The Hungarian economic reform introduced on 1 January 1968 was an attempt to reduce the intervention of the state in the economy and to enlarge enterprises' independence without undermining the political regime, despite having an inevitable liberalising impact. The reform also desired to create a so-called 'socialist market economy', in which the administration governed the production and distribution of goods by enterprises, primarily by means of so-called 'indirect economic regulations and legal instructions'. Twenty years of cyclical repression and relative freedom – mostly due to international and economic–political circumstances – failed to achieve the success that would have proved the validity of a 'third socialist way' different from that of the Soviet model. One indisputable merit of the system was, however, that it fostered the development of the basic institutions of a market economy so that the transition into a 'civil' market economy – when international conditions warranted it – was significantly eased.

2.2   Main developments

We can distinguish twelve key dimensions to this change:

1   The *regulation of state-owned property* in the Civil Code. Although its dominant role has remained, the field of operations belonging exclusively to state ownership and the sphere of state monopolies has noticeably shrunk since 1980.

2   The *increased autonomy of the state-owned enterprises*, even if prejudicial to the centralised administration, has been a crucial principle of the Hungarian economic reform. This was confirmed first of all by the 11/1967 (X.13) Decree of Government, then Act No. VI, 1977 on state-owned enterprises (the autonomy of enterprises having been declared in an amendment attached to the constitution in 1971 and executed by Act No. I, 1972). The amendment of 1984–5, the so-called company management reform (22/1984 Law Decree), was a landmark in the status of state-owned enterprises. As a result, a mere 20 per cent of enterprises have remained under central state adminis-

trative control; about 80 per cent became so-called *self-governing enterprises*, whereby almost all the state's ownership rights were transferred to the enterprises. These ownership rights are exercised by the so-called Council of Enterprise in the majority of these self-governing enterprises; in the rest, a direct *self-administration* by employees has been introduced (in 10 per cent, the enterprise is managed by a General Meeting or by a Meeting of Delegates).

3   Act No. II, 1967, on *Agricultural Producing Cooperatives*, significantly increased the autonomy of these cooperatives, guaranteed by an opportunity of *household farming* (half-private) for their members. Act No. IV, 1967 on Lands created the possibility of a separate cooperative type of land ownership. Cooperatives have extended to the fields of industry, trade, house maintenance, and savings banks, among others, as one of the forms of joint private activity. In Hungary, unlike in any other East European country, a *unified cooperative Act* had already been passed by the early 1970s (Act No. III, 1971) and the constitution declared the equality of state and cooperative ownership (in practice, this has not been fully accomplished). The amendments of the 1970s and 1980s have eased restrictions further – although cooperative members were still denied a proprietary status – and more flexible new cooperative forms have been generated: cooperative side activities, small cooperatives, and cooperative specialised groups – which are the forerunners of the present private enterprises. Act No. I, 1987 on Land cancelled the permanent land use provisions and the distinction between personal and private property, and pulled down the barriers to the acquisition of ownership: another great step forward.

4   The *Labour Code* elaborated in Act No. II, 1967 also notably enlarged the autonomy of both contracting parties – employees and enterprises – in negotiations over labour relations. Among other things, it transferred the right to a collective contract to enterprises, widened the rights of trade unions, and extended the statutory period of notice on severance.

5   The non-cooperative *private enterprises* have come to prominence only recently, in the last decade of the Hungarian economic reform. Such enterprises were established between 1979 and 1981 as additional side-business forms, distinct from the so-called socialist sector: shopkeepers, restaurants operating under contractual arrangements, civil law associations, VGKMs or in-company working pools,[1] etc. (16/1981, 15/1981, 7/1982 Law Decrees; 30/1981 (IX.14) Decree of Government).

6   The *Corporation Law* has been in process of development since the

1960s, at the beginning separately in the cooperative sector (after 1961) and later in the state sector (after 1967). The enterprises and cooperatives were allowed to form in a so-called *economic association* for the first time by the 19/1970 Law Decree and later by the 4/1978 Law Decree this was extended to commercial enterprises and newly created forms such as a *joint company* working with collateral of the members, or a *business union*, which are still existing forms.

The possibility of forming joint ventures with Western capital participation was introduced in 1972 (28/1972 (X.23) Decree of Minister of Finance), and in the form of the traditional company limited by shares, a limited liability company governed by Com.C. In practice, however, there were initially only a few such joint ventures with foreign capital participation.

7   Several statutes have departed from the classical socialist model even in the field of economic management – of course proceeding within the constraints of the socialist regime. The most significant legislation here is the Act No. VII, 1972 on the *Planning of the Economy*, which eliminated planning directives with the force of compulsion so that they did not apply even to state-owned enterprises. Act No. III, 1974 on *Foreign Trade* was even more liberalising. Act No. IV, 1972 abolished the Decision Committees, incorporating the economic courts within the unified court system. Finally, Act No. II, 1979 on *State Finances* modernised and placed on a legislative footing the regulations concerning the budget and the planning system.

8   The planning/contractual system was abolished by a comprehensive updating of the Civil Code – Act No. IV, 1977 – and disposed the *contracts between companies* to a market economy model.

9   Act No. V, 1923 on *Unfair Economic Competition* was revived by Decrees of Government after 1968, reactivating the institutions of antitrust laws and economic courts. This field was consolidated by Act No. IV, 1984 on *Prohibition of Unfair Business Activities*. Regulations on commercial administration consist of 33/1975 (XI.29) Decree of Government on Product Distribution and 38/1984 (XI.5) Decree of Government on Regulation of Prices, this latter replaced by Act No. LXXXVII, 1990.

10 The legal basis for the *protection of nature and the environment* was provided in Act No. II, 1976 and the 4/1982 Law Decree on Environmental Protection, but environmental safeguards have also been included in Act No. III, 1964 on Construction Affairs; Act No. IV, 1964 on Water Supply; Act No. III, 1960 on Mining; and Act No. IV, 1976 on Alimentation.

11 Since the end of the 1960s a relatively modern *intellectual property*

protection has been developed. The Act on *Industrial Property*, Act No. II, 1969, extends to patents and inventions and Hungarian law also recognises the protection of innovation and know-how. Act No. IX, 1969 governs the protection of trade marks and industrial design, and regulations also include those on licence contracts. Hungary is a member state of several organisations for international industrial property protection, such as the Paris Union.

12 The initiatives for the representation of *economic interests* have mostly been interpolated in other rules – for the trade unions in the Labour Code, for national and regional associations and councils of cooperatives in the Cooperative Act, etc. The Hungarian Economic Chamber (the former Chamber of Commerce) has developed through several stages and finally emerged as a body for the representation of (mainly the big) state-owned companies (it is nevertheless an open and voluntary organisation, see the 62/1980 Decree of Government).

It is therefore obvious that Hungary has entered a state of social transition with a far more sophisticated and market-oriented economy than any of the other East European countries. The majority of these statutes and other legal prescriptions (with some inevitable amendments) are not only temporarily effective: they are capable also of serving a future modern civil market economy.

3   The legal climate during the transition to a free market system

3.1   The Act on Companies (Act No. VI, 1988)

The transition phase of the economic system has been based on Act No. VI, 1988 on Companies, which came into effect on 1 January 1989. This Act consolidates the previously fragmented corporation law, provides equal conditions for domestic and foreign investments, and introduces in practice an unlimited opportunity for private enterprise. It modernises the traditional forms of companies, acknowledging both the Hungarian development of corporate form and the direction of international commercial law such as that of the EC.

The Act has also adopted an approach which might be referred to as 'rules of law in a welfare state': it leaves no way for administrative discretion since most of the rules, etc. are mandatory.

3.2   Supplementary statutes

Several supplementary statutes were later added to the Act on Companies:

1   The *Foreign Investment Act in Hungary*, Act No. XXIV, 1988. This came into force simultaneously with the Act on Companies in order to complete its civil law provisions with regulations on financial, labour and customs matters.

2   A modern, Western-type *tax system*: Act No. V, 1987 on Value Added Tax; Act No. VI, 1987 on Income Tax; Act No. IX, 1988 on Corporate Profits Tax. These had been introduced on 1 January 1988 and were incorporated in the Act on Companies on 1 January 1989 (see also Chapters 7, 8 and 9 above).

3   The *Transformation Act*, Act No. XIII, 1989. This came into effect in the middle of 1990 and provides the potential for economic transformation in two ways: on the one hand, it regulates relations between business organisations, on the other – as the first privatising Act – it transforms the state-owned enterprises into companies limited by shares or limited liability companies.

4   Rules for the *procedure of incorporation*, the 23/1989 Law Decree, and the *procedure in insolvency*, the 11/1986 and 26/1988 Law Decrees amended by s.63 of the Deregulation Act (see below), have both now come into force.

5   The amendment of the *Cooperative Act*, Act No. II, 1988. This abandoned the former rigid notions about the indivisibility of cooperative property, so that members may now for the first time possess a joint proprietorial status; the Act also makes the cooperative form more comparable to that of companies, an aim reinforced by the 1991 Act on Cooperatives.

6   The *Private Enterprise Act* was passed in January 1990. It offered the same opportunities to the individual entrepreneur – artisans and small merchants – as to companies. The compulsory personal participation of the individual in the undertaking is abolished, and there is now no limit concerning the number of employees (in 1981–2 a maximum of 30 employees could be employed by an individual; this was raised to 500 on 1 January 1989 and has now been abolished entirely).

7   The basic rules on securities were incorporated in the Civil Code in 1988, Act No. XXV, 1988. This was amplified by the *Securities and Stock Exchange Act*, Act No. VI, 1990, a statute which made it possible to open the Stock Market in Budapest in 1990.

8   Act No. VIII, 1990. This established the *State Property Agency* (SPA) to support the privatisation process. This central Agency represents

the state as the proprietor (owner). Act No. VII, 1990 on the Protection of State-Owned Property, in conjunction with the SPA, regulates the procedures by which state-owned enterprises sell or lease their assets or use them as capital contribution in kind to business organisations.

3.3   Social developments

Despite these accelerated and dynamic political changes, the necessary social consciousness, commercial culture, legal knowledge, expertise (from corporate lawyers, judges, auditors and accountants) and facilities (a building for the Court of Registration, computerised data processing, accounting/balance sheet stationery, etc.) are not yet in evidence. Anomalies, abuses, and similar undesirable phenomena are therefore inevitable, and may even be exacerbated at a time when the political climate is volatile and it is hard to make people appreciate what lessons have to be learned, and what hardships borne. A fairly intensive debate has already been generated as to whether:

(a)   abuses should be accepted temporarily, while work to develop a more liberalised culture goes on (the 'liberal' viewpoint); or whether
(b)   the state should by administrative intervention prevent these anomalies as soon as they occur (the 'etatist' viewpoint).

3.4   The MDF's position

The activity of the governing coalition steered by the winning Hungarian Democratic Forum (MDF) after the elections of May 1990 can be summarised as follows:

(a)   Amending some elements of former statutes in order to allow broader possible intervention by the state:

* This has been apparent in the recently enlarged scope of the regulations concerning the State Property Agency, Act No. LIII, 1990.
* In self-governing enterprises, state delegates are now to be sent to the Council of Enterprise, 20/1990 (VII.3) Decree of Government.
* In the Transformation Act and the Company Act, the rights of enterprises, judicial review and the compensation payable on privatisation, money now flowing into the budget, have been diluted by Acts No. LXXI and LXXII, 1990, coming into effect on 18 September 1990.
* In order to avoid abuse, the Land Act has been amended, by Acts

No. XLI and XXXVIII, 1990, in a way that has in practice caused a moratorium in the business transactions of the real estates in state ownership: regional property protecting committees may permit the sale or lease of land and its incorporation into a company as a contribution in kind.

(b)   *Obstacles created by 'etatism'*

This so-called 'government etatism' creates more obstacles for foreign investment, already criticised by the Opposition; it stems partly from the makeup of the coalition, whose basic support belongs mostly to the intelligentsia sensitive to rural rather than urban needs and with a ertain nationalist complexion. It should be emphasised, however, that the streamlining of legislation, such as the Law on Competition, is basically liberal in intent and when temporary difficulties have been overcome and the civil system is stabilised the liberalist tenor of economic legislation will probably return.

3.5   Economic deregulation

In the name of the previous 'administrative state' (between September 1989 and May 1990) a remarkable economic deregulation was carried through in Hungary, with the help of the World Bank. About 6000 lower-level Decrees of Government or Ministers were repealed, and a Deregulation Act, Act No. XXII, 1990, was passed. Unfortunately, this deregulation project, which prescribed the duties of ministries in future legislation and stated that the costs and more remote effects of any proposal would have to be analysed and appended to a Bill, was cancelled by the incoming government; hopefully after the current upheaval it will be resumed.

4   Are things looking up?

The transition to a market economy is going to be a key issue for at least the next few years.

4.1   Economic law

Economic law will retain a structure fundamentally similar to that of the 1980s, but with continuing attempts to adjust it to changing conditions. This process of adjustment should be applied to the constitution as well since there are still several older provisions in place reminiscent of Soviet-style socialism.

4.2   Financial institutions

Parliament has already passed many of the finance-related Bills outlined in 1989:

* Accounting Act (Act No. XVIII, 1991)
* Central Bank Act (Act No. LX, 1991)
* Financial Institutes' Banking Act (Act No. LXIX, 1991)
* Insolvency Act (Act No. IL, 1991)
* State Financing Act (submitted to Parliament)
* Currency Exchange Act (in preparation)
* Customs Act (in preparation).

4.3   Privatisation

Consolidating previous statutes, the *Uniform Privatising Act* has been delayed because of its controversial nature, but may be passed in 1992. According to the current privatising strategy the rather state-administered method may attempt a compromise between the former concept of leaving the initiative to enterprises and the other extreme of permitting only control to the state. These laws are unlikely to be well formulated, and continuous alteration is to be anticipated. The restitution of former ownership is not likely to be accomplished, and Acts on compensation are foreseeable (such as Act No. XXV, 1991 on Compensation).

4.4   Company legislation

The Act on Companies and its supplementary statutes will basically have to remain as they are, although some technical amendments will be needed to cope with continuing adjustments both to economic reality and to EC law. This has already been achieved in the regulation of companies and foreign investment.

4.5   Codification

Greater and more comprehensive codification is not likely to be achieved in the next two years because of the present uneasy political atmosphere and the current legislative overload. This also means that the preparation of a new Civil Code will be postponed as well. The preparation of a new Labour Code, Labour Protection Act and Social Insurance Act is also under threat. Although a Social Insurance Bill has already been passed by Parliament (and see Chapter 16 below), there is still vigorous political debate over all these areas, stemming from the practical problems posed by the burdens, costs and risks of transition.

The submission of a Bill on Representation of Economic Interests and Negotiations (trade unions, chambers of commerce) is also now uncertain. It is widely desired, but the outcome is still in doubt – the prevailing national lobbies (National Association for Entrepreneurs, Association for Managers, Agricultural Chamber, etc.) are now established in association form, as are the councils of employees, although civil law provisions are hardly effective in this field. The question of the new Land Act and Cooperation Act is no less troublesome, owing to the confusion generated by attempts to found the property of cooperatives on the basis of private property structures.

NOTE

1 The company contracts with workers use company facilities outside normal working hours (normally to permit overtime wage payments without attracting the wage tax).

14 Tax reform in Hungary

JENŐ KOLTAY

1 Introduction

The Hungarian tax reform is the first, and until now the only, comprehensive fiscal reform in the Central–Eastern European economies, initiated and implemented within the framework of the *ancien régime*. (In the case of the Eastern part of Germany we cannot speak of a genuine tax reform in one or several consecutive steps, rather of a country being suddenly subject to an organically developed tax system with some inevitable distortions and exceptions.) The resulting tax system is already comparable to the tax systems of developed market economies, though far from being in conformity with them or in harmony with the EC standards and directions to be followed by Hungary on the road towards full membership. (Hungary is associated with the EC from 1992.)

The new tax system was introduced in one major reform package, followed by frequent modifications and further reform steps. The 1988 reform, much broader and deeper than the tax reforms of developed market economies, without fully accomplishing its task, raised very clearly the problem of incompatibility of the tax system and the economic system as a whole (Koltay 1987, 1989). The former was already shaped in the pattern of market economies, the latter was moving (far) away from the command economy, but maintaining its basic features. Now, in the period of transition to a market economy the question is even more relevant: whether such an incompatibility could promote the economic transformation, and have a positive feedback on changing the whole economic system, or whether redistribution of property rights and other systemic changes are preconditions of a successful tax reform.

2   Before the tax reform

The recognition of the importance of taxation and fiscal policy had led by 1968 to the creation of a more or less structured tax system. It gained a prime role as the main economic regulator of the indirect system of central economic management which replaced the system of plan targets after the 1968 economic reform (NEM). The main function of taxation was not simply to finance public spending, but also to serve contradictory policy objectives, far from traditional functions of taxation, and to sustain the redistribution machinery of an overwhelming state.

The relative autonomy of state-owned enterprises gained in reform waves (1968 economic reform, 1985 enterprise reform) justifies us in denoting the obligatory payments of state enterprises to the state budget as *taxes* and the whole of such obligatory payments as a tax system. (For the pre-1968 period the term *levy* is appropriate to distinguish from taxes all obligatory payments where there was no change of ownership in the transfer.) The structure of this tax system was unique in comparison to both market and command economies. The bulk of government revenue was realised from direct taxes and only one-sixth came from indirect taxes. Two-thirds of tax receipts came from taxes paid by state-owned enterprises. Personal taxes constituted only a few per cent.

Enterprise taxes were differentiated, or even individualised, according to property form, organisation, sphere of activity, branch and firm size. Almost every tax was a 'multi-function' one and several taxes had similar functions (from purchasing power regulation and price control through export promotion to energy-saving and product structure change). There were many and continuously changing allowances, exemptions and smaller and larger subsidies on the expenditure side, making the system confused and opaque. Employees were levied on their wages by a social security contribution. This functioned as a quasi-income tax, with progressive rates, marginal rates being the effective ones.

A peculiarity of Hungarian indirect taxation – beyond its small weight in tax revenues – was that there was no genuine general turnover tax. The one-stage turnover tax embraced only part of products and services, and was rather a set of different consumption taxes (it best resembled the former British purchase tax). Many products and services were not only exempt from taxation but were directly subsidised. Within one product group (for example, clothes of different sizes) taxation and subsidisation could coexist. The number of individual tax and subsidy rates was at first measured in thousands, later in hundreds.

The aim of the tax reform was to change this state of affairs by easing the taxation of production and firms and shifting part of the tax burden on consumption and personal income and to re-establish a 'two-level price system', where producer prices were lower than consumer prices.

The reform was supposed to bring about transparency in the economy both for producers and consumers, with fewer exemptions and allowances, a lower number of taxes and an institutional ban on frequent alteration. New and remaining old taxes were to be fixed by law. The tax system should become thereby simpler, transparent, neutral and stable, with eventual changes predictable and the uncertainty for economic agents reduced. The main function of taxation should be to secure the indispensable revenue for the budget and horizontal and vertical equity in taxation.

3   Preparation and implementation of the tax reform

International practice had an outstanding role in preparing the tax reform and dictating the new taxes to be introduced. Effects were attributed to the envisaged tax system (e.g. 'equity in bearing the tax burden', 'making invisible income visible'), that realistically could not be claimed in the Hungarian context.

The new taxes, with much that was arbitrary and accidental in their design, were claimed to be the only workable solution for approaching sector neutrality and equal chances in competition, goals which may be attained in different ways and which cannot even be guaranteed by the chosen taxes. The detrimental effects and the hardships of implementation were underrated, or denied outright. The profession and the larger public were excluded from preparations, and the debate which later nevertheless unfolded was not exempt from the same kind of disinformation: the role of taxpayers' information in the Hungarian and similar cases is even more important than in the case of tax reforms in market economies (Buchanan, 1987).

Experiences of Western tax reforms are hard to adopt directly. In developed market economies, even if from time to time considerable transformations were undertaken, their depth and dimension were far less than that of our tax reform, and much more time and effort was devoted to their implementation. Much simpler and much more constrained tax reforms were introduced (often phased in) only after several years of preparation and public debate; sometimes reforms already announced were postponed (the case of Italy or Greece with VAT, for example).

Previous, and even recent, tax reforms of developed market economies never caused such a profound restructuring of the tax system as in Hungary. Only a few developing countries' tax reform (e.g. the 1983 tax reform of Indonesia, see Gillis, 1985) may be likened to the Hungarian one. In market economies the share of corporate taxes is nowhere more than 10–15 per cent (30 per cent with employers' social security contributions). The bulk of tax revenue has been secured for long decades by general turnover taxes and personal income taxes. Reforms only replaced and/or improved former types of turnover taxation (sales tax, purchase tax, Bruttoumsatzsteuer) and a more differentiated income taxation (schedular taxes). More recently the transformation of tax systems progressed all over the world towards simplification, globalisation, and burden reduction, first of all in personal income taxation.

The evaluation of price and wage impacts was largely substituted by references to foreign experience. Even inflationary effects were predicted referring to such experience in the absence of well-founded, detailed calculations or impact analyses. It had a soothing effect, for example, to hear that the introduction of VAT did not raise consumer prices in this or that country, but it was irrelevant for the Hungarian case where VAT was a substitute for enterprise taxes and not an improved version of the old general turnover tax.

In this context one could hear such bold and lively statements as 'tax reform may reduce the rate of price increase', adding the veiled threat that 'without it, price increase would surely be greater . . .' One could see in advance that under our circumstances a 'two-level price system' could be introduced only by slightly reducing producer prices and considerably raising consumer prices, i.e. by speeding up inflation.

Without market competition there was no way of reducing producer prices by easing direct taxation and thereby holding back the increase of consumer prices. Buyers facing monopolies and shortage had to accept higher prices, and firms could not be prevented by administrative measures from keeping for themselves the profit arising from enterprise tax reductions. In this respect the lessons of the Hungarian producer price reshuffle corroborate those experienced in monopoly markets. 'Preventive' price increases of individual firms were 'neutralised' by raising proposed tax rates before their introduction, producer prices did not fall as was forecast (by 5 or 3.3 per cent) but kept level and consumer prices rose more (by 8 instead of 6 per cent). This already foreshadowed the fact that inflation would be higher than envisaged.

The badly shaped personal income tax, introduced under unfavourable economic circumstances, contributed, directly and indirectly, to price increases. By reinforcing the pressure for wage increases it gave a cost-push impetus and/or put a constraint on work effort. The declared liberalisation of wages coupled with the introduction of personal income tax (see below) proved to be illusory. In 1988 the central wage regulation, relying on taxing profits at prohibitive rates in case of excessive wage increases (a scheme comparable to Western proposals on tax based incomes policy), became even more strict; later on it was only partially relaxed and even in 1992 can be (re)activated if macro level tripartite wage negotiations fail to replace it in controlling wage increases in an efficient way.

4   The new taxes

The 1988 reform introduced two new taxes: *personal income tax* (PIT) and *value added tax* (VAT). At the same time several enterprise taxes (wage tax, property tax, investment tax, local tax) and the one-stage turnover tax were abandoned.

The profit tax of state enterprises was only modified and a new entrepreneurial tax was introduced at a lower rate in the 'second economy' (activities based on private initiative, only loosely controlled by the state). The reform of enterprise income taxation was deferred to a later date. In 1989 a uniform *entrepreneurial profits tax* was introduced. The legal frameworks of state-owned enterprises' transformation into corporations, still maintaining constraints on private ownership, developed in parallel. After the free elections, the removal of the remaining ownership constraints and privatisation put the introduction of a *corporate income tax* on the agenda in 1992.

In the case of *social security contributions* the *employees'* progressive contribution was replaced by a flat rate one, and the rate of *employers'* contribution was raised (twice, in 1988 and in 1989). The introduction of personal income taxation and the modification of social security contributions was reinforced by a revalorisation (called 'grossing up') of pre-tax wages/salaries to secure that after-tax incomes (PIT and social security contributions deducted) remained at their former level.

The majority of the new PIT revenues was channelled to local authorities, first on a *per capita* basis, later fixed at a percentage of the previous year's PIT revenue (100 per cent in 1990, 50 per cent in 1991). From 1991 the new local governments have been granted some taxing power of their own, within the framework of a law fixing the type of taxes, maximum rates, etc. Use of the new local taxes (property taxes, communal taxes, Gewerbesteuer) is still rare, though existing local levies disappeared from 1992.

4.1   Personal income tax (PIT)

The Hungarian PIT is a global-type one. With some exceptions all income, whatever its source, is taxed (invisible income included). Tax is imposed on the total amount of income from different sources according

Table 14.1. *Changes in PIT rates, HUF per year, and brackets, 1988–92*

1988		1989	
Tax base	Tax rate	Tax base	Tax rate
0– 48 000	0	0– 55 000	0
48 001– 70 000	20	55 001– 70 000	17
70 001– 90 000	25	70 001–100 000	23
90 001–120 000	30	100 001–150 000	29
120 001–150 000	35	150 001–240 000	35
150 001–180 000	39	240 001–360 000	42
180 001–240 000	44	360 001–600 000	49
240 001–360 000	48	600 001–	56
360 001–600 000	52		
600 001–800 000	56		
800 001–	60		

1990		1991	
Tax base	Tax rate	Tax base	Tax rate
0– 55 000	0	0– 55 000	0
55 001– 90 000	15	55 001– 90 000	12
90 001–300 000	30	90 001–120 000	18
300 001–500 000	40	120 001–150 000	30
500 001–	50	150 001–300 000	32
		300 001–500 000	40
		500 001–	50

1992	
Tax base	Tax rate
0–100 000	0
100 001–200 000	25
200 001–500 000	35
500 000–	40

to a standard, progressive tax table. The unit of taxation is the individual, income of taxpayers living in the same household cannot be added up. The tax base is income net of different types of costs.

At the beginning employees of the state sector were given for every month in employment a HUF 1000 lump sum cost allowance, later

HUF 250 per month was deductible directly from the tax to be paid, all this replaced from 1992 in parallel with an increase of the zero rate bracket (see Table 14.1). For cost deductions of non-wage salary incomes there are several kinds of cost allowance schemes, the allowance either being a certain percentage of income (preference is given to art, science, innovation and small-scale agricultural production) or determined on the basis of verified costs.

Special rules apply(ied) to certain categories of income:

* Income earned on small-scale agricultural production is summed for the household and divided equally among family members above sixteen.
* Income from literary and artistic activity is allowed to be carried forward up to three years.
* Interest income on savings accounts and bonds is taxed separately, at a 20 per cent rate, by withholding at source.
* Non-regular income under HUF 2000 per item is taxed separately at a 20 per cent rate; from 1992 HUF 3000 per item may be taxed separately at the marginal rate.
* Old-age pensions (and similar incomes) are exempt from taxation, whatever the amount. Other income of pensioners is taxed aggregated with pensions. Below a certain amount of total income (in 1992, HUF 108,000) no tax is paid; above it the tax on the pension is 0 per cent but the part of income from other sources is taxed at the relevant rate in the standard tax table.
* The long list of exemptions includes social benefits, scholarships, numerous fringe benefits of employees (from 1992 the scope of the latter is being sharply reduced).

At the beginning costs of dependents could be deducted from the tax base only if the number of children was three or more. Its amount was HUF 1000/child/month. From 1992 HUF 1300/child/month is deductible for each dependent child.

In certain cases and up to a certain limit other expenses may also be deducted from the tax base. Here modifications have been frequent. From 1992, saving for housing investment (up to HUF 36,000/year) and 20 per cent of life insurance policies are no longer deductible. In the case of contributions to foundations and public institutions deductibility is somewhat reduced. A first acquisition of shares directly from the issuing company up to 30 per cent of annual aggregated income can be deducted from 1992 onwards.

In the case of wage income, it is the employer who deducts the advance tax payment and transfers it to the Tax Office. From other types of income a tax advance is to be paid quarterly. At the end of the year the final tax assessment of persons having other-than-wage income is prepared on the basis of the tax returns of those concerned. Taxpayers may make wealth statements voluntarily or at the request of the Tax Office (to be used for income tax control purposes). In 1992 there is a general obligation to do so.

4.2   Corporate income tax (CIT)

The entrepreneurial profit tax (EPT), merging the tax on state enterprise profits and the 25 per cent entrepreneurial tax, was introduced in 1989, at a rate of 50 per cent, and a 4 per cent supplement in 1991. Several industries and (small-size) firms were taxed at a reduced rate. In principle the tax was applied equally to state-owned, cooperative and private firms. Small entrepreneurs had the choice whether they wanted to be taxed according to the PIT or the EPT. In the latter case they had to follow the accounting standards of the enterprise sector. In 1990, along with the introduction of an obligatory 'dividend' payment for state enterprises (see later) the tax rate was reduced to 40 per cent, for the first HUF 3 mn of profit, to 35 per cent (this latter was valid only for one year). Dividends paid from after-tax profits to individuals, were taxed – as personal income – at the same 20 per cent rate as interest income, withheld at source.

The corporate income tax (CIT) introduced in 1992 – in parallel with a new system of business accounting – brought the accounting and taxation of profits nearer to European standards. The tax rate remained 40 per cent, the same as the new marginal rate of PIT. Preferences given in form of reduced rate and other allowances were limited or eliminated. The double taxation of dividends was eased by reducing the withholding tax to 10 per cent.

The tax is applicable to all firms in corporate forms, including the still state-owned majority (privatised or not, they are obliged to transform themselves into corporations by the end of 1992). Non-corporate private entrepreneurs, who choose to be taxed as enterprises, should return to the PIT. Important changes are imposed by the new accounting system, related first of all to the tax consequences of new depreciation rules and to the enforcement of prudent evaluation of assets.

4.3   Value added tax (VAT)

The Hungarian VAT is modelled on VAT in the EC countries. Tax falls on the final consumer of goods and services even if it is levied in every stage of the production and distribution process. Taxes on intermediate stages do not figure as a cost element. The collection of tax is realised by the tax credit method to relieve the intermediaries from the tax. Products, services and imports are taxable, the tax on exports is 0 per cent.

The standard tax rate is 25 per cent, some services (transport of goods, repair, tourism) are taxed at 15 per cent. The basic consumption goods (food, public transport, books) are taxed at a zero rate (practically an exemption with credit, as in the UK).

Financial, health, housing services, social insurance, education, culture, sport, and public administration are exempt from taxation, reducing further the coverage of VAT. Retail trade outlets (with a yearly turnover under HUF 1 mn or HUF 250,000) may apply for tax exemption. If private persons are investing in housing, canalisation, etc. they can claim back the amount of tax paid on their purchases.

The deductibility of taxes related to enterprise investments has been provisionally lifted. Up to 1992 taxes paid on such purchases could be only partly deducted, the deductible part increasing yearly by 20 per cent. Exception was made for certain investments producing hard currency exports.

The implementation of a two-rate VAT with a standard rate around 20 per cent and a lower rate around 10 per cent, both remaining within the guidelines of the related EC directives, has been postponed to 1993, mainly because of price changes and political tensions arising from the elimination of the zero rate.

4.4 Social security contributions (SSC)

Social security contributions are paid partly by employers and partly by employees. The employers' contribution was originally 43 per cent of the wage bill, raised to 44 per cent from 1992, the employees' contribution is 10 per cent. For employers the contribution paid increases their total wage cost, for employees the contribution paid is part of their taxable income when paying PIT. The tax-like character of the contributions is maintained by the fact that there are no upper limits, both contributions being levied on the whole amount of wages/salaries.

Contributions financing old age pensions, disability and sickness will be separated only from 1993; 24.5 per cent employers', 6 per cent employees' contribution will go to the pension scheme, 19.5 per cent and 4 per cent respectively to the health scheme. A new separate contribution to finance unemployment benefits (paid from the so-called Solidarity Fund) was introduced in 1991 at the rate of 1.5 per cent on the employers' and 0.5 per cent on the employees' side, increased to 5 per cent and 1 per cent respectively for 1992 (see also Chapter 16 below).

5   The taxation of personal income

The Hungarian personal income taxation system introduced in 1988 – with its high tax rates, steep progressivity, narrow brackets, many and sometimes irrational exemptions – adopted a model which is dying out in developed market economies. In Hungary the above-mentioned traits were incorporated into the PITs, sometimes with grotesque results. The progression of Hungarian PIT was similar to Western PITs of the 1960s and 1970s but income brackets were narrower, progression was steeper and marginal tax rates relatively high for large strata of the population. Unlike the majority of foreign tax systems, family size, i.e. the number of dependents, was hardly considered (the very dubious motivation being that one 'must not mix taxation with social policy').

The model of PIT introduced arose in developed market economies in the era of rapid economic growth and full employment. At that time tax rates crept upwards, and exemptions and allowances multiplied. In a period of rapidly increasing real wages and real incomes such taxation was acceptable. Institutions of control over the use of tax revenues were established in pluralistic democracies even before the expansion of taxation, or were developed in parallel with it. This had an important role in making high taxes acceptable and was a guarantee that if the economic situation changed, PIT would change (would be reduced), too.

In Hungary – in a period of shrinking GDP, high inflation, just before the appearance of mass unemployment, with monopolistic firm structure, conflicting interests without open articulation and without any political framework to give voice to taxpayer control, personal–progressive income taxation, implemented with a fiscal narrow-mindedness and budgetary greed, had particularly adverse effects.

High marginal tax rates, too high a tax burden for large strata of the population (including the non-deductible social security contributions) were untenable. Hard bargaining – backed up by strike-threats and sometimes with actual strikes – is more or less constantly used to press for allowances. To recover the revenue loss because of multiplying allowances and exemptions, the remaining taxpayers have further to be taxed at high rates, and this has 'disrupted' the PIT. It was clear from the very beginning, and examples were offered by Western tax reforms in the 1980s, that broader tax brackets, a smaller number of tax rates, milder progression, less confused regulation, a halt to the burgeoning of allowances, exemptions and reliefs are necessary elements of a contemporary PIT in Hungary too. In 1988, a unique occasion was missed to create such a tax, and avoid – at least partly – fruitless bargaining and widespread dissatisfaction.

Table 14.2. *PIT average effective rates, 1988–92, per cent*

	1988	1989	1990	1991	1992 (est.)
Total income	14.5	15.4	16.2	18.7	18.2
Tax base	16.1	16.2	17.6	19.2	18.8
GDP	5.4	5.4	6.1	6.7	6.7

Source: Ministry of Finance and Tax Office data.

Both incentive considerations and equity principles make such provisions imperative. In tax reforms of other countries when reshaping PIT, a priority was accorded to the ruling out of disincentive, effort-withholding effects. In Hungary there has been a total confusion on these issues. Small-scale agricultural production and 'some intellectual trades' were given preference to 'preserve incentives'. Further allowances, lacking any firm rationale, were abundantly accorded, but the whole problem was not thought out consistently. In the context of economic crises and of transition to a market economy it is particularly important to avoid tax effects discouraging work effort, restricting individual performance and the drive for higher income.

Recent tendencies of Western tax reform show clearly that the static approach to the relationship of taxation and income production, followed in Hungary, which takes for granted that 'higher taxes means more tax revenue', is untenable and that the relationship must be reconsidered in a dynamic context. In this field recent developments have been contradictory. On the one hand further allowances have appeared, on the other the tax table has been modified several times in a more or less downward direction, tax brackets becoming slightly wider. Taking into consideration the relatively high inflation rate over recent years, both results and outlook are rather gloomy. With increasing nominal wages (and decreasing real wages even before tax) after-tax real incomes are being reduced by the fiscal drag.

The average effective tax rate and income tax revenues have been increasing every year in comparison both with previous years' and forecast figures (see Table 14.2). This is not accidental, since in graduating the tax table and calculating the tax revenue, the inflation rate and nominal income growth were systematically under-estimated by the government and the tax table was not fully adjusted to the lower figures. For 1991 there was neither any easing in rates and brackets nor any tightening of allowances.

The last round of modifications and pressure against exemptions and allowances resulted in a lower marginal rate (bringing the corporate income tax rate down to a 40 per cent level), a broader tax base, and – paradoxically – some special allowances (e.g. for small-scale farming), not mentioned in public pronouncements but even more generous in reality.

An equally important and by no means incompatible factor is equity, especially horizontal equity. The argument put forward against consistently taking into account family size (i.e. all dependent children), by PIT, was weak. The need for such 'mixing' of tax and social policy considerations is amply proved by the experience of EC countries. Direct taxes (e.g. PIT) differ from indirect ones (e.g. VAT) precisely on this point. VAT gives no preference to those buying children's clothes (as was given by the old Hungarian turnover tax), but PIT in almost every country recognises the lower ability to pay of families with dependents. In recent Hungarian debates on personal versus family income taxation the problem of who should be the tax unit (the individual or the household) was confounded with the problem of how to take, or not to take, into account the number of dependents. By accepting that the ability to pay diminishes with the number of dependents one does not only make the tax system more equitable but also diminishes the disincentive effect of taxation. It is more than probable that the loss of tax revenue due to a broader tax allowance on dependents, valid from 1992 onwards, will be compensated by revenue increase from the tax on growing incomes produced by taxpayers with dependent children.

6   Corporate income taxation and 'dividend' payments of state enterprises

Taxation of business profits lags as far behind its Western counterparts as PIT and VAT. The same is valid for the related regulations: distributing and taxing dividends, calculating profits and depreciation for tax purposes. Here the adjustment to market economy standards is directly linked to the ongoing transformation of enterprises and the redistribution of property rights. Basic problems have already been reflected in fixing the tax rate(s). In principle a uniform profit tax with a uniform tax rate was introduced in 1989, but rate preferences proved to be persistent. Some remaining old-type special levies – another part of the heritage of enterprise-specific taxation – further differentiated the taxation of enterprise incomes.

Another structural problem was the built-in discrimination against private businesses. State and private firms paying tax at the same rate were not in the same position. The latter normally pay out a part of their (after-tax) profit to the owner(s), state-owned enterprises have no such supplementary obligation. To eliminate – at least partially – the tax discrimination resulting from this distinction, an obligatory payment was introduced for state-owned enterprises in 1990, coupled with the reduction of the tax rate. It is paid by all state enterprises, from their profits, to the state as owner, but fixed at a uniform percentage of profits and not related at all to the capital engaged, it is a tax-like payment, far from a real dividend.

Along with the transformation of enterprises, lowering of the tax rate and the implementation of the corporate income tax, differentiation and distortion in enterprise direct taxation is gradually being reduced, old-type levies and rate preferences are being suppressed, and the tax base is being widened. With ongoing privatisation, real dividend payments are slowly growing. In this process the uniform nominal rate and the average effective rate have moved closer to each other. Reducing the tax rate from 50 to 40 per cent and narrowing rate preferences in the same year as a 15 per cent 'dividend' payment was introduced, gave an average effective rate of 35.2 per cent, 36.3 per cent for private firms and, including the 'dividend' payment, 50.1 per cent for state enterprises.

The elimination of tax discrimination against private firms, resulting in a lower tax rate, is encouraging private investment and privatisation. A kind of positive discrimination has been introduced for foreign capital in the form of abundant tax incentives ranging from substantial allowances – for a wide range of activities – to full exemption – for activities on a long priority list (Koltay, 1990). Tax holidays were intended to make foreign capital investment in Hungary attractive by offsetting other serious handicaps. The massive inflow of small investments seeking short-term profits may be proof of these easy-to-get incentives, but important investors' decisions seem to be guided more by such priorities as a stable economic and political environment, a well-developed financial infrastructure, and a smoothly working administration. Despite strengthening economic legislation and relative political stability in Hungary, uncertainties and instabilities remain, especially of the region as a whole. Claims of emerging national capital and potential revenue loss have pressed government to reconsider the issue. Too generous eligibility criteria are being tightened from 1992 and are applicable only to the end of 1993; the whole scheme will then be phased out over a ten-year period.

The recession of state-owned industries, shrinking production, and collapsed Eastern trade caused important losses in revenue coming from the state enterprise sector. The compensation comes from personal income taxation, indirect taxes and not from the dynamic but small private sector where the iceberg of profits is difficult to evaluate and tax.

Table 14.3. *Government revenue from major taxes, 1988–92, HUF bn*

	1988	1989	1990	1991	1992 (est.)
PIT	79.3	103.4	139.6	188.0	230.0
CIT[1]	108.5	112.2	140.0	132.0	153.0
VAT	123.0	135.1	146.8	152.5	225.0
SSC	82.0	95.6	108.2	151.5	149.0

Note:
1. Or similar taxes.
Source: Ministry of Finance data.

Paradoxically enough, it helps to lower the unduly high part of direct taxes on enterprise income in the percentage of total tax revenue or of GDP (see Tables 14.3 and 14.5).

With a lower tax, higher dividends could, in principle, be paid, and it is a stimulus for private investments. But profit distribution of private enterprises is hit by a double taxation (first a 40 per cent corporate tax, then a 20 per cent flat rate withholding tax in personal income taxation). This can also be interpreted as a residual tax discrimination which falls if the owner enjoying the distributed profit is the state.

The list of unsolved problems closely related to corporate taxation is long: from the (re)definition of the tax base and an intelligent taxation of capital gains to the (re)evaluation of assets because of inflation and the tax treatment of depreciation. Here the implementation of the new law on business accounting will greatly help. Until now – contrary to market economies – an important part of sums normally intended for the depreciation fund to finance the replacement of assets appears as profit, and is taxed away, augmenting the state redistribution machinery. Threatened with the brutal shrinkage or the total disappearance of the tax base, the government temporarily limited the use of new depreciation rules for tax purposes.

7   General and selective consumption taxation

When preparing the introduction of a general turnover tax, VAT appeared the only feasible solution offered by international practice. VAT was presented as a panacea with over-stated advantages which could not be attained by other types of turnover taxes and would surely prevail in Hungary. It is true that VAT eliminates the cumulative effects of taxation and the inducement for vertical integration. But this is an advantage only as against the gross turnover tax (Bruttoumsatzsteuer) once used in several EC countries and cannot be assumed in the Hungarian case.

For the EC countries who started the triumphal march of VAT it was reasonable to rid themselves of the disadvantages of a multiple-stage tax by substituting it with another multiple-stage tax whose introduction and implementation did not cause – for countries having a well organised tax administration and reliable business accounting – much upheaval and additional costs. Countries which later joined the EC had no choice, even if VAT had no specific advantages for them (e.g. the UK). Other countries have chosen VAT because of similar traditions (like Austria with its gross turnover tax) or because they wanted to adapt to leading industrial economies (Scandinavian and South American countries). But adjustment to the world economy can be managed with a single-stage turnover tax, too, as has been shown by the example of Switzerland, Japan or the USA. In perspective the choice of VAT for the European countries (including Hungary) is justified only by a desire to join the EC.

It would otherwise have been much simpler to modernise our single-stage turnover tax, where fewer taxpayers are involved, the money demand is less, firms have no liquidity problems, introduction, implementation and control is cheaper, the administrative burden is less, and an ill-prepared and ill-equipped tax administration and taxpayers can better cope with it. The introduction of a multiple-stage tax like VAT, especially with several tax rates – which is an inevitable compromise – increased administration and the potential for abuse quickly appeared.

Despite textbook arguments on the 'automatic control property' of VAT its introduction does nothing to diminish tax avoidance and tax evasion: one needs only to consult Italian experience in the longer run and first impressions on (private) retail trade and services in Hungary. For Italy indirect evidence has showed 40–60 per cent evasion rate estimates in the 1970s (see Pedone, 1981). For Hungary, where ownership, national and business accounting are in turmoil, measuring VAT, PIT or CIT evasion is extremely difficult. The tax administration allows deduction from tax for the acquisition of modern cashier machines, makes obligatory the delivery of a simplified tax receipt to the customer, and tries to reinforce control measures.

The unity and neutrality of the tax was debased by the transitory regulation of turnover taxation on investments. It also happened in other countries that VAT on investment goods was – because of its disturbing effect on investment activity and the business cycle – made deductible only in a phased manner over a period of several years. But it is already a special Hungarian feature that this was not a general rule (exemptions in the case of exports) and that in the first two years it meant a greater tax burden on firms than the former system of investment taxation, and appeared as almost a direct tax on enterprises (it was to be paid from taxed profit). This is alien to VAT and gave some validity to the misapprehension that VAT was a kind of direct tax on enterprises.

It is a singular – but transitory – phenomenon that such an important part of indirect tax revenues is produced by this special taxation of investments. This tax will disappear in 1992 and there is a natural temptation to replace it either by raising VAT rates which are already high in international comparison or by reclassifying an increasing part of turnover under higher tax rates, or else by increasing further selective taxes on consumption which are already much more widely used and much more differentiated than in developed market economies. This heavy weight of excise taxes is another and long-lasting feature of Hungarian indirect taxation; in recent years the government has abused their ease of increase (see Table 14.3). In 1992, when the envisaged elimination of the VAT zero rate was postponed, increase of consumption taxes was abundantly used to fill budgetary gaps instead of relying at least partly on higher PIT revenues as in previous years.

If these peculiar features remain, indirect taxation will remain too fragmented and VAT with its relatively low weight and rather incomplete coverage will not be able to assume the role of a really neutral and genuine general turnover tax.

8   Tax reform and the budget

Successful tax reforms in market economies started from a clear-cut conception of how taxes, subsidies, other expenditures and their respective structure should be changed or modified. With unilateral changes on the revenue side or with non-harmonised changes on both sides of the budget the outcome of a tax reform will be difficult either to predict or to evaluate. In the Hungarian case the tax reform was not accompanied by coordinated changes on the expenditure side. The need for a comprehensive budgetary reform appeared in vague statements and the new taxes were shaped under the increasing pressure of revenue-raising considerations; the tax reform became more and more subordinated to short-term, budgetary problems, the need to limit the deficit. New taxes were used to reduce real income and personal consumption, thereby diversifying the arsenal of restrictive policies.

Tax reform, the introduction of new taxes, has not been linked to the reform of the expenditure side, elaborated and put on the agenda only later in several versions without having gone through the phase of legisla-

Table 14.4. *General government revenue and subsidy payments, 1985–9, per cent of GDP*

	Hungary						OECD (average)		EEC
	1985[1]	1985[2]	1988[1]	1988[3]	1989[1]	1989[2]	1965	1986	1989[2]
Personal income taxes	0.9	1	4.7	5	5.5	6	7.3	12.1	9
Enterprise income taxes	9.6	16[4]	8.4	18[5]	7.0	14[4]	2.4	3.0	4
Turnover taxes	16.7	17[6]	22.6	19[6]	17.6	18[6]	9.7	11.5	11
Customs duties	3.1	3	3	—	4	3	—	—	—
Social security contributions	15.7	13	14.4	17	14.3	16	5.0	9.3	13
Property taxes	—	3	—	—	—	—	2.0	1.8	2
Other	3.9	8[7]	0.8	1	0.5	5[7]	0.3	0.4	5
Total	49.9	60	54	60	49	61	26.6	38.1	44
Subsidy payments		21[8]		14[9]		16[8]	0.7	1.8	3

Notes:
[1] OECD estimates.
[2] Kopits' estimates.
[3] Koltay's estimates.
[4] Including other transfers.
[5] Including 'production taxes' and other levies.
[6] Including selective consumption taxes.
[7] Including non-tax revenue and grants.
[8] Including explicit product-specific price subsidies, interest rate subsidies and debt service on behalf of enterprises.
[9] Excluding consumers' subsidies.
Source: OECD (1989); Kopits (1991); Koltay (1989).

tion and implementation. However more or less loosely designed subsidy cuts started in parallel with the introduction of the new taxes. The GDP tax ratio and state redistribution through taxes (and subsidies) did not diminish (see Table 14.4) in the years of the tax reform.

Consumer price subsidies (negative turnover taxes) were the first issue of concern, and the reduction of state administration costs and of production outlays was envisaged. But no new expenditure policy or consistent subsidy reduction programme was worked out. Instead the ambitious intention to put an end in a few years to the budget deficit was announced in 1988. Due to the menacing increase of the deficit there was an abrupt decrease in the subsidisation of rouble exports, which was a very important item at that time. It was also uncertain what would be the fate of crisis industries, of agriculture and of budget-financed large investments, which absorbed a very important part of budgetary expenditures. On the revenue side the outcome of the race between the rising tax rates and increasing allowances was also uncertain.

The reduction of consumer subsidies has continued and military and central administration outlays have been somewhat reduced. In the meantime preparatory work on a comprehensive reform of the expenditure side of the budget went on, along with the decision to give autonomy to the social security system and to separate its budget from the central budget. A four-year reduction programme was announced for both producer and consumer subsidies. The scheduling of subsidy reduction and compensating social policy measures were not elaborated.

It was high time to reverse the tendency of rising subsidies (see Table 14.5). In the 1980–8 period they rose threefold, increasing production outlays by 50 per cent. And the gap between revenues and expenditures kept growing (HUF 50 bn at the time of preparing the 1989 budget, the second year of the tax reform and the last year of the *ancien régime*). Continuing high inflation has been an obstacle to limiting the increase of the deficit; large items are sharply rising with inflation (e.g. interest rate subsidies of old housing credits, paid to banks from the budget, or interest paid on increasing public debt at rates now somewhat nearer to a market level).

In the present state of the Hungarian economy the reduction of subsidies has had contradictory effects even from the point of view of the budget. First it improves the budget balance but then, as producer and consumer prices increase, high inflation partially wipes out this gain. An anti-inflation policy would thus operate subsidy cuts linked to tax reduction that could – at least partly – 'countervail', even in the short run, on inflationary effects.

The new government, along with taking further steps towards tax

Table 14.5. *Government revenue and expenditure, 1986–92, per cent of GDP, at current prices*

	1986	1987	1988	1989	1990	1991 (prel.)	1992 (est.)
Central government revenue	62.6	62.0	63.9	62.3	62.0		
Expenditure	66.8	64.8	64.6	65.2	62.1		
Deficit	− 4.2	− 2.8	− 0.7	− 2.9	− 0.1	− 4.3	− 2.2
Central government revenue	38.9	38.5	40.3	35.1			
Revenue of central funds outside the budget	2.4	2.6	1.7	2.4			
Local government revenue	7.7	8.0	8.1	7.6			
Social security revenue	13.0	12.9	13.8	17.2			

Sources: CSO, *Statistical Yearbook*, 1989, 1990, 1991. Ministry of Finance, *Main Economic Processes*, 1988, 1989. Ministry of Finance and Parliament data.

reform, continued subsidy cuts and by 1992 the bulk of subsidies, especially direct consumer subsidies, had been phased out. From 1988–92 the ratio of subsidies in GDP decreased to one-quarter of its previous level. The relative weight of social and welfare outlays in expenditures remained at the same high level. Measured by different estimates neither expenditures nor the GDP tax ratio (all obligatory payments taken into account) followed the fall in subsidies. Recent government statements refer to somewhat lower figures of tax or and/or expenditure ratio in GDP (all estimates rely on the same uncertain ground, determined by the deficiencies of the statistical system in the transformation).

In developed market economies the tax reforms of the 1980s brought important tax reductions. PITs in particular, going up with increasing real income and accelerating inflation, became dysfunctional and politically unacceptable, and were substantially lowered. Although the results are somewhat controversial, it is by and large recognised that taxes and unacceptably high budget deficits need to be reduced in parallel, and that expenditures must be reduced more than revenues. The further increase of the already high GDP: tax ratio was halted, and even reversed in several countries.

The balance or deficit of the budget does not depend on resolute fiscal manoeuvres alone. However, in Hungary, as elsewhere, increasing or decreasing revenues and expenditures largely determine how the burden of stabilisation will be shared.

9   The tax system and the economic system

The philosophy of the 1968 economic reform (NEM) and the 'indirect system of central economic management' accorded taxation the task of directly influencing economic activity. Taxes, as the main tools of economic regulation, had to assume the role of abolished plan targets, to fill the void of coordination, parallel with other (mainly informal) tools: central desires, responsibility for procurement campaigns (Soós 1985).

In the period of transition, with a shrinking but still decisive state sector, this hierarchical coordination mix has been improved by an increasing dose of market coordination. The use of taxes as economic regulators to transmit the central will has only reluctantly been abandoned. The oversized redistribution of resources through taxes and subsidies has been maintained at a somewhat lower level, positions of the central state are preserved and bankrupt state-owned firms continue to survive, with shrinking production and employment, causing great revenue losses and waste of public money. They do not pay taxes from their non-existent profits and often 'forget' to pay social security contributions, replacing thereby the subsidies that have been removed (even employees' contributions withheld at source are not forwarded to the budget). The dynamically growing, but still relatively small private sector enters the game using other stratagems, primarily tax avoidance and tax evasion. A large part of its activities do not enter the national accounts and do not produce tax revenues.

Taxes paid by profit-making state-owned firms – most of them in a monopolistic position – were normally shifted either forward to the consumer or another firm or backward on to the budget, if there was an obstacle (formerly administrative, recently market constraints) to raising prices. Until now firms with a strong enough bargaining position were successful in fighting tax increases or subsidy cuts. And the state in one way or another further increased the tax of those firms who were successful in making more profits.

All this was reflected in a huge overhang in enterprise taxes, in the steady modification of the micro structure of taxation, in frequent and capricious – sometimes retroactive – changes in tax-base definition, tax rates, exemptions and allowances, and in the persistant survival of some exemptions.

The outstanding role of taxes in economic regulation, the poor toolkit of macroeconomic management, the long neglect of monetary policy, the lack of an autonomous social policy, subordinated taxation to actual economic goals and burdened it with too many functions more or less alien to it. As a result a very complicated and too 'flexible' tax system arose in which taxes were adapted to individual circumstances, the hierarchical position, size, property form, industry affiliation, importance, etc. of taxpayers. The tax reform saw a remedy in the introduction of new taxes, matured over several decades of organic development in market economies, where the tax system had developed – if not in its details but in general – in accordance with the economic system.

The approach of the Hungarian tax reform was different. There were serious problems with the functioning of the economy, despite the many reform steps taken. The more Hungary modernised and made transparent the tax system, adopting taxes which had justified themselves in market economies, and the more radical the tax reform, the more would the working of the economy improve. But the Hungarian economy was in this, if in nothing else, similar to market economies in that the relationship actually went in a reverse direction. The Hungarian tax system before the tax reform was in accordance with the economic system, although it did not arise from a long, organic development, but was an artefact created to fit the needs of an indirect system of central economic management.

For the smooth working of the new tax system created by the tax reform the whole economic system should be changed (for comparable experiences see Flockermann, 1991). Without this even the narrow goal of the tax reform – a simpler, more rational, more neutral, more equitable taxation – cannot be really attained and the effects of a tax system designed for a market economy will inevitably be distorted in a non-market based economy.

In the early years the new Hungarian tax system was adapting itself to the old economic environment. It now depends on the scope and pace of ongoing fundamental changes how, and when, the new tax system will match the economic system. Tax reform and systemic changes should go in parallel and be coordinated.

REFERENCES

Buchanan, J.M. (1987) 'Tax reform as public choice', *Journal of Economic Perspectives*, **1(1)**.

Flockermann, P.-G. (1991) 'The experience of Germany', in P.-G. Flockermann, *The Role of Tax Reform in Central and Eastern European Economies*, Paris: OECD.

Gillis, M. (1985) 'Micro and macroeconomics of tax reform in Indonesia', *Journal of Development Economics*, **19**.

Gray, C.W. (1991) 'Tax systems in the reforming socialist economies of Europe', *Communist Economies and Economic Transformation*, **1**.

Koltay, J. (1987) 'Az általános forgalmi adóztatás helye adórendszerünkben és bevezetésének problémái' (The problems of implementing VAT in Hungary) (in Hungarian), *Közgazdaságy Szemle*, **7–8**.

— (1989) 'Az új adórendszer "korszerűségéről" és "működéséről"' (How the new tax system works and how it should be changed) (in Hungarian), *Közgazdasági Szemle*, 11.

— (1990) 'Das neue Ungarische Steuersystem und das Ungarische Steurrecht für gemischte Unternehmungen', in J. Koltay, *Joint Ventures in Hungary*, Wien: PGS.

Kopits, G. (1991) 'Fiscal reform in European economies in transition', *IMF Working Paper*, **91/43**, Washington, D.C.: IMF.

OECD (1989) *Economies in Transition. Structural Adjustment in OECD Countries*, Paris: OECD.

Pedone, A. (1981) 'Italy', in H.J. Aaron (ed.), *The Value-added Tax. Lessons From Europe*, Washington, D.C.: Brookings Institution.

Soós, A. (1985) 'Planification imperative, régulation financière, "grandes orientations" et campagnes', *Revue d'études comparatives est–ouest*, **2**.

Discussion of Part Five

ATHAR HUSSAIN

1 Introduction

Amongst several interesting issues raised in Jenő Koltay's Chapter 14 I shall concentrate on two general issues, and take them in turn. The first concerns the long-term goal of achieving a tax system similar to those in Western Europe and the second the tax system required during the transition phase. There is a pragmatic reason for adopting a Western European-type tax system: it will facilitate the membership of the EC. It is, however, interesting to ask how such a system squares with the economic principles of taxation and whether it embodies defects which Hungary and other Eastern European economies would be well advised to avoid.

On average the total tax revenue in Western Europe constitutes 30–35 per cent of GDP, although there is a very substantial range. Typically, taking social security contributions with the direct taxes, revenue comes two-thirds from direct taxes and one-third from indirect taxes. Interestingly, viewed at this level of aggregation, the breakdown of tax revenue is not dissimilar from the pre-transition command economies where the bulk of tax revenue came from taxes on profits of enterprises and turnover taxes on those enterprises. This similarity is, however, nominal. Almost all direct taxes came from enterprises rather than households, which in Western Europe are a more important source of direct taxes than companies. Moreover, if enterprise output is subject to both planning targets and government price controls, the turnover tax, the principal indirect tax in erstwhile command economies, acts as a direct tax on enterprise profits.

How well do the tax systems of Western European accord with the economic precepts of taxation? The first lesson is that indirect taxes should not fall on intermediate goods, save where final output cannot be taxed, and value added taxes (VAT), common in Western Europe, are consistent with this principle. The second principle of indirect taxation is that domestically produced and imported commodities should be treated alike. This rules out tariffs and quotas on imported commodities, though in economies where tax collection is difficult there may be an additional argument in favour of tariffs on the grounds that they are easier to collect than the alternatives. VAT fits in with this principle in that it applies to domestically produced and imported goods alike. Broadly speaking, the indirect tax structures in Western Europe are consistent with these tax principles and thus provide a reasonable long-term goal for Hungary and other transitional economies. VAT and excise taxes have the added advantage of being comparatively easy to collect.

Economic theory does not provide strong arguments for taxing corporate income, except as a component of personal income which should be included along with all the other elements of personal income. In this sense, the recent emphasis in Western tax systems on the integration of personal and corporate income taxes is consistent with theory. The reasons theory does offer for taxing corporate income, *per se*, are first, as a means for taxing monopoly rents (although these are very difficult to identify); second, as a means of taxing foreign income; and, finally, to prevent the emergence of capital gains which would be associated with the removal of such a tax, gains which might have undesirable redistributive consequences. The third reason is only an argument for not removing the existing corporate taxes, rather than for introducing them. However, companies and corporations furnish an important tax handle and withholding personal income tax at the corporate stage is a convenient method of collecting part of personal income tax.

Thus far, the Western European tax systems emerge with an apparently satisfactory theoretical bill of health. One must also ask whether they have any major weaknesses or defects? This concern applies particularly to the taxation of property (land and buildings). For a variety of historical reasons, property and land taxation in most Western European economies is far from satisfactory, the UK being a notable example. Property taxation has much to commend itself on almost all grounds relevant to taxation. It is also one which Eastern European and other transitional economies would be well advised not to neglect. The tax base is fairly easy to measure, at least relative to other taxes. The supply elasticities of buildings and land are low and the value of property owned is strongly related to wealth. The revenue potential of a property tax is also, in principle, substantial. The value of the housing stock alone in Western European economies would be around two–three times GDP. To this one should also add the value of commercial buildings and under-developed land. Transitional economies start with an advantage in that in many of them a large percentage of buildings and land is publicly-owned. Their privatisation could be coupled with the introduction of a property tax without the fear of strong resistance from existing owners.

Turning to the issues of transition, a changeover from a command economy tax system to a Western European-type tax system will involve fundamental changes in tax bases and rates which even in a well-functioning economy would raise considerable practical problems. In a transitional economy where the underlying economic structure itself is changing and is clouded with uncertainty the changeover is likely to be long-drawn-out and complicated. In the initial stages of transition, government revenue is likely to fall uncomfortably short of government expenditure. The government in a transitional economy would normally find that the erstwhile taxes (especially those on enterprises) eroded more rapidly than it was able to put in place new taxes such as a personal income tax (PIT). The speed with which Hungary has managed to introduce a wide-ranging PIT may turn out to be too ambitious for other transitional economies. And on the expenditure side the government may be faced with still considerable expenditure liabilities despite its withdrawal from the economy and an increasing expenditure on providing a social safety net. In such a situation securing tax revenue would have priority over a rapid progress towards the desired tax system. The two may not be consistent and the tax system in the transitional phase may in certain key respects have to be quite different from the long-term goal. For example, it may be difficult to achieve the 2:1 split between direct and indirect taxes usual in Western European economies whilst raising sufficient revenue. Generalising from the experience of developing economies, indirect taxes are usually easier to introduce and enforce than direct taxes. Therefore in the transitional phase, indirect taxes may have to play a more important role in raising revenue and achieving distributional objectives than they will according to the long-term tax design.

The rule that intermediate goods should not be taxed may need extensive qualification. When relative prices of inputs are heavily distorted, there is a strong case for using taxes on intermediate goods to compensate for distortions. Although it is preferable to tackle price distortions at source, an immediate removal of all major price distortions may simply not be possible. Further, until a comprehensive PIT system is firmly in place, there is a good justification for using taxes on intermediate goods as an indirect instrument for taxing incomes which might otherwise escape taxation such as those of the self-employed and small firms. This can be done easily in a VAT system by treating the economic agents outside the reach of PIT or corporate taxes as households and thus not entitled to a refund of taxes on inputs. There may also be an argument for tariffs in transitional economies from the point of view of both being comparatively easy to collect and providing protection to domestic producers as they adjust to large changes in relative prices. The usual danger of tariff protection becoming entrenched is not great in the transitional economies of Eastern Europe, since they are likely to join the EC as full or associate members in the not too distant future. Further, given that economic inequality is likely to rise during the transition, distributive considerations are likely to play a more important role in determining the rate structure of indirect taxes than they will when a comprehensive personal income tax is fully operational.

Notwithstanding the weak theoretical case for corporation tax, firms are likely to remain in transitional economies both a significant tax source and an important point for levying various taxes. The main practical problem for a profits tax is likely to be the wide latitude for misreporting provided by the absence of standard accounting practices and the wide asymmetry of information on prices and transactions available to managers and tax authorities. In such a situation it may be desirable to opt for a more transparent base for corporation tax than profits. This could be some measure of cash flow and the employed labour force. Moreover, there would seem to be a strong case not to go for an integration of personal and corporation taxes during the transitional phase. That is desirable, but only when there is a comprehensive and global personal income tax in operation.

The above discussion would seem to indicate that transitional economies ought to devote more attention to introducing a property and a land tax than they seem to have done so far. Such taxes are comparatively easy to enforce. The assessment of property values is not easy, especially in a situation where the market for buildings and land is still in its infancy. But a detailed assessment is not necessary for the introduction of a property tax. The fact that buildings and land are highly durable provides the possibility of starting with an interim assessment and revising it over time.

NOTES

These comments draw on joint work with Nicholas Stern as part of an ESRC-funded project on public finance in transitional economies.
Athar Hussain is director of the Development Economics Research Programme at the London School of Economics.

Part Six

Labour markets, unemployment and social security

15 The tranformation of shop floor bargaining in Hungarian industry

JÁNOS KÖLLŐ

1 Introduction

In this chapter we try to depict how bargaining on wages and work intensity (effort) is changing in Hungary. The major proposition of sections 2–6 of the chapter is that despite the lack of collective bargaining on wages (under state socialism) Hungarian workers had substantial individual power to bargain over effort. The wealth or utility maximizing level of effort (in the first job) was low and the set of feasible individual strategies was large. In section 7 we try to sum up recent changes, and we shall conclude that the sources of worker's individual bargaining power are drying up.

Throughout this chapter we make a clear (and perhaps oversimplified) distinction between bargaining on wages and effort: in this vision of the bargaining process wages are a matter of agreement between firms and the state and other elements of the explicit work contract (such as work time, work schedule, relative occupational wage rates, fringe benefits, pension schemes, retirement age, hiring and firing rules) are also fixed in the firm–government bargain. We shall not discuss this part of the bargaining process in detail; we shall instead focus on shop floor bargaining to see how a fixed wage offer and the worker's effort level are matched.

The role of unions will be ignored. This will hardly bias the discussion of socialism, as unions (or other institutions of collective action) then played no significant role in the bargaining process. The case is becoming more complicated now. The rise of more than 1000 registered unions in 1990–1[1] and the inclusion of (some) unions into tripartite negotiations promise a future for collective bargaining in place of the recent dualism characterised by the effective participation of union centres in legislation, but only sporadic collective action on the firm level, and the lack of communication between trade union leaderships and workers.[2] In this chapter we shall be concerned with past and present rather than with future prospects and, accordingly, we shall ignore the union while discussing the problems of firm level bargaining.

2   Managerial attitudes towards wages and effort under state socialism

Before moving to the shop floor (and to the subject of effort bargaining) we need to discuss briefly the question of managerial attitudes towards wages and worker's effort under socialism. The shift of the right of wage setting from the enterprise level to central decision-making bodies in state socialism may encourage two types of over-simplistic interpretation.

In the common concept of the *command economy* firms appear as dependent parts of the state's control machinery and capital–labour relations are interpreted as conflicts between workers and 'leaders', irrespective of the actual position the latter hold. In this interpretation wages and effort requirements (as anything else) are set by the central decision-maker. This fundamentalist approach has long ago been abandoned by social scientists who, by studying Soviet systems, inevitably met deep conflicts between managerial and central levels.

More attention should be paid to the *corporatist view* which maintains that as managers do not endeavour to minimise, nor even to constrain, the level of workers' wages, there can be a basic community of interest between the two parties. This view of the bargaining process is literally 'one-sided'. The one 'side' it emphasises is the phase of negotiations between the central authorities and managers who 'while negotiating wages behave as "union activists" not as employers' (Kornai, 1980, p. 418) that is, they fight for the highest possible benefits for 'their' workers. The phase this interpretation seems to neglect is the period between two negotiations when the manager resembles anything but a union activist.[3] Norms' revisions, bitter shop floor bargaining and open disputes in the factory were documented in a series of empirical studies (see, e.g., Haraszti 1978; Kemény, 1978; or several empirical studies in Révész, 1985).

In order to understand the seemingly paradoxical behaviour of managers it is worthwhile to distinguish between different aspects of *output*. Let us denote potential output, planned output and actual output by Q_c, Q_p and Q, respectively. Note that the actual output will be influenced by the effort (E) of workers and effort will be positively influenced by the level of wages (w), hence in the case of the Cobb–Douglas production function and N workers for instance,

$Q = A \cdot K^a \cdot [NE(w)]^{1-a}$. In the phase of negotiations the managers will try to maximise Q_c/Q_p and when doing so they will indeed try to increase the wage fund and/or to decrease the amount of work to be done. In the phase of implementation, however, their main concern will be to keep $|Q - Q_p|$ within narrow confines because substantial deviation from the plan target in either direction would adversely affect their position. (A basic difference between capitalists (owners) and socialist managers is that under free competition the former will be interested in minimising $|Q - Q_c|$.) From the point of view of conflicts between workers and managers this difference will be of little importance because the w/E ratio can be further improved (by shirking) at any particular wage rate and effort standard. The existence of a *well-defined effort standard* (irrespective of its level) seems to be a sufficient condition for conflicts and bargaining *per se*.

Despite their seemingly 'pro-worker' attitude in wage bargaining socialist managers established powerful systems of control inside and outside the factory. The repression of Hirshman's 'voice' (1970) through the early liquidation of union autonomy in these countries is well known and so are repeated attempts to render 'exit' difficult. The practices of reinforcing loyalty (socialist competition, brigade movements, etc.) are also famous for their widespread use and dubious results. Enterprise managers played an important – often initiating – role in these repressive attempts.

3 The means of bargaining

Yet the East European worker has never been completely powerless. Despite the fall of collective autonomy the logic of the economic system provided the workers (or at least a part of them) with considerable individual bargaining power. We shall refer to this set of small freedoms, forms of resistance and evasion as *everyday power*.[4] In contrast to the organised forms of collective action, everyday power is hidden, informal, and possessed by small groups or individuals. It is based on momentary chances not on established legal rights. Its rules and constraints are not public, one has to learn them by trial and error. Whereas collective action puts a great emphasis on organised protest (Hirshman's 'voice') everyday power finally stems from the option of individual 'exit'.

What we call 'everyday power' is by no means a special East European or 'socialist' category. The unorganised forms of resistance – expressed in the form of 'dissimulation, desertion, false compliance, pilfering, feigned ignorance, slander, arson, sabotage', the withholding of effort or pretence of work – have been observed in West European industrial plants as well as in Malaysian villages (see, e.g., Dubois, 1976 or Scott, 1985; the quotation is from Scott, 1989, on a Malay community, p. xvi). It was not particular to Eastern European countries either that workers possessed no other kind of power – not only large masses of the Third World are in a similar position, but some marginal groups in the West, too. What is undoubtedly specific to the East European situation is the vital contribution of the economic system to the emergence of everyday power. In a seemingly paradoxical way, the creation of a totalitarian political power – depriving workers of collective rights – brought about an economic system which in many respects biased the cost–benefit structure of individual bargaining in favour of the worker.

4   The sources of individual bargaining power

4.1   The labour market

Although unemployment still existed when the attainment of full employment was declared – and unemployment benefit was suppressed – in the USSR (1929) or Hungary (1948) it indeed ceased to be a mass phenomenon within a few years. With the exception of regions with large rural labour surpluses and/or very high birth rates (such as Central Asia) urban labour markets became increasingly supply-constrained as the massive outflow from agriculture decelerated. Labour shortages became a steady and widespread concomitant of economic development throughout the Soviet bloc.

One proxy of the tightness of labour markets could be the unemployment rate. Data on unemployment in socialist times is scarce but the available figures have always suggested low levels. In the USSR the estimated rates fell between 1.1 and 3 per cent (Wiles, 1982; Granick, 1987; Gregory and Collier, 1988). In Hungary the registered rate was 0.35 per cent as late as in 1988.[5] The first official reports on registered unemployment in 1990 (after the breakdown of communism) suggested that the rate was still below 2 per cent in all former CMEA countries except Poland.

While the unemployment rates experienced in Eastern Europe are not unprecedented in the Western world, the vacancy rates probably are. The vacancy inflow/unemployment (v/u) inflow ratio in the depressed labour market of Hungary in January–March 1989 was 3.6 and regional rates as high as 17.0 and 15.4 were registered. In contrast, the highest national rate registered in Sweden between 1964 and 1986 was 2.8, despite a predictably higher vacancy notification rate and a booming economy in 1965 (Johanesson, 1985, p. 15). In Finland the v/u ratio failed to exceed 1.0 throughout the 1970s (Makela, 1986, p. 14). The comparison with

Hungary in 1988 seems *a fortiori* valid because this country was regarded as facing 'grave' employment problems in the late 1980s. In 1986–7 the v/u ratios in Hungary were between 5 and 10 on the national level and the highest regional rates amounted to 66.8 (Budapest) and 70.2 (Csongrád region) in late 1987. What data are available from other countries suggest that these figures were not at all high in comparison with Eastern Europe. The national v/u ratio in Poland 1979, for instance, was 20.1, but as the Polish labour exchange system covered only a part of workers, a direct comparison with Western statistics would be misleading. What we know about 'tight labour markets' in Western capitalist countries, however, might urge us to regard 20.1 as an extremely high ratio, which not even the tightest regional or occupational sub-market is likely to produce in a market economy. Great Britain can serve as a good example: in the mid-1970s when Britain was considered to be 'short of manpower' the highest regional v/u rate was 5.5 in the South-East and the highest occupational rate was 5.3 (machine tool operators).[6]

The abundance of available jobs provided the East European workers with effective means of protest. Even in case of strict legal restrictions on mobility, quitting remained an available option for them mainly because the managers – when hiring labour – were not interested in enforcing the legal sanctions so precisely elaborated at a central level, hence the striking failure of many harsh attacks on voluntary labour turnover. During a political campaign and imposition of legal and moral sanctions against job hoppers in the USSR in 1929–33 the industrial quit rate fell only from 155.2 per cent to 122.4 per cent (Schwarz, 1954, pp. 87; 98). In Hungary (1950–4) voluntary quits were treated as a criminal act (arrested culprits were convicted of embezzlement) but the quit rate still exceeded 50 per cent in industry and 100 per cent in construction (see Gyekiczky, 1988, p. 50).

Quit rates decreased as casual work was step by step ousted by steady employment and large enterprises with internal labour markets became dominant. The annual rate fell below 20 per cent in Soviet industry and below 25 per cent in construction; in Poland it slightly exceeded 20 per cent on the national level; in Hungary the comparable figure was 20–24 per cent in the early 1980s, of which approximately 15–17 per cent was accounted for by voluntary mobility between firms. Labour turnover was predictably less intense in Bulgaria, Rumania, and Czecho-Slovakia and in the then GDR. What figures are available suggest that in Czecho-Slovakia the voluntary quit rate was about 8 per cent in 1984 but some firms experienced 13–17 per cent rates. A real 'success' was achieved only in the GDR where the rate of voluntary labour turnover was said to be around 4 per cent in the early 1980s and ambitious plans were under way to push it down to 2 per cent.[7]

These rates suggest that (despite a descending secular trend) 'spontaneous' labour mobility failed to disappear in Eastern Europe or, in other words, the labour market has never been replaced by bureaucratic manpower allocation.

What is important from the viewpoint of effort bargaining is that in these extremely tight labour markets the workers' expected cost of job loss was low, all the more as the hiring firms were generally reluctant to enforce the sanctions (such as a wage cut or the disbarment from seniority related benefits) aimed at increasing the expense and reducing the gains of mobility.[8] In contrast, the firm's search cost tended to be extremely high, compared with market economies.

4.2   The second economy

Hungary has always been regarded as a country with an especially large 'second' economy, but this assessment is perhaps too strong and too general. The size of the parallel economy can be measured in different ways: researchers generally use expenditure or participation rates. The estimates based on monetary flows do not support the above-mentioned evaluation: Grossmann's emigrant survey (1977), for instance, suggested that European Soviet households spent 30–40 per cent of their income on goods and services from the second economy (the respective figures were even higher in the Southern republics). In Hungary, similar estimations fall into the 13–23 per cent range for the 1970s and mid-1980s (13.2 per cent by Balázs and Laki, 1990; 16–19 per cent by Sík, 1987; a rising trend from 12 to 22 per cent by Lackó, 1991).

Hungary's unique position can better be grasped by focusing on participation rates and the mode of participation. There is general agreement among experts that within Eastern Europe Hungary was at one extreme, with only slightly less than 700 hours a year performed in the second economy by an average economically active adult (and 1022 hours by an average participant of the part-time second economy). According to time budget surveys the total labour input to the part-time second economy grew from 930 mn hours a year in 1963 to 3337 bn hours a year in 1986. As much as 3,265,000 people did part-time work in the second economy in 1985, an equivalent of two-thirds of the labour force or 41.5 per cent of the total adult population including pensioners and students.

The other extreme within the CMEA was probably the then GDR, with only 300–500 hours a year worked by small gardeners and predictably even less by the rest of the population. The proportion of households taking part in the second economy in one or another form was 30–40 per cent in the GDR but 65–70 per cent in Hungary (see Brezinski, 1987,

p. 98; Révész, 1985, p. 113; Tímár, 1988, p. 244). The comparison of Hungarian and Czecho-Slovakian time budgets by Farkas *et al.* (1988, p. 1117) suggested that in the latter country active workers spent only half as much time with secondary work as did Hungarians on weekdays (although only five minutes less on holidays). In the USSR part-time farming 'employed' 3.7 mn peasants on private plots and 10 mn urban people in 'collective gardens'. Compared with Hungary these numbers seem very low if we regard the size of the country (this conclusion is also supported by Moskoff, 1984, who reported 28 and 54 per cent working overtime in gardens in urban communities as high proportions within the Soviet Union).

Unlike Rumania, the USSR and (partly) Poland – each with either a traditionally high or an increasing newly-formed sector of illegal redistributive activities – Hungary experienced the expansion of legal and predominantly productive forms of private activities. According to estimates more than half of the labour input to the second economy fell on legal private plots and gardens, roughly one-third was performed in legal forms in construction, industry, trade and services and less than 15 per cent of the secondary work was done in an illegal way in the late 1980s.[9] More than two-thirds of the participants worked part-time.

Hungary's case within Eastern Europe was thus special in that a vast majority of its first-economy employees had access to extra income and the tolerance of the second economy by the rulers decreased the risk (or cost) of taking part in it. The second economy was integrated into the first, to a great extent, and made workers capable of building rather different strategies with varying mixtures of primary and secondary earnings and effort.

4.3   The work process under input shortages

The excess demand for inputs, energy and capital goods exerts a crucial influence on the production process. On the one hand, the competition for capital goods under the circumstances of forced growth favoured 'the labour-intensive variants of capital-intensive technologies' (Ellmann, 1979, p. 14) that is, the implementation of the productive capacity without such additional elements as control appliances, feeding systems or programming methods. For the state 'this dualism [had] the advantage of combining modern technology with some savings in scarce investment resources' (Ellmann, 1979, p. 14) and for firms such quantity-oriented projects promised a better position in the race for investment funds. The price to be paid was not only poor quality but also the transformation of standardised technologies to firm-specific systems that required perpetual intervention so as to keep them at work. Although non-standardised operating 'knacks' are essential in any production process, they are of vital importance in case of a system with missing parts.

Furthermore, frequent shortages of current inputs require frequent adaptation on the spot in the form of the retiming of process plans, the substitution of one material by another, the retooling of machines, the reallocation of the job of absent workers, etc. Much attention has been paid to this problem on the managerial level ('benign plan violation' is a central concept of Soviet studies) and one can often meet descriptions of attempts to solve the problem by informal market transactions (see reports on middlemen – 'tolkachi' – by Feldbrugge, 1983, p. 15; Brezinski, 1987, pp. 90–1; and Bicanic, 1985, p. 15 on the USSR, the GDR and Yugoslavia, respectively). Research has been less concerned with intra-firm adaptation, despite the fact that the adjustment measures in question must in practice be carried out on the shop floor mainly by workers and foremen themselves. The official system built for standardised mass production is generally too slow to eliminate these unforeseen and incalculable disturbances, and this results in the shift of certain organisational functions from management to workers. Such organisational tasks, for example, are the substitution of inputs and the necessary modification of the work process; the distribution of tasks among group members otherwise having a clear-cut official job description; the collection of tool sets or the preparation of the work-piece by friends on a reciprocal basis; additional material handling to compensate for missing auxiliary workers, etc. (see examples in Kemény, 1978; Révész, 1985; Makó, 1985; or Ladó and Tóth, 1985).

The fact that the vulnerability of the production process to input shortages brought about the erosion of formal rules and made the official job descriptions irrelevant is important from the point of view of effort bargaining. The identification of shirking became difficult and extremely costly as workers quickly learned how to disguise shirking by causing 'objective difficulties' or 'technological failure'. The socialist industrial plant was also characterised by heavy reliance on firm-specific worker skills. The total cost of firing a worker and hiring an equally productive new one was increased by the necessity of substantial on-the-job training.

5   The problems of contract enforcement

A major corollary of tight labour markets, high wage second economies and uncertainties in the production process is the high cost of work contract enforcement. Shirking tends to be very appealing under state socialist conditions. When there is a high wage Soviet-type second economy some workers will try to produce goods or to provide services for the 'grey' market directly, by using the firm's assets during official office hours; others will relax to save energy for moonlighting. As the benefits of shirking are considerable and the cost of job loss relatively low, the wealth or utility maximising level of shirking will be high compared with market economies (assuming identical detection probabilities).[10]

The firm's response to this can be to choose higher relative wages, more monitoring and/or more selective hiring practices. The socialist firm's autonomy in setting its wage level relative to its labour market competitors is rather restricted, probably more than any of its decisions. The discussion of the contract enforcement question by assuming a fixed (or random) relative wage is thus highly justified. *Monitoring* in large organisations with much production uncertainty will be rather expensive, as was discussed in 4.3 above.[11] The firm's *search cost* per hiring a worker (at least as good as the one who has been dismissed for shirking) will also be higher (consider 4.1 and 4.3 above).

If wages are constant, the firm has to find an optimal mix of (1) monitoring costs (2) screening costs and (3) lost value output due to shirking. It follows from the above that in order to remain competitive the socialist enterprise has to spend more on contract enforcement than the capitalist firm because by fixing (1) it has to waste more resources on (2) and/or (3) and vice versa. Although the reduction of the cost of monitoring and screening are also feasible solutions to this problem, there was a historical trend to absorb more and more enforcement cost in the form of lost value output. The reasons seem to lie in the nature of government control.

The firm's cost of monitoring and screening can be reduced by more state control over the production process and the labour market. This can happen in different ways.

(1) The Communist Party can involve its activists in the monitoring of effort (institutions serving this aim were, for example, the 'socialist brigade movement', 'socialist emulation drives', the 'meetings of criticism and self-criticism' and, most of all, the use of ideologically indoctrinated spies).

(2) The state can restrict labour mobility outside the Labour Office System.

(3) The state can increase the expected cost associated with detected shirking beyond the cost of job loss (it can sentence some shirkers to jail, for instance).

Such endeavours are easy to observe in the early history of state socialism but it is also apparent that these practices gradually lost their importance as rigorous central planning was replaced by soft bargaining between firms and authorities. One possible explanation could be that though 'political monitoring' and the constraining of the labour market generate positive externalities for firms, they are costly for the state and party officials who organise control. Both parties can be better off if (instead of taxing the enterprise and spending the intake on burdensome state control) they resign themselves to more shirking and the resulting loss of output and quality. With a shift to this option less effort will be required on the part of officials while the cost of production will not necessarily be higher. An alternative (and less static) explanation might argue that the governmental monitoring of workers' effort was only part (and a by-product) of an enormous system of unrestrained political control – and that with a general restriction of terror (and cutback in the number of spies) monitoring within the firm was no more practicable.

Whatever the reason, the move away from strict output planning, hard monitoring and tough sanctions was a core element of János Kádár's historical compromise. The arrangement of the contract enforcement problem was precisely characterised by the worker *bon mot*: 'We pretend to work and they pretend to pay us'. It could be argued that the total cost of contract enforcement could also be reduced by incentive payments. Indeed, payment by results was widespread in Eastern Europe despite the large average firm size.[12] But there are limits to such schemes: it is often difficult or impossible to measure individual marginal products; in case of payment by group results additional monitoring is required to combat free-riding and, especially in large industrial plants, workers will also be tempted to misuse the capital equipment.[13] If we consider, furthermore, the practices of governmental redistribution eliminating the correlation between pre-taxation and post-taxation profits (Kornai and Matits, 1985) we may cast serious doubt on the capacity of incentives to resolve the problem of shirking. Similarly, we regard the Becker–Stigler bond as a merely theoretical alternative under state socialism.

The Kádárian compromise provided a large variety of individual strategies for workers. If we assume that shirking above a critical level is unprofitable for the worker but is profitable at all levels below that critical rate, this also means there is a large set of feasible effort-shirking strategies. (This conclusion is supported by the observation of large within-group deviations of individual efforts in socialist countries[14].)

6   The erosion of individual bargaining power

The key variables of the labour market suggest the revolutionary changes we are witnessing today in Eastern Europe were not preceded by any kind of slow evolution: the labour market and the firm remained unmistakably

'East European' by nature until the very last days of communist political rule. The unemployment rate was very low throughout Eastern Europe even in 1989–90, as was discussed earlier. Despite resolute plans to close hundreds of unprofitable factories in several countries shut-downs until recently remained exceptional events.[15] Part-time employment amounted to 0.32 per cent in the USSR and 0.6 per cent in Hungary in the early 1980s and similar levels have been characteristic until recently in all the other countries, except the GDR with traditionally 'high' proportions (9 per cent in 1961, for example) (Tímár, 1988, p. 172; Moskoff, 1984, p. 27). Flexible work time was simply not allowed in the GDR and Rumania, its share recently was 1 per cent in Bulgaria, less than 5 per cent in the USSR and 6 per cent in Hungary (Frey, 1988, p. 76). The unregistered economies were (some parts of it still are) flourishing. Production input shortages failed to disappear (and as a new element, the irregular working of the energy supply was added in Bulgaria, Poland, the USSR and – in some winters – Czecho-Slovakia). The new political order, however, brought about radical and rapid change in these conditions.

6.1   The labour market

As shown by Figure 15.1 the unemployment rate increased from 1–2 per cent to 5–15 per cent in 1991 in the former CMEA bloc countries. In Hungary the national rate was 6.6 per cent in December 1991 and registered rates in hard-hit regions grew beyond 14 per cent. The average duration (of all spells) of unemployment reached 160 days in November 1991. The registered vacancy/unemployed job seeker (stock/stock) ratio fell from 1.0 in May 1990 to 0.05 in September 1991, as shown by Figure 15.2.[16]

The expected cost of job loss is thus increased by growing unemployment but decreased by the introduction of unemployment benefit (1989). The replacement ratio in Hungary is 70 per cent for twelve months and 50 per cent for a second year. A roughly estimated 'real' replacement ratio (benefit/last wage $\times$ average wage increase by time t) amounts to about 60 per cent in the 6th, 50 per cent in the 12th and 25 per cent in the 24th month, considering the annual average nominal wage increase.

A profound evaluation of the change of the expected cost of job loss would require the comparison of pre- and post-1990 dismissal and unemployment records. Unfortunately, retrospective data are more or less unavailable, so we have to refer to the common experience (and sporadic observations) suggesting that the time needed to get back to work was very short in the socialist period and therefore that the expected cost was considerably lower despite the lack of benefits.[17]

288   János Köllő

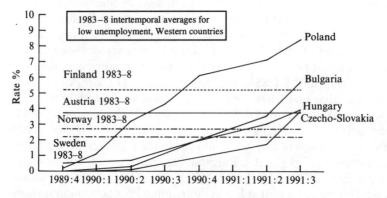

Source: Jackman and Layard (1990); Holzman (1990)
Figure 15.1   Unemployment rates, 1990–1

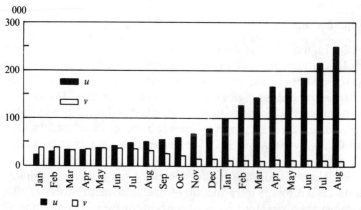

Source: Országos Munkoerôpiaci Központ (National Labour Market Centre),
Munkaerôpiaci Helyzetkép (1991/2) p. 16
Figure 15.2   Registered unemployment and vacancies in Hungary, 1990–1

Equally important from the viewpoint of contract enforcement is that, while the worker's expected cost of job loss probably increased with the appearance of unemployment, the firm's search cost presumably decreased with the growing number of available job seekers. The firm now can reallocate resources from screening to monitoring (or to paying higher wages). Other things being equal, the growing probability of detection and the increasing cost of job loss imply a higher effort level and a contracting set of available individual strategies.

6.2   The part-time second economy

The three major domains of the second economy in Hungary are private gardening/farming, house-building and services.

6.2.1 Private gardening and small farming

This has been hard-hit by falling food demand and the collapse of the Soviet market (pork and vegetable production are suffering from the contraction of home market demand; fruit and wine is also heavily affected by foregone Soviet exports). Agricultural output fell by 22.4 per cent in January–July 1991–90 and food prices were under recessionary pressure (the price index was 125 as opposed to the 136 per cent general price increase).[18] Small farming also has to face harder competition by (and less support from) the cooperative or the state farm. (In a 1991 survey of a sample of coop managers only 5 per cent said that the development of private allotment plots was a priority: *Figyelő* (25 July 1991, p. 24).

6.2.2 House-building

The long-lasting recession and the (partly retroactive) increase of housing loan interest rates from 3 to more than 30 per cent dramatically decreased the demand for construction moonlighters (house construction fell from 70,000–90,000 units a year in the early 1980s to 35,000 units a year in 1991).[19] With the massive inflow of immigrant workers labour supply on the free market increased and wages were pushed down as well (the daily rate of an unskilled construction labourer was HUF 500–700 in 1984; in Autumn 1991 the rate was still HUF 1000 at the major market of Budapest's Moscow Square, meanwhile, the average wage in industry had increased by 284 per cent).[20] Furthermore, as smaller and more flexible private firms and joint ventures appear in the housing market, the once existing competitive advantage of the 'grey' market over the legalised (or at least 'organised') sector is diminishing or disappearing altogether.

Last but not least, an important new development to be mentioned is that construction seems to have become a sector where the Soviet-type, high wage, part-time second economy is being replaced, to a considerable extent, by a Western-type black economy with an unregistered, low wage, full-time, partly immigrant workforce.

6.2.3 Services

In services, the part-time (moonlighting) second economy has to face hard competition from the expanding legal private sector and has to tackle the effects of import liberalisation. With the development of a 'buyers' market' in services the competitive advantage of legal firms or licensed craftsmen over moonlighters is becoming increasingly evident, mainly because the former promise lower search cost and reduced risk for the consumer. The impact of import liberalisation has also had harmful effects on the traditional second economy as a great part of its products and services had been devoted to adapting, complementing or substituting imported goods.

These developments suggest that a return to traditional part-time work outside the factory is decreasing and will probably further diminish with the transition to a market economy. This will increase the optimum level of effort in the first economy and reduce the set of available individual strategies.

6.3   The production process

The nature of the production process is obviously changing at a slower speed than the labour market or the second economy. Nevertheless, both the deep recession and the liberalisation of imports tend to mitigate input shortages. The rapidly growing number of small firms may have a similar impact through an improved access to subcontracting.

Western technologies and quality standards may also have an impact as, on the one hand, the increasingly important OECD markets require improved quality and tighter deadlines and, on the other, the influx of foreign capital transforms the 'labour-intensive variants of capital-intensive technologies', even in the slowly-moving state sector.

6.4   The abolition of wage increment taxation

According to an agreement made by the government and the major unions and chambers of commerce in December 1991, the separate taxation of the wage increment was to be abolished from January 1992, and the parties hope that their agreement will be efficient in constraining wage outflow. Firms increasing their wages by 28 per cent or more have to pay a prohibitive tax (of as yet unknown amount) if the *average* wage increase exceeds 23 per cent. The agreement is valid if the rate of inflation does not exceed the forecast.

It is not the aim of this chapter to solve the game imbedded in the agreement. What is important from this chapter's point of view is that the 'fixed relative wage condition' does not apply any more: with the abolition of (an almost prohibitive) wage taxation firms will be free to pay higher or lower relative wages and in the long run to develop non-equalising differentials.

7 Conclusion

If we sum up the developments of 1990–1 (and consider that some of the major changes will cause long-run transformation in the labour market or in the factory), we may conclude that the determinants of wage (and effort) bargaining are subject to dramatic change. The word 'dramatic' is not used here to imply that the Kádárian arrangement was 'good' and that the new one is 'bad', or vice versa. It simply implies that Hungarian workers face an enormous task of changing their *modus vivendi*. During forty years of communism they developed wise strategies of survival – they found a way of making profits under conditions of total legal repression. These strategies, however, were founded on conditions which seem set to vanish with communism. The cost of job loss will never again be as low (and the firm's search cost as high) as it was even a few years ago. The value of 'shirking' will probably never reach the levels it did when the Soviet-type second economy was flourishing and the search cost on the consumer's goods market was extremely high. The confused production process will no longer offer an easy way of 'sabotage'. Wage differences will probably increase. The worker will have to make rather different, unfamiliar decisions: to have paid employment or not; to try to start a business or to go into employment; to find out where the highest wages are; to accept a wage offer or to stay unemployed; to join a union or not, and so on.

Even though the road of transition merely leads from one optimum to another – and there is no reason to suppose that the new one is inferior to the old in any meaningful way – the process of finding this new optimum can be painful and full of harmful pitfalls. The challenge itself may provoke unrest and may contribute to massive disappointment and desolation directed at the new economic order.

Another conclusion is the need for more stringent incomes' policies. With less chance to absorb the cost of contract enforcement in lost output (thanks to increased competition) managers will possibly put more emphasis on relative wage rates. This would not cause any problem in a fully competitive economy, but it may do so in Hungary. The replacement of a tax-based incomes policy by centralised wage bargaining (with union centres whose influence on their local organisations is more than questionable) may not be efficient in constraining excessive wage outflow at the 'followers' whose economic performance lags behind the 'wage leaders'.

NOTES

1 The number of registered unions has not yet been 'officially' published. MSZOSZ and Liga officials estimate that the number has already exceeded 1000. The minimum membership size (sufficient for registration) is 10.

2 The latter was well shown by the failure of calls for general warning strikes by MSZOSZ. Less than 10 per cent of the alleged 1 mn MSZOSZ members joined the 'general strike' in December 1991, for instance.

3 The phases of negotiation and implementation are obviously logical stages rather than distinct time periods.

4 For a more detailed discussion of this concept and of the problems discussed in points 1–3 see Köllő (1989).

5 'Munkaerő kereslet és kínálat 1989. I. negyedév', ABMH-MIK, Budapest (1989).

6 'Skill shortages in British Industry', *Department of Employment Gazette* (May 1979) p. 433. The Polish figures are from Fallenbuchl (1982, p. 33).

7 Data sources are Adam (1982) pp. 40, 151 for the then USSR and Poland; Munkaügyi Statisztikai Zsebkönyv (Budapest, 1985, pp. 169–70) for Hungary; *Heti Világgazdaság* (26 May 1984) for Czecho-Slovakia; personal communication, Institut für Wirtschaftswissenschaft (East Berlin, 1983) for the GDR.

8 The access to voluntary change of employer in high mobility countries can also be characterised by the modest role of Labour Offices. Hirings through Offices amounted to 15–22 per cent in Hungary in 1964–80 and 1985–8 (Fazekas and Köllő, 1989, p. 113); 3–4 per cent in Poland 1954–80 (Fallenbuchl, 1982), pp. 33, 40); and 17.2 per cent in the USSR in 1976 (Schroeder, 1982, p. 11). In contrast to the general case, in the under-developed, labour-surplus Republics of the USSR voluntary mobility was successfully controlled by the authorities: this is well shown by the high proportion using the Labour Office (71.1 per cent in Kirghizia against 21.4 per cent in Latvia in 1977, see Schroeder, 1982, p. 11).

9 Own calculation, based on Révész (1985) and Petschnig (1987). This is not to say that the illegal redistribution of incomes is insignificant. According to CSO estimations and Petschnig (1987) 10–12 per cent of the population's income was spent on tips, bribery, under-the-counter sales, trading with council flats, paying 'black' interest, etc. Purchasing current consumer goods on the black market accounted for only HUF 1–2 bn, or less than 0.5 per cent of the total expenditure, however.

10 An equally important benefit of shirking is savings in consumer market transaction costs, which can be extremely high if shortages are acute and market information scarce. Other things being equal, an Eastern European worker will use more office time for consumer market transactions than do Western workers.

11 We assume that firm size is exogenous to the work contract enforcement problem – it has more to do with government control costs.

12 If firms are profit maximisers, the use of incentive pay will decrease with firm size; see Alchian and Demsetz (1972) or Stelluto (1969).

13 An interesting case study by Károly Fazekas in Révész (1984) demonstrates that a shift from time rate to piece rate in the Raba Auto Works resulted in less shirking, but a destructive use of the equipment by engine assembly workers.

14 See Révész (1984), vol. 24, pp. 25–6 on the comparison of Austrian and Hungarian weaving mills or Redor (1988), p. 214 on within-group wage dispersion in Eastern Europe.

15 In Poland the president of the State Commission of Planning announced the closing of 200–300 unprofitable firms within nine months on 28 March 1982 and forecast 700,000–800,000 unemployed workers ('Lengyel dokumentumok', *Beszélő*, 8 July 1982, p. 36). In Czecho-Slovakia the state plan of 1980 included a list of factories to be closed (Csaba, 1982). In Hungary plans to regroup hundreds of thousands of workers were formulated ('Ez azonban nem munkanélküliség', *Beszélő*, 3 March 1988). None of these plans became a reality.

16 All figures from the monthly reports of the National Labour Market Centre (OMK 'Gyorsjelentes').

17 The average duration of unemployment of the Raba workers dismissed in 1979 (Fazekas and Köllő, 1989) was 29 days, one day shorter than the period of notice for which the firm paid 100 per cent compensation. In a recently studied sample of ex-Videoton employees (Székesfehérvár) none of the interviewed workers reported unemployment experience before 1991. It should be mentioned that the figures available for time between two jobs in socialist countries (Powell, 1977; Földvári, 1983, on the USSR, and Galasi and Sík, 1982; Galasi, 1978 on Hungary) are of little use in the present context as they do not distinguish between voluntary and involuntary spells.

18 *Figyelő* (24 October 1991) p. 5 and (10 October 1991) p. 5 respectively.

19 *Figyelő* (18 July 1991) p. 9. In 1990–1 the average unit size also fell by 1.5 square metres; see *Figyelő* (10 March 1991) p. 4.

20 From HUF 5173 to an estimated net HUF 14707. The average gross wage in industry was HUF 18384 in October 1991. Compare *Statistical Pocket Book 1986*, p. 33 and *Figyelő* (31 October 1991) p. 5. We apply a 20 per cent PIT deduction.

REFERENCES

Adam, J. (ed.) (1982) *Employment Policies in the Soviet Union and Eastern Europe*, London: Macmillan.

Alchian, A. and H. Demsetz, (1972) 'Production, information costs, and economic organization', *American Economic Review*, **62**, pp. 777–95.

Balázs, K. and M. Laki (1990) '*A pénzben mért magángazdaság súlya a magyar háztartások bevételeiben és kiadásaiban*' (The private economy in terms of household expenditure and household income), *Közgazdasági Szemle*, **7–8**.

Bicanic, I. (1985) 'The influence of the unofficial economy on income inequality in Yugoslavia', University of Zagreb, mimeo.

Brezinski, H. (1987) 'The second economy in the GDR – Pragmatism is gaining ground', *Studies in Comparative Communism*, **1** (Spring) pp. 85–101.

Csaba, L. (1982) 'A csehszlovák gazdaságirányítás új vonásai' (New features of economic policy in Czecho-Slovakia), *Bankszemle*, **1**.

Dubois, P. (1976) *Le sabotage dans l'industrie*, Paris.

L

Ellmann, M.J. (1979) *Full Employment – Lessons From State Socialism*, Leiden-Antwerp: H.E. Stenfert-Kroese BV.

Fallenbuchl, Z. (1982) 'Employment policies in Poland', in Adam (1982) pp. 26–48.

Farkas, J., I. Harcsa and A. Vajda (1988) 'Csehszlovákia és Magyarország társadalmi jelzöszámainak összehasonlitása' (A comparison of social indicators for Czecho-Slovakia and Hungary), *Statisztikai Szemle*, **12**, pp. 1108–21.

Fazekas, K. and J. Köllő (1989), 'Munkaerőpiac tökepiac nélkül', PhD. thesis, Institute of Economics of the Hungarian Academy of Sciences, Budapest; published (1990) under the same title, Budapest: KJK.

—— (1990) 'The patterns of unemployment in Hungary – a case study', *Structural Change and Economic Dynamics*, **1**.

Feldbrugge, F.J.M. (1983) 'Government and shadow economy in the Soviet Union', Bielefeld Conference on 'The Economics of the Shadow Economy' (10–14 October).

Földvári, Zs. (1983) 'Vándormadarak tollvégen' (Job whoppers come to light) (in Hungarian), *Heti Vilaggazdasag*, **34**.

Frey, M. (1988) 'Kötöttöl a rugalmas munkaidörendszerek felé' (From fixed to flexible work schedules), PhD. thesis, Institute of Economics of the Hungarian Academy of Sciences, Budapest.

Galasi, P. (1978) 'A fluktuáló munkaerő néhány jellegzetessége' (Some characteristics of mobile workers), *Közgazdasági Szemle*, **6**.

Galasi, P. and E. Sík (1982) 'Vállalatközi kapcsolatok a helyi munkaerőpiacon' (Inter-firm flows on a local labour market), in P. Galasi (ed.), *A munkaerőpiac szerkezete és müködése Magyarországon* (The structure and working of the labour market in Hungary), Budapest: KJK.

Granick, D. (1987) *Job Rights in the Soviet Union: Their Consequences*, New York: Cambridge University Press.

Gregory, P. and I.L. Collier (1988) 'Unemployment in the Soviet Union : Evidence from the Soviet Interview Survey', *The American Economic Review* (September, pp. 613–32).

Grossmann, G. (1977) 'The second economy in the Soviet Union', *Problems of Communism*, **26(5)**, pp. 25–40.

Gyekiczky, T. (1988) 'A fegyelem csapdájában' (In the trap of discipline), MTA Szociológiai Intézete, Budapest.

Haraszti, M. (1978) *A Worker in a Workers' State*, New York: University Books.

Hirschman, A. O. (1970) *Exit, Voice and loyalty*, Cambridge, MA: Harvard University Press.

Holzman, R. (1990) 'Unemployment benefits during economic transition: Background, concept and implementation', paper submitted for the OECD Centre for Co-operation with the European Economies in Transition (CCEET) (November), Paris: OECD.

Jackman, R. and R. Layard (1990) 'Unemployment benefits during the transition', paper submitted for the OECD Centre for Co-operation with the European Economies in Transition (CCEET) (November), Paris: OECD.

Johanesson, J. (1985) 'Labour market policy in Sweden', PhD. thesis, University of Canberra, mimeo.

Kemény, I. (1978) 'La chaine dans une usine Hongroise', *Actes de la Recherche en Science Social*, **X**.

Köllő J. (1989) 'After a dark golden age – Eastern Europe', delivered at Harvard (11 March 1989) forthcoming in J. Schor (ed.), *Changing Production Relations – A Global Approach*, Helsinki: WIDER.

Kornai, J. (1980) 'A hiány' (The Economics of Shortage), Budapest: KJK.
Kornai, J. and A. Matits (1985) The bureaucratic redistribution of firms' profits', in J. Kornai and A. Matits, *Vision and Reality*, Market and State: New Studies on the Socialist Economy and Society, Budapest, Corvina & Hemel Hempstead: Harvester-Wheatsheaf; New York: Routledge.

Lackó, M. (1991) 'Az illegális gazdaság aránya Magyarországon 1970 és 1990 között' (The share of the illegal economy in Hungary, 1970–90), Budapest: Institute of Economics, mimeo.

Ladó, M. and F. Tóth (1985) 'A hivatalos szabályok árnyékában' (In the shade of official rules), *Mozgó Világ*, 11, pp. 4–9.

Makela, V. (1986) 'The regional differences in the excess demand for labour and its effect on the aggregate inflation rate', University of Tampere Department of Economics, **Series E.**

Makó, C. (1985) 'A társadalmi viszonyok erötere: a munkafolyamat' (The work process as a network of social relations), Budapest: KJK.

Moskoff, W. (1984) *Labour and Leisure in the Soviet Union*, London: Macmillan.

Petschnig, M.Z. (1987) 'Adalékok a második és harmadik gazdaság terjedelmének felméréséhez' (On measuring the size of the second and third economies) Budapest, manuscript.

Powell, D.E. (1977) 'Labor turnover in the Soviet Union', *Slavic Review* (July).

Redor, D. (1988) 'Les inegalités de salaires a l'est et à l'ouest', Paris: Economica.

Révész G. (ed.) (1984) 'Wage bargaining in Hungarian firms', *Studies of the Institute of Economics*, 24, Budapest.

Révész, G. (ed.) (1985) 'Wage bargaining in Hungarian firms', Budapest: *Studies of the Institute of Economics*, 27.

Schroeder, G. (1982) 'Managing labour shortages in the USSR', in Adam (1982) pp. 3–25.

Schwarz, S. (1954) *Labour in the Soviet Union*, London: Cresset Press.

Scott, J. (1985) *Weapons of the Weak*, New Haven: Yale University Press.

Sík, E. (1987) 'A láthatatlan jövedelmekről' (On invisible incomes), *Mozgó Világ*, **6.**

Stelluto, G.L. (1969) 'Report on incentive pay in manufacturing industries', *Monthly Labour Review*, **92**, pp. 49–53.

Sziráczki, G. (1984) 'Stratification of drivers and their earning in a transport company', in Rèvész (1985).

Tímár, J. (1988) *Idö és munkaidö* (Time and work-time), Budapest: KJK.

Wiles, P. (1982) 'A note on Soviet Unemployment by US definitions', *Soviet Studies*, **123** (April), pp. 619–28.

M

16 The social security crisis in Hungary

MÁRIA AUGUSZTINOVICS

Social security systems are rather insecure almost everywhere. Problems are usually explained by referring in the first place to the increased and increasing life-expectancy, and then more brutally, to the 'aging' of the population. In this chapter I shall argue that the present Hungarian crisis has little to do with demographic factors; the real sources have to be sought in the near-collapse of the economy and in the particular Hungarian means of transition to a 'market economy' – more frankly, to a capitalist society.

The focus will be on problems of retirement, and other fields of social security will be mentioned only within this context. The chapter consists of two sections. In section 1 a simple numerical example will be used to introduce major concepts and to highlight basic trends that affect a stable, fixed-benefit pension system under economic growth, stagnation and stagflation. In section 2 the real-life system will be described, referring to conclusions from section 1 but relying wherever possible on available empirical evidence. The demographic background, the social and economic expansion of the social security system, the situation of retirees at the micro level and the financial status of the system at the macro level can be reasonably well documented. In addition, reference will be made to views and ongoing debates concerning the future of the system.

1 Lessons from a simple example

Secular trends affecting the present situation cannot be consistently documented by empirical evidence since even the available time series are too short to describe a period as long as the actual life-span of today's retirees and older workers. We have therefore to rely on a simple numerical example. This is not a mere theoretical exercise: even if data were abundant, basic trends would be easier to reveal under simplifying assumptions than amidst the ever-changing reality.

296

The example assumes a *stationary population* of nine adult cohorts, each reduced to the usual 'representative' individual. They all live over *nine* years, *six* of them spent in employment and *three* in retirement. It follows that cross-sectionally there are always six cohorts in employment and three cohorts in retirement. All working cohorts receive the same wage. Workers contribute a uniform percentage of their wage to the social security system (hereafter SSS). Retirees receive a pension determined as a uniform percentage of the wage they earned in their last active year. It is a *fixed-benefit* system: the pension does not change over retirement (except for eventual compensation for inflation).

In addition to the customary growth rate, interest rate and simple averages we shall need the following concepts to describe the cross-section state of the SSS:

* *Contribution ratio*	Contribution to SSS over gross wage (wage including the portion to be contributed)
* *Entry pension*	Pension determined at retiring
* *Entry ratio*	Entry pension over last wage earned
* *E/O entrant/oldest ratio*	Entry pension over pension of oldest cohort
* *P/W pension/wage ratio*	Average pension over average wage
* *Retirement wealth*	Cumulated sum of past contributions minus pensions received, discounted to date
* *AFCR*	Actuarially fair contribution ratio, which provides zero retirement wealth at death.

Our example assumes an *entry ratio of 70 per cent*. The AFCR depends on this ratio as well as on the growth and interest rates, as demonstrated in Table 16.1.

Obviously the AFCR is a function *decreasing with the interest rate*. Less obviously, but clearly, it is a function *increasing with the growth rate*, since higher growth pushes the bulk of life-time earnings towards the end of the earning span. In the *golden rule* case (interest rate = growth rate), represented in the main diagonal of Table 16.1, the interest effect dominates: the higher the rates, the smaller are the golden rule AFCRs. Observe that *above* the main diagonal (interest rate exceeds growth rate) AFCRs are smaller than the golden rule value, both row-wise and column-wise, while *below* the diagonal (interest rate lower than growth rate) they are larger.

It should be noted that our example describes a **stable pension system** in a changing macroeconomic environment. The number of participants, the contribution and entry ratios remain constant over time, so do individual

Table 16.1. *Actuarially fair contribution ratios, entry ratio 70 per cent*

	R = 0	R = 1	R = 2	R = 3	R = 4	R = 5	R = 6	R = 7	R = 8	R = 9	R = 10	R = 11
L = 0	35.0	33.5	32.0	30.6	29.3	28.0	26.8	25.7	24.6	23.6	22.6	21.6
L = 1	35.9	34.3	32.8	31.4	30.1	28.8	27.5	26.4	25.3	24.2	23.2	22.2
L = 2	36.8	35.2	33.6	32.2	30.8	29.5	28.3	27.1	25.9	24.9	23.8	22.8
L = 3	37.6	36.0	34.5	33.0	31.6	30.3	29.0	27.8	26.6	25.5	24.5	23.5
L = 4	38.5	36.9	35.3	33.8	32.4	31.0	29.7	28.5	27.3	26.2	25.1	24.1
L = 5	39.4	37.7	36.1	34.6	33.2	31.8	30.5	29.2	28.0	26.8	25.7	24.7
L = 6	40.3	38.6	37.0	35.4	33.9	32.5	31.2	29.9	28.7	27.5	26.4	25.3
L = 7	41.2	39.4	37.8	36.2	34.7	33.3	31.9	30.6	29.4	28.2	27.0	26.0
L = 8	42.1	40.3	38.6	37.0	35.5	34.1	32.7	31.3	30.1	28.9	27.7	26.6
L = 9	42.9	41.2	39.5	37.8	36.3	34.8	33.4	32.1	30.8	29.5	28.4	27.2
L = 10	43.8	42.0	40.3	38.7	37.1	35.6	34.1	32.8	31.5	30.2	29.0	27.9
L = 11	44.7	42.9	41.1	39.5	37.9	36.3	34.9	33.5	32.2	30.9	29.7	28.5

L = growth rate; R = interest rate; all in percentages, per period.

pensions if there is no inflation. The macro level status of the system will vary solely under the impact of the changing growth and interest rates.

Our example has much in common with the life-cycle model as well as with the overlapping generations model, as initiated by Modigliani and Brumberg (1954), Ando and Modigliani (1963), Samuelson (1958), and Gale (1973). It assumes a stationary population of representative individuals, it neglects childhood and the costs of human gestation, and finally it provides for a balanced life-path with zero bequest. Nevertheless our example is somewhat more complex: it allows for economic growth and non-zero interest, hence the AFCR ratio is not simply a function of the lengths of the earning and retirement spans (as distinguished from the life-cycle model) and it does not assume a consumption–loan economy, hence a cross-section budget constraint is not enforced (as distinguished from overlapping generations).

The example demonstrates three periods of different macroeconomic conditions. Each period consists of three calendar years. For the first period (and for a sufficiently large number of preceding years), we assume a steady 5 per cent annual growth and the golden rule 5 per cent interest rate to go with it. It is also assumed that the *contribution ratio* has been fixed at its AFCR level, which makes it *31.8 per cent.*

In Table 16.2, cross-section flows and stocks resulting from these assumptions are normed to the average wage of the first year, taken as 1000. Retired cohorts are accounted for individually, denoted by upper-case consecutive letters of the alphabet; cohorts in work appear only at the aggregate level. Pensions received are registered as negative contributions.

Column (1) represents the current account of the SSS. Columns 2–5 describe retirement wealth, whether it is indeed funded or just imputed. 'Change of wealth' is the algebraic sum of contribution and interest accrued; it explains the difference between opening and year-end wealth.

In this simple golden age world aggregate pensions (indicated by Σ Retired) and wages grow at the same rate, hence all ratios remain constant. Obviously the P/W ratio is lower than the 70 per cent entry ratio and the E/O ratio is higher than 100 per cent: in both cases the gap corresponds exactly to two years of growth.

Trivially, because of the golden rule assumption, the AFCR results in zero cross-sectional balance for the SSS: incoming contributions cover exactly the pensions to be paid by the system. It is well known in economic theory that in the golden age there is no significant difference between a pay-as-you-go and a funded system; see, for example, Bourgeois-Pichat (1978). Interest accrued on retirement wealth can be

Table 16.2. Golden age growth

Year 1 — Growth 5%, Interest 5%, Average wage 1000, Average pension 635, Pension/wage 63.5%, Entrant/oldest 110.2%

	Contribution (1)	Wealth, opening (2)	Interest accrued (3)	Change of wealth (4)	Wealth, year-end (5)
Cohort A	−605	576	29	−576	605
B	−635	1181	59	−576	1240
C	−667	1815	91	−576	1844
Σ Retired	−1906	3572	179	−1728	
Employed	1906	4539	227	2133	6672
Total		8111	406	406	8516

Year 2 — Growth 5%, Interest 5%, Average wage 1050, Average pension 667, Pension/wage 63.5%, Entrant/oldest 110.2%

	Contribution (1)	Wealth, opening (2)	Interest accrued (3)	Change of wealth (4)	Wealth, year-end (5)
Cohort B	−635	605	30	−605	635
C	−667	1240	62	−605	1302
D	−700	1906	95	−605	1937
Σ Retired	−2002	3751	188	−1814	
Employed	2002	4766	238	2240	7006
Total		8516	426	426	8942

Year 3 — Growth 5%, Interest 5%, Average wage 1102, Average pension 701, Pension/wage 63.5%, Entrant/oldest 110.2%

	Contribution (1)	Wealth, opening (2)	Interest accrued (3)	Change of wealth (4)	Wealth, year-end (5)
Cohort C	−667	635	32	−635	667
D	−700	1302	65	−635	1367
E	−735	2002	100	−635	2033
Σ Retired	−2102	3938	197	−1905	
Employed	2102	5004	250	2352	7356
Total		8942	447	447	9389

accumulated and aggregate wealth – opening as well as year-end – is increasing with the overall growth rate.

The important fact to be observed is, however, that *aggregate and average pensions grow* while individual pensions do not. This phenomenon is generally known as the **pension paradox**. The 'burden' on SSS – or, as it is usually put, the burden on the working generations who 'support' the elderly – is steadily growing with the economy, without any living retired soul being better off than he or she was in the previous year.

The paradox is due to the natural turnover among retired cohorts in a fixed-benefit system. The oldest cohort with its smallest pension exits and the newly retiring cohort's entry pension is the largest because of the increased wage level. Thus aggregate and average pensions grow, while each retired individual is falling more and more behind the average living standards of an increasingly affluent society. Pensioners become *relatively* poorer, continuously over the retirement span, while individual pensions do not change in absolute terms. The E/O ratio measures the strength of the turnover effect as well as the magnitude of income differentials among pensioners.

This has been the sole purpose of our golden age exercise: to demonstrate that the paradox occurs even under the simplest conceivable conditions. We may now turn to the second period in our example. For sake of simplicity we assume zero growth, i.e. stagnation, but the major trends would appear very similar under any kind of *slowdown* (see Table 16.3). The 5 per cent real interest is sustained so the golden rule does not any more apply.

Wages, and thus contributions to SSS as well as entry pensions, stop growing. The relative position of pensioners in society is being stabilised, not because they themselves are better off but because wages are also stagnating.

However, the *turnover effect keeps working*, it takes as many years for it to level off as the number of cohorts in retirement. Aggregate and average pensions continue to increase until Year 6 when finally all individual pensions become equal. Hence the P/W ratio is increasing until it reaches the 70 per cent entry ratio. The E/O ratio sinks gradually to 100 per cent, implying that the turnover effect is gradually weakening and pension differentials decreasing.

The major feature of the slowdown period is that the SSS develops an increasing **deficit** on its current account. The reason is obvious: contributions follow *current* wages while aggregate pensions follow the growth trend of the *previous* period by the turnover effect. Revenues thus fall behind expenditures. If the SSS operates as a *pay-as-you-go* system then the deficit must be financed from the government's budget and the

Table 16.3. *Stagnation*

		Contribution (1)	Wealth, opening (2)	Interest accrued (3)	Change of wealth (4)	Wealth, year-end (5)
Year 4	Cohort D	−700	667	33	−667	700
Growth 0% Interest 5%	E	−735	1367	68	−667	1435
Average wage 1102	F	−772	2102	105	−667	2135
Average pension 736	Σ Retired	−2207	4135	207	−2000	
Pension/wage 66.7%	Employed	2102	5254	263	2364	7619
Entrant/oldest 110.2%	Total	−105	9389	469	364	9754
Year 5	Cohort E	−735	700	35	−700	735
Growth 0% Interest 5%	F	−772	1435	72	−700	1527
Average wage 1102	G	−772	2189	109	−662	2262
Average pension 759	Σ Retired	−2278	4324	216	−2062	
Pension/wage 68.9%	Employed	2102	5429	271	2373	7802
Entrant/oldest 105%	Total	−177	9754	488	311	10 064
Year 6	Cohort F	−772	735	37	−735	832
Growth 0% Interest 5%	G	−772	1527	76	−695	1604
Average wage 1102	H	−772	2263	113	−659	2436
Average pension 772	Σ Retired	−2315	4525	226	−2089	
Pension/wage 70%	Employed	2102	5540	277	2379	7918
Entrant/oldest 100%	Total	−214	10 064	503	290	10 354

growing burden of 'supporting' the elderly becomes irritating in a world of stagnation.

The capital account of retirement wealth, of course, tells a different story. The life-path of those retired cohorts that contributed in the previous period is still balanced (cohorts D, E and F die with zero retirement wealth). Those who are retiring in this period (cohorts G and H) will predictably leave a positive bequest at death because the contribution ratio has not been reduced with the growth rate, hence prior to retirement they contribute at a rate which is higher than AFCR. Pensions are thus actually financed from the life-time retirement saving of the pensioners and the interest accrued on it. Retirees are not 'supported' by anyone except themselves.

If the SSS operates as a *funded system*, then the capital income on wealth more than adequately covers the current deficit. Although pensioners withdraw their wealth by enjoying pension benefits, savings by cohorts in work keep the aggregate retirement wealth growing. The change of wealth is still positive, the capital account shows a healthy surplus and there is no need for government intervention. For the SSS **access to retirement wealth** and to the interest accrued on it is the natural instrument to cope with the turnover effect and the resulting current deficit in a slowdown period. (As long as each generation provides for its own life-path, the same is true for current deficits resulting from demographic upheavals, not considered in our simple example.)

The stagnation period of our example has served to demonstrate the significance of access to retirement wealth, the difference between a pay-as-you-go and a funded system. Now we turn to the third period when a severe depresson hits the economy, with 5 per cent annual contraction accompanied by 20 per cent inflation. Nominal growth thus appears at a 14 per cent rate. We assume a reduced but still positive gap of 3 percentage points between the interest and growth rates, and thus a 17 per cent nominal interest.

For completeness, we should consider cases when pensions are fully indexed for inflation, or at least for keeping up with nominal wages. Rather, to make a long story somewhat shorter, we turn directly to the more typical case when pensioners are compensated for inflation to a smaller extent than workers – at 10 per cent annually in our example. (New entrants are of course not compensated, the entry pension is determined with respect to current wages thus considered adequate at the current price level.)

In stagflation (see Table 16.4) aggregate, average and entry pensions are again *growing* over time, at least nominally. This time *the E/O ratio* neither remains constant nor decreases, it is *increasing*, and the gap

Table 16.4. *Stagflation*

		Contribution (1)	Wealth, opening (2)	Interest accrued (3)	Change of wealth (4)	Wealth, year-end (5)
Year 7						
Growth 14%	Interest 17%					
Average wage	1257					
Average pension	823					
Pension/wage	65.5%					
Entrant/oldest	90.9%					
	Cohort G	− 849	832	141	− 708	124
	H	− 849	1604	273	− 576	1028
	I	− 772	2321	395	− 377	1943
	Σ Retired	− 2470	4756	809	− 1661	3095
	Employed	2396	5598	952	3347	8945
	Total	− 74	10354	1760	1686	12041
Year 8						
Growth 14%	Interest 17%					
Average wage	1433					
Average pension	888					
Pension/wage	61.9%					
Entrant/oldest	94.2%					
	Cohort H	− 934	1105	188	− 746	359
	I	− 849	1943	330	− 519	1425
	J	− 880	2640	449	− 431	2209
	Σ Retired	− 2663	5689	967	− 1695	3993
	Employed	2731	6305	1072	3803	10108
	Total	69	11994	2039	2108	14101
Year 9						
Growth 14%	Interest 17%					
Average wage	1633					
Average pension	968					
Pension/wage	59.3%					
Entrant/oldest	107.4%					
	Cohort I	− 934	1502	255	− 678	824
	J	− 968	2209	376	− 592	1617
	K	− 1003	2989	508	− 495	2494
	Σ Retired	− 2905	6700	1139	− 1765	4935
	Employed	3114	7119	1210	4324	11443
	Total	209	13819	2349	2558	16378

Table 16.5. *Golden age growth, stagnation and stagflation*

	Golden age growth	Stagnation	Stagflation
Real wage	Increasing	Constant	Decreasing
Real value of pensions	Constant	Constant	Decreasing
Status of pensioners	Relative poverty	Constant	Relative and absolute poverty
P/W ratio	Constant	Increasing	Decreasing
E/O ratio	Constant	Decreasing	Increasing
SSS current account	Balanced	Deficit	Surplus

between the new entrant and older pensioners widens. In many ways the situation resembles the case of real growth when retirees keep falling behind the average of society, except that now their impoverishment is absolute as well as relative since they are losing 10 per cent of their real income while workers lose 'only' 5 per cent of the real wage annually. This is reflected in the *decrease of the P/W ratio* that remained constant over the golden period of real growth and increased in stagnation.

The most important fact to observe is, however, the improving situation of the SSS current balance. After the first year's smaller deficit, inherited from the period of stagnation, the balance turns positive and the surplus is increasing. **Inflation is favourable** for the current status of the SSS, inasmuch as nominal wages grow faster than nominal pensions, no matter what happens to real wages and pensions. This is the lesson from stagflation with under-compensated retirees.

Our example could be continued endlessly. We could account for economic recovery, the end of the 2-digit inflation and the beginning of some modest real growth. The current account of the SSS, however, has nothing to do with real trends, it reflects nominal growth. In nominal terms the recovery would be nothing else but a *slowdown* with all the consequences of the second period, already discussed. Aggregate pensions would grow rapidly by the turnover effect, contributions would fall behind because of the slower growth of nominal wages, current deficits would replace current surpluses. There is no need to repeat all this.

Summing up the major trends of the three periods considered, we have the position in Table 16.5.

The moral of the story told by our example is that (1) the *turnover effect*, (2) the *access to retirement wealth or lack of it*, and (3) the *level of inflationary compensations* are the dominant factors that determine the status of the SSS. This status may change dramatically with economic conditions, even if a stable pension system is assumed.

The turnover effect and the impact of inflationary compensation are due to the fact that a fixed-benefit system has been considered. None of these factors would have any role to play in a *wage-indexed* pension system where all pensions would automatically follow the average nominal wage. In such a system there would be no source of generational conflicts, all generations would smile or cry together and the current balance of the SSS would be changing exclusively because of demographic fluctuations, with retirement wealth as a convenient buffer if the system was funded.

In contrast, the status of a fixed-benefit SSS can be said to be critical, its situation termed a **crisis**, if the relative and absolute impoverishment of pensioners is excessive *yet* the current account is in severe deficit *and* the system has no access to retirement wealth. There was no such period in our simple, logical example – it takes real life to accomplish a real crisis.

2   The real-life system

2.1   Demography

The demographic transition reached Hungary belatedly. Life-tables from the turn of the century indicate a lag of at least 70–100 years with respect to the pioneer countries of the transition. However, progress was rapid until the late 1960s. In 1966 life-expectancy at birth was 70.4 years (average, both sexes), only some two years less than in England. These six decades were characterised by processes of the *first phase of demographic transition*: life-expectancy increased mostly by rapid improvement in infant and child mortality (see Table 16.6).

The normal course of the transition process has been halted, even somewhat reversed since the late 1960s. In spite of much speculation, this fact has remained without consistent scientific explanation. While infant and child mortality continues to improve mortality in many adult and elderly age-groups has been deteriorating. **Life-expectancy at age 60 has stagnated** since 1960, markedly decreased for males and somewhat increased for females. The latter are more numerous so the average is practically unchanged. If there is trouble, it is not that retirees live longer.

The *number of people in retirement age* keeps slowly increasing since more numerous cohorts are reaching retirement age, due partly to the rapidly improving infant and child mortality in the first decades of the century, partly to smaller World War II losses in presently retiring cohorts. However, the 1970s added only 79,000 and the 1980s 93,000 persons to their numbers. On average **9300 persons annually added** over

Table 16.6. *Demographic indicators, 1900–90*

		1900	1950	1960	1970	1980	1990
Life-expectancy	Male	36.1	59.3	65.9	66.3	65.4	65.1
at birth	Female	39.1	63.4	70.1	72.1	72.7	73.7
Infant mortality (000 persons)		222.8	85.7	47.6	35.9	23.2	14.8
Life-expectancy	Male	11.8	16.3	16.8	15.2	15.1	14.7
at age 60	Female	12.1	17.7	18.0	18.2	18.8	19.0
Population (000 persons)			9293	9961	10 322	10 710	10 354
In retirement age (000 persons)			1307	1677	2116	2195	2288
per cent of population			14.1	16.8	20.5	20.5	22.0

the last ten years to an army of 2.2 mn can hardly be blamed for a severe social security crisis. The percentage increase from 1980 to 1990 was due less to this real increase than to the decrease of the population. An unknown part of the latter is genuine natural decrease but it is widely known that the 1990 Census was not the most exact in the history of Hungarian demography.

2.2 Expanding system

Until 1949 three separate, large retirement and health insurance systems existed in Hungary apart from a few smaller institutions: one for *blue-collar* and one for *white-collar* workers (both excluding agriculture) and a third one for *civil servants*. All existing systems were funded but their funds were mainly invested in urban real estate, demolished or badly damaged in World War II. *Farmers and most agricultural workers*, over 50 per cent of the labour force in 1949, were not covered at all.

In 1949 a major reform established a *single, unified, pay-as-you-go pension system* and incorporated it into the central budget. (Actually it took a few years to combine all previous institutions into this giant.) The system covered all those groups that had been previously insured but still excluded agriculture, except for employees of state-owned large farms. From 1949 onwards, the budget directly financed the various branches of *health services*. The supply of such services was free for those insured and their families, later extended over the entire population as a citizen's right. Since health services were – until quite recently – separated from the social security system, their problems are beyond the scope of this chapter.

During the 1950s the traditionally insured group was significantly expanded by increasing employment. In the early 1960s the retirement system was extended over members of *agricultural cooperatives* – practically the entire agricultural labour force and their families, including those already of retirement age. In the five years between 1960 and 1965 nearly 400,000 new retirees entered the system from the ranks of previously uninsured, old peasant men and women. Initially the rules were somewhat different for them, the age-limit higher and the entry pension lower than for the traditionally insured group. Nevertheless, one has to admit that a funded system could never survive such a blow as the admittance of several hundreds of thousands of people who had not previously contributed to the system.

All this resulted in a rapidly **growing number of people covered** by the system. Growth was particularly pronounced in the number of insured in their own – rather than in their families – right because women's participation in the labour force continued to increase until the mid-1970s.

The *retirement age* (lower limit) was determined in 1949 *as age 60 for men and 55 for women* in the traditionally insured groups, sustained until the present day. While this had its rationale at that time it seems to be unusually low today. The lower limit should have been gradually increased over decades of improving living standards and permanent labour shortage – it will now have to be increased in times of contracting real wage and increasing unemployment.

At the beginning, the system required only ten years in employment for admission into retirement at the proper age and offered a base pension at 15 per cent of the wage earned in the last 3–5 years of employment, plus a premium of 2 per cent of the base for each year spent in work after 1945. In 1954 the base ratio was increased to 50 per cent and the premium reduced to 1 per cent. In 1958 the criterion for the 50 per cent base became 25 completed years in employment but each year served since 1929 became eligible for the premium. In 1975 rules for the traditionally insured groups and agricultural cooperative members were unified. Base and premium were merged, and the entry pension became a more or less continuous function of years served and earnings. As an upper limit, with 42 years completed in service the system granted an entry pension equal to 75 per cent of labour income earned over the last three (or most favourable three of the last five) years in employment. More exact descriptions of these details are of course available in Hungarian, e.g. Szabó (1991).

Changing legislation, together with a rapidly increasing participation ratio and the passing of time – that gave more people more and more years served – resulted in a gradually **increasing entry ratio** from the mid-1960s until the early 1980s (see Table 16.7).

Table 16.7. *The system in expansion, 1950–80*

	1950	1960	1965	1970	1975	1980
Insured (per cent of population)						
In own right	25.8	44.2	52.6	59.9	66.1	65.7
Family members	21.5	41.1	44.1	37.0	33.9	34.3
Altogether	47.3	85.3	96.6	96.9	100.0	100.0
Entry ratio		53.0	48.3	48.7	61.8	70.9

The unifying, comprehensive Social Security Act, passed in 1975, completed the 25-year long expansion of the system and codified what will be referred to in this chapter as the 'old deal' between state and population. The deal provided the state with a labour force employed at a relatively low wage-share and high surplus-share, on the other hand it granted safety in old age at a satisfactory entry ratio, free education, health service and other social security benefits, eg. children's and maternity allowances. The high surplus went almost entirely into the central budget and all benefits were paid from there. This fact was criticised almost from the beginning. Over-centralised income redistribution resulted in over-centralised economic power, in lack of transparency and efficiency. Nevertheless, the social merits of the deal, the safety for participants and the relatively high level of benefits were generally appreciated at that time.

2.3 Withdrawal

No more than three years later, in 1978, general economic conditions started to deteriorate. Economic policy, aware of the seriousness of the foreign debt situation, changed its first priority from 'improving living standards' to 'improving the current account' – a reasonable goal but greatly mismanaged over the following decade. Among economic policy-makers there was an obsession with 'over-consumption', while the real problem was 'under-production' in terms of structure and efficiency. How actually to reduce consumption became the central issue, and inflation became the major instrument.

In this climate the 1975 Social Security Act became increasingly seen by economists as too generous, the old deal as obsolete. All through the 1980s there was general agreement and much talk on how a social security reform was inevitable. Yet consistent outlines for a comprehensive 'new deal' were never worked out and to revise the 1975 Act seemed politically infeasible. So the state begins to withdraw, to *break the old deal* covertly, in small steps, hiding mainly behind inflation.

In 1982 the entry pension was made step-wise degressive, with successive income brackets adding less and less percentages to a person's entry pension. The original intention was to forestall 'too high' entry pensions, but the nominal limits of the brackets have never been changed. With nominal wages increasing rapidly in the inflationary process, larger and larger portions of the income gradually fall into higher brackets, so more and more medium and even low income people suffered heavy losses in their entry pensions. Moreover, previous earnings were not adjusted, so the average nominal income of the last three years spent in work became much lower than the actual income at retirement.

Consequently since the late 1980s a **decreasing trend in the entry ratio** can be observed. By 1990 the average entry ratio for workers and employees had sunk to 64 per cent. This figure may be somewhat downward biased because of technical problems in the SSS information system, but undoubtedly the present entry ratio is much lower than the 70.9 per cent of 1980 and the top level 73.8 per cent of 1984.

Reducing the entry ratio is a powerful but slowly working instrument. The bulk of pension payments in any given year consists of pensions determined many years ago and – without relegislating acquired rights – those can be reduced only by undercompensation for inflation.

In a study based on the reconstruction of more than 800 individual pension histories from 1975 to 1990 Berényi, Borlói and Réti (1990) established that *compensation* in higher and medium pension categories worked effectively as an **increasingly progressive tax**, since it was increasingly falling behind not just the consumers' price index but also the nominal wage increase.

Take for example a pension, determined on the basis of 42 years served, with an average 5000 forints/month earning in the last years. For those who retired between 1975 and 1980 this pension lost almost half of its purchasing power over 10–15 years. For those in the same category who retired in 1987 the real value was reduced to 71 per cent by 1990. (The 1990/87 price index was 75 per cent, so compensation in this category must have been around 24 per cent in three years.) But 5000 forints/month equalled 157 per cent of the current average wage in 1975, 110 per cent in 1980 and only 72 per cent in 1987.

Severe inflationary losses, affecting first the higher income pensioners, have thus been gradually reaching the middle and lower-middle income categories. At the same time the lowest pensions enjoyed not only full compensation but some of them even gained in purchasing power by over-compensation. The conclusion from this study is that 'solidarity', a

Table 16.8. *Absolute poverty, end of 1991*

Minimum subsistence income (HUF/month)		
Rural 2 retired persons' household	6463	
Urban 1 retired person's household		8416
Persons whose pension is less		
Number (000 persons)	728	1843
In per cent of all retirees	30	78

virtue often called for in issues of social security, has not been shown *towards* pensioners as a group but has been forced *within* the group. Preservation of the bare subsistence level for the lowest income pensioners has been paid for by higher income, and increasingly by average income, pensioners. Pension differentials have thereby been drastically reduced, and today they have already little to do with differences in personal histories, number of years served and labour income achieved. This is part of what Hungarian sociologists call the impoverishment of the 'middle class'.

Unfortunately it is impossible to establish the aggregate, average magnitude of these processes since the SSS information system does not provide the proper weights by which reconstructed, individual histories could be consolidated into macroeconomic aggregates. Neither is it possible to reconstruct longitudinal paths at the macro level from aggregate data because in the recent period legislation has been erratically changing from year to year, motivated by the actual situation of the budget rather than by any regard for a consistent pension system. New and newer detailed and differentiated rules, exceptions from the rules and exceptions from the exceptions are legislated by the dozen annually while no one can tell how much a measure taken two years ago costs today or how much a present measure will cost two years from now.

There is one fact that can be taken for granted. The last phase of our numerical example applies to the period from 1978 until now: retirees are *absolutely and relatively impoverished* (see Table 16.8).

Overhead costs are highest in urban one-person households, lowest in rural two-person households hence these two figures can be considered as the lower and upper limits of the *minimum subsistence income bracket* for retirees. The figures are those published by the Central Statistical Office for June 1991 but increased by a modest 10 per cent to account for further price increases until the end of the year. The average pension equalled 7774 forints. We do not know exactly, however, how many of the pensioners live in what type of households. So all that can be said definitely is that by the end of 1991 the **average pension was within the**

Table 16.9. *Real growth and inflation, annual average rates, 1950–90, per cent*

	1950–60	1961–78	1979–89	1990
Average wage	4.4	2.8	– 1.0	– 5.0
Average pension	7.9	4.9	1.8	– 2.4
Entry pension		3.8	– 0.1	– 12.0
GDP	5.1	5.5	1.4	– 4.2
Consumers' prices	4.9	1.9	8.9	28.7

minimum subsistence bracket and some 48 per cent of all retirees received pensions around the minimum subsistance level while at least 30 per cent received less.

2.4   Turnover effect

In spite of all efforts to control pension payments, notwithstanding the resulting mass poverty among individual pensioners, *aggregate pension exenditures were increasing* even in real terms until 1990. This could be hardly explained without the lessons from our numerical example in section 1. In our example the turnover effect was attributed simply to economic growth and the number of cohorts in retirement was only three. In real life the expansion of the system, the growing number of people covered and the increasing entry ratio of the 1960s and 1970s amplifies the pension paradox. Also, in real life the number of cohorts in retirement exceeds forty, thus the turnover effect carries the impact of past periods through long decades.

Already in the early 1970s there was a large group of retirees whose pension hardly exceeded the subsistence level of that period. However, the situation of the people commonly called the 'small pensioners' did not become really tragic as long as the economy kept growing and consumers' prices were relatively stable. This old group of original 'small pensioners' was gradually disappearing in the 1970s and 1980s while new entrants occupied their place in increasing numbers, at higher wage levels and with entry ratios that – although already decreasing in the 1980s – certainly exceeded the ratios of the 1950s and 1960s.

No withdrawal policy can completely circumvent the pension paradox, as indicated by the arrows in Table 16.9. While the real value of *individual* pensions was rapidly decreasing, the *average* pension increased even in real terms during the 1980s, so strong was the turnover effect in nominal terms.

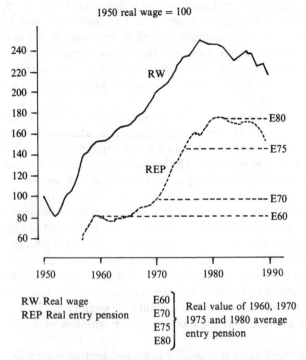

1950 real wage = 100

RW Real wage
REP Real entry pension

E60
E70
E75
E80

Real value of 1960, 1970
1975 and 1980 average
entry pension

Figure 16.1   The turnover effect in real terms, 1950–90

Even in 1990 the decrease in the real value of the average pension was only half the decrease in the real wage. The inflationary blow in this year would be seen more clearly if there were a way *directly* to calculate the turnover effect, i.e. if we knew how the average pension *should have increased* by pure turnover, without measures taken to reduce it.

Figure 16.1 presents a bird's-eye view on the working of the turnover effect over four decades; hopefully, it is self-explanatory. It should be noted that Figure 16.1 displays the relative real value of the *entry pension* of the year indicated – not the present real or nominal pension of people who retired in those years.

2.5   Contribution and wealth

So far, we have discussed the receiving side of the pension system. Now let us turn to the contributing side. The *employees'* contribution ratio varied between 3 and 15 per cent of labour income over the past four decades. It changed many times, from linear to progressive, then back again to linear.

It was called an insurance fee, but regarded as rather a kind of tax. In recent years it has been a flat, linear 10 per cent. The *employers'* contribution has changed even more dramatically. Since the bulk of the net surplus of state-owned enterprises went into the central budget anyway, the sum or ratio of what was called 'contribution to SSS' did not really matter. A few years ago the employers' contribution ratio was raised to 44 per cent of the notional wage.

Altogether this is generally viewed as outrageous, unheard of: 54 per cent, 10 from employees and 44 from employers, heavily attacked by the newly emerging entrepreneurial class. But this is facile arithmetic since the '100' in the calculation does not exist. The employer pays gross 144, the worker receives net 90 and the 54 that goes to the SSS is *37.5 per cent of the gross wage.*

Beginning with 1992, 56 per cent of all contributions will serve retirement and the remaining 44 per cent will go into the envisaged health insurance system. This leaves the retirement system with a **21.2 per cent contribution ratio**. Whether this is high or low could be established only by detailed calculations that were not carried out prior to determining the overall ratio and allocating it between the two systems. Such calculations should account for several factors, but first of all they would have to rely on a clear vision of the future of the pension system which is presently lacking.

The present contribution ratio is probably not consistent with even the preservation of today's reduced pension levels. It is more consistent with ultra-conservative views concerning the 'new deal' to be made between state and population. There are influential groups who argue that in a 'genuine market economy' the state-guaranteed pension system is nothing more than the ultimate 'safety-net' providing basic subsistence – otherwise people should take care of themselves by private retirement saving. The new deal is seen as offering at most 35–40 per cent entry ratios, maybe less. In this case the employers' contribution ratio could be reduced in the name of competitiveness on the world markets and the additional private retirement savings should be financed from the unchanged *net wage.* How to reconcile this with the low net wage-share inherited from the old deal is a question not usually asked.

Even if a consistent new deal can be worked out along these lines, it can be offered only to younger generations who still have a chance to adjust to it. It cannot be extended over generations near to or already in retirement. These generations did not have the opportunity for, and did not feel the necessity of, significant, additional private retirement saving. They have already contributed according to the old deal, at low net wage-share and high surplus-share.

Called SSS contribution or tax or anything else, the bulk of the high surplus went into the budget and served whatever purposes the total budget revenue served. For this reason it is often argued that retirement wealth in Hungary does not exist as SSS contributions have not been accumulated. This argument is, however, fallacious, since it assumes that whatever went into the budget went down the drain. Some money was undoubtedly wasted but the budget was also financing the bulk of **aggregate net capital formation** over four decades, directly in the state-owned sector of the economy and by subsidising investment in agricultural cooperatives as well as in private housing.

Taking this into account one could say that the Hungarian retirement system was a strange animal: a **funded pay-as-you-go system**. Viewed *cross-sectionally* it worked as a pay-as-you-go system but the government guarantee was backed by vast accumulated, state-owned wealth. (This is a major difference from Western countries where the govenment guarantee relies on tax revenues while the bulk of retirement wealth is accumulated in corporate, union, institutional and private retirement funds.) Viewed *longitudinally*, people who worked over 20, 30 or 40 years were undoubtedly producing a surplus at least as large as the proper amount of their own retirement saving. If that saving has been invested in state-owned property then that property *belongs to them* to the extent of their retirement wealth, and it could be used to create a funded system.

There are two major obstacles to this argument. One is that this retirement wealth is indeed not visible, not recorded, it must be *imputed* by calculations. This immediately becomes a matter of assumptions, methodology and data. Originally I planned to include my own estimates in this chapter, but explaining the assumptions and listing the data sources would require another chapter to itself; the interested reader might refer to Augusztinovics (1989). Other people and institutes have their own estimates, e.g. Bod (1992). Days or weeks could be spent arguing about the exact figures; no one questions, however, that the lowest possible estimate for the magnitude of the retirement wealth is **40–50 per cent of the net tangible national wealth** (natural resources and consumers' durables excluded, foreign debt deducted). Surely a methodological consensus could be reached if there was political interest and will.

Hence the second obstacle is the decisive one. *The ongoing privatisation process in Hungary does not provide for the social security system to receive its share* from state property. Some insignificant sums will be handed over to the SSS over the coming three years but nothing will happen that will be comparable with the real magnitude of retirement wealth. There are people who say that it is too late anyway, that the profitable part is already gone and that the SSS could not make use of what is left. Whether this is true or not, I do not know, but it is an additional good excuse for not altering the course of the privatisation process.

2.6   Independence

By lessons from our numerical example the SSS ought to have a comfortable surplus in this period of 2-digit inflation and under-compensated retirees. Judging by parliamentary debates and newspaper reports, it is in a critical state of severe deficit.

The envisaged social security reform of the 1980s resulted only in one actual measure: in 1990 the SSS was formally detached from the government budget. It is now formally independent and its own budget is separately legislated by the Parliament. Furthermore, in February 1992 a partial revision of the 1975 Social Security Act created *two* legally separate, self-governing systems: old-age insurance and health insurance. This had been partially prepared by previous budget manoeuvres but essentially the separation of the two systems and the conversion of both into true *insurance* systems is yet to be accomplished.

On the revenue side the SSS budget is practically limited to employees' and employers' contributions (apart from insignificant small sums). Before looking at the expenditures, a few more details must be introduced.

Traditionally the SSS chapter of the central budget was responsible for cash benefits: pensions (including disability benefits), sick pay, children's and maternity allowances. Health services, as already mentioned, were financed from the budget of the appropriate branch of government – let us just call it the Welfare Office, since its name has been changing almost as frequently as pension rules. Already in 1988 subsidies to be paid on medicine bought by the population were transferred from the Welfare Office budget to the SSS budget without compensation.

The real divorce, however, came at the formal separation in 1990. The Welfare Office took over children's allowances, and the financing of health services were transferred to the SSS. At that moment the two sums, as expected for 1990, were roughly equal so the action was called an exchange of equal burdens. However, it was obvious at first sight that health costs would be increasing almost uncontrollably in the coming years, while children's allowances would show a decreasing trend (at least in real terms) because of the demographic situation, and in any case they could be legislated at will.

Another detail that the reader must be made familiar with is the popular Hungarian game of 'queueing'. We are not queueing in the shops for bread, but enterprises, and everybody else is queueing in the banks for

Table 16.10. *Current account of the social security system, 1989–91,*
HUF bn

	1989	1990	1991
SSS contributions due	290.7	372.6	429.3
Other	5.7	7.8	29.4
Total revenues due	296.4	380.4	458.7
Pensions	156.5	202.1	263.8
Maternity and children's allowances	67.9	82.5	104.5
Sick pay	21.1	24.3	28.7
Other	4.7	6.1	7.7
Total traditional expenditures	250.2	315.0	404.8
Invisible balance	46.2	65.4	53.9
SSS contributions not received		− 20.2	− 19.1
Health service costs	− 19.0	− 95.4	− 128.1
Contribution to extra-SSS funds		− 14.7	− 6.5
Children's allowances not paid		64.3	80.7
Visible balance	27.2	− 0.6	− 19.0

their own money because the debtors cannot pay. Most often debtors
cannot pay because their debtors cannot pay and the third debtor is
actually the creditor of the first debtor so actually it is not a queue, it is a
vicious circle. The SSS has practically no means of collecting employers'
contributions due if the employer is not able to pay or is financing more
urgent expenditures by not paying to the SSS.

We are now ready to compile two current accounts for the SSS. One as it
would be along the traditional lines of sharing expenditures with the
Welfare Office, and if things went normally, the other one as it is (see
Table 16.10).

The would-be current account results in a surplus shown on the line
'Invisible balance'. This is the surplus to be expected in times of inflation
and under-compensated beneficiaries. What happened to the invisible
surplus? This is shown in the following lines. 'Contributions not received'
is due to the queueing game. The items 'Health service costs' and 'Children's allowances not paid' with a positive sign must be clear since the
'exchange of equal burdens' has been explained. Nevertheless, after
accounting for all these heavy losses, some surplus was left in 1989 and
should have been left in 1990, while the 1991 deficit could have been much
smaller.

However, most of the 1989 surplus had to be spent on purchasing
non-marketable bonds issued by the government's extra-budget housing

fund. 'Contribution to extra-SSS funds' meant in 1990 a loan to the government in the form of *still* paying children's allowances over the first quarter of the year while *already* financing health services. In 1991 it was the mandatory and really desirable 'reserve fund formation', except that it is shown as a current expenditure, increasing the deficit.

Naturally these budget tricks were not contrived in some diabolical plot against the independent SSS, they were simply intended to lighten the pressure on the government budget, the major target of IMF vigilance. They conceal the fact that the independence of the two, newly created insurance systems had not been prepared by and based on actuarially fair calculations. The independence of the SSS was accomplished in an act of *exchanging unequal burdens*, an act that **absorbed the inflationary gains** achieved by under-compensation of pensioners and other social security beneficiaries – or rather funnelled these gains from the SSS budget into the government budget.

At the same time the disappearance of the proper inflationary surplus helped to convince Parliament and the public that 'gigantic' expenditures on these large social service systems must be reduced since the SSS was in deficit up to its neck – when it was not, at least not yet.

2.7   The future

Genuine trouble will come for the independent SSS when inflation cools down and a modest real growth begins. As pointed out in section 1, this will be a *slowdown period* in nominal terms and the SSS budget is sensitive only to nominal trends. By the turnover effect aggregate and average pensions will be growing with the high nominal growth rates of the previous, inflationary period. It will not be possible to damp this growth by under-compensating retirees since there is no compensation if there is no inflation. (Increasing the retirement age may help in the long run, but it must be done gradually so the gain in the first decade will be marginal.) Even if contributions increased with the modest rate of real growth, even if the system remained more or less stable in its basic principles, increasing **slowdown deficits** on the current account would become inevitable.

However, the system is not likely to remain stable. If the conservative concept of the 'new deal' gains support then contribution ratios will probably be significantly reduced. Naturally entry and average pensions will also sink for generations that might come under the new deal – beginning not sooner than twenty years from now. Until then, the bulk of pension payments will go to generations whose past contributions and pension rights resulted from the old deal, who cannot retroactively change their course of life. Thus a 'transitory' period of at least two decades must be envisaged, a period when SSS revenues will be low according to the new deal while expenditures will be high according to the old deal. A *pay-as-you-go system* is supposed to pay current benefits from current incomes, it cannot endure such a schizophrenic **gap between deals**. Something will have to be done about the 'burden of the old pensions'.

Logically there are not too many options. Either (1) the 'burden' is relieved by retroactive legislation that reduces acquired pension rights drastically, or (2) the government budget accepts responsibility for the 'old' pensions, or (3) the SSS is transformed into a funded system where all retired generations are satisfied from, and in accordance with, their own previously accumulated retirement wealth.

Option (1) does not seem feasible politically and anyway, considering present pensions, with their average level falling in the minimum subsistence bracket, it would drastically increase the need for 'social policy' (or, rather, charity instruments) to support the needy. Option (2) does not seem attractive with respect to the 'balancing the budget' requirement, and it would make the independence of SSS and the 'insurance principle' a fiction. Moreover, the government itself would have no access to capital income on retirement wealth since that would already have been privatised, so government support, whether in form (1) or form (2), would initiate *higher taxation* (which would just compensate for lower SSS contributions).

Option (3) would require immediate action, changing the rules in the privatisation process *now*, before it is too late. Besides, if the SSS as a funded system gained access to the retirement wealth accumulated under the old deal then this wealth would be gradually used up in the future. Naturally the retirement savings of the younger generations would be accumulated in parallel, but at the extremist new deal level they would probably not provide adequate compensation. Over the transition period the capital account would probably be in deficit – in other words, aggregate retirement wealth under SSS jurisdiction would decrease. Since that wealth is now invested in tangible assets, the withdrawn part would have to be substituted by other forms of saving.

It should be noted that the ultimate macroeconomic consequences do not differ significantly under the various options. The exact magnitude may vary slightly but in any case **there is a bill to pay**. It might be moved from one department to the other but in the final analysis it cannot be escaped except by genocide. *Who exactly is paying* depends, of course, on the selected option, and in this sense the social consequences might be very different in each case.

Precisely the usual 'no-decision, no-solution' outcome seems therefore to be the most likely. The contribution ratio will be reduced, but not sufficiently to satisfy entrepreneurs. Pensions will be further reduced, but not sufficiently to eliminate the problem. Some government subsidies will have to be paid for by the taxpayers. The SSS will be given some property, but not sufficient to make it a funded system so it will remain formally independent under self-governing bodies but actually always dependent on the government. After all, the sharing of the bill is not necessarily irrational – one should hope that it will be done in a more or less rational way.

REFERENCES

Ando, A. and F. Modigliani (1963) 'The "Life Cycle" Hypothesis of Saving: Aggregate Implications and Tests', *The American Economic Review* (March).
Augusztinovics, M. (1989) 'The Costs of Human Life', *Economic Systems Research*, **1(1)**.
Berényi, Sándorné, Rudolf Borlói and János Réti (1990) *A nyugdijak nagyságának. arányainak és reálértékének alakulása az elmult 15 évben* (Magnitude, proportions and real value of pensions over the past 15 years), Országos Társadalombiztositási Föigazgatóság Közgazdasági Föosztály (July), Budapest.
Bod, Péter (1992) 'Mennyibe kerül egy társadalombiztositási nyugdijrendszer müködtetése? (The costs of a social security pension system), *Közgazdasági Szemle*, **2** and **3**.
Bourgeois-Pichat, J. (1978) 'Le financement des retraites par capitalisation', *Population*, **6**.
Gale, D. (1973) 'Pure Exchange Equilibrium of Dynamic Economic Models, *Journal of Economic Theory*, **6**.
Modigliani, F. and R. Brumberg (1954) 'Utility Analysis and the Consumption Function: An Interpretation of Cross-Section Data', in K.K. Kurihara (ed.), *Post-Keynesian Economics*, New Brunswick, N.J.: Rutgers University Press.
Samuelson, P.A. (1958) 'An Exact Consumption–Loan model of Interest With or Without the Social Contrivance of Money', *Journal of Political Economy*, **LXVI(12)**.
Szabó, Sándorné (1991) 'A nyugdijrendszer elvi és gyakorlati kérdései' (Principal and practical problems of the pension system), *Közgazdasági Szemle,* **12**.

Discussion of Part Six

DAVID M. G. NEWBERY

One of the key allocative decisions facing an economy is the balance between consumption now and consumption in the future, which can be simplified as the choice between wages and pensions, or consumption and investment. The socialist regime in Hungary was characterised by an inefficient use of labour in the state sector, a very efficient extraction of the surplus, but a rather inefficient investment of that surplus. Confronted with the slow-down in growth, the economy borrowed abroad, so that the net accumulation of assets after allowing for the growing claims represented by foreign debt was falling and hence the ability of the economy to finance future consumption (and the social security system including pensions) was already under threat. The market economy towards which Hungary aspires should lead to the more efficient use of labour, though in the transition there will be the inefficiency costs of possibly high unemployment. It should also increase the efficiency of investment, but the appropriation of the surplus by direct ownership and through the tax system will be significantly lower than in the previous system. The problem of meeting pension obligations will have in effect changed from a system in which these payments were met from the returns on the investment of the state (as in a funded system) to meeting these obligations out of taxation (more like a pay-as-you-go system). While it may be possible in the long run to transfer the responsibility of providing pensions to the private sector, for the next twenty years or so before such a transition can be made the state will be left with significant liabilities.

Hungary is not alone in facing difficulties in financing social security payments and pension obligations, which have increased as a share of GNP in most Western countries with improved coverage and increased longevity. Hungary has, however, three special features. First, it has had a stagnant and recently declining population for a longer period than most Western countries, so that the ratio of the retired to the working tends to be higher. In addition, the retirement age has been retained at the relatively low levels of 60 for men and 55 for women. Finally, offsetting these adverse tendencies, life expectancy after surviving birth has remained low by Western standards. If, as one must hope, the health of the population improves, the first two factors will then work to increase the burden of the retired on the working population.

Mária Augusztinovics has shown clearly in Chapter 16 the problems of interpreting the state of the social security fund and the reasonableness of pension payments. If the economy is growing, and the system is one in which retirement pensions are frozen at retirement, the relative income of a given pensioner will fall relative to the average population. Of course, one could index pension payments to the average wage rate, but this would either raise the cost and contribution ratio, or require a lower initial ratio of pensions to final wages. In a growing economy, the worry will then concern the relative deprivation of the increasingly elderly. When the econmy is stagnating, pensioners may then appear relatively better off than those working, and the temptation will be to raid the social security fund by a failure to index against inflation, as in Hungary at present.

We can look at the equity issue of the well-being of pensioners compared to wage earners in two different ways. If pension payments come out of a fully funded scheme which is protected against declines in real value and returns during recessions (a very strong requirement) then generations which had prosperous working lives will also have prosperous retirements, while unlucky generations experiencing low wages while working will also have low pensions. Inequality between generations will thereby be amplified. A pay-as-you-go system will tend to make those well off during their working life who enter retirement when the current population is adversely affected rather poorer, and the currently poor workers may look forward to better pensions if their successors are more successful. To that extent, different generations may be treated more equitably. The interesting question in Eastern Europe is whether one considers the younger generation today as looking forward to eventually much happier times than their parents experienced under socialism, or whether the costs of the transition will be borne for so long that those costs should be shared with the previous generation who suffered under socialism.

An alternative way to look at the problem of providing for pensions (and also for other claimants on the state's benevolence such as the sick, young children, etc.) is to look at the assets and liabilities of the state. On the liability side, there is the US$ 20 bn external debt and the commitments to pensioners whose contributions were made under state socialism. These liabilities stretch forward for the foreseeable future. On the asset side, the state accumulated capital, which generated dividends, and it has the power to levy taxes. The problem that has become more evident during the transition is that the net value of the capital stock *less* the foreign claims may be substantially lower than was thought, and the process of privatisation will transfer the dividend-generating aspect beyond the range of the government. As already remarked, the tax system has become less potent, as the inevitable counterpart of encouraging increased efficiency. Hungary, through the political process, will have to decide how to apportion the claims of the decreased revenue amongst investment, other forms of social security, and pensioners. At present, inflation is providing a concealed method of taxing pensioners to balance the budget, and as Mária Augusztinovics points out, a fall in inflation would make this hidden tax explicit. The obvious solution of raising the retirement age may be essential in the long run, and is apparently under consideration, but in the short run it may have little impact on the budget, as early retirement is likely to be a strategy for dealing with the rapid rise in unemployment. Whether a worker has retired early or remains unemployed makes little difference to the claims on the budget. The idea of transferring the shares, or part of the shares, in the newly privatised enterprises to a pension fund is attractive, but is unlikely to produce sufficient revenue and will in any case have no effect on the overall budget. The evidence of the past decade is that although reform of social security has been pressing for some time, and the problems could have been, and were, readily forecast, the political will to deal with the problem in a just way was absent, for perfectly understandable reasons. The political process is not well placed to mediate between competing claims on an existing resource. Pensioners are not unique in having just claims on the revenue of the state, but they may be relatively less well placed to exercise those claims.

DAVID WINTER

Köllő's Chapter 15 provides an excellent summary of the conditions faced by workers in the Hungarian economy prior to the collapse of communism. At the heart of the argument lies the belief that although the Hungarian economy had ostensibly abandoned central planning for over twenty years, the relationship between enterprise managers and the centre were not substantially changed during that period. As a result many features of the labour market under central planning persisted in Hungary.

Excess demand for labour which allowed high labour turnover and high v/u ratios enabled workers to bargain over the level of effort which they provided. The incentives, which were the result of the continuous negotiations between enterprise managers and the centre, meant that managers would sometimes collude with workers in an effort to reduce the production possibility set of an enterprise, or at least as this was perceived by the centre.

Köllő provides some data on turnover rates and v/u ratios to support this position. I am not sure that I find these statistics convincing in themselves, but I am prepared to believe that although the Hungarian economy has been engaged in the reform of central planning for many years, this portrayal of labour market conditions is at least plausible. Indeed the reforms, by making enterprises less dependent on the centre, may have had the effect of increasing the power of workers to bargain over the effort they supplied. Workers were able to optimise within the constraints that Kádárism provided.

The labour market environment of the transitional economy is clearly very different. Unemployment can be expected to rise to levels at least as high (if not higher) than OECD averages. Firms will now be able to screen workers effectively and, by threatening dismissal, provide incentives for workers for which firms do not bear the cost. Even if real wages of those in employment do not fall, workers will suffer losses since the expected gains from shirking are a great deal lower. This seems obvious.

The final strand of Köllő's argument concerns the second economy. He provides strong evidence that the second economy was exceptionally widespread under Kádár. The excess demand by enterprises for material inputs and low productivity in agriculture provided many opportunities for a thriving second economy. In the later part of the chapter Köllő also argues that with the transition from communism and the resulting recession, the secondary economy has been faced with a substantial drop in demand.

This is to be expected. The second economy was itself a market response to the peculiarities of the previous economic system. With the demise of that system, the second economy will find that it, too, will have to adjust as it becomes part of the first economy. Although such adjustments may well be painful for those involved, they do seem to be unavoidable.

Second economies in Western market economies are usually the consequence of the structure of taxes. Köllő mentions the abolition of wage increment taxation, he does not discuss new taxation systems where workers are taxed directly a great deal more than they have been in the past. Given the fact that a high proportion of Hungarians have had experience of the second economy, new taxation systems will have to be designed to deal with the possibility of widespread evasion.

How the labour market will evolve during the period of transition is a fascinating question to which we do not yet know many, if any, answers. It might seem obvious that the degree of dispersion in relative earnings will have to increase. Nevertheless we observe that amongst market economies there are considerable differences in the dispersion of relative earnings. The size of the economy, its past history and culture all have a role to play. If relative wages' differences are market based signals to ensure that labour markets work efficiently, then the degree of relative differences which provides the necessary incentives are determined by preferences. Economists know very little about how such preferences are determined.

One final point concerns unemployment. Köllő briefly describes the unemployment benefit system as it is now supposed to operate. Whether the government will be able to provide either the institutional structure or the funds adequately to cope with unemployment rates significantly above 10 per cent is to be doubted. Hungary's foreign creditors will have to be extremely understanding if widespread poverty is to be avoided. However if Köllő is correct in arguing that workers adapted successfully to the incentives provided by the compromises of Kádárism, perhaps they will be equally successful in the new environment in which they find themselves.

Part Seven

State desertion

17 State desertion and convertibility: the case of Hungary

ISTVÁN ÁBEL and JOHN P. BONIN

1 Introduction: the economic black hole

The rapid disintegration of social, political and economic organisations in the previously socialist bureaucratically managed countries creates new challenges to economic theory and policy. Attempts to describe the situation in the transforming countries provide a great variety of policy suggestions for choosing the 'road to a free economy'. Some scholars focus on immediate and deep change, dubbed 'Shock Therapy' or 'The Big Bang', while others take a longer-run more gradualistic view in connection with economic restructuring,[1] called by Nordhaus 'The Longest Road'. These two distinct policy prescriptions have taken on an adversarial role in the literature. Neglected in this debate over the correct way to begin has been a crucial issue – the consequences of the *changing economic role of the state*.

Privatisation is a good example of the necessity of a managed transformation from the socialist planned or bureaucratically managed economy to a capitalist market economy based on private initiative. Without the appropriate infrastructure and property rights' legislation, privatisation is fraught with problems. In political arenas in all of the transforming countries, voices have been raised against privatisation and in favour of renationalisation and state administration. This backlash is often supported by a '*reductio ad absurdum*' argument. Foreign ownership is unacceptable for nationalistic reasons. Wealthy domestic buyers are tainted either by previous ties to the old regime (*nomenklatura*) or by profiteering in black markets. The conclusion drawn is to return state assets to the government for custody during the period necessary to educate a new managerial/entrepreneurial class.

Even amongst groups sympathetic to privatisation in these countries,

N

proposals are often ill-conceived and practices often amount to little more than selling state assets at bargain-basement prices in transactions that involve abusive insider trading. Proposals to distribute state assets to the general populace using a voucher system and follow-up auctions are likely to have little impact on the agency incentive problem. The object of privatisation should be corporate restructuring, not wealth redistribution. Conventional wisdom indicates that takeovers play an important disciplinary role against managerial malfeasance in Western stock markets, yet the existence of independence corporate raiders in the emerging nascent stock markets in the transforming countries seems to be decades away.

The conversion of enterprises from state-owned, and more importantly state-dependent, units to companies driven by private initiative to search out profitable opportunities (in the West) is a critical aspect of the transformation. According to Kornai (1990a), before an efficient private ownership system can function an entrepreneurial class must be in place. The emergence of a vibrant entrepreneurial class endowed with technical and managerial know-how involves complex cultural and institutional changes (Kornai calls the process 'embourgeoisement') that cannot be accelerated beyond a certain pace because such an entrepreneurial class has to grow 'organically': the 'mere imitation of the most refined legal and business forms of the leading capitalist countries is not sufficient to ensure their general application'. Consequently Kornai concludes that the recommended road is a gradual transition, which he estimates will take twenty years in Hungary, to a dual economy involving both market and bureaucratic forces.

State desertion results in companies being set adrift in uncharted seas with a real possibility of many disappearing into an 'economic black hole'. Not all of these companies are dinosaurs incapable of operating under modern economic conditions, some are simply encumbered by the old ways. The *quid pro quo* of bilateral bargaining between the state and its offspring enterprises often resulted in financial rewards (subsidies) for companies that assisted the state in meeting its CMEA obligations at prices determined by the state. Set adrift, the only option is to search for new markets. But this requires the very entrepreneurial expertise that Kornai finds non-existent in the transforming economies. However, if extensive foreign participation in privatisation is deemed unacceptable by nationalistic political parties so that foreign direct investment is excluded or significantly curtailed, the opportunities available from combining the 'know-how' of local business situations provided by current managers and modern managerial techniques plus the modernised production technology associated with Western companies will be foregone.

The rapid disintegration of the economy in the wake of 'state desertion' creates serious economic problems that threaten to erode popular support for the transformation. We use the term 'state desertion' to characterise the abrupt and discontinuous change in the state's financial involvement in social and economic activities. Along with the socialist political system, the economic order begins to collapse as the state abrogates its economic paternalism. To what extent, and how rapidly, should the state withdraw? What *alternative types of state intervention* are required to keep the transformation on course? These are crucial questions that are beginning to be addressed in detail in Hungary, as the chapters in this volume indicate. The issue of social security financing is an example where the abrupt change is difficult to manage.[2] When the state withdrew its backing from the pension system, alternative sources of financing had to be found. The previous system of state-managed resource allocation precluded the need for (and perhaps prevented) such systems accumulating adequate wealth to back claims against them.

Although increasing unemployment is an unavoidable consequence of the necessary structural adjustments, state intervention to provide a 'safety net' to ameliorate the cost to individuals rather than leaving the displaced to the mercy of market forces may be difficult to finance as fiscal budgets are trimmed back. Even the state-owned enterprises cannot be held fully accountable for the financial conditions and accumulated debt inherited from the past, the cleaning-up of company balance sheets will require state involvement. Nonetheless, some state withdrawal and a significant structural change in the state budget are necessary for the transformation to proceed. Such a policy was eschewed on purpose by 'some enlightened government officials'[3] during the 1980s and it has not been promoted actively by the leaders of transforming countries at the beginning of the 1990s. It was rather macroeconomic conditions and external events in the bloc that initiated the process against the wishes of officials and policy-makers.

Given the 'great economic expectations' generated by the political upheavals in Eastern Europe, some 'short-term fix' is also necessary. Otherwise political parties may not survive the time period required for the new wave of embourgeoisement to bring forth flowers. Yet a call for 'shock therapy' may not be appropriate. As Williamson (1991, p. 73) argues:

> The main lesson of the Hungarian experience seems to be that gradualism does not deserve the contemptuous dismissal that it has tended to receive in much recent discussion. Under certain circumstances it does provide a feasible road to reform.

The conclusion seems to be that the state must manage its own withdrawal to foster a smooth transition from the state-controlled planned economy to the market. This chapter focuses on the Hungarian experience, primarily from 1985 to the present, to draw lessons on state management of the transformation for all the Central European countries.

Section 2 establishes the primary importance of the fiscal budget in the Hungarian economy prior to the transformation, and examines the deep structural distortions reflected in its size and structure. As the state withdraws, the inflationary impact of price liberalisation and subsidy reduction is examined. Section 3 discusses Hungary's policy of gradual establishing currency convertibility as an example of the state managing its own withdrawal. A brief concluding section 4 compares the Hungarian and Polish policies on convertibility as prototypes of the two approaches to the transformation.

2   The fiscal budget: state desertion and inflation

In many of the transforming countries, inflation interferes with rapid market liberalisation. In several of the economic policy proposals concerning the transformation, two phases are distinguished. In the first phase, *monetary stability* is achieved by reducing inflation and bringing the balance of payments into a manageable state. In the second phase (post-stabilisation), the key issues become *industrial restructuring* and ownership reform. Monetary overhang – that is, too much accumulated liquidity in the household sector – is often a major problem in the first phase. Somewhat paradoxically, the major difficulty encountered in the post-stabilisation phase is a lack of domestic savings to support enterprise privatisation. The apparent contradiction between monetary overhang from too much accumulated savings and a lack of domestic financing for privatisation within a reasonable time horizon goes unaddressed in the literature.

In Hungary, monetary overhang is not relevant; rather the root of the inflationary pressure is monetised *fiscal deficits*. Ábel and Székely (1988) study the financial flows in the pre-transformation period by considering three money circuits. The total money stock is defined conventionally, so that compulsory reserve funds of the enterprises (used by the government to confiscate profits but only up to 1984) and the clearing accounts of the fiscal budget (a discretionary instrument of fiscal policy and not the monetary system) are excluded; however, saving notes (a bond that acts like a savings deposit) held by the households are included in broad money (M2). The household money circuit consists of currency, demand deposits, time and savings deposits held by the households. The enterprise money is defined as liquid enterprise deposits (with the exception of the compulsory reserve fund deposits referred to above). Flows in the government money circuit are equated with the fiscal deficit which is monetised directly by the national bank.

Using quarterly data for the period 1974–86, Ábel and Székely find that the household money and the enterprise money circuits are separate, in the sense that no causal relationship between these two circuits in either direction is detected by Granger causality tests. However, the authors find strong causality running from the government money circuit to enterprise money and weak causality from government money to household money. Consequently, they conclude that fiscal deficits significantly influence the other two money circuits while the household and business sectors are not connected by financial flows. In essence, monetised fiscal deficits provide liquidity to the economy.

The central government fiscal budget deficit in Hungary did not rise above 4 per cent of GDP in the 1980s. The highest deficit for this period was 3.97 per cent of GDP recorded in 1987 – a year in which the world average was 4.1 per cent and the average for developing countries was 6.05 per cent. However, such a statistic does not indicate that Hungarian fiscal policy was on the right track. Only in Hungary was central government expenditures higher than 55 per cent of GDP for the entire period of the 1980s. Other countries experienced years in which this ratio was higher than in Hungary but none of them maintained such a high percentage for the whole period.[4] In Hungary during the 1980s, the fiscal budget redistributed a large percentage of the national income. Subsidies and other current transfers represented 66.46 per cent of central government expenditures in 1988. In this year, subsidies alone accounted for about 13 per cent of GDP. Disaggregated into broad categories and measured as a per cent of GDP, consumer subsidies equalled 3 per cent, housing subsidies 4.8 per cent, and producer subsidies 5.2 per cent, of which agricultural subsidies were 3.2 per cent of GDP. A subsidy reduction programme was initiated in 1989, having as its aim the elimination of all price subsidies in four years.

Coincidental with the subsidy reduction programme was a continuing policy of price liberalisation to decrease the proportion of prices regulated by the Price Office over time.[5] The inflationary impact of price liberalisation and subsidy reduction is apparent from the data. In 1987, the inflation rate on an annual basis was 8.6 per cent. Price liberalisation began in 1988 with a series of January price increases. Although at annualised rates inflation soared to over 35 per cent by mid-1991, the basic component of inflation in each year was the first-quarter price spikes followed by much smaller changes in the subsequent three quarters (single-digit on an annual basis). Much of the recent inflation in Hungary is due to a series of 'one-shot' price adjustments that coincide with price liberalisation but are not accompanied by any mechanism for transmitting the inflationary spikes into hyperinflation. However, this series of shocks produced an accelerating trend through 1991, although inflation was expected to remain constant or fall slightly in 1992.

To this point in Hungary, state desertion consisting of price liberalisation and significant subsidy elimination has been paired with fiscal and monetary austerity. Inflation has accelerated to moderately high annual rates (35 per cent), real output has fallen by around 20 per cent since the beginning of 1990, and unemployment stands at more than 8.5 per cent. The shock induced by the dismembering of CMEA resulted in a decline in exports from Hungary to these areas of 60 per cent and a decline in GDP in 1991 that was twice as large as in 1990. To what extent is the increased inflation and unemployment along with the decline in real output attributable to state desertion? In some sense, the answer must be that state desertion is responsible for the entire change as the continued existence of CMEA is incompatible with state desertion. A more fundamental question, to which we have no answer, might be 'just how much disruption is necessary for the transformation to proceed with sustainable momentum?' In section 3, we focus on the state's role in foreign economic transactions to examine Hungary's gradual policy of convertibility.

3   State-managed convertibility

The management of the progress toward convertibility remains an open question in the debate over the proper road to a market economy. To establish a precise definition of convertibility, Williamson (1991) discusses the difference between the Western and East European concepts. The former distinguishes unrestricted convertibility, which allows unrestricted capital flows from current account convertibility, which requires that no restriction be placed on obtaining currency for current account transactions including tourism and the repatriation of foreign investment incomes. The latter distinguishes internal convertibility, which is the right of domestic residents to exchange currency at official rates from external convertibility, which gives the same right to foreigners.

Kornai (1990a) favours full liberalisation of the private sector, a notion that approaches unrestricted convertibility. Yet Hungary's experience with opening up the travel account in 1989 led to the reimposition of stringent controls on households. From a net surplus of $41 mn in 1988, the travel account in the convertible currency balance of payments deterioriated to a deficit of $349 mn. The government responded by suspending official exchange allowances to households for travel purposes (from 3 November until 20 November 1989). At that time, a new system of foreign exchange allocation was introduced, limiting Hungarian residents to. a foreign exchange allowance of $300 for a four-year period. The travel component of the convertible currency balance of payments rebounded in 1990 to a surplus of $345 mn. Current account convertibility combined with a prohibition of capital outflows and a recognition that this may require some limitations on households to prevent the circumvention of the capital account constraint is the definition that we use in what follows.

After macroeconomic stabilisation is attained and while restructuring accompanied by privatisation is proceeding at a natural pace, what are the proper policies to adopt regarding the integration of these countries into the global economy? Most commentators agree on the importance of export-led growth as the primary engine of economic expansion and the necessity of direct foreign investment to revitalise industry. However, no consensus emerges concerning the appropriate exchange rate regime or the extent and timing of trade liberalisation. Should an under-valued fixed exchange rate like the one used as the nominal anchor in the Polish stabilisation programme be retained during the interim (medium) term? Is Hungary's managed exchange rate and gradualist approach to convertibility a more appropriate strategy?

According to Portes (1991), a commitment to early convertibility of the currency raises the stakes and enhances policy-makers' credibility. Blommestein, Marrese and Zecchini (1991) support current account convertibility at an early stage in the transformation to expose domestic producers to foreign competition. The Polish 'shock therapy' programme is based on trade liberalisation and a nominal exchange rate anchor designed to 'import' such competition from abroad and blunt the monopoly power of producers in highly concentrated domestic industries. Nuti (1990) disagrees on both counts; he supports a real (rather than a nominal) exchange rate anchor and slower progress toward liberalisation. For Nuti, the sluggish domestic import and export price elasticities that are legacies of the old system constrain the speed with which currency convertibility and trade liberalisation can be pursued. Nuti is also sceptical of these countries' ability to defend a nominal exchange rate for any reasonable period of time.

Several strong arguments have been advanced against a freely floating exchange rate for the transforming countries, at least in the medium term. Bofinger (1990) poses the following dilemma: a compatible monetary policy is a necessary condition for floating yet its basic components (e.g. demand for money, propensity to save) are extremely unstable in these countries. Williamson (1991) claims that a floating exchange rate can function effectively only in the presence of the well-developed capital markets which these countries lack.

The argument in favour of a fixed exchange rate is often associated with the Polish stabilisation programme in which this nominal 'anchor' was designed to 'import' a rational structure of relative prices. However, fixed exchange rates are credible only if they are defensible. The 1991 Polish devaluation of the zloty by about 14.5 per cent casts doubt on the feasibility of defending a fixed rate over the medium term, even with substantial support from the international financial community (which Poland received), and even when the rate chosen initially is significantly under-valued to improve the chances of defending it. Indeed, the latter condition is problematic since the benefit of international competition accruing from convertibility is blunted if the exchange rate is seriously under-valued. Moreover, the change from an over-valued to a significantly under-valued exchange rate induced an inflationary shock in Poland, the legacies of which seem to be continuing inflation at a rate of about 10 per cent per month.

So what exchange rate regime should be chosen after macroeconomic stabilisation has been achieved in a transforming country? Williamson (1991) favours a crawling peg tied to the ecu, a policy that requires periodic devaluations to offset any inflation differential with the EC countries. Since the latter half of the 1980s, the Hungarian exchange rate policy can be viewed as choosing a real exchange rate anchor and supporting it by a 'crawling peg' policy of periodic devaluations to offset differential inflation. Consequently, the Hungarian laboratory beginning in the mid-1980s provides useful insights for evaluating Williamson's crawling peg proposal in the context of a gradualist programme toward convertibility.

The official exchange rate in Hungary is (and was throughout the 1980s) somewhat over-valued despite periodic devaluations (see Ábel and Bonin, 1992, for details). The National Bank of Hungary (NBH) pursues are exchange rate policy in which the HUF is pegged to a basket of ten convertible currencies with a large weight given to the US dollar. In 1989, the central bank's scope of authority to adjust the peg was increased from a margin of ± 1 per cent to one of ± 5 per cent. From mid-March to mid-April 1989, the HUF was devalued twice by the maximum allowable amount bringing about a rather steep decline in the real effective rate as measured by the IMF index. Charting the IMF real effective exchange rate by quarter from 1988 to 1990 indicates that the NBH maintained fluctuations within a relatively narrow band of 2.5 per cent. Exchange rate policy in Hungary for the past three years appears to be consistent with a real anchor approach. However, the nominal rate remained somewhat over-valued in 1990 and the HUF was still supported by some exchange controls.

Beginning in 1991, only 10 per cent of Hungarian imports appear on the list of restricted goods and services. With import liberalisation almost completed, the HUF is mostly convertible for domestic corporations wishing to buy foreign goods and services (see Bokros, 1991, for details). However, progress toward complete current account convertibility was gradual; the NBH still maintains control over foreign exchange transactions. Domestic non-financial institutions generally did not have the right to hold foreign exchange accounts or to retain a portion of their export earnings in hard currencies; the NBH maintained the exclusive right to buy these receipts. Decentralisation of foreign exchange transactions within the banking sector began in 1990, but only a limited number of financial institutions were involved. The joint venture banks always had a virtually unrestricted licence to execute foreign transactions abroad and to buy and sell almost unlimited amounts of HUF in exchanges with the central bank. Some of the Hungarian-owned banks were granted the licence to engage in a limited scope of current foreign transactions, mainly related to foreign trade. These banks could collect foreign exchange deposits but they were required to conduct their foreign business with a very low working balance in cash at home and in deposits abroad (Bokros, 1991).

Convertibility has been established as a medium-term goal of the official government gradualist programme. In the second half of 1991, the NBH established a domestic interbank foreign exchange market. Instead of forcing companies to relinquish their foreign exchange earnings from export activity, the central bank now must purchase the hard currency it needs to service the debt from the commercial banks. At the same time, the commercial banks sell hard currency to their corporate customers to purchase imports. This internal market has virtually eliminated the premium in black-market currency in hard currency transactions.

Despite the travel account restrictions mentioned above, Hungarian citizens are permitted to deposit unlimited amounts of hard currency holdings in a legally accepted account with any of the authorised banks. Such deposits were encouraged by the tax exempt status of interest payments and a positive real interest rate. In 1990, unrequited (unilateral) transfers increased by $600 mn, reflecting significant increases in deposits to such foreign currency accounts. When combined with the change from 1989 in the travel component of almost $700 mn, a large proportion of the change from a convertible currency current account deficit of $1437 mn in 1989 to a surplus in 1990 of $127 mn is attributable to these two policies. For the first eight months of 1991, unrequited transfers totalled $591 mn, up from $393 mn over the same period in

1990. The positive current balance for the first six months is due in large part to these transfers, as the trade balance was in deficit by $148 mn.

The government's adoption of an explicitly gradualist programme toward convertibility is based primarily on its concern for meeting its foreign debt obligations given the extremely thin existing financial markets. Hungary has accumulated substantial foreign debt over the past decade. By 1989, *per capita* net foreign debt using OECD measures was $1837 and the net interest to export ratio was 26 per cent. As a percentage of fiscal expenditures, interest payments on the debt were 10.8 per cent in 1990 and were forecast to be 12.9 per cent in 1991. However, the full burden of the debt is not conveyed accurately by these fiscal figures. The government liabilities to the NBH pay a below-market, HUF denominated interest rate. The NBH in turn is responsible for meeting the foreign currency requirements of the debt service, which in 1991 was $4.1 bn, $2.4 bn of which was principal repayment.

By August 1991, foreign exchange reserves in convertible currency totalled $2.2 bn or more than half of the total obligation (principle plus interest). However, the trade balance for the first eight months of 1991 was a deficit of $148 mn compared to a surplus of $571 mn for the first six months of 1990. Given the debt albatross in Hungary, the need to manage and monitor movement toward convertibility remains.

4   Conclusion: 'shock therapy' versus 'slow but steady'

The Polish stabilisation programme introduced on 1 January 1990 included a significant devaluation of the official exchange rate. By setting the official exchange rate at the free market rate of 9500 zloty to the dollar (almost a 40 per cent devaluation from the previous level of 6000 zloty to the dollar), the government effectively under-valued the zloty. As a result, Polish exports to hard currency areas increased significantly from $8.5 bn in 1989 to $11.4 bn in 1990. Imports decreased in 1990 due to a combination of the reduction in real income from the stabilisation programme and an imposition of import duties and taxes. An interest rate policy designed to yield a positive real return on hard currency deposits and a policy requiring exporting companies to sell foreign exchange to commercial banks induced a significant increase in foreign exchange reserves. For the first three quarters of 1990, reserves increased from $2.6 bn to $3.7 bn and then to $5.2 bn. Hence, Poland's nominal exchange rate anchor initially needed no defence.

A major objective in fixing the nominal anchor in Poland was the 'importation' of the correct relative price structure from the rest of the world. However, the under-valued zloty encouraged export expansion and import substitution. Coupled with high tariffs, the official nominal rate discouraged imports. The choice of a nominal or a real exchange rate anchor for stabilisation has been hotly debated. The hypothesised benefit of the fixed nominal anchor is the 'importation' of both a (correct) relative price system and the inflation rate of the country or region to which the exchange rate is fixed. An initial over-shooting (under-valuation) might be desirable to make this commitment credible and to allow some time for the inflation rate to be brought down to the target level. However, Poland was not successful in reining in domestic inflation, as the appreciation in its real exchange rate immediately following the implementation of the stabilisation programme bears witness. By the first quarter of 1991, the real effective exchange rate in Poland was 73 per cent higher than at the beginning of the stabilisation programme. The zloty was devalued in May 1991, indicating that the nominal anchor (at an initially under-valued rate) was not sufficient to harness inflationary pressures in Poland. On the contrary, the substantial devaluation on 1 January 1990 introduced an inflationary shock leading to continuing inflationary pressure.

By contrast, fluctuations in the real effective exchange rate in Hungary resemble outcomes that would be expected from a policy based on a real anchor. From 1988 to 1990 several devaluations in the nominal exchange rate were required to maintain a relatively stable real rate in the face of inflationary shocks stemming from the price liberalisation policies. However, adjustments in the nominal exchange responded to rather than transmitted inflationary pressures in Hungary. The prospects for reining in inflation in the near future seems brighter in Hungary now that price liberalisation is virtually complete.

Hungary, the prototype of the gradualist strategy, seems to have been relatively successful in its exchange rate policy by avoiding large volatile swings in the real effective exchange rate. Given its debt albatross, the cautious movement to full convertibility in the 1990s may have been a sound policy. Poland, the prototype of the 'Big Bang' strategy, may have missed an opportunity to move more quickly to a flexible market-determined exchange rate after the debt forgiveness package had been negotiated in 1990. Indeed the Polish experience with the under-valued nominal anchor and subsequent rapid increase in the real effective exchange rate may be indicative of a policy 'shock without much therapy'. Significant institutional and legal changes accompanied the gradualist policies in Hungary during the 1980s and early 1990s, whereas Poland may be suffering from the lack of institutional development and a 'legislative lag' (Schaffer, 1990). Gradualism, like the 'slow but steady' tortoise, deserves more serious consideration as a strategy for the trans-

340 István Ábel and John P. Bonin

formation. However, whatever strategy is chosen, the state has a role to play in managing the smooth transition to a market economy.

NOTES

Research conducted under the auspices of CEPR's research project on Economic Transformation in Eastern Europe, supported by a grant from the Commission of the European Communities under its SPES Programme (No. E/90100033/PRO) and its ACE Programme (No. CT91-0050), whose help is gratefully acknowledged. We also wish to thank the Pew Charitable Trust Foundation, MTA-OTKA Research Fund and the Wesleyan University for support for this research. An early version of this chapter was presented at the CEPR Conference 'Hungary – An Economy in Transition', London (7–8 February 1992). Comments on that version from Professors David Begg and Robert E. Rowthorn are greatly acknowledged; they helped us to revise the chapter significantly.

1 Kornai (1990a); Lipton and Sachs (1990); Nordhaus (1990).
2 See more details in Augusztinovics, Chapter 16 in this volume.
3 Kornai (1990b).
4 The following countries had higher fiscal expenditure:GDP ratios than Hungary for one or more years in the 1980s but each of these countries exhibited ratios lower than a 55 per cent ratio for other years in that decade: Belgium, Guinea–Bissau, Guyana, Israel, the Netherlands, Nicaragua, Tonga. (GFS, 1990, pp. 90–1.)
5 In 1991, the Price Office was reorganised and renamed the Competition Office. As the price regulatory functions have been eliminated, the office has taken on a different role somewhat analogous to an anti-trust office (see Chapter 7 in this volume).

REFERENCES

Ábel, I. and J.P. Bonin (1992) 'The "Big Bang" versus "Slow But Steady"': a comparison of the Hungarian and the Polish transformation', CEPR, *Discussion Paper*, **626** (January) London: CEPR.
Ábel, I. and I. Székely (1988) 'Money and causality in CPEs', Budapest University of Economics, *Working Paper*, **88/3**.
Augusztinovics, M. (1993) see Chapter 16 in this volume.
Blanchard, O., R. Dornbusch, P. Krugman, R. Layard and L. Summers (1990) 'Reform in Eastern Europe and the Soviet Union', UN–Wider Report, Washington, D.C.: UN.
Blommestein, H.J. and M. Marrese (eds) (1991) *Transformation of Planned Economies: Property Rights' Reform and Macro Stability*, Paris: OECD.
Blommestein, H.J., M. Marrese and S. Zecchini (1991) 'Centrally planned economies in transition: an introductory overview of selected issues and strategies', in Blommestein and Marrese (eds) (1991) pp. 11–28.
Bofinger, P. (1990) 'A multilateral payments union for Eastern Europe', Washington, D.C.: IMF, mimeo.

Bokros, L. (1991) 'Gradual progress towards currency convertibility in Hungary', in Williamson (ed.) (1991).

GFS (1990) *Government Finance Statistics, 1989*, Washington, D.C.: IMF.

Kornai, J. (1990a) *The Road to a Free Economy – Shifting from a Socialist System: The Case of Hungary*, New York: Norton.

(1990b) 'The affinity between ownership form and coordination mechanisms: the common experience of reform in socialist countries, *Journal of Economic Perspectives*, **4(3)** (Summer), pp. 131–47.

Lipton, D. and J. Sachs (1990) 'Creating a market economy in Eastern Europe: the case of Poland', *Brookings Papers on Economic Activity*, **1990(1)**, pp. 75–147.

NBH (1991) *National Bank of Hungary Annual Report, 1990*, Budapest: NBH.

Nordhaus, W.D. (1990) 'Soviet economic reform: the longest road', *Brookings Papers on Economic Activity*, **1990(1)**, pp. 287–318.

Nuti, D.M. (1990) 'Internal and international aspects of monetary disequilibrium in Poland', *European Economy*, **43** (March), pp. 169–82.

OECD (1991a) *Financial Market Trends*, Paris: OECD (February).

(1991b) *Hungary, OECD Economic Surveys*, Paris: OECD.

Portes, R. (1991) 'The transition to convertibility for Eastern Europe and the USSR', CEPR, *Discussion Paper*, **500** (January), London: CEPR.

Schaffer, M.E. (1990) 'State-owned enterprise in Poland: taxation, subsidization and competition policies', *European Economy*, **43** (March), pp. 183–202.

Williamson, J. (1991) 'The Economic Opening of Eastern Europe', Washington, D.C.: Institute for International Economics.

Williamson, J. (ed.) (1991) 'Currency Convertibility in Eastern Europe', Washington, D.C.: Institute for International Economics.

Discussion of Part Seven

DAVID BEGG

Chapter 17's title includes the vivid phrase 'state desertion'. It is a good phrase, and it deserves discussion. In places, the authors seem to mean the entire package of 'shock therapy' policies which accompany a strategy of rapid transition to the market economy, as in Poland or Czecho-Slovakia. Elsewhere, they imply more specific notions, such as a vacuum in corporate governance once the shackles of central planning have been thrown off and 'companies are set adrift in uncharted seas with a real possibility of many disappearing into an "economic black hole"'. The formal definition of state desertion put forward by the authors involves yet a third notion 'the abrupt and discontinuous change in the state's financial involvement in social and economic activities'.

Of these three possible meanings, I like least the formal definition proposed by Ábel and Bonin. In many instances, a closer examination of what is actually taking place in Central and Eastern Europe reveals not a withdrawal of the state's financial involvement but rather a redefinition of the form it takes. The authors mention both fiscal retrenchment (subsidy reduction) and monetary stabilisation (financial austerity and convertibility of the currency) as examples of state desertion. Yet the fact remains that, in spite of the apparent withdrawal of state support, hardly a single one of the state-owned enterprises has been driven into bankruptcy. How can this be?

Two related phenomena help square the circle. The first is an explosion of interenterprise credit, the second is a proliferation of non-performing loans from the state banks to state-owned enterprises. Indeed, without the second, it is unlikely that the first would be observed to the same extent: if enterprises really were under pressure to meet promised payments to banks they would be less keen to extend trade credit to other enterprises.

Thus, in spite of apparently tight monetary and fiscal policy, enterprises, not only in Hungary but also in neighbouring countries such as Poland and Czecho-Slovakia, are not yet subject to hard budget constraints. Financial support from the state continues. In large part, it has switched from the direct and visible channel of subsidies to the indirect, and much harder-to-monitor, channel of a cumulation of the true indebtedness of enterprises to the state banking system. Recapitalising the banks will eventually require either a severe drain on the fiscal budget or a further bout of inflation.

I conclude that portraying state desertion as the withdrawal of financial support of the state misses at least part of what is going on. I would have liked to see the authors discuss more fully the second notion of state desertion set out above, namely the potential vacuum of corporate control until new ownership structures emerge. One could argue that this problem may be more important in Hungary than elsewhere. One reason other countries aim to move rapidly is precisely to put in place a new (private) framework to corporate governance; whether such plans will in fact be fulfilled speedily is, of course, another matter. My own view is that privatisation is likely to proceed less quickly than was hoped, and in any case fails to address the question of how the state should manage the (inevitably large) number of state-owned enterprises which will remain in state hands for the foreseeable future. There is a real danger that this issue will receive much less attention than it deserves.

That leaves us with the first interpretation of state desertion, the general package of 'shock therapy' policies in pursuit of a rapid transition to the market. Ábel and Bonin provide a brief survey of fiscal and monetary policy (including exchange rate policy) during the last decade in Hungary, and find favour with Hungarian gradualism essentially because it implies a lower degree of state desertion. They justify their discussion by claiming to investigate lessons of the Hungarian experience for other countries: I am not sure they really do justice to this claim.

We know Hungary began reforms much earlier than its neighbours and therefore was able to proceed more slowly. In so doing, it has escaped the extreme severity of recession experienced by Poland and Czecho-Slovakia. But what conclusions should we draw from this? It may or may not be the case that other countries would have been wiser to go more slowly. This depends on many considerations: the degree of political consensus and expectations as to how long it can be sustained; the need to establish the credibility of the commitment to reform; the extent of initial centralisation and planning; and so on. Without further discussion of such issues, there is no way to draw many lessons from the Hungarian experience for other countries.

Let me conclude by examining in more detail the issue of exchange rate policy, which occupies a good portion of the authors' discussion. Essentially, they argue that the attempt to fix the nominal exchange rate failed in Poland, and that Hungary pursued a wider policy of a crawling peg which helped stabilise its real exchange rate. I am inclined to agree that Poland (and Czecho-Slovakia) initially devalued too much. Choosing an exchange rate which could last a long time meant choosing one initially so under-valued that any notion of importing world prices 'at a stroke' became as much rhetoric as reality. That said, I think the authors press their argument rather too far.

In Poland, the initial task was to stop a hyperinflation, not an inherited circumstance in which it is possible (or necessary) to be too precise about where that targeted nominal anchor is pitched. Prices, and the real exchange rate are endogenous, and gradually respond to market forces. Given the extent of initial Polish inflation, it was a substantial achievement to bring inflation down to 'Hungarian levels', and that seems to me a triumph, not a failure. That policy was forced to switch eventually to a crawling peg was the inevitable (and foreseen) result of a fairly good stabilisation which had failed to eradicate inflation completely. In neighbouring Czecho-Slovakia, the outcome was even more dramatic. Since the devaluation at the end of December 1990 and price liberalisation in January 1991, there has been about a 50 per cent one-off increase in prices but no continuing inflation; and the exchange rate has held. Indeed, such has been domestic wage discipline to date that the real exchange rate remains highly competitive. In contrast, in Hungary inflation remains over 30 per cent. Preservation of the real exchange rate is a recipe for monetary accommodation. It is not obvious that its neighbours should look on this aspect of Hungarian policy as something to emulate.

ROBERT E. ROWTHORN

Ábel and Bonin's Chapter 17 is an interesting study for two reasons. It identifies an important, but rather neglected, aspect of the transformation in Eastern Europe. This concerns the disintegration of economies following the abrupt and discontinuous change in the financial involvement of the state in social and economic activities. To characterise such a withdrawal, the authors employ the graphic term 'state desertion'. Following their brief remarks on this phenomenon, the authors go on to consider the Hungarian experience of currency convertibility, which they use to support the case for gradual reform rather than shock therapy.

  Much of the debate within Eastern Europe, and much of the advice coming from the West, has been both ill-conceived and highly ideological in character. It has been dogmatically assumed that the role of the state should be reduced as quickly and as far as possible – sometimes to little more than a 'nightwatchman' function. Under the pressure of events, the economic and social implications of this doctrinaire position are becoming obvious, and disillusionment in Eastern Europe with liberal utopianism is now widespread. 'Big Bang' or 'shock therapies' are falling into disrepute as they are blamed, probably to an exaggerated extent, for the economic catastrophe now engulfing Eastern Europe. Hopefully, this disillusionment will lead to a more balanced approach to the question of the state and its role in the economies of Eastern Europe.

  By coining the term 'state desertion' Ábel and Bonin have made an important contribution to the evolution of such a balanced approach. Without a suitable language, serious intellectual discussion in any field is difficult, and nowhere is this more true than in the theory of the state. From a purely linguistic point of view the present chapter is therefore to be welcomed. In addition, the authors' discussion of state desertion is also thought-provoking. Unfortunately, it is extremely sketchy and I hope that in a future paper they will go on to explore the topic in greater depth.

Throughout their chapter, Ábel and Bonin urge caution and pragmatism in dealing with the question of state involvement in economic and social life. One area which they do not discuss, but which is obviously very important, is that of privatisation. Many small-scale enterprises have been privatised in Eastern Europe, but relatively few large enterprises have been sold off. The failure to sell off large firms is not in the least surprising. There is an acute shortage of domestic citizens with the skills required to take over large state companies and make a success of them under present economic conditions. There is also a shortage of suitable foreigners. In some cases East European countries do not wish to sell their most prized firms to foreigners, but the main obstacle to takeovers by outsiders is quite simply a shortage of suitable applicants. Eastern Europe (including the former Soviet Union) is a gigantic region, and even under the most propitious economic and political circumstances it would be difficult to find suitable outsiders willing to buy more than a modest fraction of large-scale industry. Under present circumstances, the task is virtually impossible.

Given the lack of suitable domestic or foreign purchasers, wholesale privatisation of large firms in Eastern Europe at the present time would involve one of two things. They could be sold to unsuitable new owners who would then be allowed to go bankrupt, asset strip or close down most of their operations. This would mean a virtual collapse of the local economy, as has happened for somewhat different reasons in East Germany, but would be socially and politically intolerable in independent countries which cannot expect the kind of external aid which East Germany has received. The alternative would be to give protection and large subsidies to the newly privatised firms to prevent them from collapsing or shedding most of their labour. This would defeat the purpose of privatisation and would make longer-term restructuring of these enterprises even more difficult than if they had remained in the state sector.

Despite urgings from the West to press ahead with privatisation as fast as possible, political realities in much of Eastern Europe are likely to ensure that a substantial part of large-scale industry will remain in the public sector for many years to come. The crucial issue during this period will not be how to privatise these companies, but how to operate and restructure them whilst they remain in the public sector. The concept of 'state desertion' is of obvious relevance in this context. Insistence on the rapid elimination of protection and financial support for public enterprise may result in further large reductions in output and employment, causing more human suffering and damaging longer-term economic prospects by closing down potentially viable activities. It is also a dangerous path to take because of the political backlash it may provoke.

The above comments suggest that much of large-scale enterprise in Eastern Europe will remain in state hands for the foreseeable future. Moreover, it will take a considerable time to restructure the public sector and make it fully able to compete on the open market. In the meantime financial support or protection will be required to prevent a collapse of employment. This raises a difficult problem. If an abrupt transformation of the state sector is ruled out, what can be done to ensure that a gradual programme for transforming this sector is actually implemented? Past attempts at gradual reform in Eastern Europe under communist regimes have run out of steam and failed to live up to their initial promise. What guarantee is there that this will not happen again under the new regimes? I believe that Ábel and Bonin are right to stress the dangers of state desertion and to support gradualism as opposed to shock therapy. Indeed, I think that for both economic and political reasons there is simply no realistic alternative to gradualism. I also believe that shock therapy will eventually be rejected throughout most of Eastern Europe. However, as we all know, gradualism has its own dangers in the form of stagnation and loss of momentum. The crucial question which supporters of gradualism must answer is: how can this danger be avoided, or at least reduced to acceptable proportions? It is, after all, despair at the past failures of gradualism which has driven some of its former supporters to advocate 'Big-Bang' type solutions. I hope that Ábel and Bonin will take up this question in a future paper.

Conclusion

ADAM RIDLEY

I wish here to make some personal, and selective, comments on the issues raised by this volume.

1   Enterprise regulation, privatisation and competition policy

Járai's Chapter 5 and its subsequent discussion brought home to me three important points which might be summarised as follows. Despite Járai's optimism about the extent to which the private sector is likely to grow (for one reason or another) in the immediate future, policy has been, and remains, weak in three respects:

(a)   *Commercialisation of state-owned enterprises (SOEs)*
      This process could be pursued much more systematically and effectively.

(b)   *Restructuring*
      Hungarian policy and law make little or no provision for such restructuring, nor does the government machine practise it much – be it via ministries or the State Property Agency (SPA).

(c)   *Privatisation methods*
      Whatever may be the impression created by the scale and growth of foreign investment, the privatisation process is failing to exploit fully the opportunities available for attracting foreign investment.

In seeking to understand this dilemma, various conversations have led me to conclude that one of the key problems in all three critical processes – commercialisation, restructuring and privatisation – lies (still) in the *law for transformation of enterprises into joint stock companies* and their *subsequent status*. This would seem to give some or all of management, unions' workers, workers' councils and supervisory councils a great deal of power. In particular, it gives them enough power to derail, destabilise or hamstring the privatisation policy being pursued by the SPA for a given firm. It may be impossible at this point to envisage any change in these legal provisions, but the signs are that it is highly desirable. Both theory and practice suggest that management and workers' representatives should not have so much power in such matters.

A more general comment is that the privatisation process is being undertaken in too anarchic a way. The experience of successful privatisers, even in relatively liberal and well-established market economies such as the UK, demonstrates that a great deal of planning and preparation is needed or, at the least, is of great value before one can launch an enterprise effectively and confidently as a private company in free market conditions. (I recall personally that the privatisation of the British Post Office's Girobank took nearly five years' hard work; yet it was only a relatively modest part of the Thatcher government's privatisation strategy.)

Stadler's Chapter 7 made it clear that competition policy has been approached with much more coherence, and is already founded firmly on a solid intellectual basis. However the policy now urgently needs a competitive economy in which to be able to develop on a firm practical foundation!

2   Reform of tax and legal systems

Standing behind Koltay's fascinating and masterly account of Hungarian tax reform in Chapter 14 was a recognition that the tax burden was impossibly high if sustained for the long term and that public spending (and the public deficit) would have to be cut. But there was, in addition, an anxiety about the evasion and avoidance strategies which spring up in response to unacceptably high levels of taxation. This prompts a comparison with the British experience in the 1960s and 1970s, which suggests several lessons which could be of direct relevance in the Hungarian context.

(a)   *Morality and paying taxes*
Avoidance and evasion increased dramatically in the 1960s and 1970s as the tax burden rose, particularly the weight of income tax and social security contributions on employees. It became clear that personal morality and self-control quickly deteriorated when the burden rose beyond a certain point. Legislation, investigations into evasion and punishment of malefactors became deeply unpopular, ineffective, and indeed counter-productive, until the level of personal taxation and public spending fell to less intolerable levels. The same must be true of Hungary. If and as the tax and spending burden falls, there does come a point (the UK is now well past it) when investigation and enforcement can be pursued vigorously and at the same time attract general public support. But not before.

(b) *Investigating tax evasion*

This depends to an enormous degree on having sensible procedures for tax collection, and sound records from which tax liability can be determined. It is obvious that procedures such as deduction from salaries of income tax and social security contributions by employers are crucial; but so, too, is the move from a cash economy to one where not only enterprises but most citizens use the banking system. The cash economy is the enemy of all efficient and equitable taxes, even VAT.

(c) *Self-employment*

Even if a sound system of deduction of income and social security contribution by employers is in place, the response of individuals could well be a mass exodus into self-employment. This degenerates into a farcical world in which mysterious individuals work as contractors rather than workers, and are known to the tax authorities (as in the UK) only by names such as Ronald Reagan, Richard Nixon, Mickey Mouse, Mikhail Gorbachev or Margaret Thatcher. Once civil liberties become properly entrenched, it can be curiously difficult to cope with such absurdities!

3   Foreign trade and payments

Csaba's Chapter 2 made it clear that the USSR's collapse was inevitable, and offered intriguing grounds for being sceptical about the constant parading of the 'collapse of CMEA trade' as the excuse for all the problems of the ex-Communist economies. However, he did not demonstrate (nor try to demonstrate) that further weakening of ex-CMEA trade would be trivial in future. In this connection, the discussions of the earlier Central European Payments Union proposals considered by Mizsei in Chapter 3 were understandably unproductive, and curiously beside the point. The place in which payments unions are most needed is the ex-USSR, where barter has long been king and, *faute de mieux*, is about to become emperor for life.

Halpern and Székely's study of export supply and import demand in Chapter 4 produced the reassuring conclusion that exchange rates do matter. One must hope that such findings do not tempt the Hungarian authorities into reliance on devaluation as the principal cure for trade deficits!

4   The political economy of transformation

Chapters 17 by Ábel and Bonin, 5 by Járai and 6 by Mihályi on 'state desertion' and privatisation, and the subsequent discussion of them, underlined anxieties about the treatment of unprivatised SOEs. This issue seems almost to be an embarrassing one which people would rather not address directly, or at length; such evasiveness could be dangerous.

In the process of enterprise reform and privatisation, the easiest things are being done first. This is both normal and logical, but one possible consequence is the creation of a seductive and misleading impression of progress. As the stock of easy tasks shrinks, the difficult ones which remain will become more and more dominant – and many of them will get worse as time passes. Yet underlying the policy leading to the phenomenon of 'state desertion' (which is visible in Czecho-Slovakia and Poland as well as Hungary), is an implicit optimistic hypothesis of a very different kind: that the number of problem cases will shrink, and their problems diminish.

Any Western observer will be mindful of the decades since World War II spent by OECD countries struggling with problem sectors such as coal, steel, textiles, and shipbuilding. Indeed, their problems have still not been fully resolved in market economies enjoying free trade and with the added benefits of membership of EFTA or the EC!

5   Labour markets, unemployment and the social safety net

Maria Augusztinovics' Chapter 16 presented a very powerful analysis of some extremely important practical issues which rarely attract the attention they deserve. The discussions underlined how important it is that the authorities debate and deal with these issues directly, and as soon as possible.

There are few more serious policy areas than pensions or social security. Yet it is an almost universal experience that both subjects are normally left to specialists, and decisions on them are postponed and postponed almost everywhere – often on the illogical grounds that what is at stake is 'long-term structural change'. Economists of all kinds have a duty to join in such debates, and to force the rest of society to face up to and deal with the issues.

6   The financial system, monetary policy and savings

Chapters 8 and 9 by Király and Várhegyi, and their discussion, raised many questions about policy for the banking sector:

(a)   It was striking to outsiders how little was written or said about what should be done.
(b)   There seemed at times to be an obsessive interest in the problems of *writing off bad loans*, and a tendency to treat the matter as one

necessarily having major implications for resources and the real economy. Like Richard Portes and others, I find it difficult to see why the loans should not be written down in recognition of reality, as has been done repeatedly for state-owned firms in the West. The act of writing them off does not solve the bank supervisors' problems of capital adequacy. But nor does it claim to; that issue of banking capital can, in principle, be dealt with in numerous ways, as can be seen from experience in the USA, Spain and elsewhere.

(c) It was in a sense surprising to discover substantial support for the view that interenterprise credit poses serious and unsolved *theoretical* problems. To many Western observers the theoretical questions are neither very mysterious nor of great relevance, and the problem strikes one as essentially a *practical* one. In the normal market economy such credit is constrained by:

   (i) the need to agree with a company's accountants realistic assessments of the *credit status* of all payables and receivables
   (ii) the need for a company's board to ensure it stays unequivocally *liquid*, and above all, solvent at all times
   (iii) the insistence of a company's financiers, in particular its banks, on frequent, regular *accounting information* to inform them of its balance sheet (including a realistic assessment of payables/receivables), liquidity and solvency.

The Hungarian authorities have no doubt been moving in this direction, but such forces and processes have yet to be really unleashed.

(d) There could be an interesting sequencing issue here. Intuitively it would seem right to rein in and 'put right' interenterprise credit very early on in the market reform process and, whatever else, *before* having a final decisive purge of the bad debts on the banks' balance sheets. To privatise the bulk of commercial banks *before* cleaning up the Augean stable of interenterprise credit would be to leave the whole banking system exposed to the dangers of domino effects as and when the enterprise credit bubble is finally pricked.

(e) It is understandable that Hungarian observers should be concerned about the relatively slow development of banking services to the corporate sector. To the outsider, it is not at all surprising that the commercial banks should make little progress in offering profitable banking services to companies. Under present conditions, they have to be able to compete with the zero-cost, zero-risk credit provided by enterprises to one another. There is an obvious 'chicken and egg' problem here if one asks how this position is to be altered. But it would seem certain that it would be unwise for the banks to try (or be pressed by the authorities to try) to enter new commercial banking markets until it is clear that they have a chance of doing so profitably.

7   Savings and household portfolios

Ábel and Székely's Chapter 10 demonstrated that there are interesting and significant changes to explain, and rational explanatory hypotheses look plausible. Among the many interesting questions prompted by this work, one noted the following:

(a) *The low level of personal savings*
     Could this spell trouble both for the early development of personal, discretionary, pension-type savings? And what does a low *level* of personal savings imply for privatisation?
(b) *Investors' preferences*
     The launch of the first privatisation vouchers in Czecho-Slovakia early in 1992 suggested that most Czech investors were risk-averse. Are Hungarian investors likely to be similar? What kinds of assets would they like to hold – equity-type, deposits or bonds?

8   International finance convertibility

We were reassured by both Oblath's Chapter 11 and Riecke's Chapter 12 that Hungary's indebtedness could be managed given a sufficient inflow of private capital, and reasonable economic growth. These two conditions cannot, however, be taken for granted:

(a) The private investment inflow will have to be won in an increasingly competitive market place. The present rather disorganised methods of promoting inward investment opportunities in Hungary could well prove less than adequate.
(b) Reasonable growth will be a function of *supply-side* successes – in other words of effective restructuring and reform of SOEs – about which one cannot but remain anxious

As so often, everything turns out to depend on everything else!

Glossary

AFCR	actuarially fair contribution ratio
ATM	automatic teller machine
BOP	balance of payments
CD	certificate of deposit
CEPU	Central European Payments Union
CIS	Commonwealth of Independent States – the former USSR
CIT	corporate income tax
CMEA	Council for Mutual Economic Assistance, or COMECON, the Socialist trading bloc
COMECON	*see* CMEA
CPE	centrally planned economy
CPI	consumer price index
CSO	Central Statistical Office
E/O	entry pension/pension of oldest cohort
EBRD	European Bank for Reconstruction and Development
EC	European Community
EFTA	European Free Trade Area
EPT	entrepreneurial profit tax
ESOP	Employees Stock Ownership Plan
FDI	foreign direct investment
GDP	gross domestic product
GDR	German Democratic Republic or East Germany
GVH	Competition Agency of Hungary
HUF	Hungarian forint
IBRD	International Bank for Reconstruction and Development (World Bank)
IMF	International Monetary Fund
JV	joint venture
KSH	Hungarian Central Statistical Office
MDF	Hungarian Democratic Forum (party in power)

MIER	Ministry of International Economic Relations
NBH	National Bank of Hungary
NEM	New Economic Mechanism (1968 reform in Hungary)
NICA	non-interest current account
NMP	net material product
NRT	net resource transfer
OECD	Organisation for Economic Cooperation and Development
OTP	National Savings Bank of Hungary
P/W	pension/wages
PHARE	EC programme of aid originally for Poland and Hungary
PIT	personal income tax
SOE	state owned enterprise
SPA	State Property Agency
SSC	social security contributions
SSS	social security system
TB	Treasury bill
TR	transferable rouble
UT	unrequited transfers
VAT	value added tax
VGMK	Enterprise Business Partnership, special legal form for incorporation (see Chapter 13, p. 241) of in-company working pools introduced in Hungary

Index